chard **Rudgley** was born in Hampshire in 1961. After
eiving a degree in social anthropology and religious studies at
University of London, he continued his studies in ethnology,
museum ethnography and prehistory at the Institute of Social
and Cultural Anthropology, University of Oxford. He is
ently undertaking research into the prehistoric and ancient
of psychoactive plants. In 1991 he became the first winner
he British Museum Prometheus Award which resulted in the
lication of his first book, *The Alchemy of Culture: Intoxicants in*
ety. His equally well-received book, *The Encyclopaedia of*
hoactive Substances, was published in 1998. He is married
a daughter and a son and lives in Notting Hill.

Also by Richard Rudgley

The Alchemy of Culture: Intoxicants in Society

The Encyclopaedia of Psychoactive Substances

Lost Civilisations of the Stone Age

WILDEST DREAMS

An Anthology of
Drug-Related Literature

Richard Rudgley

An *Abacus* Book

First published in Great Britain by
Little, Brown and Company in 1999
This edition published by Abacus in 2001

A CIP catalogue record for this book
is available from the British Library

ISBN 0 349 11138 3

For reasons of space, permissions
appear on pp. 419–422.

Typeset in Meridien by M Rules
Printed and bound in Great Britain by
Clays Ltd, St Ives plc

Abacus
A Division of
Little, Brown and Company (UK)
Brettenham House
Lancaster Place
London WC2E 7EN

www.littlebrown.co.uk

To Dave, Dominic, Doug, Nassa, Neil and Tom

Contents

PART TWO
PORTABLE ECSTASIES

PART THREE
*CANNABIS – FROM THE PYGMY VILLAGE
TO GREENWICH VILLAGE*

PART FOUR
EXTRACTS OF OPIUM

Contents

Part Five
LIQUID, GAS, SMOKE AND POWDER

Part Six
HALLUCINATING HISTORY

Part Seven
CHEMISTRY SET

Contents

INTRODUCTION

CHEMICAL CUT-UP

Consciousness is a cut-up
William S. Burroughs

In my previous books on psychoactive drugs, *The Alchemy of Culture: Intoxicants in Society* (1993) and *The Encyclopaedia of Psychoactive Substances* (1998), I concentrated on the cultural and historical influences of these substances on humankind. I was concerned, among other things, to dispel the ridiculous yet widely held belief that 'it all started in the sixties'. Nothing could be further from the truth. The earliest example of drug-related literature included in this anthology comes from *The Golden Ass* by Apuleius, written in the second century A.D. Yet the use of drugs was old hat even in antiquity, and prehistorians now recognise that a host of substances were used by Stone Age people.

The earliest firm evidence of the human use of psychoactive plants dates back to around 13,000 years ago. Archaeologists working under the leadership of Tom D. Dillehay at the site of Monte Verde in the temperate rain forest of southern Chile discovered the remains of a hut that appeared to have been that of a medicine man or woman. Over twenty types of medicinal plants were found inside, including two with reported hallucinogenic properties (*Drosera* sp. and *Peumus boldus*). Monte Verde is also the earliest generally accepted evidence of the human occupation of the Americas, indicating that people entered the New World equipped with knowledge of hallucinogenic plants.

However, even this very early date can hardly be seen as the beginning; it would be absurd to think that the excavators chanced upon the evidence of humankind's first experience with psychoactive drugs. In fact, this period is better seen as the tail-end of an evolutionary chain which plunges us atavistically into our remote animal past. For we are hardly the only species to partake in the psychoactive experience – bears and reindeer are known to be partial to the stimulating and hallucinogenic properties of the fly-agaric toadstool (*Amanita muscaria*) and even bees who have drunk the dark nectar of belladonna cannot have escaped the effect of the nightshade's spell. If we were to truly seek an origin for the drug-induced state we would have to place it somewhere in the primeval past, long before the emergence of humanity.

Whilst observers have noticed that animals seek out such substances for themselves, it is also the case that the human use of psychoactive agents has often attracted their attention. In *Opium: The Diary of a Cure* Jean Cocteau writes:

> *All animals are charmed by opium. Addicts in the colonies know the danger of this bait for wild beasts and reptiles.*
>
> *Flies gather round the tray and dream, the lizards with their little mittens swoon on the ceiling above the lamp and wait for the night, mice come close and nibble the dross. I do not speak of the dogs and monkeys that become addicted like their masters.*
>
> *At Marseilles, among the Annamites [i.e. Indo-Chinese people], where one smokes with implements calculated to confuse the police (a gas-pipe, a sample bottle of benedictine with a hole in it, and a hat-pin), the cockroaches and the spiders form a circle in ecstasy.*

Humans have also encouraged animals' interest in drugs by

conducting experiments upon them. In this volume there are passing references to this practice, for example, Aldous Huxley's evidence that some rats are born alcoholics whilst others are teetotallers in *Drugs that Shape Men's Minds*, and Henri Michaux's excursion into the altered states of web weaving in *Drugged Spiders*. Not only can animals take drugs of their own accord as well as via humans, they can also be the source of such drugs. The puffer fish is desired by Japanese gourmets for its flesh and feared by the same for its poison, to which many an oriental ichthyophagist has fallen victim. An inversion of these interests in the puffer fish is shown by malevolent sorcerers in Haiti who desire its poison (tetrodotoxin) to create a powder which can, according to Wade Davis in *Zombie Poisons of Haiti*, transform a human subject into a zombie.

Even the highest of the mammals, *Homo sapiens sapiens*, is not free from the insatiable desires of his fellow man's quest for new highs. In *Fear and Loathing in Las Vegas: A Savage Journey to the Heart of the American Dream*, Hunter S. Thompson has his crazed travellers lusting after a fresh adrenal or pineal gland, and Terry Southern's story, *The Blood of a Wig*, concerns a quest to score some schizophrenic's blood. Such tales plunge us into the strange world of psychoactive vampirism and cannibalism. Whilst these are fictional accounts it is known that the powerful hallucinogen 5-MeO-DMT is naturally present in toad venom, and, in much lesser amounts, in human cerebrospinal fluid. Some scientific research indicates that the levels of 5-MeO-DMT (and DMT, another hallucinogen) *may* be higher in schizophrenics.

Whilst the radically altered states of consciousness experienced by schizophrenics are largely involuntary, those of the shaman who takes hallucinogenic plants are clearly intentional. Shamans in various parts of the world – most notably in the hallucinogen-rich Amazon Basin – seek to transform themselves into animals in order to attain the power of other species. According to Carlos Castaneda and his followers, such magical activities are examples of genuine communication between species. Such transformations were also common among European witches who believed themselves changed into birds and beasts after having anointed themselves with 'flying ointments' made from a mixture of hallucinogenic plants including henbane, mandrake and belladonna. The use of such an ointment is described in *The Golden Ass*, when the sorceress Pamphile changes herself into an owl. From the Middle Ages onwards witch-finders viewed these transformations as delusions of the devil, whilst to the more sceptical observer they were merely delusions. In *To Make a Man Out of His Senses for a Day*, the sixteenth-century scientist John Baptista Porta describes how he made a potion similar to the 'flying ointments' and tried it out on his chamber-fellows to his own amusement and to their consternation.

From Apuleius to Burroughs, descriptions of such transformations are commonplace in Western literary tradition, at least amongst those authors who took drugs themselves or who have their characters do the dirty work for them. Thus, the lizard-boys and other sexual chimeras that litter the pages of Burroughs' *oeuvre*, and the female shark which Lautréamont's *Maldoror* makes love with, are distant descendants of the owl-woman Pamphile in *The Golden Ass*. If Burroughs was indeed following in a literary tradition of animal transformations (which both shamanism and mythology inform us preceded *The Golden Ass* by millennia), he was, nevertheless, breaking with it when *Naked Lunch* was first published in 1959. The book was certainly novel, introducing his now famous 'cut-up' style, in which disparate texts were fused and others cut to pieces and rearranged. Whilst texts had literally been cut up by the Dadaist poet Tristan Tzara in the early part of the twentieth century, Burroughs cited the artist Brion Gysin as his direct influence for this experimental technique. Not all of his peers approved of this radical method; Burroughs himself reported that

Samuel Beckett dismissed it as more akin to plumbing than true writing.

For Burroughs cut-up was a seditious operation performed, in part, to break through the totalitarian state imposed by the structures of the written word. Like some kind of literary Dr Frankenstein (or perhaps more appropriately Dr Benway, Burroughs' own character signifying medical incompetence combined with the most draconian form of patient 'care'), Burroughs attempted to inject life into the composition created by the pieces of text he had previously hacked apart. The title of the book was suggested by Jack Kerouac and, says Burroughs, 'means exactly what the words say: NAKED Lunch – a frozen moment when everyone sees what is on the end of every fork'. In stating that 'consciousness is a cut-up' he was announcing that the incorporation of the technique into his writings allowed his work to better reflect the world as we perceive it. When we walk through a busy street market we overhear fragments of conversations with no knowledge of what was said before or after the chance phrases that reached our ear; when flipping through television channels numerous parts of unconnected programmes flash across the screen in a meaningless sequence; when we daydream our mind flits between a number of unrelated objects of thought.

The protean nature of consciousness is compounded by the introduction of psychoactive drugs into the body. Such substances alter the state of consciousness of the user and, particularly in the case of hallucinogens, notions of self, space and time can change dramatically. Not only are hallucinations visual, they may also be aural, olfactory, gustatory and tactile. The discontinuities of life often become more apparent during drug-induced states – sensory derangement, ecstasy, paranoia, panic, panoramic vistas and interaction with the beings that inhabit inner space, may all contribute to a radically different perspective than that experienced in the ordinary waking state.

The anthology is, by its very nature, bound to include some

elements of the cut-up, and the compiler or editor must decide where to cut and where to paste. The writers have very different takes on the overall theme – some experiences are reported by observers and some by participants, some in sobriety and others in frenzy, guilt or wilful indulgence iced with jet black humour. The anthology, then, takes the form of a chimera, a composite creature made from other texts and other worlds of experience and imagination.

What is not too bizarre to happen? I'm told there are men who live far to the North and bathe in some sacred pool Minerva has graced. They do this nine times, and then on their bodies the down and feathers of birds sprout out. Who knows if it's true? There are also accounts of Scythian women who use some ointment or emollient oil on their skins with the same peculiar result. Sober and trustworthy men of science report observations we all accept as true of things that are no less amazing.

From *The Metamorphoses of Ovid*
(translation by David R. Slavitt)

Among the witches of Europe the most popular means of inducing an altered state of consciousness was to mix a whole host of psychoactive substances together to make a hallucinogenic paste known as 'flying ointment'. Depending upon availability, personal choice and local tradition, these substances might include opium, cannabis, tobacco, aconite, cat's brains or bat's blood, but almost always one or more of the nightshade family. Nightshades such as henbane, belladonna or mandrake all contain essentially the same hallucinogenic agents, namely the tropane alkaloids. When smeared on the body of the witch these magical ointments caused her to experience wild hallucinations and narcotic trances. Some of the witches reported sensations of flying off to visit demons and participate in orgiastic rites, whilst others transformed into animals.

The earliest detailed account of the use of such an ointment is in *The Golden Ass* by Apuleius. Apuleius was born in the 120s A.D. in a Roman colony in what is now Algeria where his father was an important magistrate. He pursued his interest in philosophy by travelling to Greece, Rome and then to Egypt when he was about thirty. On his way to Alexandria he fell sick and decided to stay with friends at Oea, now Tripoli in Libya. Whilst there he met a rich widow whom he was accused of bewitching by means of love-philtres in order to persuade her to marry him. He was put on trial for magic (then a capital offence) but defended himself successfully and was acquitted. Whilst the accusations turned out to be unfounded, the extract from *The Golden Ass* clearly shows that the author had an in-depth knowledge of the darker by-ways of sorcery and enchantment. In *The Ointments of Pamphile*, Lucius, the hero of the book, uses his lover Photis to gain access to the magical ointments of her mistress Pamphile. In the process he literally makes an ass of himself.

Inquisition in the Pigsty is a much later account of the witches' flying ointments. It comes from the pen of Bartolommeo Spina (*c*. 1475–1546), a Dominican and leading theologian of his day whose main work, *Quaestio de Strigibus* ('On Witches'), is concerned with cases of witchcraft in Italy. *Women are Made to Cast Off Their Clothes and Go Naked* and *To Make a Man Out of His Senses for a Day* have been extracted from *Natural Magick*, written by the early scientist and polymath John Baptista Porta (*c*. 1535–1615). Porta claimed to have written the first version of the book at the ripe old age of fifteen, but the fact that it was first published in Naples in 1558 indicates that he most probably wrote it during his early twenties. The book covers a bewildering variety of subjects ranging from metallurgy, chemistry and the use of lenses (Porta claimed to have invented the telescope before Galileo), to cookery, cosmetics and magical spells. His precocious knowledge of the witches' ointments and the black arts in general led to him being called to Rome by Pope Paul V in order to account for himself. He was let off with a caution, having justified his interests by citing them as a means of exposing charlatans and conjurers. The appeal of *Natural Magick* was enormous and it was an instant best-seller. As well as going through at least six editions in Latin within a decade of its first publication, it was also translated into Italian, French, Spanish, English, Dutch and Arabic.

The two recipes entitled *The Ant Wine Aphrodisiac* come from a book by the physician John Heydon, published in 1662 with the snappy title *The Holy Guide: Leading the Way to the Wonder of the World: (A Compleat Phisitian) teaching the Knowledge of all things, Past, Present, and to Come: Viz. Of Pleasure, long Life, Health, Youth, Blessedness, Wisdome and Virtue; and to Cure, Change and Remedy all Diseases in Young and Old*. As if the claims contained here were not enough, the title page also informs us that many of the remedies and potions given in the book are genuine Rosicrucian medicines (quite clearly an attempt to cash in on the inordinate reputation of this secret esoteric order of alchemists and hermetic doctors). Yet most of the contents of this medical miscellany are of a highly questionable nature, as the recipes for making aphrodisiacs from ants and wood lice reveal. Heydon was also responsible for various other formulas allowing the reader to create artificial flesh out of bread crumbs, which were heated and then hermetically sealed for two months, or to bring a dead bird back to life like a phoenix by reducing it to ashes and then putrefying it in horse dung, or, if your aims were more modest, simply the method of refining sugar.

Whilst Heydon's recipes for aphrodisiacs are unintentionally amusing, the opposite is true of *Anti-Aphrodisiacs According to the Physician Rondibilis* from *Gargantua and Pantagruel* by François Rabelais (*c.* 1495–1553). In this extract Panurge, overcome with lustful thoughts, seeks advice from Rondibilis who suggests a number of psychoactive substances to treat his condition, among them wine, cannabis and the mandrake plant. Another early masterpiece of European literature, the *Decameron* by Giovanni Boccaccio (1313–1375) includes a tale entitled *The Powder of Marvellous Virtue* about a less than holy guide, a lustful monk from an abbey in Tuscany. Armed with a narcotic powder containing the drug used by the Old Man of the Mountain (*see* Part Three – *The Old Man of the Mountain* by Marco Polo, which Boccaccio draws from), the monk sends a man to purgatory in order to gain access to his wife.

Montague Summers, who wrote numerous books on witchcraft and demonology in the first half of the twentieth century, provides the story of *The Satanic Nun*. In his gothic and sensationalistic prose he describes the malevolent goings-on (witches' ointments, poisonings, hauntings, poltergeist activity) in a German convent in the mid-eighteenth century. King James I of England (1566–1625) had already denounced the work of the devil in a book entitled *Demonology* before he set about denouncing the growing habit of smoking in *A Counter-blaste to Tobacco* published in 1604. From the extracts herein it is clear that he saw tobacco smoking as a devilish pastime and, quite rightly, bad for the health. His tract is also one of the earliest examples of racist arguments used to vilify exotic substances, for it is virulently anti-Indian. When the anti-drug lobbies denounced opium as intimately linked to the 'yellow peril' and marijuana as a seditious indulgence of immigrant populations, they were simply continuing an ignoble tradition stemming back to King James.

The Ointments of Pamphile

Apuleius

I thirstily applied my mouth to the moist and trembling eyes of my Photis, which were languid with uncontrolled desire, and were now half-closed as I pressed hungry kisses upon them.

Her high spirits now restored, 'Please wait a moment,' she said, 'until I carefully close the bedroom door. I don't wish to commit a grievous error by carelessly and sacrilegiously letting my tongue run free.' As she spoke, she thrust home the bolts and fastened the hook securely. Then she came back to me, and took my neck in both her hands. In a low and quite restrained voice, she said: 'I am fearful and mortally terrified of revealing the secrets of this house, and of exposing the hidden mysteries wrought by my mistress. But I have considerable trust in you and your learning. In addition to the noble distinction of your birth and your outstanding intellect, you have been initiated into several sacred cults, and you are certainly aware of the need for the sacred confidentiality of silence. So all that I entrust to the sanctuary of your pious heart you must for ever enclose and guard within its confines, and thus repay the ingenuous trust of my revelations with the steadfast security of your silence. The love which holds me fast to you compels me to reveal to you things which I alone know. You are now to gain acquaintance with the entire nature of our household, with the wondrous and secret spells of my mistress. To these

the spirits hearken and the elements are enslaved, and by them
the stars are dislocated and the divine powers harnessed. But
for no purpose does my mistress have recourse to the power of
this art so much as when she eyes with pleasure some young
man of elegant appearance, and indeed this is a frequent practice of hers.

'At the moment she is passionately obsessed with a young
and extremely handsome Boeotian, and she eagerly deploys
every device and every technique of her art. Only this evening
I heard her with my own ears threatening the sun itself with
cloud cover and unbroken darkness because it had not retired
from the sky quickly enough, and had yielded to nightfall too
late for her to practise the enticements of magic. Yesterday,
when she was on her way back from the baths, she happened
to catch sight of the young man sitting in the barber's, and she
ordered me to remove secretly his hair which had been snipped
off by the scissors and was lying on the floor. As I was carefully
and unobtrusively gathering it, the barber caught me at it. Now
we in this city have a bad name for practising the art of sorcery,
so he grabbed me brusquely and rebuked me. "You brazen
hussy, is there no end to your repeatedly stealing the hair of eli-
gible young men? If you don't finally stop this criminal practice,
I'll have you up at once before the magistrates." He followed up
his words with action; he thrust his hands between my breasts,
felt around, and angrily extracted some hair which I had
already hidden there. I was extremely concerned at this turn of
events, remembering my mistress's usual temper. She often
gets quite annoyed if she is frustrated in some way, and she
takes it out on me most savagely. I actually thought of running
away from her, but the thought of you at once caused me to
reject the idea.

'I was just returning dispirited and afraid to go back empty-
handed from the barber's, when I saw a man paring some
goatskins with scissors. Once I watched the skins inflated, tightly
tied, and hanging up, and the hair from them lying on the
ground and of the same blonde colour as that of the young

Boeotian, I abstracted a quantity of it and passed it to my mistress, concealing its true provenance. So it was that in the first hours of darkness, before you returned from your dinner, my mistress Pamphile in a fit of ecstatic madness climbed up towards the overlapping roof. On the far side of the house there is an area which is uncovered and exposed to the elements. It commands every view on the eastern side, as well as those in other directions. So it is especially convenient for those magical arts of hers, and she practises them there in secret. First of all she fitted out her infernal laboratory with the usual supplies, including every kind of aromatic plant, metal strips inscribed with unintelligible letters, the surviving remains of ill-omened birds, and a fairly large collection of corpses' limbs, earlier mourned over by relatives and in some cases even buried. Noses and fingers were in a heap in one place, and in another, nails from the gibbet to which there still clung flesh from the men hanged there. In yet another place the blood of slaughtered men was kept, and also gnawed skulls, torn from the fangs of wild beasts.

'Then, after chanting spells over quivering entrails, she poured propitiating offerings of various liquids – now spring-water, now cow's milk, now mountain-honey; she also poured out mead. She twisted and entwined the locks of hair with each other, and placed them on live coals to be burnt with a variety of fragrant plants. Immediately, through this combination of the irresistible power of her magic lore and the hidden energy of the harnessed deities, the bodies from which the hair was crackling and smoking acquired human breath, and were able to feel and walk. They headed for the place to which the stench from the hair they had shed led them, and thus they took the place of the Boeotian youth in barging at the doors, in their attempt to gain entrance. At that moment you appeared on the scene, drunk with wine and deceived by the darkness of the sightless night. You drew your short sword, and armed yourself for the role of the mad Ajax. But whereas he inflicted violence on living cattle and lacerated whole herds, you much more courageously dealt the death-blow to three inflated goat-skins. Thus you laid low the enemy without shedding a drop of blood, so that I can embrace not a homicide but an utricide.'

This elegant remark of Photis made me smile, and I responded in the same joking spirit. 'Well then,' I said, 'I can regard this as the first trophy won by my valour, in the tradition of Hercules' twelve labours, for I can equate the body of Geryon which was in triplicate, or the three-formed shape of Cerberus, with the like number of skins that I slew. But to obtain as you desire my forgiveness willingly for the entire error by which you involved me in such great distress, you must grant me the favour which is my dearest wish. Let me watch your mistress when she sets in train some application of her supernatural art. Let me see her when she summons the gods, or at any rate when she changes her shape. I am all agog to witness magic from close up. Mind you, you yourself do not seem to be a novice wholly innocent of such things. I have come to be quite convinced of this, for your flashing eyes and rosy cheeks, your shining hair, your kisses with parted lips, and your fragrant breasts hold me fast as your willing slave and bondsman, whereas previously I always spurned the embraces of matrons. So now I have no thought of returning home or planning my departure there; there is nothing which I count better than spending a night with you.'

'Lucius,' she replied, 'I should dearly love to grant your wish, but her surly disposition aside, Pamphile invariably seeks solitude and likes to perform such secret rites when no one else is present. However, I shall put your wish before my personal danger. I shall watch out for a favourable occasion, and carefully arrange what you seek. My only stipulation, as I said at the beginning, is that you must promise to maintain silence in this momentous matter.'

As we chatted away, our desire for each other roused the minds and bodies of us both. We threw off the clothes we wore until we were wholly naked, and enjoyed a wild love-orgy. When I was wearied with her feminine generosity, Photis offered me a boy's pleasure. Finally this period of wakefulness caused our eyes to droop; sleep invaded them, and held us fast until it was broad daylight.

After we had spent a few nights in such pleasurable pursuits, one day Photis came hurrying to me trembling with excitement. Her mistress, she said, was having no success in her love-affair by other means, and so she intended on the following night to invest herself with a bird's plumage, and to join her beloved by taking wing. I should accordingly be ready to observe with due circumspection this astonishing feat. So just as darkness fell, Photis led me silently on tiptoe to that upper chamber, and instructed me to witness what was happening there through a chink in the door.

Pamphile first divested herself of all her clothing. She then opened a small casket and took from it several small boxes. She removed the lid from one of these, and extracted ointment from it. This she rubbed for some time between her hands, and then smeared it all over herself from the tips of her toes to the crown of her head. She next held a long and private conversation with the lamp, and proceeded to flap her arms and legs with a trembling motion. As she gently moved them up and down, soft feathers began to sprout on them, and sturdy wings began to grow. Her nose became curved and hard, and her nails became talons. In this way Pamphile became an owl; she uttered a plaintive squawk as she tried out her new identity by gradually forsaking the ground. Soon she rose aloft, and with the full power of her wings quitted the house.

This was how Pamphile deliberately changed her shape by employing techniques of magic. I too was spellbound, but not through any incantation. I was rooted to the ground with astonishment at this event, and I seemed to have become something other than Lucius. In this state of ecstasy and riveted mindlessness, I was acting out a waking dream, and accordingly I rubbed my eyes repeatedly in an effort to discover whether I was awake. Finally I returned to awareness of my surroundings, and seizing Photis' hand I placed it on my eyes. 'While the chance allows,' I begged her, 'do please allow me one great and unprecedented boon bestowed by your affection. Get me, my honey-sweet, a little ointment from that same box – by those dear breasts of yours I beg you. Bind me as your slave for ever by a favour which I can never repay, and in this way ensure that I shall become a winged Cupid, drawing close to my Venus.'

'Is that what you're after, my foxy lover?' she asked. 'Are you trying to force me to apply an axe to my own limbs? When you are in that vulnerable state, I can scarcely keep you safe from those two-legged Thessalian wolves! And where shall I seek you, when shall I see you, once you become a bird?'

'The gods preserve me from perpetrating such an outrage,' I replied. 'Even if I were to fly through the entire heavens on the soaring wings of an eagle, as the appointed messenger or happy squire from highest Jove, would I not sweep down from time to time from the enjoyment of such distinction on the wing to this fond nest of mine? I swear by this sweet knot that binds your hair and has enmeshed my heart, there is no other girl I prefer to my dear Photis. A second thought comes to my mind: once I have smeared myself and have become a bird like that, I shall have to keep a safe distance from all habitations. What a handsome and amusing lover I should make for matrons to enjoy when I'm an owl! If those night-birds do get inside a house, the residents, as we see, take care to catch them and nail them to their doors, to expiate by their sufferings the threatened destruction to the household occasioned by their ill-omened flight. But I almost forgot to ask: what word or action do I need to discard those feathers and return to my being Lucius?' 'You have no worries in ensuring that,' she answered, 'for my mistress has shown me each and every substance that can restore to human form those who have adopted such shapes. Do not imagine that she did this out of mere goodwill; it was so that I could aid her with an efficacious remedy on her return. Observe with what cheap and everyday herbs such a great transformation is achieved. You wash yourself with water in which a sprig of dill and some bay-leaves have been steeped, and drink some of it.'

She made this claim repeatedly, and then with great apprehension she crept into the chamber, and took a box from the casket. First I hugged and kissed it, and prayed that it would bring me happy flying hours. Then I hastily tore off all my clothes, dipped my hands eagerly into the box, drew out a good quantity of the ointment, and rubbed all my limbs with it. I then flapped my arms up and down, imitating the movements of a bird. But no down and no sign of feathers appeared. Instead, the hair on my body was becoming coarse bristles, and my tender skin was hardening into hide. There were no longer five fingers at the extremities of my hands, for each was compressed into one hoof. From the base of my spine protruded an enormous tail. My face became misshapen, my mouth widened, my nostrils flared open, my lips became pendulous, and my ears huge and bristly. The sole consolation I could see in this wretched transformation was the swelling of my penis – though now I could not embrace Photis.

As I helplessly surveyed the entire length of my body, and came to the realization that I was not a bird but an ass, I tried to complain at what Photis had done to me. But I was now deprived of the human faculties of gesture and speech; all I could do by way of silent reproach was to droop my lower lip, and with tearful eyes give her a sidelong look. As soon as she saw what I had become, she beat her brow with remorseful hands and cried: 'That's the end of poor me! In my panic and haste I made a mistake; those look-alike boxes deceived me. But the saving grace is that the remedy for this transformation is quite easy and available. Just chew some roses, and you will stop being an ass and at once become my Lucius again. I only wish that I had plaited some garlands this evening as I usually do, and then you would not have had the inconvenience of even one night's delay. But as soon as dawn breaks, the remedy will be set before you with all speed.'

She kept wailing on like this. Though I was now a perfect ass, a Lucius-turned-beast, I still preserved my human faculties, and I gave long and serious thought to whether I should end the life of that most nefarious and abominable woman by kicking her repeatedly with my hooves and by tearing her apart with my teeth. But second thoughts deterred me from that rash course, for I feared that if Photis suffered the punishment of death, I should lose all my prospects of saving help. So angrily shaking my drooping head from side to side, I swallowed the indignity for the time being, and submitted to this most bitter of misfortunes. I retired to the stable to join the horse which had served as my trusty mount.

Inquisition in the Pigsty
Bartolommeo Spina

First, indeed, there should be adduced the thing that happened to the illustrious Prince N., within the lifetime of those who are now alive. A certain witch, who said that she had often been carried on the journey, was being held in the prison of some cleric Inquisitor. The Prince, hearing of this, desired to find out whether these claims were true or dreams. He summoned the Inquisitor D., and finally prevailed upon him to let the woman be brought forth and anoint herself with her usual ointment in their presence and in the presence of a multitude of nobles. When the Inquisitor had given his consent (even if in error), the witch asserted in their presence that, if she might anoint herself as before, she would go and be carried off by the Devil. Having anointed herself several times, however, she remained motionless; nor did anything extraordinary manage to happen to her. And many noble eye-witnesses of the matter survive to this very day. From this fact, it is obviously false that witches are carried on the ride as part of their pact; it is rather that when they think that they are so carried, it happens by a delusion of the Devil.

There are many other testimonies of this, and now it is my pleasure to adduce examples which are said to have happened in our own times. Dominus Augustinus de Turre, of Bergamo, the most cultivated physician of his time, told me a few years ago in his home at Bergamo, that when he was a youth at his studies in Padua, he returned home one night about midnight with his companions. He knocked, and when no one answered or opened the door, he climbed up a ladder and finally got into the house by a window. He went to look for the maid and finally found her lying in her room, supine upon the floor, stripped as if a corpse, and completely unconscious, so that he was in no way able to arouse her. When it was morning, and she had returned to her senses, he asked her what happened that night. She finally confessed that she had been carried on the journey; from which it is manifestly clear that they [witches] are deluded not bodily, but mentally or in dreams, in such a way that they imagine they are carried a long distance while they remain immobile at home.

Something similar to this last was told to me at Saluzzo a few years ago by Dr. Petrus Cella, formerly vicar of the Marchese of Saluzzo and still living: like things had happened to his own maidservant, and likewise he had discovered that she was deluded.

But there is also a story commonly told among us, that at the time when the Inquisition in the diocese of Como was being carried on by our people, in the walled city called Lugano, it happened that the wife of a notary of the Inquisition was accused by due process of law of being a witch and a sorceress. Her husband was exceedingly troubled at this, since he had thought her a holy woman. Then, through the will of the Lord, early on Good Friday, since he could not find his wife, he went to the pigsty. There he found her naked, in some corner, displaying her genitals, completely unconscious and smeared with the excrement of the pigs. Now then, made more certain of that which he had not been able to believe, he drew his sword in sudden wrath, wishing to kill her. Returning to himself, however, he stood waiting for a little while that he might see the outcome of all this. And lo, after a little while she returned to her senses. When she saw that her husband was threatening to kill her, she prostrated herself before him and, seeking pardon, promised that she would reveal the whole truth to him. So she confessed that she had gone that night on the journey, etc. Hearing these things, her husband left at once and made an accusation of her in the house of the Inquisitor, so that she might be given to the fire. She, however, though sought at once, was nowhere to be found. They think that she drowned herself in the lake above whose shore that area is situated.

Women are Made to Cast Off Their Clothes and Go Naked

John Baptista Porta

To let nothing pass that Jugglers and Impostors counterfeit, They set a Lamp with Characters graved upon it, and filled with Hare's fat; then they mumble forth some words, and light it; when it burns in the middle of women's company, it constrains them all to cast off their clothes, and voluntarily to shew themselves naked unto men; they behold all their privities, that otherwise would be covered, and the women will never leave dancing so long as the Lamp burns: and this was related to me by men of credit. I believe this effect can come from nothing but the Hare's fat, the force whereof perhaps is venemous, and penetrating the brain, moves them to this madness. Homer saith, The Massagetæ did the like, and that there are Trees whose fruit cast into the fire, will make all that are neer to be drunk and foolish; for they will presently rise from their seats, and fall to leaping and dancing.

The Ant Wine Aphrodisiac
John Heydon

The First:

Take of Pismires [an obsolete word for ants] or Ants (the biggest, that have a sowrish smell, are the best) two handfuls, spirit of Wine a gallon, digeste them in a glasse vessel close shut the space of a month, in which time they will be dissolved into a Liquor, then distil them in *Balneo* [i.e. in a bain-marie] till all be dry. Then put the same quantity of Ants as before, digest and distil them in the said Liquor as before: do this three times, then aromatize the spirit with some Cinnamon.

. Note that upon the spirit will float an oyl, which must be separated.

This spirit is of excellent use to stir up the Animal spirit; in so much that John Casimire Palsgrave of the Rhene, and Seyfrie of Collen, General against the Turks, did alwayes drink of it when they went to fight, to encrease magnanimity and courage, which it did, even to admiration.

This spirit doth also wonderfully irritate them that are sloth-ful to Venery.

The Second:

Take of ants of Pismires a handful, of their Eggs two hundred, of Millepedes, i.e. Wood-lice one hundred, of Bees one hundred and fifty, digest all these in two pints of spirit of Wine, being very well impregnated with the brightest Soot. Digest them together the space of a month, then pour off the clear spirit, and keep it safe. This water or spirit is of the same vertue as the former.

To Make a Man Out of His Senses for a Day

John Baptista Porta

After these Medicines to cause sleep, we will speak of those which make men mad: the business is almost the same: for the same Plants that induce sleep, if they be taken in a larger proportion, do cause madness. But we will not tell those things which breed it for ever, onely which may make us sport for a day, and afterwards leave no harm. We will begin with,

How to make men mad with Mandrake.

We have told you, That a small dose brings sleep; a little more, madness; a larger, death. *Dioscorides* saith, That a Drachm of Motion will make one foolish: we will easilier do it with Wine, which is thus made: Take the Roots of Mandrake, and but put them into new Wine, boyling and bubling up: cover it close; and let them infuse in a warm place for two months. When you would use it, give it to somebody to drink; and whosoever shall taste it after a deep sleep, will be distracted, and for a day shall rave: but after some sleep, will return to his senses again, without any harm: and it is very pleasant to behold. Pray make trial. We may do the same.

With Stramonium, or Solanum Manicum:

The Seeds of which, being dried and macerated in Wine, the space of a night, and a Drachm of it drank in a Glass of Wine, (but rightly given, lest it hurt the man) after a few hours will make one mad, and present strange visions, both pleasant and horrible; and of all other sorts: as the power of the potion, so doth the madness also cease, after some sleep, without any harm, as we said, if it were rightly administered. We may also infect any kinde of meat with it, by strowing thereon: three fingers full of the Root reduced into powder, it causeth a pleasant kinde of madness for a day: but the poysonous quality is allayed by sleep, or by washing the Temples and Pulses with Vinegar, or juice of Lemmon. We may also do the same with another kinde of Solanum, called

Bella Donna,

A Drachm of the Root of which, amongst other properties, hath this; that it will make men mad without any hurt: so that it is a most pleasant spectacle to behold such mad whimsies and visions; which also is cured by sleep: but sometimes they refuse to eat. Nevertheless, we give this precaution, That all those Roots or Seeds which cause the Takers of them to see delightful visons, if their Dose be increased, will continue this alienation of minde for three days: but if it be quadrupled, it brings death. Wherefore we must proceed cautiously with them. I had a Friend, who, as oft as he pleased, knew how

To make a man believe he was changed

into a Bird or Beast; and cause madness at his pleasure. For by drinking a certain Potion, the man would seem sometimes to be changed into a Fish; and flinging out his arms, would swim on the Ground: sometimes he would seem to skip up, and then to dive down again. Another would believe himself turned into a Goose, and would eat Grass, and beat the Ground with his Teeth, like a Goose: now and then sing, and endeavour to clap his Wings. And this he did with the aforenamed Plants: neither did he exclude Henbane from among his Ingredients: extracting the essences by their Menstruum, and mix'd some of their Brain, Heart, Limbs, and other parts with them. I remember when I was a young man, I tried these things on my Chamber-Fellows: and their madness still fixed upon something they had eaten, and their fancy worked according to the quality of their meat. One, who had fed lustily upon Beef, saw nothing but the formes of Bulls in his imagination, and them running at him with their horns: and such-like things. Another man also by drinking a Potion, flung himself upon the earth, and like one ready to be drowned, struck forth his legs and arms, endeavouring as it were to swim for life: but when the strength of the Medicament began to decay, like a Shipwrack'd person, who had escaped out of the Sea, he wrung his Hair and his Clothes to strain the Water out of them; and drew his breath, as though he took such pains to escape the danger. These, and many other most pleasant things, the curious Enquirer may finde out: it is enough for me only to have hinted at the manner of doing them.

Anti-Aphrodisiacs According to the Physician Rondibilis

François Rabelais

How the physician Rondibilis counselleth Panurge

Panurge, continuing his discourse, said, The first word which was spoken by him who gelded the lubbardly quaffing monks of Saussiniac, after that he had unstoned Friar Cauldaureil, was this, Now for the rest. In like manner, I say, Now for the rest. Therefore, I beseech you, my good master Rondibilis, should I marry or not? By the raking pace of my mule, quoth Rondibilis, I know not what answer to make to this problem of yours.

You say that you feel in you the pricking strings of sensuality, by which you are stirred up to venery. I find in our faculty of medicine, and we have founded our opinion therein upon the deliberate resolution and final decision of the ancient Platonics, that carnal concupiscence is cooled and quelled . . . several ways.

First, by the means of wine. I shall easily believe that, quoth Friar John, for when I am well whittled with the juice of the grape, I care for nothing else, so I may sleep. When I say, quoth Rondibilis, that wine abateth lust, my meaning is, wine immoderately taken; for by intemperance proceeding from the excessive drinking of strong liquor, there is brought upon the body of such a swill-down bouser, a chillness in the blood, a slackening in the sinews, a dissipation of the generative seed, a numbness and a hebetation of the senses, with a perversive wryness and convulsion of the muscles; all of which are great lets and impediments to the act of generation. Hence it is, that Bacchus, the god of bibbers, tipplers, and drunkards, is most commonly painted beardless, and clad in a woman's habit, as a person altogether effeminate, or like a libbed eunuch. Wine, nevertheless, taken moderately, worketh quite contrary effects, as is implied by the old proverb, which saith, – That Venus takes cold, when not accompanied with Ceres and Bacchus. This opinion is of great antiquity, as appeareth by the testimony of Diodorus the Sicilian, and confirmed by Pausanias, and universally held amongst the Lampsacians, that Don Priapus was the son of Bacchus and Venus.

Secondly, The fervency of lust is abated by certain drugs, plants, herbs, and roots, which make the taker cold, maleficiated, unfit for, and unable to perform the act of generation; as hath been often experimented in the water-lily, Heraclea, Agnus Castus, willow-twigs, hemp-stalks, woodbine, honeysuckle, tamarisk, chaste-tree, mandrake, bennet, keck-bugloss, the skin of a hippopotamus, and many other such, which, by convenient doses proportioned to the peccant humour and constitution of the patient, being duly and seasonably received within the body, – what by their elementary virtues on the one side, and peculiar properties on the other, – do either benumb, mortify, and beclumpse with cold the prolific semence, or scatter and disperse the spirits, which ought to have gone along with, and conducted sperm to the places destinated and appointed for its reception, – or lastly, shut up, stop, and obstruct the ways, passages, and conduits through which the seed should have been expelled, evacuated, and ejected. We have nevertheless of those ingredients, which, being of a contrary operation, heat the blood, bend the nerves, unite the spirits, quicken the senses, strengthen the muscles, and thereby rouse up, provoke, excite, and enable a man to the vigorous accomplishment of the feat of amorous dalliance. I have no need of those, quoth Paurge, God be thanked, and you, my good master. Howsoever, I pray you, take no exception or offence at these my words; for what I have said was not out of any ill will I did bear to you, the Lord, he knows.

The Powder of Marvellous Virtue

Giovanni Boccaccio

Know then that there was and still is in Tuscany an abbey, situate, as we see not a few, in a somewhat solitary spot, wherein the office of abbot was held by a monk, who in all other matters ordered his life with great sanctity, save only in the commerce with women, and therein knew so well how to cloak his indulgence, that scarce any there were that so much as suspected – not to say detected it – so holy and just was he reputed in all matters. Now the abbot consorted much with a very wealthy contadino, Ferondo by name, a man coarse and gross beyond measure, whose friendship the abbot only cared for because of the opportunities which it afforded of deriving amusement from his simplicity; and during their intercourse the abbot discovered that Ferondo had a most beautiful wife; of whome he became so hotly enamoured that he could think of nought else either by day or by night. But learning that, however simple and inept in all other matters, Ferondo shewed excellent good sense in cherishing and watching over this wife of his, he almost despaired. However, being very astute, he prevailed so far with Ferondo, that he would sometimes bring his wife with him to take a little recreation in the abbey-garden, where he discoursed to them with all lowliness of the blessedness of life eternal, and the most pious works of many men and women of times past, insomuch that the lady conceived a desire to confess to him, and craved and had Ferondo's leave therefor. So, to the abbot's boundless delight, the lady came and seated herself at his feet to make her confession, whereto she prefixed the following exordium: – 'If God, Sir, had given me a husband, or had not permitted me to have one, perchance 'twould be easy for me, under your guidance, to enter the way, of which you have spoken, that leads to life eternal. But, considering what manner of man Ferondo is, and his stupidity, I may call myself a widow, while yet I am married in that, so long as he lives, I may have no other husband; and he, fool that he is, is without the least cause so inordinately jealous of me that 'tis not possible but that my life with him be one of perpetual tribulation and woe. Wherefore, before I address myself to make further confession, I in all humility beseech you to be pleased to give me some counsel of this matter, for here or nowhere is to be found the source of the amelioration of my life, and if it be not found, neither confession nor any other good work will be of any avail.' The abbot was overjoyed to hear her thus speak, deeming that Fortune had opened a way to the fulfilment of his heart's desire. Wherefore he said: – 'My daughter, I doubt not that 'tis a great affliction to a lady, fair and delicate as you are, to have a fool for a husband, and still more so that he should be jealous: and as your husband is both the one and the other, I readily credit what you say of your tribulation. But, to come to the point, I see no resource or remedy in this case, save this only, that Ferondo be cured of his jealousy. The medicine that shall cure him I know very well how to devise, but it behoves you to keep secret what I am about to tell you.' 'Doubt not of it, my father,' said the lady: 'for I had rather suffer death than tell any aught that you forbade me to tell. But the medicine, how is it to be devised?' 'If we would have him cured,' replied the abbot, 'it can only be by his going to purgatory.' 'And how may that be?' returned the lady; 'can he go thither while he yet lives?' 'He must die,' answered the abbot; 'and so he will go thither; and when he has suffered pain enough to be cured of his jealousy, we have certain prayers with which we will supplicate God to restore him to life, and He will do so.' 'Then,' said the lady; 'am I to remain a widow?' 'Yes,' replied the abbot, 'for a certain time, during which you must be very careful not to let yourself be married to another, because 'twould offend God, and when Ferondo was restored to life, you would have to go back to him, and he would be more jealous than ever.' 'Be it so then,' said the lady; 'if he be but cured of his jealousy, and so I be not doomed to pass the rest of my days in prison, I shall be content: do as you think best.' 'And so will I,' said the abbot; 'but what reward shall I have for such a service?' 'My father,' said the lady, 'what you please; so only it be in my power. But what may the like of me do that may be acceptable to a man such as you?' 'Madam,' replied the abbot, ''tis in your power to do no less for me than I am about to do for you: as that which I am minded to do will ensure your comfort and consolation, so there is that which you may do which will be the deliverance and salvation of my life.' 'If so it be,' said the lady, 'I shall not be found wanting.' 'In that case,' said the abbot, 'you will give me your love, and gratify my passion for you, with which I am all afire and wasting away.' Whereto the lady, all consternation, replied: – 'Alas! my father, what is this you crave? I took you for a holy man; now does it beseem holy men to make such overtures to ladies that come to them for counsel?' 'Marvel not, fair my soul,' returned the abbot; 'hereby is my holiness in no wise diminished, for holiness resides in the soul, and this which I ask of you is but a sin of the flesh. But, however it may be, such is the might of your bewitching beauty that love constrains me thus to act. And, let me tell you, good cause have you to vaunt of your beauty more than other women, in that it delights the saints, who are used to contemplate celestial beauties; whereto I may add that, albeit I am an abbot, yet I am a man even as others, and, as you see, not yet old. Nor need this matter seem formidable to you, but rather to be anticipated with pleasure, for, while Ferondo is in purgatory, I shall be your nightly companion, and will give you such solace as he should have given you; nor will it ever be discovered by any, for all think of me even as you did a while ago, or even more so. Reject not the grace that God accords you; for 'tis in your power to have, and, if you are wise and follow my advice, you shall have that which women not a few desire in vain to have. And moreover I have jewels fair and rare, which I am minded shall be yours and none other's. Wherefore, sweet my hope, deny me not due guerdon of the service which I gladly render you.'

The lady, her eyes still downcast, knew not how to deny him, and yet scrupled to gratify him: wherefore the abbot, seeing that she had hearkened and hesitated to answer, deemed that she was already half won, and following up what he had said with much more to the like effect, did not rest until he had persuaded her that she would do well to comply: and so with some confusion she told him that she was ready to obey his every behest; but it might not be until Ferondo was in purgatory. The abbot, well content, replied: – 'And we will send him thither forthwith: do but arrange that he come hither to stay with me to-morrow or the day after.' Which said, he slipped a most beautiful ring on her finger, and dismissed her. Pleased with the gift, and expecting more to come, the lady rejoined her attendants, with whom she forthwith fell a talking marvellous things of the abbot's sanctity, and so went home with them.

Some few days after, Ferondo being come to the abbey, the abbot no sooner saw him than he resolved to send him to purgatory. So he selected from among his drugs a powder of marvellous virtue, which he had gotten in the Levant from a great prince, who averred that 'twas wont to be used by the Old Man of the Mountain, when he would send any one to or bring him from his paradise, and that, without doing the recipient any harm, 'twould induce in him, according to the quantity of the dose, a sleep of such duration and quality that while the efficacy of the powder lasted, none would deem him to be alive. Whereof he took enough to cause a three days' sleep, and gave it to Ferondo in his cell in a beaker that had still some wine in it, so that he drank it unwittingly: after which he took Ferondo to the cloister, and there with some of his monks fell to making merry with him and his ineptitudes. In no long time, however, the powder so wrought, that Ferondo was seized in the head with a fit of somnolence so sudden and violent that he slept as he stood, and sleeping fell to the ground. The abbot put on an agitated air, caused him to be untrussed, sent for cold water, and had it sprinkled on his face, and applied such other remedies as if he would fain call back life and sense banished by vapours of the stomach, or some other intrusive force; but, as, for all that he and his monks did, Ferondo did not revive, they, after feeling his pulse and finding there no sign of life, one and all pronounced him certainly dead. Wherefore they sent word to his wife and kinsfolk, who came forthwith, and mourned a while; after which Ferondo in his clothes was by the abbot's order laid in a tomb. The lady went home, saying that nothing should ever part her from a little son that she had borne Ferondo; and so she occupied herself with the care of her son and Ferondo's estate. At night the abbot rose noiselessly, and with the help of a Bolognese monk, in whom he reposed much trust, and who was that very day arrived from Bologna, got Ferondo out of the tomb, and bore him to a vault, which admitted no light, having been made to serve as a prison for delinquent monks; and having stripped him of his clothes, and habited him as a monk, they laid him on a truss of straw, and left him there until he should revive. Expecting which event, and instructed by the abbot how he was then to act, the Bolognese monk (none else knowing aught of what was afoot) kept watch by the tomb.

The day after, the abbot with some of his monks paid a pastoral visit to the lady's house, where he found her in mourning weeds and sad at heart; and, after administering a little consolation, he gently asked her to redeem her promise. Free as she now felt herself, and hampered neither by Ferondo nor by any other, the lady, who had noticed another beautiful ring on the abbot's finger, promised immediate compliance, and arranged with the abbot that he should visit her the very next night. So, at nightfall, the abbot donned Ferondo's clothes, and, attended by his monk, paid his visit, and lay with her until matins to his immense delight and solace, and so returned to the abbey; and many visits he paid her on the same errand; whereby some that met him, coming or going that way, supposed that 'twas Ferondo perambulating those parts by way of penance; and fables not a few passed from mouth to mouth of the foolish rustics, and sometimes reached the ears of the lady, who was at no loss to account for them.

As for Ferondo, when he revived, 'twas only to find himself he knew not where, while the Bolognese monk entered the tomb, gibbering horribly, and armed with a rod, wherewith, having laid hold of Ferondo, he gave him a severe thrashing. Blubbering and bellowing for pain, Ferondo could only ejaculate: – 'Where am I?' 'In purgatory,' replied the monk. 'How?' returned Ferondo, 'am I dead then?' and the monk assuring him that 'twas even so, he fell a bewailing his own and his lady's and his son's fate, after the most ridiculous fashion in the world. The monk brought him somewhat to eat and drink. Of which when Ferondo caught sight, 'Oh!' said he, 'dead folk eat then, do they?' 'They do,' replied the monk; 'and this, which I bring thee, is what the lady that was thy wife sent this morning to the church by way of alms for masses for thy soul; and God is minded that it be assigned to thee.' 'Now God grant her a happy year,' said Ferondo; 'dearly I loved her while I yet lived, and would hold her all night long in my arms, and cease not to kiss her, ay, and would do yet more to her, when I was so minded.' Whereupon he fell to eating and drinking with great avidity, and finding the wine not much to his taste, he said: – 'Now God do her a mischief! Why gave she not the priest of the wine that is in the cask by the wall?' When he had done eating, the monk laid hold of him again, and gave him another sound thrashing with the rod. Ferondo bellowed mightily, and then cried out: – 'Alas! why servest thou me so?' 'God,' answered the monk, 'has decreed that thou be so served twice a day.' 'For why?' said Ferondo. 'Because,' returned the monk, 'thou wast jealous, notwithstanding thou hadst to wife a woman that has not her peer in thy countryside.' 'Alas,' said Ferondo, 'she was indeed all that thou sayest, ay, and the sweetest creature too, – no comfit so honeyed – but I knew not that God took it amiss that a man should be jealous, or I had not been so.' 'Of that,' replied the monk, 'thou shouldst have bethought thee while thou wast there, and have amended thy ways; and should it fall to thy lot ever to return thither, be sure that thou so lay to heart the lesson that I now give thee, that thou be no more jealous.' 'Oh!' said Ferondo; 'dead folk sometimes return to earth, do they?' 'They do,' replied the monk; 'if God so will.' 'Oh!' said Ferondo; 'if I ever return, I will be the best husband in the world; never will I beat her or scold her, save for the wine that she has sent me this morning, and also for sending me never a candle, so that I have had perforce to eat in the dark.' 'Nay,' said the monk, 'she sent them, but they were burned at the masses.' 'Oh!' said Ferondo, 'I doubt not you say true; and, of a surety, if I ever return, I will let her do just as she likes. But tell me, who art thou that entreatest me thus?' 'Late of Sardinia I,' answered the monk, 'dead too; and, for that I gave my lord much countenance in his jealousy, doomed by God for my proper penance to entreat thee thus with food and drink and thrashings, until such time as He may ordain otherwise touching thee and me.' 'And are we two the only folk here?' inquired Ferondo. 'Nay, there are thousands beside,' answered the monk; 'but thou canst neither see nor hear them, nor they thee.' 'And how far,' said Ferondo, 'may we be from our country?' 'Oh! ho!' returned the monk, 'why, 'tis some miles clean out of shit-range.' 'I'faith,' said Ferondo, 'that is far indeed: methinks we must be out of the world.'

In such a course, alternately beaten, fed and amused with idle tales, was Ferondo kept for ten months, while the abbot, to his great felicity, paid many a visit to the fair lady, and had the jolliest time in the world with her. But, as misfortunes will happen, the lady conceived, which fact, as soon as she was aware of it, she imparted to the abbot; whereupon both agreed that Ferondo must without delay be brought back from purgatory to earth and her, and be given to understand that she was with child of him. So the very next night the abbot went to the prison, and in a disguised voice pronounced Ferondo's name, and said to him: – 'Ferondo, be of good cheer, for God is minded that thou return to earth; and on thy return thou shalt have a son by thy lady, and thou shalt call him Benedetto; because 'tis in answer to the prayers of thy holy abbot and thy lady, and for love of St Benedict, that God accords thee this grace.' Whereat Ferondo was overjoyed, and said: – 'It likes me well. God give a good year to Master Lord God, and the abbot, and St Benedict, and my cheese-powdered, honey-sweet wife.' Then, in the wine that he sent him, the abbot administered enough of the powder to cause him to sleep for four hours; and so, with the aid of the monk, having first habited him in his proper clothes, he privily conveyed him back to the tomb in which he had been buried. On the morrow at daybreak Ferondo revived, and perceiving through a chink in the tomb a glimmer of light, to which he had been a stranger for full ten months, he knew that he was alive, and began to bellow: – 'Let me out, let me out;' then, setting his head to the lid of the tomb, he heaved amain; whereby the lid, being insecure, started; and he was already thrusting it aside, when the monks, matins being now ended, ran to the spot and recognized Ferondo's voice, and saw him issue from the tomb; by which unwonted event they were all so affrighted that they took to flight, and hied them to the abbot: who, rising as if from prayer, said: – 'Sons, be not afraid; take the cross and the holy water, and follow me, and let us see what sign of His might God will vouchsafe us.' And so he led the way to the tomb; beside which they found Ferondo standing, deathly pale by reason of his long estrangement from the light. On sight of the abbot he ran and threw himself at his feet, saying: – 'My father, it has been revealed to me that 'tis to your prayers and those of St Benedict and my lady that I owe my release from purgatorial pain, and restoration to life; wherefore 'tis my prayer that God give you a good year and good calends, to-day and all days.' 'Laud we the power of God!' said the abbot. 'Go then, son, as

God has restored thee to earth, comfort thy wife, who, since thou didst depart this life, has been ever in tears, and mayst thou live henceforth in the love and service of God.' 'Sir,' answered Ferondo, ''tis well said; and, for the doing, trust me that, as soon as I find her, I shall kiss her, such is the love I bear her.' So saying he went his way; and the abbot, left alone with his monks, made as if he marvelled greatly at the affair, and caused devoutly chant the Miserere. So Ferondo returned to his hamlet, where all that saw him fleeing, as folk are wont to flee from spectacles of horror, he called them back, asseverating that he was risen from the tomb. His wife at first was no less timorous: but, as folk began to take heart of grace, perceiving that he was alive, they plied him with many questions, all which he answered as one that had returned with ripe experience, and gave them tidings of the souls of their kinsfolk, and told of his own invention the prettiest fables of the purgatorial state, and in full folkmoot recounted the revelation vouchsafed him by the mouth of Ragnolo Braghiello before his resuscitation.

Thus was Ferondo reinstated in his property and reunited to his wife, who, being pregnant, as he thought, by himself, chanced by the time of her delivery to countenance the vulgar error that the woman must bear the infant in the womb for exactly nine months, and gave birth to a male child, who was named Benedeto Ferondi. Ferondo's return from purgatory, and the report he brought thence, immeasurably enhanced the fame of the abbot's holiness. So Ferondo, cured of his jealousy by the thrashings which he had gotten for it, verified the abbot's prediction, and never offended the lady again in that sort. Wherefore she lived with him, as before, in all outward seemliness; albeit she failed not, as occasion served, to forgather with the holy abbot, who had so well and sedulously served her in her especial need.

The Satanic Nun
Montague Summers

It was towards the end of the year 1746 that Sister Cecilia, a professed nun of the Convent of Unterzell, was attacked by a mysterious and unaccountable malady. At first an obscure nervous complaint was suggested and appropriate measures for the relief of the patient were commenced. However, other symptoms soon appeared. The sufferer was seized by painful cramps in every member, her body swelled as if from dropsy, the muscles contracted and were again suddenly relaxed so as to cause her intense agony, hallucinations of the senses, sight, hearing, touch, succeeded and developed into actual delirium. Although the senior nuns took every precaution that the details of Sister Cecilia's illness should not be known, and although the infirmary was isolated under even stricter regulations than usual, before long strange stories began to be whispered among the community. Shadowy figures had been seen at night in the corridors; mocking laughter was heard which suddenly died away in an awesome silence; the cries of animals, a porcine grunting, the deep baffing of huge hounds, the angry miauling of cats, sounded in the refectory, but when the doors were hastily opened the room was empty and still; and, as so often in poltergeist hauntings, articles of furniture moved here and there, seemingly of their own volition, chairs being overthrown without any visible agency, whilst a huge oak chest no two men could shift was overturned with a loud crash that rang through the vaulted cloisters. An atmosphere of indefinable terror possessed the place. Other and unseen inhabitants, not of this earth nor from heaven, had occupied those hallowed walls.

Cecilia Pistorini, the sick religious, was originally from Hamburg, the descendant of an Italian family which had long been settled there. During her novitiate at Unterzell she was distinguished by her fervour and piety, but, as is not unusual in these cases, in order to test her constancy her solemn profession had been deliberately deferred. Whilst the question was under discussion by the Mothers it was remarked that the Sub-Prioress Maria-Renata Sænger showed a most determined and even violent opposition to the young novice, even voting for her dismissal from the convent. In order that they should make no mistake, to assure themselves that her zeal for the cloister was no mere romantic enthusiasm, her superiors, says Father Loschert, legitimately 'made her submit to hard, not to say harsh, trials of her patience, which gave her ample opportunity of practising the virtue of humility. It was noticed that prominent among the Mothers who advocated this strict probation was Renata who, when possession or some demoniac malice came to be suspected in Sister Cecilia's illness, openly declared that there were neither witches nor occultists, that possession was a fable – rationalistic arguments many Satanists use as a wicked blind to compass their ends – and that Sister Cecilia was an hysterical subject who had brought about her own sickness, for which she deserved to be punished rather than consoled.' As Görres says: 'Renata distinguished herself throughout the whole community by the hatred she displayed towards Sister Cecilia.' So here we have a nun of high position in the convent who not only expresses herself in scoffing and atheistical language but shows herself full of malice and rancour which she is ready to visit in every possible way upon a simple and pious girl, a novice of the Order. It might seem that Renata had some presentiment that through this humble Sister, who was eventually admitted to take solemn vows in 1745, her own evil life would be dragged to the light of day.

Suddenly as the religious were reciting their office in Choir several of the nuns collapsed in their stalls uttering raucous cries and even piercing yells. They shook from head to foot as if with an ague, their bodies were convulsed, they rained blows upon invisible enemies who assailed them, they foamed at the mouth, wrestled, and struggled with a more than human strength. It was wellnigh impossible to stifle the scandals of some years' continuance any longer. Yet with praiseworthy anxiety for the good name of her house and tenderest love for her little flock whom the wolf had so foully ravaged, the Prioress, awful suspicions gnawing at her heart, heroically endeavoured to bear the burden without complaint, without appeal. At length, however, the whole business was inevitably and immediately exposed. One of the elder sisters was stricken with a mortal disease. Upon her death-bed she revealed to her confessor, a Canon of Oberzell, that the illness which had sapped her life was the result of the secret machinations of the Sub-Prioress, whom for a number of years she had recognized as a Satanist, an adept in black magic, a worker of enchantments and noxious spells. The dying woman attested that Renata by the employment of certain herbs and drugs had contrived to affect four choir nuns and a lay sister with lingering complaints. There can be little doubt, in fact, that the Sub-Prioress was a skilled poisoner, versed in the horrid crafts of the Roman witch Hieronyma Spara, her companion La Graziosa, and the infamous Toffania, whose *acqua tofana* dispersed half over Europe under the name of 'Oil of S. Nicolas of Bari' was regulated so that the victims would die in a week, a month, a year according to the strength and doses.

At first the confessor, appalled at these monstrous accusations, refused to give credit to the tale; he remonstrated with his penitent, reminded her that she lay on a bed of death, and adjured her by that living God Whose judgement she was so soon to endure to speak the truth, the just truth only concerning these dark matters. The aged nun in most solemn tones reiterated that all she had revealed, nay more, she declared that she must tell her story in the presence of witnesses so that it should not be for ever lost under the seal of Sacramental Confession. Accordingly when the Host was brought into her chamber, then in the very presence of her Maker, before the numerous persons who had assembled there, she repeated every detail already whispered to the priest, openly denouncing Renata as author of these hideous crimes, and invoking God, Whom she was about to receive as Viaticum, to attest her sincerity and faith. The scene must have been intensely dramatic in its impressiveness and terror. The failing woman is stretched upon her pallet in the humble room, her wrinkled cheeks and trembling veined hands almost as pale as the snowy counterpane over which they feebly strayed or the spotless pillows which propped her high; strange broken accents fall hesitatingly and slow from her parched gasping lips, words at which the sisters kneeling all round blanch and quiver with fear what time the star-capped tapers shake in their grasp; tempered by the fire of a thousand confessions the grave priest in his white robe and flowing surplice of goffered lawn down which hangs the purple stole, a narrow splash of colour, stands silent by the bed; in the centre of all, upon a table covered with damask and fair linen, ablaze with wax flambeaux is the golden ciborium scintillating in the candlelight, the ciborium whereon are fixed the dim-mantled eyes of the expiring nun.

'Even yet,' says Father Loschert, 'the community was loth openly to accuse the Sub-Prioress to denounce her to the authorities. They preferred to suffer in patience rather than allow themselves to be persuaded that a religious, at any rate a person wearing the religious habit, could be guilty of such abominations. However, the demon declared by the mouth of a possessed nun that he seized Renata even in her mother's womb, that she was his slave and a cursed thing.'

Maria-Renata Sænger von Mossau was born at Munich about 1680, and she had commenced her postulancy with the

Premonstratensians of Unterzell at the age of nineteen. It afterwards came to light that she had been devoted to Satan when
only seven years old, a ceremony repeated with binding oaths
two years later. An old woman had instructed her in occult lore
and magic, and no doubt in the art of poisoning as well. At
eleven she had lent herself to the foul desires of a man of high
estate, and at thirteen she was engaged in a disgusting intrigue
with two lewd officers. A little later she was baptized with the
Devil's baptism by a woman of ill life, one of her father's household, a Satanist, who introduced her to that horrid society. A
woman of rank, whose name was not revealed, became her
mistress in the most intimate arcana of goetic lore, and it was
finally under this tutelage that she became a skilled chemist, a
very Locusta in her knowledge of herbs and venomed drugs.
She entered the convent only to sow dissension and evil in the
very strong-holds of God's kingdom, to debauch and torment
souls essaying the perfect life. She was, indeed, as Joannes
Scherr says, 'no ordinary woman,' a virago as strong for evil as
some have been for good. For fifty years had she hidden her
abnormal wickedness under a cloak of cunningest hypocrisy.
None so regular as she at office, in chapter, at refectory; none so
devout in choir; none so attentive, so punctual, so reserved.
She seemed the very model of a good religious. It was this mas-
querade which had gained her the position of Sub-Prioress. She
would even have been elected Prioress, had not an indefinable
something, not a suspicion, not a suggestion, but yet a vague
shadow of mistrust hindered the community from appointing
her to that all-important office.

This was providential, as I believe in the exactest sense of the
word. From the very first hour she had entered the convent
Renata had secretly been in touch with the Satanists of
Würzburg; sometimes before, sometimes after Matins she had
stolen out to their assemblies; they had supplied her with poisonous roots and *acqua tofana*, with magical screeds and amulets,
of which not a few, including the witches' unguent, were found
concealed in her room. Indeed, the continual visits to the

Convent of an old beldame who sought to hold long confer-
ences with Renata in private gave rise to gossip. It seems certain
that by their aid she had procured duplicate keys to the doors,
both exterior and interior. Impressions could easily be obtained
with a little soft wax, and then the thing were done. Father
Loschert relates that in her youth Renata almost nightly frequented the local Sabbat, that the Grand Master of the Satanists
of Würzburg had welcomed her there, that in the presence of all
that accursed society she renounced Almighty God and His
Blessed Mother, that her name Maria whereat Satan trembles
and is afraid was changed to Ema, under which nomenclature
she was inscribed in the Black Book, that she was marked on
the back with the brand of hell. As I have said elsewhere,
although the role of Devil at such Sabbats was often undertaken by the chief officer, the leader of the Satanists, in any
particular locality, I have no doubt that there was on occasion
an actual manifestation of the materialized evil power, who was
adored by his worshippers with filthy blasphemies and mysterious rites.

Immediately after the death-bed revelations of the aged nun,
who had denounced Renata, special prayers, novenas and
tredicinas, mortifications, rigid fasts, litanies, penitential psalms,
were ordered for the community. The Blessed Sacrament was
solemnly exposed and the *Miserere* sung in choir to obtain grace
and guidance during those dark and troubled days. On
Christmas Day the almoner of the convent, a pious and discreet priest, determined to proceed to the solemn exorcism of
the afflicted nuns. For three days he continued his efforts, and
the morning of Holy Innocents, certain of whose Relics were
shown for the veneration of the religious, a terrible scene took
place. All were in chapel, the almoner had begun the formula of
exorcism when the possessed women fell into frenzied convulsions. They rolled on the ground howling and snapping like
mad curs. Hideous blasphemies mingled with their raucous
yells. At length they shrieked out: 'Our time is come! Our time
is come! We cannot longer lie hid!' As in the days of our Divine

Lord the demons were speaking through the mouths of their miserable victims.

Diabolic possession was proven. 'Nobody,' says Father Loschert, 'could from this moment doubt but that the six nuns were possessed by the Devil; one could only in all humility wonder that Heaven had permitted so terrible a curse to fall upon a convent where day and night the occupation of all was the praise of God and prayer. This hour, however, had been ordained by Providence to expose that foul witch who hid her sorceries beneath the holy habit, to expel her from that fair community to which in spirit and in truth she had never belonged.'

Another solemn exorcism of the afflicted sisters took place in full choir. The evil spirits when adjured revealed their names in the kingdom of darkness – fantastic, hideously grotesque labels – Datas Calvo, Dusacrus, Nataschurus, Nabascurus, Aatalphus, Elephatan. Renata was present, and it is said that in horror at her stony silence, the contemptuous smile that curled her lip, her flashing eyes, the Prioress and the nuns, even the priest himself, shrank from the blast of malice and hate that seemed to encompass her and dart malevolently from such hellish fury.

As may be well supposed Renata concentrated her rage upon the almoner, who had been so largely instrumental in discovering the Satanist.

The Lord Abbot of Oberzell forthwith made a formal visitation of the convent, in the course of which he ordered Renata to be confined in a room apart, straitly charging that she should be allowed no communication with the rest of the community. This quick move filled her with apprehension, as well it might, and when she was immediately put under restraint before she had the opportunity of returning to her own room, she began to lose her stoic attitude and to show signs of distress. She earnestly pleaded to be allowed to furnish herself with certain books of devotion, a mere subterfuge as shortly appeared. 'She asked that she might go to her room,' reports Father Loschert, 'in order to get a few articles of pious use, but this was a flimsy pretext, and it was soon evident that she was anxious to destroy various unhallowed objects she had concealed there, ingredients for her spells and sorceries. Leave was denied.' On the other hand grave suspicions were aroused by her pertinacity and manifest uneasiness. Several learned priests made a thorough examination of the chamber, and there they found not only noxious herbs and phials containing potions and lotions, which when analysed by skilled chemists were discovered to be swift poisons, but also a number of pots of ill-savoured ointment, the witches' unguent, and above all a yellow robe curiously embroidered with cabalistic sigils and signs, which, as she afterwards confessed, Renata wore at the conclaves of Satanists she was wont secretly to frequent. It will not be impertinent to note that Weyer has preserved for us three formulæ of 'witch' ointment:

1. Du persil, de l'eau de l'Aconite, des feuilles de Peuple, et de la suye.
   (Parsley or rather hemlock, water of aconite, poplar leaves, and soot.)
2. De la Berle, de l'acorum vulgaire, de la Quintefeuille, du sang de chauvesouris, de la Morelle endormante, et de l'huyle.
   (Water hemlock, sweet flag, cinquefoil, bat's blood, deadly nightshade, and oil.)
3. De graisse d'enfant, de sue d'Ache, d'Aconite, de Quintefeuille, de Morelle, et de suye.
   (Baby's fat, juice of cowbane, aconite, cinquefoil, deadly nightshade, and soot.)

'These prescriptions,' says Professor A. J. Clark, 'show that the society of witches had a very considerable knowledge of the art of poisoning.'

As Renata continued to display such a violent animosity toward the almoner of Unterzell it was resolved that a confessor extraordinary should be applied for, whose ministrations and ghostly counsel might prevail upon her to relieve her guilty soul by a frank and free acknowledgement of her crimes. This is strictly in accordance with the provision of the Council of Trent: 'Præter ordinarium autem confessorem alius extraordinarius ab Episcopo et aliis superioribus bis aut ter in anno offeratur qui omnium confessiones audire debeat.' Sessio XXV.cap.10. (In addition to the ordinary confessor, another priest, a confessor extraordinary may be provided by the Bishop or other superiors twice or thrice a year, and he shall then hear the confessions of the Community.) The Prince-Bishop of Würzburg, when formal application was made, at once authorized a confessor extraordinary to visit the convent, and with the approbation of his Abbot, Dom Maurus, a learned and experienced director, a Benedictine of the Würzburg monastery, undertook the task. There were many religious houses in the city, Augustinians, Franciscans, Dominicans, Jesuits, and others, but of them all the Benedictine family was reputed to be the most scholarly, the most deeply versed in things mystical, true monks, true contemplatives, not mingling with the world, but wholly devoted to the interior life, walking in heavenly places. Dom Maurus enjoyed the reputation of a Saint; his knowledge of the spiritual life, his gentleness, his charity, had won him not only the love but also the reverence of the whole district. At his first interview with the unhappy Renata his holy admonitions so touched her heart, that she unburdened her conscience of the load of guilt and poured forth a tale of blackest infamy. This she related openly, not under the sacramental seal, and later her long and terrible confession was reduced to thirteen heads: (1) She acknowledged that she was a Satanist; (2) that she had made a covenant with the Demon, changing her name Maria, as especially hateful to Satan, to Ema, under which title she had been entered on the local roll of witches; (3) that she was marked on her body with the Devil's character; (4) that at night she frequently rubbed her body with the witches' ointment, and attended the Sabbat, wearing the yellow robe which had been discovered in her room; (5) that at these assemblies she had abjured God, our Blessed Lady, the Sacraments; (6) that she had had carnal intercourse with a Demon and with Satanists at the Sabbat; (7) that she had enticed three persons outside the convent to join the hellish society; (8) that she was accompanied by a familiar, a rat; (9) that she attempted to cast spells upon the almoner of the convent and the Lord Abbot of Oberzell, but in this instance she had failed; (10) that by her enchantments [and, doubtless, by her poisons] she had caused six persons in the house and several persons not of the house to fall ill of wasting diseases, that she had stricken several with paralysis and other ailments; (11) that she was responsible for the diabolic possession of six nuns; (12) that she had ensorceled Father Gregory of the monastery of Ebrach and Father Nicolas Venino of Ilmstadt; (13) that at her communions she was wont not to swallow the Sacred host but to keep It, and then to throw It into the fish-ponds or on a midden, or again down the latrines, or not unseldom to carry It to her secret rendezvous when the company would stab and pierce It with bodkins and needles in their insensate hatred of God. It was, in truth, this last and most horrible confession which sealed her doom.

The unhappy woman showed every sign of a sincere and complete penitence, but the evil she had wrought could not be so soon undone. The afflicted nuns were still tortured and tormented by the devils, for as was divinely said in days of old: 'Hoe genus in nullo potest exire, nisi in oratione et ieiunio.' (This kind can go out by nothing, but by prayer and fasting.) The Prince-Bishop, to whom a full report was addressed, now ordered the transference of Renata to the fortress of Marienberg where she was kept under strict ward. Her religious habit was taken away and she was dressed in a dark robe of secular fashion. Several pious priests visited her and spent long hours in exhortation and prayer, and 'although they knew she had been a hardened and infamous malefactor, nevertheless they believed that she had truly repented of her crimes, since she gave such unmistakable signs of contrition and a change of heart.' The unclean spirits, furious at their prey being thus snatched from them, raved more madly and foully from the mouths of the possessed, tearing and rending their poor victims in hideous convulsions and paroxysms of frenzy.

An ecclesiastical tribunal sat to judge the case. The assessors were two priests of tempered experience and probity, of whom one was Father Loschert; two Jesuit fathers; Dom Maurus and the almoner of the convent. After long deliberations, which lasted several weeks, Renata was condemned as guilty of sorcery, heresy, apostasy, and of having defiled the Host in the Manichæan manner. She was degraded from religion and handed over to the secular courts. 'After a new inquiry, a report was submitted to His Highness the Prince-Bishop [23 May, 1749] and the prisoner was condemned to be burned for her crimes; this punishment, however, Monsignor, in consideration of the extreme youth of the accused when she was first seduced to the heinous sin of Witchcraft mitigated to death by the headsman's sword within the precincts of the prison, and that her body should afterwards be publicly burned upon a great pyre.' Renata heard her sentence calmly, accepting it without a murmur as the just penalty of her crimes.

On 21 June, 1749, between the hours of eight o'clock and nine, the prisoner was carried in a chair to the place of execution, a bastion of the castle. She wore a long black dress, a white apron, a white gorget, and a coif of black and white. Two priests, Dom Maurus, her confessor, and the almoner of the prison, Father Gaar, S.J., walked by her side, to comfort and exhort her in this extremity. An eye-witness, who was officially present as the representative of a civic corporation, relates that she showed a truly perfect and humble resignation at the last, and the executioner most dextrously severed her neck with one swift sudden sweep of his sword.

The body was then conveyed by two serjeants, 'night watchmen,' to the other side of the Main, and there on a hill locally dubbed 'Sorcerers' Square,' perpetuating the fact that a century and a half before numbers of witches had perished at the stake on that spot, it was consumed in an immense fire of faggots, brushwood, and tar-barrels, which had been built up the preceding day. A vast crowd had assembled to witness the event, and Father Gaar, mounting a movable pulpit, first addressed the throng in an eloquent and admirably reasoned discourse. He impressed upon his hearers that sorcery although a rare was none the less a very real offence, that unclean spirits might yet possess and torment persons even as in the days of Our Lord, that the Devil even now 'tamquam leo rugiens circuit, quærens quem deuoret,' 'as a roaring lion, goeth about seeking whom he may devour.'

The whole account of Maria-Renata Sænger is recorded with the utmost clarity without passion, without partiality. There are ample documents, and the train of events is perfectly simple and logical. It is obvious that she was a Satanist, who had early been introduced into that dark society, that for years she was trained in all their evil secrets, and that at last discovery came almost by an accident.

A Counter-blaste to Tobacco

King James I

That the manifolde abuses of this vile custome of *Tobacco* taking, may the better be espied, it is fit, that first you enter into consideration both of the first originall thereof, and likewise of the reasons of the first entry thereof into this Countrey. For certainely as such customes, that have their first institution either from a godly, necessary, or honorable ground, and are first brought in, by the meanes of some worthy, vertuous, and great Personage, are ever, and most justly, holden in great and reverent estimation and account, by all wise, vertuous, and temperate spirits: So should it by the contrary, justly bring a great disgrace into that sort of customes, which having their originall from base corruption and barbarity, doe in like sort, make their first entry into a Countrey, by an inconsiderate and childish affectation of Noveltie, as is the true case of the first invention of *Tobacco* taking, and of the first entry thereof among us. For *Tobacco* being a common herbe, which (though under divers names) growes almost everywhere, was first found out by some of the barbarous *Indians*, to be a Preservative, or Antidot against the Pockes, a filthy disease, whereunto these barbarous people are (as all men know) very much subject, what through the uncleanly and adust constitution of their bodies, and what through the intemperate heate of their Climate: so that as from them was first brought into Christendome, that most detestable disease, so from them likewise was first brought this use of *Tobacco*, as a stinking and unsavorie Antidot, for so corrupted and execrable a Maladie, the stinking Suffumigation whereof they yet use against that disease, making so one canker or venime to eate out another.

And now good Countrey men let us (I pray you) consider, what honour or policie can moove us to imitate the barbarous and beastly maners of the wilde, godlesse, and slavish *Indians*, especially in so vile and stinking a custome? Shall wee disdaine to imitate the maners of our neighbour *France* (having the stile of the first Christian Kingdom) and that cannot endure the spirit of the Spaniards (their King now being comparable in largenes of Dominions to the great Emperor of *Turkie*). Shall wee, I say, that have bene so long civill and wealthy in peace, famous and invincible in Warre, fortunate in both, we that have bene ever able to aide any of our neighbours (but never deafed any of their ears with any of our supplications for assistance) shall we, I say, without blushing, abase our selves so farre, as to imitate these beastly *Indians*, slaves to the *Spaniards*, refuse to the world, and as yet aliens to the holy Covenant of God? Why doe we not as well imitate them in walking naked as they doe? in preferring glasses, feathers, and such toyes, to golde and precious stones, as they do? yea why do we not denie God and adore the Devill, as they doe?

And as for the vanities committed in this filthie custome, is it not both great vanitie and uncleanenesse, that at the table, a place of respect, of cleanlinesse, of modestie, men should not be ashamed, to sit tossing of *Tobacco pipes*, and puffing of the smoke of *Tobacco* one to another, making the filthie smoke and stinke thereof, to exhale athwart the dishes, and infect the aire, when very often, men that abhorre it are at their repast? Surely Smoke becomes a kitchen far better then a Dining chamber, and yet it makes a kitchen also oftentimes in the inward parts of men, soiling and infecting them, with an unctuous and oily kinde of Soote as hath bene found in some great *Tobacco* takers, that after their death were opened. And not onely meate time, but no other time nor action is exempted from the publicke use of this uncivill tricke: so as if the wives of *Diepe* list to contest with this nation for good maners their worst maners would in all reason be found at least not so dishonest (as ours are) in this point. The publike use whereof, at all times, and in all places, hath now so farre prevailed, as divers men very sound both in judgement, and complexion, have bene at last forced to take it also without desire, partly because they were ashamed to seeme singular (like the two Philosophers that were forced to duck themselves in that raine water, and so become fooles as well as the rest of the people) and partly, to be as one that was content to eate Garlicke (which he did not love) that he might not be troubled with the smell of it, in the breath of his fellowes. And is it not a great vanitie, that a man cannot heartily welcome his friend now, but straight they must bee in hand with *Tobacco*? No it is become in place of a cure, a point of good fellowship, and he that will refuse to take a pipe of *Tobacco* among his fellowes, (though by his own election he would rather feele the savour of a Sinke) is accounted peevish and no good company, even as they doe with tippeling in the cold Easterne Countries. Yea the Mistresse cannot in a more manerly kinde, entertaine her servant, then by giving him out of her faire hand a pipe of *Tobacco*. But herein is not onely a great vanitie, but a great contempt of God's good giftes, that the sweetenesse of mans breath, being a good gift of God, should be willfully corrupted by this stinking smoke, wherein I must confesse, it hath too strong a vertue: and so that which is an ornament of nature, and can neither by any artifice be at the first acquired, nor once lost, be recovered againe, shall be filthily corrupted with an incurable stinke, which vile qualitie is as directly contrary to that wrong opinion which is holden to the wholesomnesse thereof, as the venime of putrifaction is contrary to the vertue Preservative.

Moreover, which is a greater iniquitie, and against all humanite, the husband shall not bee ashamed, to reduce thereby his delicate, wholesome, and cleane complexioned wife, to that extremetie, that either shee must also corrupt her sweete breath therewith, or else resolve to live in a perpetuall stinking torment.

Have you not reason then to bee ashamed, and to forbeare this filthie noveltie, so basely grounded, so foolishly received and so grossely mistaken in the right use thereof? In your abuse thereof sinning against God, harming yourselves both in persons and goods, and taking also thereby the markes and notes of vanitie upon you: by the custome thereof making your selves to be wondered at by all forraine civil Nations, and by all strangers that come among you, to be scorned and contemned. A custome lothsome to the eye, hateful to the Nose, harmefull to the braine, dangerous to the Lungs, and the blacke stinking fume thereof, neerest resembling the horrible Stigian smoke of the pit that is bottomelesse.

Here was the secret of happiness, about which philosophers had disputed for so many ages, at once discovered; happiness might now be bought for a penny, and carried in the waistcoat-pocket; portable ecstasies might be had corked up in a pint-bottle; and peace of mind could be sent down by the mail.

From *Confessions of an English Opium-Eater*
by Thomas De Quincey

Psychoactive substances, the portable ecstasies to which De Quincey refers, have, since prehistoric times, moved with remarkable rapidity across geographical and cultural divides as humankind has sought new pleasures and exotic cures for its pains. In this section are a number of travellers' tales of strange plants and poisons, and the equally strange individuals and societies that have made use of them. The anthropologist James Mooney collected two versions of a Cherokee myth entitled *How They Brought Back Tobacco*. In these tales it can be seen that the Indian view of tobacco is in sharp contrast to that of King James I.

Early travellers to the New World found many similarities between the practices of the native inhabitants and those of European witches. A book by José de Acosta (*c.* 1539–1600), first published in England in the same year as King James's tobacco tract, gives an account of *The Abominable Unction of the Mexican Priests*. Not only does he describe an Indian counterpart to the flying ointment of the European witches but also the 'devilish' use of the hallucinogenic plant, morning glory. Later travellers among the Mexican Indians have been less prone to damn the native priests, among them the French writer and one-time surrealist Antonin Artaud (1896–1948) whose *The Peyote Dance* is a highly personal account of his experiences among the Tarahumara Indians of Mexico. Artaud had sought release from his mental and physical turmoil, his opium habit and his alienation from society by partaking in the ceremonial use of the hallucinogenic peyote cactus. He saw the peyote rite as imparting to its participants a more authentic experience of life than was available in the decaying civilisation of Europe. Yet sadly his own participation could not liberate him from his suffering and, on his return to Europe, he was confined in an asylum whilst writing this account of his Mexican experiences.

Anthropologists, ethnobotanists and other travellers in Amazonia have long been struck by the sheer number of hallucinogenic plants used by the natives. The bizarre cultural use of such plants is described in *The Hallucinogenic Snuff of the Muras Indians* written by Johann Baptist von Spix (1781–1826) and Carl Friedrich Philip von Martius (1794–1868). This text is a description of a hallucinogenic ceremony that goes on for eight days and nights during which time the Indians literally whip themselves into a frenzy. The great Colombian anthropologist Gerardo Reichel-Dolmatoff collected numerous tales from the shamans of the Desana people, including one entitled *Narcotic Snuff and First Origins*. This story tells of how narcotic snuff was used by the ancestors to induce visions at the beginning of time.

Contrary to modern science, many Amazonian peoples believe that the ordinary world which we see as real is but an illusion, and that the states of consciousness achieved by shamans with the help of psychoactive plants give them access to a reality that is unknown to those who dwell solely in the mundane world. Among these peoples are the Jívaro, famous for their eclectic science of shrinking the heads of their enemies, and users of numerous hallucinogens such as the jungle vine *ayahuasca* and the datura plant which contains the same alkaloids as the henbane, belladonna and deadly nightshade plants used by the European witches. *Hallucinogens of the Jívaro Headhunters* by the American anthropologist Michael Jo Harner describes the magical world of the shamans, their bewitchments and their cures.

Two different preparations of the poisonous powders used by the *bokor* (the name given to a malevolent priest or sorcerer of a Voudon society) in order to turn unfortunate victims into zombies are described by the remarkable Canadian ethnobotanist Wade Davis in *Zombie Poisons of Haiti*. Whilst the dark sorcery of the *bokor* brings the victim closer to death, the shaman in the next tale – *Mushrooms in Kamchatka* – brings an ailing Polish brigadier back from the brink of death with the help of the fly-agaric mushroom. In the late 1790s Joseph Kopeć, the man in question, was travelling in the Kamchatka peninsula in eastern Siberia, when he clambered into a *yurt* (a native dwelling) whilst running a fever. It was then that he was cured by the Kamchadal shaman or 'evangelist' as Kopeć refers to him.

How They Brought Back Tobacco

James Mooney

In the beginning of the world, when people and animals were all the same, there was only one tobacco plant, to which they all came for their tobacco until the Dagûl'kû geese stole it and carried it far away to the south. The people were suffering without it, and there was one old woman who grew so thin and weak that everybody said she would die unless she could get tobacco to keep her alive.

Different animals offered to go for it, one after another, the larger ones first and then the smaller ones, but the Dagûl'kû saw and killed every one before he could get to the plant. After the others the little Mole tried to reach it by going under the ground, but the Dagûl'kû saw his track and killed him as he came out.

At last the Hummingbird offered, but the others said he was entirely too small and might as well stay at home. He begged them to let him try, so they showed him a plant in a field and told him to let them see how he would go about it. The next moment he was gone and they saw him sitting on the plant, and then in a moment he was back again, but no one had seen him going or coming, because he was so swift. 'This is the way I'll do,' said the Hummingbird, so they let him try.

He flew off to the east, and when he came in sight of the tobacco the Dagûl'kû were watching all about it, but they could not see him because he was so small and flew so swiftly. He darted down on the plant – *tsa!* – and snatched off the top with the leaves and seeds, and was off again before the Dagûl'kû knew what had happened. Before he got home with the tobacco the old woman had fainted and they thought she was dead, but he blew the smoke into her nostrils, and with a cry of *'Tsâ'lû!* [Tobacco!]' she opened her eyes and was alive again.

SECOND VERSION

The people had tobacco in the beginning, but they had used it all, and there was great suffering for want of it. There was one old man so old that he had to be kept alive by smoking, and as his son did not want to see him die he decided to go himself to try and get some more. The tobacco country was far in the south, with high mountains all around it, and the passes were guarded, so that it was very hard to get into it, but the young man was a conjurer and was not afraid. He travelled southward until he came to the mountains on the border of the tobacco country. Then he opened his medicine bag and took out a hummingbird skin and put it over himself like a dress. Now he was a hummingbird and flew over the mountains to the tobacco field and pulled some of the leaves and seed and put them into his medicine bag. He was so small and swift that the guards, whoever they were, did not see him, and when he had taken as much as he could carry he flew back over the mountains in the same way. Then he took off the hummingbird skin and put it into his medicine bag, and was a man again. He started home, and on his way came to a tree that had a hole in the trunk, like a door, near the first branches, and a very pretty woman was looking out from it. He stopped and tried to climb the tree, but although he was a good climber he found that he always slipped back. He put on a pair of medicine moccasins from his pouch, and then he could climb the tree, but when he reached the first branches he looked up and the hole was still as far away as before. He climbed higher and higher, but every time he looked up the hole seemed to be farther than before, until at last he was tired and came down again. When he reached home he found his father very weak, but still alive, and one draw at the pipe made him strong again. The people planted the seed and had the tobacco ever since.

The Abominable Unction of the Mexican Priests

José de Acosta

'*Of the abominable unction which the Mexicaine priests and other Nations used, and of their witchcraftes.*'

God appoynted in the auntient Lawe the manner how they should consecrate *Aarons* person and the other Priests, and in the Lawe of the Gospel wee have likewise the holy creame and unction which they use when they consecrate the Priestes of Christ. There was likewise in the auntient Lawe a sweete composition, which God defend should be employed in anie other thing then in the divine service. The Divel hath sought to counterfet all these things after his manner as hee hath accustomed, having to this end invented things so fowle and filthie, whereby they discover wel who is the Author. The priests of the idolles in *Mexico* were annoynted in this sort, they annointed the body from the foote to the head, and all the haire likewise, which hung like tresses, or a horse mane, for that they applyed this unction wet and moyst. Their haire grew so as in time it hung downe to their hammes, so heavily that it was troublesome for them to beare it, for they did never cut it untill they died, or that they were dispensed with for their great age, or being employed in governments or some honorable charge in the commonwealth. They carried their haire in tresses, of six fingers breadth, which they died blacke with the fume of sapine, or firre trees, or rosine; for in all Antiquities it hath bin an offring they made unto their idolls, and for this cause it was much esteemed and reverenced. They were always died with this tincture from the foote to the head, so as they were like unto shining Negroes, and that was their ordinary unction: yet, whenas they went to sacrifice and give incense in the mountaines, or on the tops thereof, or in any darke and obscure caves where their idolls were, they used an other kinde of unction very different, doing certaine ceremonies to take away feare, and to give them courage. This unction was made with diverse little venomous beastes, as spiders, scorpions, palmers, salamanders, and vipers, the which the boyes in the Colledges tooke and gathered together, wherein they were so expert, as they were always furnished when the Priestes called for them. The chiefe care of these boyes was to hunt after these beasts; if they went any other way and by chaunce met with any of these beasts they stayed to take them, with as great paine as if their lives depended thereon. By the reason whereof the Indians commonly feared not these venomous beasts, making no more accompt than if they were not so, having beene all bred in this exercise. To make an ointment of these beastes they took them all together, and burnt them upon the harth of the Temple, which was before the altare, untill they were consumed to ashes; then did they put them in morters with much Tobacco or *Petum* (being a hearbe that Nation useth much to benumme the flesh that they may not feele their travell), with the which they mingle the ashes, making them loose their force; they did likewise mingle with these ashes scorpions, spiders and palmers alive, mingling all together; then did they put to it a certaine seede being grownd, which they called *Ololuchqui*, whereof the Indians make a drinke to see visions, for that the vertue of this hearbe is to deprive man of sence. They did likewise grinde with these ashes balcke and hairie wormes, whose haire only is venomous, all which they mingled together with blacke, or the fume of rosine, putting it in small pots which they set before their god, saying it was his meate. And therefore, they called it a divine meate. By means of this oyntment they became witches, and did see and speake with the Divell. The priestes being slubbered with this oyntment lost all feare, putting on a spirit of cruelty. By reason whereof they did very boldely kill men in their sacrifices, going all alone in the night to the mountaines and into obscure caves, contemning all wilde beasts, and holding it for certayne and approved that both lions, tigres, serpents, and other furious beasts which breede in the mountaines and forrests fledde from them, by vertue of this *Petum* of their god.

And in trueth, though this *Petum* had no power to make them flie, yet was the Divelle's picture sufficient whereinto they were transformed. This *Petum* did also serve to cure the sicke and for children, and therefore all called it the Divine Physicke; and so they came from all partes to the superiors and priests, as to their saviors, that they might apply this divine physicke, wherewith they anoynted those parts that were grieved. They said that they felt heereby a notable ease, which might be, for that Tobacco and *Ololuchqui* have this propertie of themselves, to benumme the flesh, being applied in manner of an emplaister, which must be by a stronger reason being mingled with poysons; and for that it did appease and benumme the paine, they helde it for an effect of health, and a divine virtue. And therefore ranne they to these priests as to holy men, who kept the blind and ignorant in this error, perswading them what they pleased, and making them runne after their inventions and divellish ceremonies, their authority being such, as their wordes were sufficient to induce beliefe as an article of their faith. And thus made they a thousand superstitions among the vulgar people, in their manner of offering incense, in cutting their haire, tying small flowers about their necks, and strings with small bones of snakes, commanding them to bathe at a certain time; and that they should watch all night at the harth lest the fire should die, that they should eate no other bread but that which had bin offered to their gods, that they should upon any occasion repaire unto their witches, who with certaine graines tolde fortunes, and divined, looking into keelers and pailes full of water. The sorcerers and ministers of the divell used much to besmere themselves. There were an infinite number of these witches, divines, enchanters, and other false prophets. There remaines yet at this day of this infection, althogh they be secret, not daring publikely to exercise their sacrileges, divelish ceremonies, and superstitions, but their abuses and wickednes are discovered more at large and particularly in the confessions made by the Prelates of *Peru*.

The Peyote Dance
Antonin Artaud

The Race of Lost Men

In northern Mexico forty-eight hours from Mexico City, there is a race of pure red Indians called the Tarahumara. Forty thousand people are living there in a style that predates the Flood. They are a challenge to this world in which people talk so much about progress only because they despair of progressing.

This race, which ought to be physically degenerate, has for four hundred years resisted every force that has come to attack it: civilization, interbreeding, war, winter, animals, storms, and the forest. The Tarahumara live naked in the winter in mountains that are made impassable by snow, in defiance of all medical theories. Communism exists among them in a feeling of spontaneous solidarity.

Incredible as it may seem, the Tarahumara Indians live as if they were already dead. They do not see reality and they draw magical powers from the contempt they have for civilization.

[. . .] The whole life of the Tarahumara revolves around the erotic Peyote rite.

The root of the Peyote plant is hermaphroditic. It has, as we know, the shape of the male and female sexual organs combined. It is in this rite that the whole secret of these savage Indians resides. To me, its force seemed to be symbolized by the rasping stick, a piece of curved wood covered with notches which, for whole nights, the Peyote sorcerers rhythmically scrape with little sticks. But the strangest part is the way in which these sorcerers are recruited. One day, an Indian will feel *called* to handle the rasp. He goes to a sacred hiding place in the mountains, where for thousands of years there has lain an incredible collection of rasps which other sorcerers have buried. They are made of wood, the wood of warm soil, it is said. The Tarahumara will spend three years living on this plantation of rasps and, at the end of the third year, he returns – the possessor of the essential rite.

Such is the life of this strange people over whom no civilization will ever gain control.

The Peyote Rite among the Tarahumara

[. . .] It was on a Sunday morning that the old Indian chief awakened my consciousness with a prick of the sword between the spleen and the heart. 'Have confidence,' he said to me, 'have no fear, I will do you no harm,' and he quickly retreated three or four steps and, after describing a circle in the air behind him with his sword, rushed forward and leaped at me with all his strength, as if he meant to destroy me. But the point of his sword barely grazed my skin and drew only a tiny drop of blood. I felt no pain whatsoever, but I did have the impression of awakening to something for which until then I had been ill endowed and ill prepared, and I felt filled with a light which I had never before possessed. It was a few days later that one morning at dawn I entered into relation with the priests of Tutuguri and two days after that I finally made contact with Ciguri.

'To sew you back together in your wholeness, without God who assimilates you and creates you, as if you were creating yourself, and as you yourself create yourself out of nothingness and in spite of Him at every moment.'

These are the very words of the Indian chief and I am merely reporting them, not as he said them to me, but as I have *reconstructed* them under the fantastic illuminations of Ciguri.

Now if the Priests of the Sun behave like manifestations of the Word of God, or of his Logos, that is, Jesus Christ, the Priests of Peyote allowed me to experience the actual Myth of the Mystery, to become immersed in the original mythic arcana, to enter through them into the Mystery of Mysteries, to look upon the face of those extreme operations by which THE FATHER MAN, NEITHER MAN NOR WOMAN, created all things. To be sure I did not catch all this immediately and it took me a while to understand it, and indeed, many of the dance movements, many of the attitudes or the shapes which the priests of Ciguri draw in the air as if they were imposing them on the darkness or drawing them from the caves of night, they themselves do not understand, and in performing them they are merely obeying on the one hand a kind of physical tradition, and on the other the secret commands issued to them by the Peyote whose essence they absorb before they start dancing, in order to achieve a trance state. I mean that they do what the plant tells them to do; they repeat it like a kind of lesson which their muscles obey, but which they no longer understand in the relaxation of their nerves, any more than their fathers or grandfathers before them. For the function of every nerve is strained. This did not satisfy me and when the Dance was over I wanted to find out more. For before witnessing the Rite of Ciguri as it is performed by living Indian priests, I had questioned many Tarahumara on the mountain and had spent the night with a young family of whom the husband was an adept of this rite and seemed to know many of its secrets. And I received from him some marvellous explanations and extremely precise elucidations of the way in which Peyote revives throughout the nervous system the memory of certain supreme truths by means of which human consciousness does not lose but on the contrary regains its perception of the Infinite. 'The nature of these truths,' this man told me, 'it is not my business to show you. But it is my business to reawaken them in the mind of your human existence. The mind of man is tired of God, because it is bad and sick, and it is up to us to make it hungry for Him. But as you see,

Time itself refused us the means. You will be shown tomorrow what we still can do. And if you wish to work with us, perhaps with the aid of the Good Will of a man who has come from the other side of the sea and who is not of our Race, we shall succeed in breaking down one more barrier.' CIGURI is a name which Indian ears do not like to hear pronounced. I had with me a *mestizo* guide, who also acted as my interpreter with the Tarahumara, and he had warned me to mention it to them only with respect and caution because, he told me, *they are afraid of it*. But I observed that if there is any emotion that is alien to them in this connection it is fear, and that, on the contrary, the word awakens in them that sense of the sacred which European consciousness has lost, and this is the root of all our misfortunes, for here people no longer respect anything. And the series of attitudes the young Indian assumed before my eyes when I uttered the word CIGURI taught me many things about the potentialities of human consciousness when it has retained the sense of God. I will admit that a terror emanated from his gestures, but the terror was not his own, for it covered him as if with a shield or a mantle. He seemed happy as one is only in the supreme moment of existence, his face overflowing with joy and adoration. So must they have stood, the First Born of a humanity still in childbirth when the spirit of MAN UNCREATED rose in thunder and flames over the eviscerated world; so must they have prayed in the catacombs, those skeletons to whom it is written that MAN himself appeared.

He joined his hands and his eyes kindled. His face became transfixed and closed. But the more he withdrew into himself, the more I had the impression that a strange and legible emotion radiated physically from him. He moved two or three times. And each time his eyes, which had become almost fixed, returned to a point next to him, as if he wanted to be aware of something that was to be feared. But I realized that what he might be afraid of was falling short of the respect he owed to God, through some sort of negligence. And I observed two very important things: the first was that the Tarahumara Indian does not attach the same value to his body that we Europeans do, and that he has an entirely different notion of it. 'It isn't I at all,' he seemed to say, 'who am this body,' and when he turned to stare at something next to him it was his body itself that he seemed to examine and observe.

'Where I am myself and what I am, it is Ciguri who tells it to me and dictates it to me, and you who lie and disobey. What I feel in reality you are never willing to feel, and you give me contrary sensations. You want nothing of what I want. And what you propose to me most of the time is Evil. You have been nothing but a transitory ordeal and a burden. Someday I shall command you to leave when *Ciguri* himself will be free, but,' he said suddenly, weeping, 'you must not leave altogether. *It was Ciguri*, after all, who made you and many times you have provided me with a refuge from the storm, *for Ciguri would die if he did not have me.*'

The second thing I observed in the middle of this prayer – for this series of movements in front of himself and as if beside himself which I had just witnessed, and which took much less time to perform than I have taken to report it, constituted the Indian's impromptu prayer at the mere sound of the name *Ciguri* – the second thing that struck me is that if the Indian is the enemy of his body, he seems also to have sacrificed his consciousness to God, and it seems that the habit of Peyote guides him in this work. The emotions which radiated from him, which passed across his face one after the other, and which could be read, *were manifestly not his own*; he did not attribute them to himself, he no longer identified with what for us is a personal emotion, or rather he did not do it in our way, as the result of a choice and of an instant flashing incubation as we do. Among all the ideas that pass through our heads there are those we accept and those we do not accept. On the day when our self and our consciousness are formed there is established within this incessant movement of incubation a distinctive rhythm and a natural choice whereby only our own ideas remain in the field of consciousness, and the rest automatically vanish. It may take us time to carve out of our emotions and isolate from them our own face, but the way we think on the most important points is like the *totem* of an indisputable grammar that measures its terms word for word. And our self, when we question it, always responds in the same way: like someone who knows that it is he who answers and not another. It is not like this with the Indian.

A European would never allow himself to think that something he has felt and perceived in his body, an emotion which has shaken him, a strange idea which he has just had and which has inspired him with its beauty, was not his own, and that someone else has felt and experienced all this in his own body – or else he would believe himself mad and people would probably say that he had become a lunatic. The Tarahumara, on the contrary, systematically distinguishes between what is his own and what is of the Other in everything he thinks, feels, and does. But what makes him different from a lunatic is that his personal consciousness has expanded in this process of internal separation and distribution to which Peyote has led him and which strengthens his will. Although he may seem to know what he is *not* much better than what he is, he does know what he is and who he is much better than we know what we are and what we want. 'There is,' he said, 'in every man an ancient reflection of God in which we can still contemplate the image of that infinite force which one day flung us into a soul and this soul into a body, and it is to the image of this Force that Peyote has led us because Ciguri calls us back to him.' [. . .]

I arrived at the little Indian village where I had been told that the Rite of Peyote was to be shown to me. It took place after dark. The priest arrived with two assistants, a man and a woman, and two young children. He drew on the ground a kind of large semicircle inside which the revels of his assistants were to take place and he closed this semicircle with a stout beam on which I was permitted to sit. To the right, the arc of the circle was bounded by a kind of retreat in the shape of an 8 which I understood constituted for the priest the Holy of Holies.

To the left, there was the Void: this is where the children stood. It was in the Holy of Holies that the old wooden pot containing the Peyote roots was placed, for the Priests do not use the whole plant for their special Rites, or at least not any more.

The Priest had a cane in his hand and the children had little sticks. Peyote is taken after a certain number of dance movements and when, by the religious performance of the Rite, its adepts have achieved a state in which Ciguri wishes to enter into them.

I observed that the assistants were having trouble starting to move, and I had the impression that they would not dance or would dance badly if they did not know that at the appropriate moment Ciguri was going to descend upon them. For the Rite of Ciguri is a Rite of creation, which explains how things *are* in the Void and how the Void is the Infinite, and how they emerged from it into Reality, and were made. And the Rite is completed at the moment when, at God's command, the things have taken on Being in a body. This is what the two assistants danced, but this did not take place without a long discussion.

'We can no longer understand God unless he first touches our souls, and our dance will be nothing but a mockery, and the PHANTOM,' they screamed, 'the PHANTOM which pursues CIGURI will be born here once again.'

The Priest took a long time making up his mind, but finally he drew from his breast a small bag and poured into the Indians' hands a kind of white powder which they immediately consumed.

Whereupon they began to dance. Seeing their faces after they had taken this powdered Peyote, I realized that they were going to show me something which I had never experienced before. And I gave all my attention so that I would miss nothing of what I was going to see.

The two assistants lay down on the ground facing each other like two inanimate balls. But the old Priest must have taken the powder himself, for an inhuman expression had stolen over his face. I saw him stretch and stand very tall. His eyes kindled and began to take on an expression of unusual authority. With his cane he made two or three dull thuds on the ground, then entered the 8 he had drawn to the right of the Ritual Field. Now the assistants seemed to emerge from their inanimate state. First the man shook his head and struck the ground with the palms of his hands. The woman shook her back. Then the Priest spat: not saliva, but his breath. Noisily he expelled his breath between his teeth. Under the influence of this pulmonary vibration, the man and woman simultaneously came to life and rose to their feet. But from the way they stood facing each other, especially from the way each stood in space as they might have stood in the pockets of the void and the cracks of the infinite, it was clear that it was no longer a man and a woman who were there but two principles: the male, mouth open, gums smacking, red, flaming, bloody, as if lacerated by the roots of the teeth, which were translucent at that moment like tongues of command; the female, toothless larva, molars filed down, like a she-rat in its cage, imprisoned in her own heat, shifting and turning in front of the hirsute male; and it was also clear that they were going to collide, smash frantically into one another just as material things, after facing each other for a time and making war, finally intermingle before the *indiscreet* and *guilty* eye of God, whom their action will gradually replace. 'For *Ciguri*,' they said, 'was MAN, MAN AS SELF-CREATED, HIMSELF in the space HE *was constructing* FOR HIMSELF, when God murdered him.'

This is exactly what took place.

But one thing struck me particularly in the way they threatened each other, avoided each other, collided with each other, and finally consented to unite. This is that these principles were not in the body, never reached the body, but obstinately remained like two immaterial ideas suspended outside of Being, eternally opposed to HIM, and which moreover made *their own bodies*, bodies in which the idea of matter is volatilized by CIGURI. As I watched them, I remembered everything I had been told about Indian religion and culture by the poets, teachers, and artists of all kinds whom I knew in Mexico, and what I had read in all the books I had borrowed about the metaphysical traditions of the Mexicans.

'The Evil Spirit,' says the Initiate Priests of Ciguri, 'has never been able or willing to believe that God is not accessibly and exclusively a Being and that there is something more than Being in the inscrutable essence of God.'

But this was exactly what this Peyote Dance was in the process of showing me.

For in this dance I thought I could see the point where the universal unconscious is sick. And that it is outside of God. The priest would touch his spleen or his liver with his right hand while with his left hand he struck the ground with his cane. Each of his gestures evoked from the man and the woman a distant attitude – now of desperate and haughty affirmation, now of enraged denial. But when the Priest, who now held his cane in both hands, struck several rapid blows, they advanced rhythmically towards each other with their elbows apart and their hands joined, so that they formed two triangles in motion. At the same time their feet drew on the ground circles, and something that resembled the limbs of a letter, an S, a U, a J, a V. Figures in which the 8 shape recurred most often. Once, twice they did not meet but passed one another with a tentative greeting. The third time their greeting became more certain. The fourth time they joined hands, circled each other, and the man's feet seemed to search on the ground for the places where the woman's feet had struck it.

They repeated this sequence eight times. But after the fourth time their faces, which had taken on a lively expression, never ceased to be radiant. The eighth time they looked towards the Priest, who then moved with a dominating and menacing air to the furthest end of the Holy of Holies, where things are in contact with the North. And with his cane he drew in the air a huge 8. But the scream that he uttered at that moment could have overthrown *the hellish labor pains of the dead man black with his ancient sin*, in the words of the old buried poem of the Maya of Yucatán; and I do not remember ever in my life hearing anything that revealed more clearly or resonantly to what depths the human will descends to raise its foreknowledge of night. And I seemed to see again in the Infinite and as if in a dream the raw matter from which God called forth Life. This scream of the Priest seemed meant to sustain the path of the cane in the air. Screaming this way, the Priest moved and he drew with his whole body in the air and with his feet on the ground the shape of the same 8 until he had closed the figure at the Southern end.

The dance was almost over. The two children who had remained to the left of the circle all this time asked whether they could go, and the Priest gave them a sign with his cane as if to scatter and disappear. But neither of the two had taken Peyote. They made a vague gesture that resembled a dance movement, then gave up and disappeared as if to go home.

As I said at the beginning of this account, all this did not satisfy me. I wanted to find out more about Peyote. I walked over to the Priest to question him.

'Our last Festival,' he told me, 'could not take place. We are discouraged. Nowadays we do not take Ciguri for the Rites but as a vice. Soon our whole Race will be sick. Time has grown too old for Man. It can no longer sustain us. What are we to do, what is to become of us? Already our people are turning away from God. As a priest, I cannot help feeling it. You see me in despair.'

I told him about the agreement that had been made with the director of the native school and that this time their next great festival could take place.

I also told him that I had not come to visit the Tarahumara as a tourist but to regain a Truth which the world of Europe is losing and which his Race had preserved. This disarmed him completely and he told me some wonderful things about Good and Evil, about Truth and Life.

'Everything I say comes from *Ciguri*,' he told me, 'and it was *Ciguri* that taught it to me.

'Things are not as we see them and experience them most of the time, but they are as *Ciguri* teaches them to us. They have been taken over by Evil, by the Evil Spirit since time began, and without *Ciguri* it is impossible for man to return to the Truth. In the beginning they were true, but the older we grow the more false they become, because the more they are taken over by Evil. The world in the beginning was completely real, it resounded in the human heart and with the human heart. Now the heart is no longer in it, nor is the soul because God has withdrawn from it. To see the things of the world was to see the Infinite. Now when I look at the light I have trouble thinking of God. And yet it is He, Ciguri, who made everything. But Evil is in all things and I, as a man, can no longer feel pure. There is inside me something horrible which rises and which does not come from me, but from the shadows that I have in me, where the soul of man does not know where the *I* begins and where it ends, or what made it begin as it sees itself. And this is what *Ciguri* tells me. With *Ciguri* I no longer know untruth and I no longer confuse *that which wills* truly in every man with that which does not will but mimics being with ill will. And soon that is all there will be,' he said, retreating several steps: 'this obscene mask of someone sniggering between the sperm and the dung.'

These words of the Priest which I have just reported are absolutely authentic; I found them too important and too beautiful to allow myself to change them in any way, and if I have not reported them word for word the difference is very slight, for you must understand that they impressed me profoundly and that my recollection on this point has remained extremely precise. As I said before, he had just taken Peyote and I was not surprised at his lucidity.

When this conversation was over he asked me whether I would like to taste Ciguri myself and in this way to come closer to the Truth I was seeking.

I told him that this was my fondest desire and that I did not think that without the help of Peyote one could reach everything which eludes us and from which we are becoming more and more alienated by time and material things.

Into my left hand he poured a quantity the size of a ripe almond, 'enough,' he said, 'to see God two or three times, for God can never be known. To enter into his presence one must come under the influence of Ciguri at least three times, but each dose must not exceed the size of a pea.'

So I spent another day or two among the Tarahumara to deepen my experience of Peyote, and it would require a large volume to report everything I saw and felt under its influence and everything that the priests, their assistants, and their families told me on the subject. But a vision which I had and which impressed me was declared *authentic* by the Priest and his family; it concerned, apparently, the one who must be *Ciguri* and who is God. But one arrives at such a vision only after one has gone through a tearing and an agony, after which one feels as if turned around and *reversed* to the other side of things, and one no longer understands the world that one has just left.

I said *reversed* to the other side of things, as if a terrible force had granted that you be *restored* to that which exists on the other side. You no longer feel the body which you have just left and which secured you within its limits, but you feel much happier to belong to the limitless than to yourself, for you understand that what was yourself has come from the head of this limitless, the Infinite, and that you are going to see it. You feel as if you were in an effervescent wave which gives off an incessant crackling in all directions. Things which seem to have emerged from what was your spleen, your liver, your heart, or your lungs keep breaking away and bursting in this atmosphere which wavers between gas and water, but which seems to summon forth material things and command them to combine.

The things that emerged from my spleen or my liver were shaped like the letters of a very ancient and mysterious alphabet chewed by an enormous mouth, but terrifyingly obscure, proud, *illegible*, jealous of its invisibility; and these signs were swept in all directions in space while I seemed to ascend, but not alone. Aided by a strange force. But much freer than when on the earth I was alone.

At a given moment something like a wind arose and space shrank back. On the side where my spleen was, an immense void was hollowed out which was painted gray and pink like the shore of the sea. And at the bottom of this void there appeared the form of a stranded root, a kind of J that had at its summit three branches surmounted by an E that was as sad and luminous as an eye. Flames came out of the left ear of the J and, passing behind it, seemed to push all things to the right, to the side where my liver was, but far beyond it. I saw no more and everything vanished or it was I who vanished as I returned to ordinary reality. In any case, it seems that I had seen the very Spirit of Ciguri. And I believe that this must have objectively corresponded to a *painted* transcendental representation of the ultimate and highest realities; and the Mystics must go through similar states and images before they reach, according to the formula, the supreme burnings and rendings after which they fall beneath the kiss of God like whores, no doubt, into the arms of their procurers.

This experience inspired a number of reflections on the psychic effects of Peyote.[1]

Peyote leads the self back to its true sources. Once one has experienced a visionary state of this kind, one can no longer confuse the lie with the truth. One has seen where one comes from and who one is, and one no longer doubts what one is.

[1] I mean that although these mystical ideas may once again impose themselves on my thinking, Peyote, on the other hand, does not lend itself to these fetid spiritual assimilations, for MYSTICISM has never been anything but the copulation of a very learned and refined hypocrisy against which PEYOTE as a whole protests, for with Peyote MAN is alone, desperately scraping out the music of his own skeleton, without father, mother, family, love, god, or society.

And no living being to accompany him. And the skeleton is not of bone but of skin, like a skin that walks. And one walks from the equinox to the solstice, buckling on one's own humanity. [Note added by Artaud in 1947.]

There is no emotion or external influence that can divert one from this reality.

And the whole series of lustful fantasies projected by the unconscious can no longer oppress the true breath of MAN, for the good reason that Peyote is MAN not born, but INBORN, and that with it the atavistic and personal consciousness is summoned and supported. It knows what is good for it and what is of no use to it: it knows which thoughts and feelings it can receive without danger and *with profit*, and which are harmful to the exercise of its freedom. Above all, it knows just how far its own being goes, and just how far *it has not yet gone* OR HAS NOT THE RIGHT TO GO WITHOUT SINKING INTO THE UNREAL, THE ILLUSORY, THE UNMADE, THE UNPREPARED.

To take one's dreams for realities (a state into which Peyote will never let you sink) is where one might confuse perceptions taken from the depths – fleeting, uncultivated, not yet ripe, not yet arisen from the hallucinatory unconscious – with the images and emotions of the real. For there is in consciousness a *Magic* with which one can go beyond things. And Peyote tells us where this Magic is, and after what strange concretions, whose breath is atavistically compressed and obstructed, the Fantastic can emerge and can once again scatter in our consciousness its phosphorescence and its haze. And this Fantastic is of noble quality, its disorder is only apparent, it really obeys an order that is fashioned mysteriously and on a level which normal consciousness does not reach but which *Ciguri* allows us to reach, and which is the very mystery of all poetry. But there is in human existence another level, obscure and formless, where consciousness has not entered, and which surrounds it like a mysterious extension or a menace, as the case may be. And which itself gives off adventurous sensations, perceptions. These are those shameless fantasies which affect an unhealthy mind, which abandons itself to them and dissolves in them completely if it finds nothing to hold it back. And Peyote is the only barrier that Evil encounters on this terrible frontier.

The Hallucinogenic Snuff of the Muras Indians

*Johann Baptist von Spix and
Carl Friedrich Philip von Martius*

The Muras Indians, a wandering tribe, have a very strange custom, peculiar only to them. This is the use of the *paricá* snuff. For preparing the *paricá* powder, they use the dried seeds of the *Parica üva*, an *Inga* species. First, the effect of the powder is exciting, then, narcotic. Once a year, when the seeds are ripe, the members of each tribe use the *paricá* for eight days. This practice is accompanied by constantly drinking intoxicating beverages, dancing and singing. For this feast the whole tribe assembles in a spacious, open house, where the women animate the men with *cujas* of the *cajiri*, abundantly supplied, or with other vegetable drinks. Then the men arrange themselves in pairs, according to their choice, and whip one another with leather straps until they draw blood. This odd whipping is not a hostile act, but, on the contrary, an act of friendship. This entire excess, as we were told, may be considered a misdirected sexual relationship. After this bloody operation, lasting for several days, is over, the pairs blow one another *paricá* powder into their nostrils with a tube made of a hollow tapir bone, one foot long. They blow with such a force and so continuously, that sometimes some men die, either suffocated with the fine dust thrust up to their frontal cavity, or, from being over-excited from the narcotic effect of the powder. With unparalleled rage the pairs fill the *paricá* from large bamboo pipes (*tabocas*) in which the powder is kept. A hollow crocodile tooth serves as a measure for each insufflation. With their knees drawn close to one another, the men blow and stuff the powder into their nostrils. The effect of this is a sudden exaltation, nonsensical talking, screaming, singing, wild jumping and dancing. Having been stupefied by drinks and all kinds of dissipation, the men then fall into a beastly drunkenness. It is said that a decoction of *paricá* is also used as a clyster producing a similar, though weaker effect.

Paricá snuffing may also be found with the Mauhés Indians, but since this is a more civilized tribe, it is taken in a more refined manner.

Narcotic Snuff and First Origins
Gerardo Reichel-Dolmatoff

1. In the beginning our grandfather *boreka* had visions from narcotic snuff.
2. In the beginning he emerged from the rock crystal, protected by [the colors] of the crab, and in this manner people began to emerge; that was it, that is what our grandfather said when conversing, younger brother./Is this what they said, elder brother?/Yes.
3. This vital element, this snuff was also present in the penis of the sun.
4. Because in the beginning Sun Person bequeathed this to our elder brother *boreka* and to Blood Person, by means of snuff, as a vital element; he too inherited it from him; this is what they said when conversing, younger brother./Is this what they said, elder brother?
5. This is how we inherited this element from our grandfathers; this is what they said when talking, younger brother./This is what they said, elder brother?
6. This is what they adopted for their germinating adornment, the ear-pendants of the umbilic cord, the [color] red of the ants, which give origin to the adornments of the ritual dialogues; this is what they said when conversing, younger brother./Was this what they said, elder brother?
7. This is why Day Person, being the germinator and progenitor,

bequeathed to our elder brothers, on that incomparable
day, the exalted children of repletion, and thus conceived
them.

8. This is how the present people [acquired] this heritage from
our fathers; this is how they came to an arrangement with
our elder brother *boreka*, he being the one who obtained
the value concepts for my entire line of kinsmen; while all
of them thus became illuminated, here [on earth] started
the [canoe] of procreation, developing the gestating powers
it possessed, for its heritage; and he proclaimed: 'I am the
chief:' this is how they spoke, younger brother.

9. They said: 'How shall we handle this [heritage]?' Our
fathers already spoke of this; as inheritors they carried on
the tradition. That is true, younger brother, this is what
they said./They said this, elder brother?

10. It was our elder brother who spoke about all this; it was he
who acquired these values and who then went up to the
house of procreation, to settle with complementary people;
this is what they said, younger brother./Is this what they
did, elder brother?

11. Thus he acted, there, in the clearings of the houses of our
ancestors where he had settled; going on from there he
found [other] houses, he found thatch and fiber ropes, and
he stayed, younger brother; and so he was feeling well:
this is what they said when talking, younger brother./This
is what they said, elder brother.

12. As it befits an elder brother and an inheritor he procreated
and had kinsmen; he had his complementary people and
his servants, and he was a leader of people; and then he
established himself in other settlements and clearings and
hence he went to settle at *biasipuru*, founding there two
houses: at *merenyokhoamë*, where he left two houses: at the
rock of *gaabëgë* and at *merepamuru*; there he settled down
and came to make the ornaments of macaw feathers; this is
what he did, younger brother./This is what he did, elder
brother.

13. This is what they said and we inherited their words; this is what they said and we possess it, younger brother; and this is what happened, elder brother.

14. This is what happened, elder brother; I won't say more, son.

Hallucinogens of the Jívaro Headhunters

Michael J. Harner

The Jívaro believe that witchcraft is the cause of the vast major-
ity of illnesses and non-violent deaths. Practically the only
diseases not attributed to witchcraft are 'white man's diseases'
(*suŋurä*), normally of an epidemic nature, such as whooping
cough, measles, colds, and some mild diarrheas. The normal
waking life, as noted before, is simply 'a lie', or illusion, while
the true forces that determine daily events are supernatural and
can only be seen and manipulated with the aid of hallucinogenic drugs. A reality view of this kind creates a demand for
shamans, part-time specialists who can cross over into the 'real'
world at will to help others to deal with the forces that influence
and even determine the events of the waking life.

Jívaro shamans (*uwišin*) are of two types: bewitchers and
curers. Both kinds take a hallucinogenic drink, whose Jívaro
name is *natemä*, in order to enter the supernatural world. This
brew, commonly called *yagé* or *yajé* in Colombia, *ayahuasca*
(Inca: 'vine of the dead') in Ecuador and Peru, and *caapi* in
Brazil is prepared from segments of a species of the vine
Banisteriopsis, a genus belonging to the Malpighiaceae. The
Jívaro boil it with the leaves of a similar vine, *yahi*, which probably is also a species of *Banisteriopsis*, to produce the cooled
natemä tea that contains the powerful hallucinogenic alkaloids
harmaline, harmine, d-tetrahydroharmine, and quite possibly

N,N-dimethyltryptamine (DMT). These compounds have chemical structures and effects similar, but not identical to, LSD, mescaline of the peyote cactus, and psilocybin of the psychotropic Mexican mushroom.

Shamans prefer to use *natemä* rather than *maikua* (*Datura arborea*) for going into trances, because the potency of the latter is too great for the shaman to be able to function ritually in singing, sucking, and the accompanying social interaction. Also, since the shaman must go into trances with frequency, he does not like to use *Datura* for that purpose because the strength of the plant is such that its repeated use is believed to lead to insanity. As an illustration of this danger, one informant said, 'My father told me that a long time ago a man took *maikua* all the time. As a result, he lost his mind and would go walking in the forest to speak with the spirits.' For these reasons, the shaman tends to use the less strong *Banisteriopsis* drink *natemä*. In *arutam* seeking, however, a person in a trance does not need to perform ritual or interact with others, and therefore *Datura*, precisely because of its strength to produce visions, is the drug of choice.

The use of the hallucinogenic *natemä* drink among the Jívaro makes it possible for almost anyone to achieve the trance state essential for the practice of shamanism. Given the presence of the drug and the felt need to contact the 'real', or supernatural, world, it is not surprising that approximately one out of every four Jívaro men is a shaman. Any adult, male or female, who desires to become such a practitioner, simply presents a gift to an already practicing shaman, who administers the *Banisteriopsis* drink and gives some of his own supernatural power – in the form of spirit helpers, or *tsentsak* – to the apprentice. These spirit helpers, or 'darts,' are the main supernatural forces believed to cause illness and death in daily life. To the non-shaman they are normally invisible, and even shamans can perceive them only under the influence of *natemä*.

The origin of knowledge about the use of *tsentsak* is attributed to Tsuŋi, the mythological first shaman who is believed still to be alive today living underwater in a house whose walls are formed, like palm staves, by upright anacondas, and where he sits, using a turtle as a stool. He is described as a white-skinned man with long hair, but he also seems capable of transforming himself into the anaconda. From time to time he is reputed to supply particular shamans with special quartz crystal *tsentsak* (*namurä*) which are particularly deadly, and, on rare occasions to kill shamans with whom he is angry. No shaman is believed capable of defending himself from the *tsentsak* of Tsuŋi.

Laymen are not able to cure or bewitch, because they do not have these magical darts in their control. Laymen can treat the 'white man's diseases,' previously mentioned, with herb remedies, but such treatment of illness is little developed in the society. Shamans never use herb remedies.

Shamans send these spirit helpers into the victims' bodies to make them ill or to kill them. At other times, they may suck such spirits sent by enemy shamans from the bodies of tribesmen suffering from witchcraft-induced illness. The spirit helpers also form shields that protect their shaman masters from attacks. The following account presents the ideology of Jívaro shamanism from the point of view of the shamans themselves.

To give the novice some *tsentsak*, the practicing shaman regurgitates what appears to be – to those who have taken *natemä* – a brilliant substance in which the spirit helpers are contained. He cuts part of it off with a machete and gives it to the novice to swallow. The recipient experiences pain upon taking it into his stomach and stays on his bed for ten days, repeatedly drinking *natemä*. The Jívaro believe they can keep magical darts in their stomachs indefinitely and regurgitate them at will. The shaman donating the *tsentsak* periodically blows and rubs all over the body of the novice, apparently to increase the power of the transfer.

The novice must remain inactive and not engage in sexual intercourse for several months. If he fails in self-discipline, as some do, he will not become a successful shaman. At the end of the first month, a *tsentsak* emerges from his mouth. With this magical dart at his disposal, the new shaman experiences a tremendous desire to bewitch. If he casts his *tsentsak* to fulfil this desire, this means he will become a 'bewitching' shaman (*wawek*, or *yahaučï uwišin*). If, on the other hand, the novice can control his impulse and reswallow this first *tsentsak*, he will become a curing shaman (*peŋer uwišin*). This will only be possible if the shaman who gave him his *tsentsak* is a curer himself.

If the shaman who gave the *tsentsak* to the new man was primarily a bewitcher, rather than a curer, the novice likewise will become a bewitcher. This is because a bewitcher's magical darts have such a desire to kill that their new owner will be compelled to adopt their attitude. One informant said that the urge to kill felt by bewitching shamans came to them with a strength and frequency similar to that of hunger.

Only if the novice shaman is able to abstain from sexual intercourse for five months, will he have the power to kill a man (if he is a bewitcher) or cure a victim (if he is a curer). A full year's abstinence is considered necessary to become a really effective bewitcher or curer.

During the period of sexual abstinence, the new shaman collects all kinds of insects, plants, and other objects, which he now has the power to convert into *tsentsak*. Almost any object, including living insects and worms, can become a *tsentsak* if it is small enough to be swallowed by a shaman. Certain small spiders become *tunčï*, a special kind of *tsentsak*. Different types of *tsentsak* are used to cause different kinds and degrees of illness, and the greater the variety of these objects that a shaman has in his body, the greater is his ability.

According to Jívaro concepts, each *tsentsak* has a natural and a supernatural aspect. The magical dart's natural aspect is that of an ordinary material object as seen without drinking the drug *natemä*. But the supernatural and 'true' aspect of the *tsentsak* is revealed to the shaman by taking *natemä*. When he does this, the magical darts appear in new forms as demons and with new names. In their supernatural aspects, the *tsentsak* are not simply objects but spirit helpers in various forms, such as giant butter-flies, jaguars, or monkeys, who actively assist the shaman in his tasks.

Bewitching is carried out against a specific, known individual and this is usually done to neighbors or, at the most, fellow tribesmen. Normally, as is the case with intra-tribal assassina-tion, bewitching is done to avenge a particular offense committed against one's family or friends. Both bewitching and individual assassination contrast with the large-scale head-hunting raids conducted against entire households of enemy tribes.

To bewitch, the shaman takes *natemä* and secretly approaches the house of his victim. Just out of sight in the forest, he drinks green tobacco water, enabling him to regurgitate a *tsentsak*, which he throws as his victim comes out of his house. If the *tsentsak* is strong enough and is thrown with sufficient force, it will pass all the way through the victim's body, causing death within a period of a few days to several weeks. More often, however, the magical dart simply lodges in the victim's body. If the shaman, in his hiding place, fails to see the intended victim, he may instead bewitch any member of the intended victim's family who appears, usually a wife or child. When the shaman's mission is accomplished, he returns secretly to his own house.

One of the distinguishing characteristics of the bewitching process among the Jívaro is that, as far as could be learned, the victim is given no specific indication that someone is bewitching him. The bewitcher does not want his victim to be aware that he is being supernaturally attacked, lest he take protective measures by immediately procuring the services of a curing shaman. Nonetheless, shamans and laymen alike steadfastly claimed, in interviews, that illness invariably follows the bewitchment, although the degree of illness can vary considerably.

Zombie Poisons of Haiti
Wade Davis

The bokor of Léogane prepared two poisons. The more toxic, by his account, was made solely from human remains. It consisted of ground legbone, forearm, and skull mixed with dried and pulverized parts of a cadaver. Having rubbed his or her hands with a protective lotion – a mixture of lemons, ammonia, and clairin – the user sprinkled the powder in the form of a cross on the ground while naming the intended victim. The recipient then needed only to walk over that cross to be seized with violent convulsions. If the powder was placed in the victim's food, it caused an immediate reaction.

The second preparation was a mixture of centipedes (Spirobolida, Polydesmida), tarantulas (Theraphosidae), and lizards including *miti verde* (*Anolis coelestinus* Cope) and *mabouya* (*Epicrates striatus* Fischer). In place of the buga toad, the bokor added two locally recognized forms of the common tree frog (*Osteopilus dominicencis* Tsudi). These were known as the *crapaud blanc* – the white toad – and the *crapaud brun* – the brown toad. In addition – acknowledged as the most essential animal ingredient – were two species of puffer fish, one named *bilan* (*Diodon holacanthus*) and the other the *crapaud du mer* (*Sphoeroides testudineus*).

Both poisons prepared at Léogane consisted only of animal constituents. As had been the case with the three preparations obtained at Saint Marc, the puffer fish and sea toads were sun-dried, carefully heated, and placed in a mortar. Fresh specimens of the two local varieties of tarantulas and the three nonven-omous lizards were roasted with the two tree frogs, the *crapaud brun* and *crapaud blanc*. The bokor at Léogane especially empha-sized the toxicity of the human remains and included both ground human bones and dried pieces of human cadaver in the preparation. The final product was a sifted powder, somewhat coarser than the Saint Marc products. Of note at Léogane were the extraordinary precautions taken by the poison makers themselves; they rubbed all surfaces of their bodies with oil emulsion, placed cotton plugs in their nostrils, and wrapped hemp sacks around their entire bodies. Both men wore large protective hats.

According to the bokor the onset of the poison was charac-terized by a feeling of ants crawling beneath the skin, precisely the way Narcisse [a man who had been given the drug and who had become a zombie] had described his first sensations. The bokor also indicated the importance of correct dosage. He mentioned that the animal poison was most effective if it was ingested by the victim, and he cautioned that the two prepara-tions should never be mixed.

Mushrooms in Kamchatka

Joseph Kopeć

Hardly a few moments had passed when a sudden change of air brought about a great change in my sick body. The air of this closed *yurta*, always stinking, mixed with the acrid scent of whale-fat used as lamp oil, made me so weak that I thought the hour of my death would strike. Thus abandoning the fire and tea I called for my evangelist in the hope of getting some help from this man, a bit more educated, as I understood, than other people in the art of healing. After having learned about my mishap, the evangelist comes a little later, he approaches the fire, and ordering me to sit up he tells me first to drink my tea. While I am doing this, the Kamchadals bring from the middle of the tent a large number of ermine hides and deer skins. Feeling a bit revived, I ask what is the meaning of this. To which the evangelist, complying with my curiosity, says to me:

'Before I give you the medicine, I must tell you something important. You have lived for two years in Lower Kamchatka but you have known nothing of the treasures of this land. Here,' opening some birch bark in which a few mushrooms were wrapped, 'are mushrooms that are, I can say, miraculous. They grow only on a single high mountain close to the volcano and they are the most precious creations of nature.'

'Take into account, Sir,' the evangelist goes on, 'that the hides brought by local people I receive as gifts in exchange for these mushrooms. They would even give all their possessions, had I many of them and if only I sought to take advantage of the situation. These mushrooms have a special and as though supernatural quality. Not only do they help the man who uses them but he sees his own future as well. Since you are weak you should eat one mushroom. It will give you the sleep you are lacking.'

Hearing so many strange things about the merits of that mushroom, I was in doubt for a long time whether I should make use of it. However, the wish to recover my health and above all to sleep overcame my fears, and so I ate half my medicine and at once stretched out, for a deep sleep overtook me. Dreams came one after the other. I found myself as though magnetized by the most attractive gardens where only pleasure and beauty seemed to rule. Flowers of different colours and shapes and odours appeared before my eyes; a group of most beautiful women dressed in white going to and fro seemed to be occupied with the hospitality of this earthly paradise. As if pleased with my coming, they offered me different fruits, berries, and flowers. This delight lasted during my whole sleep, which was a couple of hours longer than my usual rest. After having awakened from such a sweet dream, I discovered that this delight was an illusion. I was distressed that it had disappeared, as if it had been true happiness. These impressions made pleasant for me the few hours that remained until the end of the day. Having received such bewitching support from the miraculous mushroom and even having been fortified by sleep such as I had not had for a long time, I started to have confidence in its supernatural qualities (as my evangelist had taught me to do), and with the approach of night I asked my physician for a second helping. He was pleased with my courage and at once bearing the offering of his friendly benevolence, he gave me a similar whole mushroom. Having eaten this stronger dose, I fell soundly asleep in a few minutes. For several hours new visions carried me to another world, and it seemed to me that I was ordered to return to earth so that a priest could take my

confession. This impression, although in sleep, was so strong
that I awoke and asked for my evangelist. It was precisely at the
hour of midnight and the priest, ever eager to render spiritual
service, at once took his stole and heard my confession with a
joy that he did not hide from me. About an hour after the confession I fell asleep anew and I did not wake up for twenty-four
hours. It is difficult, almost impossible, to describe the visions I
had in such a long sleep; and besides there are other reasons
that make me reluctant to do so. What I noticed in these visions
and what I passed through are things that I felt I had seen or
experienced some time before, and also things that I would
never imagine even in my thoughts. I can only mention that
from the period when I was first aware of the notions of life, all
that I had seen in front of me from my fifth or sixth year, all
objects and people that I knew as time went on, and with whom
I had some relations, all my games, occupations, actions, one
following the other, day after day, year after year, in one word
the picture of my whole past become present in my sight.
Concerning the future, different pictures followed each other
which will not occupy a special place here since they are
dreams. I should add only that as if inspired by magnetism I
came across some blunders of my evangelist and I warned him
to improve in those matters, and I noticed that he took these
warnings almost as the voice of Revelation.

It is not for me to argue about the usefulness and the influence on human health of this miraculous mushroom. But I can
state that its medical usefulness, had it been known among
more educated peoples, should have earned it a place among so
many known remedies of nature in the matter of fighting
human maladies. Can anyone deny that in spite of our vast
knowledge (relative to our forces) of natural phenomena, there
still exist almost countless phenomena about which we can
only guess? Can one put a limit to nature at a point that delimits
the possibilities of inquiries and discoveries of human research?
Innumerable effects of recently discovered magnetic
forces, effects that cannot be detected by physical means nor

pinpointed with any degree of precision to some specification on the human body, seem to reconcile in some measure the controversy concerning this mushroom. It is then possible that in sleep brought by the influence of this mushroom, a man is able to see at least some of his real past and if not the future at least his present relations. If someone can prove that both the effect and the influence of the mushroom are non-existent and erroneous, then I shall stop being a defender of the miraculous mushroom of Kamchatka.

Whatever may be the nature and qualities of the above-mentioned mushroom, I must confess that the taking of it had a powerful effect on my mind, as well as a strong impression [on my senses], so that I grew disquieted to a certain degree, from which passing into anxiety I became finally gloomy. This credulity having even the power of faith was based first of all on the conviction of the evangelist that my truthful visions were a true warning of heaven, and, secondly, on a conviction coming from within me, when later I perceived, being awake, the confirmation of what the dreams had predicted. This led me to have confidence in the dependability of my dreams about the future. However, as time passed, during my travels, this faith started to slacken and when its influence on my mind ended, a peace of soul returned to me together with better health.

PART THREE

CANNABIS – FROM THE PYGMY VILLAGE TO GREENWICH VILLAGE

Anyone who takes hashish as an experiment-witness after taking mescaline leaves a racing automobile or a long distance electric locomotive for a pony. A pony, however, is capable of surprises not to be looked for from a locomotive.

From *Miserable Miracle: Mescaline* by Henri Michaux (1963)

The hemp plant (*Cannabis*), a native of Central Asia, has been used since the Stone Age for its fibre and psychoactive properties. Prehistoric farmers in both Europe and Asia cultivated cannabis, and in a revealing footnote (*In Defense of the Pygmies*) to *The Dragons of Eden* Carl Sagan speculates on its possible role in the origin of agriculture and civilisation. A very different account of the ancestry of cannabis is given in *The Origin of Ganja*, a folk tale from India. In this story hemp first grew from the juice of the hallucinogenic datura plant. At a marriage party attended by numerous animals we are told that whilst bears and tigers like their drink, snakes and scorpions prefer to use cannabis!

There are numerous folk tales concerning the wise fool Nasreddin Khoja throughout the Middle East and Muslim Central Asia. His humorous escapades typically conceal his wisdom and these short tales have been used by the mystical Sufi orders as a means of transmitting their teachings. In this instance we have a simple anecdote about the distorting effects of hashish and how the user perceives his own actions as quite normal whilst onlookers see the naked truth!

The Venetian merchant Marco Polo, like many other early travellers to exotic regions, has been accused of telling tall tales. In 1273 his journey to the east took him through Persia where he heard the legends concerning the mountain fortress of Mulehet (Alamut) which had once been the headquarters of the 'heretic' Aloadin, a.k.a. 'The Old Man of the Mountain'. Here, according to Polo's informants, Aloadin drugged his disciples to make them believe they had been transported to paradise, only to bring them back to the land of the living in order to assassinate his political adversaries. In this form the legend of the Assassins reached Western ears and became intimately linked to the consumption of hashish. The tale, as told here, is based on truth for there is a ruined castle in the Elburz mountains and it was there that Ala al-Din Muhammad (i.e. Aloadin) took over leadership of the Nizari Ismaili Islamic sect in 1221. The written records of the dominant branch of Islam, the Sunni, describe him as a drunken maniac who, rather ironically, was assassinated by his own followers. But in the West he has been closely associated with hashish. It is with the use of this drug that he is thought to have made his followers believe in his artificial garden paradise (the word paradise actually derives from an ancient Iranian word meaning 'garden'). Whilst both Iranian and Western scholars have shown that many elements of the Venetian travellers' tale are factually inaccurate it is the Marco Polo version that caught the romantic imagination in the nineteenth century.

Le Club des Haschishins was formed in Paris in 1844 and was largely the brainchild of the early psychopharmacologist Dr Jean-Jacques Moreau de Tours (1804–1884) and the leading literary figure Théophile Gautier (1811–1872). In suitably decadent and luxurious surroundings Moreau, playing the part of the 'Prince of the Assassins', would dispense the green hashish paste from a crystal vase, announcing to the club members that 'this will be deducted from your share in paradise'. The distinguished membership included Alexandre Dumas, Honoré de Balzac, Gérard de Nerval and Charles Baudelaire. Baudelaire (1821–1867) wrote a number of works on what he described as drug-induced 'artificial paradise' (echoing the garden of Aloadin). Among these is *The Poem of Hashish* which was first published in 1858. As a poetic description of the hashish state it remains unsurpassed.

In 1857, a year before Baudelaire's *Poem* was published, another remarkable account of cannabis appeared in America – *The Hasheesh Eater: Being Passages from the Life of a Pythagorean* by Fitzhugh Ludlow (1836–1870). Ludlow abandoned his early attempts to hold down careers in teaching and law to become a drama critic and writer. His early death has been falsely attributed to his hashish use but was actually due to tuberculosis. Whilst the book had little influence in his lifetime it is now seen as a precursor of much of the later American 'drug literature'. The extract given here is the chapter entitled *The Night Entrance* in which Ludlow gives a fascinating account of his personal initiation into the pleasures and pains of hashish.

Since the nineteenth century there has been a steady stream of hashish users visiting the East in search of paradise. In *Baluchistan Garden*, taken from Brian Barritt's recently published psychedelic autobiography, the author describes how in 1966 he participated in the hashish clubs that held their meetings in the teahouses of the Afghan-Pakistan border region. The open enjoyment of hashish that he experienced in the East is in stark contrast to his greeting by London airport customs officials on his return to the West. Among the exhibits at his court appearance were, as Barritt says, 'seven and one quarter pounds of hash on the table, smelling of intrigue and Assassins'. In *Identity Crisis*, an extract from *Mr Nice*, the autobiography of the mercurial hash smuggler Howard Marks, the numerous passports, reputations and identities (including the nickname Marco Polo) of the author are shuffled to evade the unwanted attentions of MI6, the IRA, the Thames Valley Police and a host of other agencies.

In Defense of the Pygmies
Carl Sagan

In defense of the Pygmies, perhaps I should note that a friend of
mine who has spent time with them says that for such activities
as the patient stalking and hunting of mammals and fish they
prepare themselves through marijuana intoxication, which
helps to make the long waits, boring to anyone further evolved
than a Komodo dragon, at least moderately tolerable. Ganja is,
he says, their only cultivated crop. It would be wryly interesting
if in human history the cultivation of marijuana led generally to
the invention of agriculture, and thereby to civilization. (The
marijuana-intoxicated Pygmy, poised patiently for an hour with
his fishing spear aloft, is earnestly burlesqued by the beer-
sodden rifle-men, protectively camouflaged in red plaid, who,
stumbling through the nearby woods, terrorize American sub-
urbs each Thanksgiving.)

The Origin of Ganja
Verrier Elwin

[Gond (India) *Barratola, Mandla District*]

In Jhinjhgarh lived Korwassi Dewar the Baiga and his wife Andaro. They had a daughter whose name was Suknibai. Mahadeo came to serve for her as Lamsena and worked for five years in her house. But the Dewar and his wife did not give the boy proper food to eat, with the result that he grew very thin.

When the five years' service was completed, the Dewar and his wife said to Mahadeo, 'Now go and call your relatives and we will celebrate your marriage'. Mahadeo called for tigers, bears, snakes, scorpions and brought them in his marriage party. The Dewar had collected a great quantity of food and liquor and when he saw the animals and reptiles in Mahadeo's marriage-party he was very angry, for he said, 'Who will eat the feast that I have provided?' Then Mahadeo by his magic power caused the animals to say that they would drink the Baiga's liquor but the snakes and scorpions said, 'We must have ganja'.

The Baiga gave the pots of liquor to the bears and tigers to drink but he had no ganja and wondered how to get some. Finally he sent his wife to pick datura leaves and when she brought them to the house he rubbed and rubbed them till a drop of juice fell to the ground. From this drop was born the hemp plant. Then the Baiga got the water of twelve tanks and made a pipe as big as twelve threshing-floors. He mixed the datura leaves with the water and filled the pipe and gave it to the snakes and scorpions to drink. They soon became drunk and began to dance. As the snakes danced – in those days they went upright like men – their backs broke and ever since they have gone flat along the ground.

Nasreddin Khoja
Taner Baybars

The Hodja was very curious to know how he would react to hashish. One day he plucked up the courage and bought himself a handful from the apothecary's, smoked it and then went to a Turkish bath. Some time passed, but he felt no change in himself. 'They must have given me the wrong thing,' he kept on saying. 'I must go and find out. I'm not going to be cheated like this.'

So he rushed out naked.

'Hodja, what is the matter?' people asked him. 'Where are you going like this, with nothing on?'

'Don't ask me,' he said. 'I thought smoking hashish would do something to me. But as you can see, I'm still what I was. I'm going to get the real stuff from the apothecary's. I have a feeling he's cheated me.'

The Old Man of the Mountain

Marco Polo

Of the Old Man of the Mountain. Of His Palace and Gardens
Mention shall now be made of the Old Man of the Mountain. The district in which his residence lay obtained the name of Mulehet, signifying in the language of the Saracens, the place of heretics, and his people that of Mulehetites, or holders of heretical tenets; as we apply the term of Patharini to certain heretics amongst Christians. The following account of this chief, Marco Polo testifies to having heard from sundry persons. He was named Aloadin, and his religion was that of Mahomet. In a beautiful valley enclosed between two lofty mountains, he had formed a luxurious garden, stored with every delicious fruit and every fragrant shrub that could be procured. Palaces of various sizes and forms were erected in different parts of the grounds, ornamented with works in gold, with paintings, and with furniture of rich silks. By means of small conduits contrived in these buildings, streams of wine, milk, honey, and some of pure water, were seen to flow in every direction. The inhabitants of these palaces were elegant and beautiful damsels, accomplished in the arts of singing, playing upon all sorts of musical instruments, dancing, and especially those of dalliance and amorous allurement. Clothed in rich dresses they were seen continually sporting and amusing themselves in the garden and pavilions, their female guardians being confined within doors

and never suffered to appear. The object which the chief had in view in forming a garden of this fascinating kind, was this: that Mahomet having promised to those who should obey his will the enjoyments of Paradise, where every species of sensual gratification should be found, in the society of beautiful nymphs, he was desirous of its being understood by his followers that he also was a prophet and the compeer of Mahomet, and had the power of admitting to Paradise such as he should choose to favour. In order that none without his licence might find their way into this delicious valley, he caused a strong and inexpugnable castle to be erected at the opening of it, through which the entry was by a secret passage. At his court, likewise, this chief entertained a number of youths, from the age of twelve to twenty years, selected from the inhabitants of the surrounding mountains, who showed a disposition for martial exercises, and appeared to possess the quality of daring courage. To them he was in the daily practice of discoursing on the subject of the paradise announced by the prophet, and of his own power of granting admission. And at certain times he caused opium to be administered to ten or a dozen of the youths; and when half dead with sleep he had them conveyed to the several apartments of the palaces in the garden.

How the Old Man used to Train His Assassins

Upon awakening from the state of stupor, their senses were struck with all the delightful objects that have been described, and each perceived himself surrounded by lovely damsels, singing, playing, and attracting his regards by the most fascinating caresses, serving him also with delicate foods and exquisite wines; until intoxicated with excess of enjoyment amidst actual rivulets of milk and wine, he believed himself assuredly in Paradise, and felt an unwillingness to relinquish its delights. When four or five days had thus been passed, they were thrown once more into a drugged state, and carried out of the garden. Upon their being introduced to his presence, and questioned by him as to where they had been, their answer was, 'In Paradise, through the favour of your highness:' and then before the whole court, who listened to them with eager curiosity and astonishment, they gave a circumstantial account of the scenes to which they had been witnesses. The chief thereupon addressing them, said: 'We have the assurances of our prophet that he who defends his lord shall inherit Paradise, and if you show yourselves devoted to the obedience of my orders, that happy lot awaits you.' Animated to enthusiasm by words of this nature, all deemed themselves happy to receive the commands of their master, and were forward to die in his service. The consequence of this system was, that when any of the neighbouring princes, or others, gave offence to this chief, they were put to death by these his disciplined assassins; none of whom felt terror at the risk of losing their own lives, which they held in little estimation, provided they could execute their master's will. On this account his tyranny became the subject of dread in all the surrounding countries. He had also constituted two deputies or representatives of himself, of whom one had his residence in the vicinity of Damascus, and the other in Kurdistan; and these pursued the plan he had established for training their young dependents. Thus there was no person, however powerful, who, having become exposed to the enmity of the Old Man of the Mountain, could escape assassination.

How the Old Man came by His End

His territory being situated within the dominions of Alaù, the brother of the Great Khan Mangu, that prince had information of his atrocious practices, as above related, as well as of his employing people to rob travellers in their passage through his country, and in the year 1252 sent one of his armies to besiege this chief in his castle. It proved, however, so capable of defence, that for three years no impression could be made upon it; until at length he was forced to surrender from the want of provisions, and being made prisoner was put to death. His castle was dismantled, and his garden of Paradise destroyed. And from that time there has been no Old Man of the Mountain.

The Poem of Hashish

(from *Paradise by Artifice*)

Charles Baudelaire

I   The Longing for the Infinite

Any man skilled in the study of his own nature, and able to retain the impression that life has made upon him – any man capable, as Hoffmann was, of constructing his own spiritual barometer – has now and then noticed, from the Observatory of his intellect, various seasons of fine weather, daytimes of happiness, minutes of delight.

There are days when a man wakes up full of a young, vigorous inspiration. With the dust of sleep scarcely out of his eyes, the material world offers him, in bold relief, an amazing clearness of outline and wealth of colour. The world of the spirit opens up huge perspectives, full of new glimpses. A man granted this blessed privilege, which unfortunately is rare and fleeting, feels himself more creative and more moral – a nobler being, in short.

But the oddest thing about this uncommon state of the soul and senses – a state that I can describe without exaggeration as paradisal, if I compare it with the heavy darkness of communal and day-to-day existence – is that it is due to no easily visible or definable cause.

Is it the result of well-cared-for health and a sensible diet? This is the first explanation that occurs to the mind; but we are compelled to recognise that often this wonder – this miracle, so to speak – comes into existence as if produced by a superior and invisible force, external to the man himself, and after a period in which he has actually been abusing his physical faculties.

Shall we say, then, that it is the reward of assiduous prayer and spiritual fervency? It is certainly true that a constant uplifting of desire, a taut striving of the soul towards heaven, would be the most suitable regimen for the creation of this brilliant and glorious spiritual health. But what absurd law permits it sometimes to appear after shameful orgies of the imagination – or after a sophisticated and deliberate abuse of the mental powers, an abuse that bears the same relation to the proper and reasonable use of these as a contortionist's tricks do to healthy gymnastics? That is why I prefer to regard this abnormal state of the mind as a true 'gift of grace'; as a magic mirror in which the recipient is invited to see himself in all his beauty – that is to say, as he should and could be; as a sort of angelic bidding, a fall-in-on-parade couched in complimentary terms. It is just so that a certain religious school, which has representatives in England and America, regards super-natural phenomena such as ghostly apparitions, hauntings, etc., as manifestations of the Divine Will intent on reawakening in man's spirit the memory of invisible realities.

It may be remarked that this strange and delightful state, in which all the forces are in equilibrium, so that the imagination, although wondrously powerful, does not drag the moral sense after it into perilous adventures, nor is the exquisite sensibility tortured by sick nerves – this marvellous state, as I was saying, has no precursory symptoms. It is as unexpected as a phantom. It is a kind of haunting visitation, but an intermittent one, from which we should gain, if we were wise, the certainty of a better existence, and the hope of attaining it by a daily exercise of our will.

This mental acumen, this inspiration of the soul and senses, must always have seemed to mankind the chief of blessings. That is why man has always sought – in all climes and at all times, and without disturbing himself with the thought that he was breaking the laws of his nation – to find in physical science, in pharmacy, in the grossest liquors or the subtlest perfumes, the means to escape, if only for a few hours, from his habitation in the mire, and, as the author of *'Lazare'* puts it, 'to capture Paradise at a stroke'.

How sad that man's vices, however horrible we may conceive them to be, themselves contain the proof (be it only in their infinite ramifications!) of his longing for the Infinite.

The trouble is that this longing often goes astray. The common proverb: 'All roads lead to Rome' might be metaphorically interpreted to apply in the sphere of morals. Everything leads to reward or punishment – two forms of eternity. The human spirit overflows with passion; it has 'enough and to spare' of it to use another trivial expression. But this unfortunate spirit, whose natural depravity is as great as its sudden and almost paradoxical inclinations towards charity and the most arduous virtues, is rich in paradoxes that allow it to employ this overflowing surplus of passion in the service of Evil.

The spirit never believes that it is selling itself wholesale. It forgets, in its infatuation, that it is playing against an opponent subtler and stronger than itself; and that, if one lets the Spirit of Evil but grasp a hair of one's head, he is not slow to carry off the head itself.

This visible lord of visible nature (man, I mean) has therefore sought to construct Paradise from drugs or fermented drinks – like a maniac using stage-sets, painted on canvas and mounted on frames, as a substitute for real furniture and gardens. In this corruption of the sense of the Infinite lies, in my view, the reason for all culpable excess: from the solitary and concentrated drunkenness of the writer who has been forced to seek relief from physical pain in opium, and, having thus found a source of unwholesome pleasures, has gradually made of it his only means of physical refreshment, and the sun of his spiritual life – to the most squalid tipsiness of some suburban drinker ridiculously sprawling, with his brain alight with fire and glory in the filth of the street.

Amongst the drugs that best serve to create what I call 'the artificial Ideal' – if we leave aside liquors that quickly drive a man into physical furore and deliver a knock-out blow to the strength of his spirit, or inhalants whose excessive use, whilst making a man's imagination more subtle, gradually exhausts his physical powers – apart from these, the two most effective agents, and those whose employment is most convenient and most ready to hand, are hashish and opium. The purpose of this study is to analyse the mysterious effects and morbid delights that these drugs can engender; the inevitable retribution resulting from their prolonged use; and, lastly, the essential immorality implicit in this pursuit of a false ideal.

The definitive work on opium has already been written, and in so brilliant a fashion, at once poetic and medically sound, that I would not dare to add anything to it. I shall therefore confine myself to offering, in another article, an analysis of this incomparable work, which has never been translated into French in its entirety. The author, a famous writer, of powerful and exquisite imagination, who is today living in silent retirement, has dared, with tragic candour, to give a full account of the delights and tortures that, in his time, he has discovered in opium; and the most dramatic part of his book is that in which he speaks of the superhuman efforts of will that he had to put forth in order to escape the doom to which he had recklessly condemned himself.

Today I shall speak only of hashish. My account of it will be based on a great quantity of detailed information, extracts from written or verbal statements by intelligent men who were for a long time addicts. I shall simply blend these various documents into a sort of monograph, selecting a single soul – one that, for choice, is easy to explain and define – as a typical victim of experiences of this nature.

II   What is Hashish?

The tales of Marco Polo – which it is a mistake to deride like those of some other ancient travellers – have been verified by scholars, and merit our belief. I shall not repeat his story of how the Old Man of the Mountain used to intoxicate his young disciples with hashish (whence the word 'Hashishin' or 'Assassins') and then shut them up in a garden full of delights, with the object of giving them a foretaste of Paradise, and thus exacting from them, in exchange, a passive and unthinking obedience. On the subject of the secret society of the Hashishin the reader may consult the book by M. de Hammer, and the study by M. Sylvestre de Sacy contained in Volume XVI of the *'Studies by the Academy of Inscriptions and Belles Letters'*; also concerning the etymology of the word 'assassin', the latter gentleman's letter to the editor of the *Moniteur* published in issue No. 359 of the year 1809.

Herodotus reports that the Scythians used to collect piles of hemp-seed, on which they threw red-hot stones. In this way they got a sort of steam-bath, more deliciously perfumed than that of any Greek hot-room, and the pleasure was so keen that it moved them to shouts of joy.

Hashish does, in fact, come to us from the East. The stimulating properties of hemp were well known in ancient Egypt, and its use is very widespread, under different names, in India, Algeria and Arabia Felix. But we also have in our own midst curious examples of the intoxication caused by herbal fumes. It is known that children, after romping and rolling on heaps of mown lucern, often undergo odd spells of dizziness, and it is also known that during the hemp harvest the male and female reapers have similar experiences. The harvest seems to give off a miasma that malignantly disturbs their brains. The reaper's head is filled with whirling eddies, or sometimes heavy with dreamy fancies. At certain moments the limbs grow weak and refuse to function. We have heard of fairly frequent cases of somnambulism amongst Russian peasants, caused, it is said, by the use of hemp-seed oil in their cooking. Who is not familiar with the extravagant behaviour of chickens that have eaten hemp, or the mettlesome eagerness of peasant's horses at fairs and on saints' days, when their masters have prepared them for a steeplechase with a dose of hemp-seed, sometimes mixed with wine?

Nevertheless, French hemp is unsuitable for conversion into hashish – or at least, as frequent experience has shown, it is incapable of producing a drug of equal power.

Hashish, or Indian hemp, *cannabis indica*, is a plant of the nettle tribe, similar in all respects, except that it grows less high, to the hemp of our climes. It has most extraordinary properties of intoxication, which for several years have been in France an object of study by scientists and by people of good society. The esteem in which it is held varies with its place of origin: the hemp of Bengal is that most valued by connoisseurs; but those of Egypt, Constantinople, Persia, and Algeria possess the same properties, only in lesser degree.

The 'herb' (for this is the meaning of the word 'hashish' – the 'herb' par excellence – as if the Arabs had wished to sum up in a single word the source of all non-physical pleasures) bears different names according to its composition and the mode of preparation it has undergone in the country where it was harvested: in India, 'bhang'; in Africa, 'teriaki'; in Algeria and Arabia Felix, 'madjound', etc. The season of year at which it is gathered makes a big difference: it is when the plant is in flower that it possesses the greatest potency. Consequently, only its flowery tops are used in the various preparations that I shall now briefly describe.

The 'rich extract' of hashish, as prepared by the Arabs, is obtained by cooking the tops of the plant, while still fresh, in butter with a little water. When all humidity has evaporated, the residue is passed through a sieve. Thus is obtained a preparation looking like a yellow-greenish hair-oil and retaining a disagreeable odour of hashish and rancid butter. In this form it is taken in little pellets of two to four grammes; but, because of its revolting smell, which continually grows stronger, the Arabs encase the rich extract in sweetmeats.

The most common of these sweetmeats, the 'dawamesk', is a mixture of rich extract, sugar and various flavourings, such as vanilla, cinnamon, pistachio, almond and musk. Sometimes even a little cantharides is added, with a purpose quite at variance from the normal purposes of hashish.

In this form, hashish is completely rid of its disagreeable quality, and can be taken in doses of fifteen, twenty or thirty grammes, either wrapped in a wafer or immersed in a cup of coffee.

The object of experiments by Messrs. Smith, Gastinel and Decourtive was to discover the active principle of hashish. Despite their efforts, its chemical components and their inter-reaction are as yet little known; but its properties are generally ascribed to a resinous substance that is present in fairly substantial quantity – in a proportion of about ten per cent. To obtain this resin, the plant is dried, ground to a coarse powder and washed several times in alcohol, which is then distilled in order to draw off a part of it. The substance is then dried off until it has the consistency of an extract. This extract is treated with water, which dissolves the gummy foreign bodies, and the residue is the pure resin.

This product is soft in texture, of a dark-green colour, and possesses to a high degree the characteristic odour of hashish. Five, ten or fifteen hundredths of a gramme are enough to produce surprising effect.

Another form of the drug, hashishin, can be taken in chocolate-coated pastilles or little ginger-flavoured pills. It produces, like the dawamesk or like rich extract, effects of varying intensity and character, according to the temperament and nervous susceptibility of the taker. Still better, the result varies in one and the same individual: sometimes it will be an immoderate and irresistible gaiety, sometimes a sensation of well-being and plenitude of life; at other times a dubious and dream-shot half-slumber. Certain phenomena, however, are fairly constant, especially amongst people of similar temperament and education. There is a sort of unity within variety – which is the reason why I shall not have too much difficulty in compiling the monograph, of which I was just now speaking, on this particular form of intoxication.

In Constantinople, in Algeria, and even in France, some people smoke hashish mixed with tobacco; but in their cases the phenomena I mentioned occur only in a very mild and, so to speak, sluggish form. I have heard it said that recently it has been found possible, by a process of distillation, to extract from hashish an essential oil that appears to have a much more active character than any preparation known hitherto. But this product has not been sufficiently investigated to enable me to describe its results with any certainty.

It is hardly necessary to add that tea, coffee and spirituous liquors are all powerful adjuvants and accelerate, in greater or less degree, the flowering of this mysterious intoxication.

It is truly superfluous, after all that has been said here, to insist on the immorality of hashish. If I compare it to suicide, a slow suicide, a weapon that is always sharp and bloody, no reasonable person will wish to contradict me. If I liken it to sorcery or magic, those arts that seek – by operating upon matter, and by occult methods whose falsity is proved by nothing so much as by their very effectiveness – to win an empire forbidden to man, or permitted only to him who is judged worthy, no philosophic soul will have fault to find with this comparison. When the Church condemns magic and sorcery, it is because these militate against the intentions of God; because they blot out the work of time and seek to make superfluous the disciplines of purity and morality; and because she, the Church, regards only those riches as legitimate and genuine that are earned by assiduous seeking.

To describe a gambler who has found a method of betting on a certainty, we use the term 'swindler'. What shall we call a man who seeks to buy happiness and genius for a small sum of money? It is the very infallibility of the method that constitutes its immorality; just as it is the alleged infallibility of magic that imposes upon it the stigma of hell. I need scarcely add that hashish, like all other solitary delights, makes the individual useless to mankind, and also makes society unnecessary to the individual, who is driven ceaselessly to admire himself, and is daily brought nearer to that glittering abyss in which he will gaze upon the face of Narcissus.

But what if, at the price of his dignity, his honour and his powers of free discernment, a man could obtain from hashish great mental benefits – could make of it a machine for thinking, a richly productive instrument? This is a question that I have often heard asked, and I shall now answer it. First of all, as I have explained at length, hashish reveals to the individual nothing except himself. It is true that this individual is, so to speak, enlarged to the power of three; and, since it is also quite true that the memories of his impressions survive the orgy, the hopes of the 'utilitarian' theorists might not at first sight seem entirely unreasonable. But I shall beg them to remember that the thoughts of the hashish-taker, from which they count on obtaining so much, are not really so beautiful as they appear under their momentary guise, clad in the tinsel of magic. They have much more of earth than of heaven in them, and owe a great part of their seeming beauty to the nervous excitement and avidity with which the mind hurls itself upon them.

These people's hopes form, therefore, a vicious circle. Let us grant for a moment that hashish gives, or at least augments, genius – they forget that it is in the nature of hashish to weaken the will; so that what hashish gives with one hand it takes away with the other; that is to say, it gives power of imagination and takes away with the other: that is to say, it gives power of imagination and takes away the ability to profit by it. Even if we imagine a man clever and vigorous enough to gain the one without losing the other, we must bear in mind a further and terrible danger, which attaches itself to all habits. They all soon turn into necessities. He who has recourse to poison in order to think will soon be unable to think *without* poison. How terrible the lot of a man whose paralysed imagination cannot function without the aid of hashish or opium!

In all its philosophical investigations the human mind, like the stars in their courses, has to travel in a curve leading back to its point of departure. The conclusion is the closing of a circle.

At the beginning of this essay I spoke of the marvellous state of mind into which a man sometimes finds himself projected, as if by a special dispensation. I said that, in his ceaseless yearning to rekindle his hopes and uplift himself towards the Infinite, man has displayed, in all places and at all times, a frantic predilection for any substances, however dangerous, that might personally exalt him and thus for a moment evoke for him that adventitious paradise upon which all his desires are fixed. And I remarked that this foolhardy instinct, which urges him, all unbeknownst, towards Hell, is of itself a proof of his natural sublimity. But man is not so forsaken, so lacking in honourable means of attaining to Heaven, that he should be obliged to resort to pharmacy or witchcraft. He has no need to sell his soul to pay for the intoxicating caresses and affections of oriental houris. What, after all, is a paradise bought at the price of one's eternal salvation?

I imagine to myself a man – a Brahman, shall I say, a poet or a Christian philosopher – who has scaled the arduous Olympus of the spirit. Around him the Muses of Raphael or Mantegna reward him for his long fastings and constant prayers by joining in their noblest dances and gazing upon him with their gentlest looks and loveliest smiles. The god Apollo, master of all knowledge – he of Francavilla, Albrecht Dürer, Goltzius, whomsoever you please: has not every man who merits it his own Apollo? – is enticing from his bow its most vibrant chords. Below this man, at the foot of the mountain, amidst the briars and the mud, the human herd, the pack of Helots, is grimacing with false delight and howling in the pangs of its poison. And the poet sadly thinks 'These unfortunates, who have neither fasted nor prayed, who have refused redemption by toil, are demanding of black magic the means of raising themselves all of a sudden to superhuman existence. The magic makes dupes of them, shedding upon them a false happiness and a false light. Whereas we, the poets and philosophers, have redeemed our souls by unremitting toil and contemplation. By the constant exercise of our wills and the enduring nobility of our devotion we have created for our use a garden of true beauty. Trusting in the Saying that faith moves mountains, we have performed the only miracle for which God has given us leave.'

The Night Entrance
Fitzhugh Ludlow

About the shop of my friend Anderson the apothecary there always existed a peculiar fascination, which early marked it out as my favourite lounging-place. In the very atmosphere of the establishment, loaded as it was with a composite smell of all things curative and preventive, there was an aromatic invitation to scientific musing, which could not have met with a readier acceptance had it spoken in the breath of frankincense. The very gallipots grew gradually to possess a charm for me as they sat calmly ranged upon their oaken shelves, looking like a convention of unostentatious philanthropists, whose silent bosoms teemed with every variety of renovation for the human race. A little sanctum at the inner end of the shop, walled off with red curtains from the profane gaze of the unsanative, contained two chairs for the doctor and myself, and a library where all the masters of physic were grouped, through their sheet and paper representatives, in more friendliness of contact than has ever been known to characterize a consultation of like spirits under any other circumstances. Within the limits of four square feet, Pereira and Christison condensed all their stores of wisdom and research, and Dunglison and Brathwaite sat cheek by jowl beside them. There stood the Dispensatory, with the air of a business-like office, wherein all the specifica of the materia medica had been brought together for a scientific conversazione, but, becoming enamored of each other's society, had resolved to stay, overcrowded though they might be, and make an indefinite sitting of it. In a modest niche, set apart like a vestibule from the apartments of the medical gentlemen, lay a shallow case, which disclosed, on the lifting of a cover, the neatly-ordered rank of tweezers, probe, and lancet, which constituted my friend's claim to the confidence of the plethoric community; for, although unblessed with metropolitan fame, he was still no

'Cromwell guiltless of his country's blood.'

Here many an hour have I sat buried in the statistics of human life or the history of the make-shifts for its preservation. Here the details of surgical or medical experiment have held me in as complete engrossment as the positions and crises of romance; and here especially, with a disregard to my own safety which would have done credit to Quintus Curtius, have I made upon myself the trial of the effects of every strange drug and chemical which the laboratory could produce. Now with the chloroform bottle beneath my nose have I set myself careering upon the wings of a thrilling and accelerating life, until I had just enough power remaining to restore the liquid to its place upon the shelf, and sink back into the enjoyment of the delicious apathy which lasted through the few succeeding moments. Now ether was substituted for chloroform, and the difference of their phenomena noted, and now some other exhilarant, in the form of an opiate or stimulant, was the instrument of my experiments, until I had run through the whole gamut of queer agents within my reach.

In all these experiences research and not indulgence was my object, so that I never became the victim of any habit in the prosecution of my headlong investigations. When the circuit of all the accessible tests was completed, I ceased experimenting, and sat down like a pharmaceutical Alexander, with no more drug-worlds to conquer.

One morning, in the spring of 185–, I dropped in upon the doctor for my accustomed lounge.

'Have you seen,' said he, 'my new acquisitions?'

I looked toward the shelves in the direction of which he pointed, and saw, added since my last visit, a row of comely pasteboard cylinders inclosing vials of the various extracts prepared by Tilden & Co. Arranged in order according to their size, they confronted me, as pretty a little rank of medicinal sharpshooters as could gratify the eye of an amateur. I approached the shelves, that I might take them in review.

A rapid glance showed most of them to be old acquaintances. 'Conium, taraxacum, rhubarb – ha! what is this? Cannabis Indica?' 'That,' answered the doctor, looking with a parental fondness upon his new treasure, 'is a preparation of the East Indian hemp, a powerful agent in cases of lock-jaw.' On the strength of this introduction I took down the little archer, and, removing his outer verdant coat, began the further prosecution of his acquaintance. To pull out a broad and shallow cork was the work of an instant, and it revealed to me an olive-brown extract, of the consistency of pitch, and a decided aromatic odor. Drawing out a small portion upon the point of my penknife, I was just going to put it to my tongue, when 'Hold on!' cried the doctor; 'do you want to kill yourself? That stuff is deadly poison.' 'Indeed!' I replied; 'no, I can not say that I have any settled determination of that kind;' and with that I replaced the cork, and restored the extract, with all its appurtenances, to the shelf.

The remainder of my morning's visit in the sanctum was spent in consulting the Dispensatory under the title 'Cannabis Indica.' The sum of my discoveries there may be found, with much additional information, in that invaluable popular work, Johnston's Chemistry of Common Life. This being universally accessible, I will allude no further to the result of that morning's researches than to mention the three following conclusions to which I came.

First, the doctor was both right and wrong; right, inasmuch as a sufficiently large dose of the drug, if it could be retained in the stomach, would produce death, like any other narcotic, and the ultimate effect of its habitual use had always proved highly injurious to mind and body; wrong, since moderate doses of it were never immediately deadly, and many millions of people daily employed it as an indulgence similarly to opium. Second, it was the hasheesh referred to by Eastern travelers, and the subject of a most graphic chapter from the pen of Bayard Taylor, which months before had moved me powerfully to curiosity and admiration. Third, I would add it to the list of my former experiments.

In pursuance of this last determination, I waited till my friend was out of sight, that I might not terrify him by that which he considered a suicidal venture, and then quietly uncapping my little archer a second time, removed from his store of offensive armor a pill sufficient to balance the ten grain weight of the sanctorial scales. This, upon the authority of Percira and the Dispensatory, I swallowed without a tremor as to the danger of the result.

Making all due allowance for the fact that I had not taken my hasheesh bolus fasting, I ought to experience its effects within the next four hours. That time elapsed without bringing the shadow of a phenomenon. It was plain that my dose had been insufficient.

For the sake of observing the most conservative prudence, I suffered several days to go by without a repetition of the experiment, and then, keeping the matter equally secret, administered to myself a pill of fifteen grains. This second was equally ineffectual with the first.

Gradually, by five grains at a time, I increased the dose to thirty grains, which I took one evening half an hour after tea. I had now almost come to the conclusion that I was absolutely unsusceptible of the hasheesh influence. Without any expectation that this last experiment would be more successful than the former ones, and indeed with no realization of the manner in which the drug affected those who did make the experiment successfully, I went to pass the evening at the house of an intimate friend. In music and conversation the time passed pleasantly. The clock struck ten, reminding me that three hours had elapsed since the dose was taken, and as yet not an unusual symptom had appeared. I was provoked to think that this trial was as fruitless as its predecessors.

Ha! what means this sudden thrill? A shock, as of some unimagined vital force, shoots without warning through my entire frame, leaping to my fingers' ends, piercing my brain, startling me till I almost spring from my chair.

I could not doubt it. I was in the power of the hasheesh influence. My first emotion was one of uncontrollable terror – a sense of getting something which I had not bargained for. That moment I would have given all I had or hoped to have to be as I was three hours before.

No pain anywhere – not a twinge in any fibre – yet a cloud of unutterable strangeness was settling upon me, and wrapping me impenetrably in from all that was natural or familiar. Endeared faces, well known to me of old, surrounded me, yet they were not with me in my loneliness. I had entered upon a tremendous life which they could not share. If the disembodied ever return to hover over the hearth-stone which once had a seat for them, they look upon their friends as I then looked upon mine. A nearness of place, with an infinite distance of state, a connection which had no possible sympathies for the wants of that hour of revelation, an isolation none the less perfect for seeming companionship.

Still I spoke; a question was put to me, and I answered it; I even laughed at a bon mot. Yet it was not my voice which spoke; perhaps one which I once had far away in another time and another place. For a while I knew nothing that was going on externally, and then the remembrance of the last remark which had been made returned slowly and indistinctly, as some trait of a dream will return after many days, puzzling us to say where we have been conscious of it before.

A fitful wind all the evening had been sighing down the

chimney; it now grew into the steady hum of a vast wheel in accelerating motion. For a while this hum seemed to resound through all space. I was stunned by it – I was absorbed in it. Slowly the revolution of the wheel came to a stop, and its monotonous din was changed for the reverberating peel of a grand cathedral organ. The ebb and flow of its inconceivably solemn tone filled me with a grief that was more than human. I sympathized with the dirge-like cadence as spirit sympathizes with spirit. And then, in the full conviction that all I heard and felt was real, I looked out of my isolation to see the effect of the music on my friends. Ah! we were in separate worlds indeed. Not a trace of appreciation on any face.

Perhaps I was acting strangely. Suddenly a pair of busy hands, which had been running neck and neck all the evening with a nimble little crochet-needle over a race-ground of pink and blue silk, stopped at their goal, and their owner looked at me steadfastly. Ah! I was found out – I had betrayed myself. In terror I waited, expecting every instant to hear the word 'hasheesh.' No, the lady only asked me some question connected with the previous conversation. As mechanically as an automaton I began to reply. As I heard once more the alien and unreal tones of my own voice, I became convinced that it was some one else who spoke, and in another world. I sat and listened; still the voice kept speaking. Now for the first time I experienced that vast change which hasheesh makes in all measurements of time. The first word of the reply occupied a period sufficient for the action of a drama; the last left me in complete ignorance of any point far enough back in the past to date the commencement of the sentence. Its enunciation might have occupied years. I was not in the same life which had held me when I heard it begin.

And now, with time, space expanded also. At my friend's house one particular arm-chair was always reserved for me. I was sitting in it at a distance of hardly three feet from the centre-table around which the members of the family were grouped. Rapidly that distance widened. The whole atmosphere seemed ductile, and spun endlessly out into great spaces surrounding me on every side. We were in a vast hall, of which my friends and I occupied opposite extremities. The ceiling and the walls ran upward with a gliding motion, as if vivified by a sudden force of resistless growth.

Oh! I could not bear it. I should soon be left alone in the midst of an infinity of space. And now more and more every moment increased the conviction that I was watched. I did not know then, as I learned afterwards, that suspicion of all earthly things and persons was the characteristic of the hasheesh delirium.

In the midst of my complicated hallucination, I could perceive that I had a dual existence. One portion of me was whirled unresistingly along the track of this tremendous experience, the other sat looking down from a height upon its double, observing, reasoning, and serenely weighing all the phenomena. This calmer being suffered with the other by sympathy, but did not lose its self-possession. Presently it warned me that I must go home, lest the growing effect of the hasheesh should incite me to some act which might frighten my friends. I acknowledged the force of this remark very much as if it had been made by another person, and rose to take my leave. I advanced towards the centre-table. With every step its distance increased. I nerved myself as for a long pedestrian journey. Still the lights, the faces, the furniture receded. At last, almost unconsciously, I reached them. It would be tedious to attempt to convey the idea of the time which my leave-taking consumed, and the attempt, at least with all minds that have not passed through the same experience, would be as impossible as tedious. At last I was in the street.

Beyond me the view stretched endlessly away. It was an unconverging vista, whose nearest lamps seemed separated from me by leagues. I was doomed to pass through a merciless stretch of space. A soul just disenthralled, setting out for his flight beyond the farthest visible star, could not be more overwhelmed with his newly-acquired conception of the sublimity of distance than I was at that moment. Solemnly I began my infinite journey.

Before long I walked in entire unconsciousness of all around me. I dwelt in a marvelous inner world. I existed by turns in different places and various states of being. Now I swept my gondola through the moonlit lagoons of Venice. Now Alp on Alp towered above my view, and the glory of the coming sun flashed purple light upon the topmost icy pinnacle. Now in the primeval silence of some unexplored tropical forest I spread my feathery leaves, a giant fern, and swayed and nodded in the spice-gales over a river whose waves at once sent up clouds of music and perfume. My soul changed to a vegetable essence, thrilled with a strange and unimagined ecstasy. The palace of Al Haroun could not have bought me back to humanity.

I will not detail all the transmutations of that walk. Ever and anon I returned from my dreams into consciousness, as some well-known house seemed to leap out into my path, awaking me with a shock. The whole way homeward was a series of such awakenings and relapses into abstraction and delirium until I reached the corner of the street in which I lived.

Here a new phenomenon manifested itself. I had just awakened for perhaps the twentieth time, and my eyes were wide open. I recognized all surrounding objects, and began calculating the distance home. Suddenly, out of a blank wall at my side a muffled figure stepped into the path before me. His hair, white as snow, hung in tangled elf-locks on his shoulders, where he carried also a heavy burden, like unto the well-filled sack of sins which Bunyan places on the back of his pilgrim. Not liking his manner, I stepped aside, intending to pass around him and go on my way. This change of our relative positions allowed the blaze of a neighbouring street-lamp to fall full on his face, which had hitherto been totally obscured. Horror unspeakable! I shall never, till the day I die, forget that face. Every lineament was stamped with the records of a life black with damning crime; it glared upon me with a ferocious wickedness and a stony despair which only he may feel who is entering on the retribution of the unpardonable sin. He might have sat to a demon painter as the ideal of Shelley's Cenci. I seemed to grow blasphemous in looking at him, and, in an agony of fear, began to run away. He detained me with a bony hand, which pierced my wrist like talons, and, slowly taking down the burden from his own shoulders, laid it upon mine. I threw it off and pushed him away. Silently he returned and restored the weight. Again I repulsed him, this time crying out, 'Man, what do you mean?' In a voice which impressed me with the sense of wickedness as his face had done, he replied, 'You *shall* bear my burden with me,' and a third time laid it on my shoulders. For the last time I hurled it aside, and, with all my force, dashed him from me. He reeled backward and fell, and before he could recover his disadvantage I had put a long distance between us.

Through the excitement of my struggle with this phantasm the effects of the hasheesh had increased mightily. I was bursting with an uncontrollable life; I strode with the thews of a giant. Hotter and faster came my breath; I seemed to pant like some tremendous engine. An electric energy whirled me resistlessly onward; I feared for myself lest it should burst its fleshly walls, and glance on, leaving a wrecked frame-work behind it.

At last I entered my own house. During my absence a family connection had arrived from abroad, and stood ready to receive my greeting. Partly restored to consciousness by the naturalness of home-faces and the powerful light of a chandelier which shed its blaze through the room, I saw the necessity of vigilance against betraying my condition, and with an intense effort suppressing all I felt, I approached my friend, and said all that is usual on such occasions. Yet recent as I was from my conflict with the supernatural, I cast a stealthy look about me, that I might learn from the faces of the others if, after all, I was shaking hands with a phantom, and making inquiries about the health of a family of hallucinations. Growing assured as I perceived no symptoms of astonishment, I finished the salutation and sat down.

It soon required all my resolution to keep the secret which I had determined to hold inviolable. My sensations began to be terrific – not from any pain that I felt, but from the tremendous mystery of all around me and within me. By an appalling introversion, all the operations of vitality which, in our ordinary state, go on unconsciously, came vividly into my experience. Through every thinnest corporeal tissue and minutest vein I could trace the circulation of the blood along each inch of its progress. I knew when every valve opened and when it shut; every sense was preternaturally awakened; the room was full of a great glory. The beating of my heart was so clearly audible that I wondered to find it unnoticed by those who were sitting by my side. Lo, now, that heart became a great fountain, whose jet played upward with loud vibrations, and, striking upon the roof of my skull as on a gigantic dome, fell back with a splash and echo into its reservoir. Faster and faster came the pulsations, until at last I heard them no more, and the stream became one continuously pouring flood, whose roar resounded through all my frame. I gave myself up for lost, since judgment, which still sat unimpaired above my perverted senses, argued that congestion must take place in a few moments, and close the drama with my death. But my clutch would not yet relax from hope. The thought struck me, Might not this rapidity of circulation be, after all, imaginary? I determined to find out.

Going to my own room, I took out my watch, and placed my hand upon my heart. The very effort which I made to ascertain the reality gradually brought perception back to its natural state. In the intensity of my observations, I began to perceive that the circulation was not as rapid as I had thought. From a pulseless flow it gradually came to be apprehended as a hurrying succession of intense throbs, then less swift and less intense, till finally, on comparing it with the second-hand, I found that about 90 a minute was its average rapidity. Greatly comforted, I desisted from the experiment. Almost instantly the hallucination returned. Again I dreaded apoplexy, congestion, hemorrhage, a multiplicity of nameless deaths, and drew my picture as I might be found on the morrow, stark and cold, by those whose agony would be redoubled by the mystery of my end. I reasoned with myself; I bathed my forehead – it did no good. There was one resource left: I would go to a physician.

With this resolve, I left my room and went to the head of the staircase. The family had all retired for the night, and the gas was turned off from the burner in the hall below. I looked down the stairs: the depth was fathomless; it was a journey of years to reach the bottom! The dim light of the sky shone through the narrow panes at the sides of the front door, and seemed a demon-lamp in the middle darkness of the abyss. I never could get down! I sat me down despairingly upon the topmost step.

Suddenly a sublime thought possessed me. If the distance be infinite, I am immortal. It shall be tried. I commenced the descent, wearily, wearily down through my league-long, year-long journey. To record my impressions in that journey would be to repeat what I have said of the time of hasheesh. Now stopping to rest as a traveler would turn aside at a wayside inn, now toiling down through the lonely darkness, I came by-and-by to the end, and passed out into the street.

Baluchistan Garden
Brian Barritt

The drop-outs of the community are called Malungs, Moslem equivalents to the Hindu sadhus, and fanatical devotees to Madam Charas. Pot is legal in the tribal territories, non-addictive and good for spiritual and physical health. Alcohol is banned by the Koran and full of evil spirits. Opium is for illness and the O smokers are likely to cultivate a very solid habit.

The tea house in Quetta, Baluchistan, is an open fronted cafe with a big brass samovar by the entrance and several blue and white teapots perched at angles on the coals. It's only incidentally for passers-by, its real raison d'etre is for the smokers in the inner room who, after a serious hookah or two, might need a pot of tea to straighten themselves out.

At the rear of the tea house is a high walled garden about twenty feet square with a clay seat running round three sides and a small well at the far end. Next to the entrance is a meter high cube of red stone with a huge Pathan tribesman, in spotless white shirt and Ali Baba trousers, seated cross legged on it.

Spread out in front of him on the stone is a square of white cloth, not much bigger than a pocket handkerchief, with a selection of several kinds of hashish upon it. The atmosphere is quiet and refined, a million decibels away from the noisy English pub, the only sounds issuing from an antique stringed instrument player and a boy harmonising with finger symbols and crooning softly in Arabic.

With a bow we are introduced to the Pathan seated on the block of stone facing the entrance. At Jebal, the owner's, prompting I take a rupee and place it on the cloth and receive four small cubes of hashish in return. I am just going to pick them up when Jebal taps me on the shoulder. He points to a mint bush growing next to the block of stone, and indicates that I should purify my hands first by rubbing them amongst the leaves, before handling the hash and entering the garden.

Omar Khayam would have liked it here; the garden is a carpet woven in flowers, a rectangular mandala with a big old hookah minus its stems standing in the centre filled with choice blooms. From the beginning we got along well with Habibullah Khan and Jebal, the owners of the tea house. When we first strolled in Jebal welcomed us as if we were expected, ushering us in with smiles and pointing to a photograph hanging on the wall which showed a waterfall tumbling down a rocky cliff.

Over the next few days we spend many afternoons in the cafe and garden, becoming familiar with the inhabitants who, it turned out, came from all over Pakistan, Afghanistan and Persia. Most of the Malungs were of Pathan stock, tall, hard, sunswept men exuding a quiet equanimity. Over their robes or long shirts they often wore waistcoats covered with a motley of postage stamp sized squares of cloth. If they liked the colour of something you were wearing they might ask you for a piece of it, and offer you a piece of theirs as a token of friendship.

Although they looked barbaric, carried short spears, rifles, or cudgels covered with bells, they were considerate and polite – everyone existed for and by hashish.

In the evenings they would generally sit in the garden for a while and then mosey through a door next to the well and, so we imagined, trail off into the night. It was a week before we were invited into the room behind the pump that led into the lair of the really serious smokers, the Inner Room.

Twenty men sat shoulder to shoulder on wooden benches in

a low ceilinged, narrow room thick with hash smoke. In the centre, its two stems reaching up from a fat bowl, stands the hookah. Squatting on the floor next to the hookah is a Malung we have not seen before, a gaunt creature, wearing a heavy steel chain coiled around his waist instead of a loin-cloth and a similar chain coiled round his head instead of a turban. His limbs are like black sticks, his face a hawk's. Two fanatical eyes burn a slow madness as he replenishes the chillum with fresh hash and fits it over the stem of the pipe.

Jebal rises from his seat and extinguishes the small lamp that is the only light. Simultaneously the fakir squatting on the floor blows hard on the dish of glowing charcoal and, picking up a coal in his bare fingers, places it in the hookah's chillum.

'Aha!'

Habibullah is standing in a half-crouch over the pipe, his two hands clutching the stems, legs spread apart to take firm hold. The scene is lit by fire and glowing charcoal, the silver of the fakir's chains gleam against a background of faces seen through writhing smoke and the water in the hookah's bowl gurgles like a happy baby.

Belching smoke, Habibullah staggers back coughing to his place on the bench and instantly the next smoker is pouncing on the pipe. The hoary old pipe passes from hand to hand, standing immobile in the centre while the room moves around it. When it reaches Paula there is a guffaw of laughter at her weak draw, likewise with myself. We are not used to smoking in this dense atmosphere of hash, charcoal and hot crowded darkness and after the first toke the room and its occupants start revolving in opposite directions. The Malungs become prophets from the Old Testament; hennaed beards sway and blend together through the smoke and darkness and closeness into a single organism, a one-celled being whose nucleus is the hookah.

Each cube of hashish is a black stone of Mecca, an enlightened chemical, purified earth. It is placed on the coals of the element fire, pulled through water and sucked up the stem by air to transmute the alchemist into the fifth element.

As the evening wears on the huge Pathan, who spends his days seated on the block of stone, begins massaging the heads of the smokers. He pours oil on my head and after a few minutes of heavy pressing and rubbing takes it between his massive hands and crushes it to pulp. At least that's how it felt as his giant paws closed over my skull, but somehow he restrained himself and afterwards the oozy feeling of too much togetherness, evaporated.

After the last pipe of the evening the fakir leaps up from his squatting crouch and snatches the hot chillum from the hookah. With a flourish he spreads a trail of glowing charcoal across the floor and tells someone's fortune with the dying embers.

We go regularly to the Inner Room after our initial introduction and find that the vibes change often. Our first trip had been to that cosmic place where everything and everyone are part of the same eternal essence, but as we became a regular feature everyone relaxed in our presence and other trips evolved.

One Malung, who was never parted from a great gnarled club bound round with copper wire, freaked out one evening into a warrior from Moslem myth and held a terrible battle with an imaginary demon in the middle of the room. He ran yelling and striking at the imaginary Djinn for ten minutes (earth time) without decapitating a single smoker. Everyone sat relaxed and watched placidly until he was convinced that he had slain his adversary and slumped back exhausted on the bench.

Other trips turned sexual so that the hookah glass became the buttocks of a she-devil standing on her head, the two stems open legs jutting from the infernal cauldron between her thighs. A Malung holds her two stems wide apart as he sucks the nipple of her toe, the water laughs deep in her belly. There was also the fakir's trip, when all attention was focused on the chain-clad penitent leaping and hopping like a JuJu man, uttering weird cries and predictions of which we didn't understand a word but somehow picked up on the meaning.

Identity Crisis
Howard Marks

In April 1974 I was sitting in a flat near the top of a high-rise building in the Isle of Dogs, overlooking the River Thames and Greenwich naval station. I was skipping bail. Over my Amsterdam lawyer's protests, the Dutch police had put me aboard a BEA flight to Heathrow. Her Majesty's Customs and Excise Officers came on the plane at Heathrow and took me to Snowhill Police Station, where I was charged under the hitherto unenforced Section 20 of the Misuse of Drugs Act, 1971, with assisting in the United Kingdom in the commission of a United States drug offence. Californian James Gater, who had been arrested at Heathrow airport a couple of days before my arrest, and a few of James Morris's workers were my co-defendants. After three uneventful weeks in Her Majesty's Prison, Brixton, I was granted bail for sureties totalling £50,000. On bail, I lived with Rosie and the children at 46, Leckford Road, Oxford, premises formerly rented and occupied by William Jefferson Clinton, who was to become the President of the United States. The evidence against me was strong, partly because I had been daft enough to admit to Her Majesty's Customs and Excise my documented illegal activities in Holland in the hope that my offence would be treated as a Dutch rather than a British one. That strategy had backfired, and my solicitor, Bernard Simons, was certain I would get convicted and was not too optimistic of my getting less than three years in prison.

The East End flat belonged to Dai, my old school-teaching companion. Thames Valley Police must obviously have made some enquiries into my whereabouts, but no one seemed to be getting very excited. I had written a note to Bernard Simons so that everyone could know that nothing untoward had happened. I had just skipped bail. The trial had started without me the previous day, May 1st, 1974. My co-defendants pleaded guilty and got sentences ranging from six months to four years. Ernie had promised to pay off any sureties demanded by the judge as the result of my skipping bail. He felt indebted to me because at the time of my arrest in Amsterdam I was the only person in the world who knew his whereabouts, and I had not disclosed them to the authorities. I was biding my time.

Dai had woken me up early before going to school.

'Howard, you've been on the news.'

'What! What did it say?'

'Well, there were only three headlines: one about Prime Minister Harold Wilson, one about President Nixon, and one about you. I couldn't take it all in. Something about MI6 and the IRA. I'll go out and get the newspapers.'

The *Daily Mirror*'s entire front page was devoted to a story about me headlined WHERE IS MR MARKS?, describing how I was an MI6 agent, with arrest warrants out for me in seven countries, who had been kidnapped, beaten up, told to keep my mouth shut, and persuaded to become an IRA sympathiser. There was no clue as to how the *Daily Mirror* had got hold of the information that I had worked for MI6. There were general statements claiming that I had told some friends I was a spy. In fact I had told only Rosie, my parents, and McCann. Rosie, when interviewed by the press, categorically stated there was no connection between me and the IRA or the security services. Her Majesty's Customs and Excise had been made aware of my MI6 involvement: Mac's telephone number had appeared in the telephone records of an Amsterdam hotel, and

I had successfully used my promise of not mentioning MI6 in court as a lever to secure bail. HM Customs would have been unlikely to spill all to a *Daily Mirror* reporter. The *Daily Mail*'s front-page headline was YARD FEAR NEW IRA ABDUCTION, and the text claimed that I had last been seen in the company of two Customs Officers and that police were now investigating the possibility that I had been executed by the IRA. Later the same day, Thames Valley Police vehemently denied that I had been an MI6 agent spying on the IRA, and Bernard Simons kept saying he'd heard from me, and that I was not being held against my will. But the media took no notice. That was too boring. In fairness, the *Daily Mirror* felt obliged at least to present an alternative theory: the next day's front page was headlined THE INFORMER, and the report stated that I had been kidnapped by Mafia drug smugglers to prevent me from appearing at the Old Bailey and grassing them up. Other reports suggested I had staged my own kidnap. The public, though, preferred the spy/IRA theory, and that's what the television and radio news stations gave them. Who were my enemies? – the police because they were being forced to look for me everywhere, the IRA because I'd smuggled dope, the Mafia because they thought I was going to talk about them, Her Majesty's Customs and Excise because I didn't turn up to get my conviction, Her Majesty's Secret Service for my switching of loyalties, or the media for reasons I didn't understand? Did it matter? All I had intended to do was change my appearance and carry on scamming. I already had a bit of a moustache. All this off-the-wall publicity would just make me more careful. Still, it all felt rather unreal and occasionally scary.

The media circus stopped as suddenly as it had begun. The Old Bailey trial judge deferred any decision regarding the estreat-ment of the bail sureties. I might have been abducted, he said, and therefore could not be termed an absconder. My main duty was to ensure that my family knew for certain that I was unharmed. Dai was not keen on my using his telephone for any purpose, and I assumed that most of my family's telephones were tapped as a result of the nation-wide search for me. Through circuitous and complex manoeuvres involving conversations with my sister in Wales, I was able to have clandestine meetings with Rosie, Myfanwy, and my parents while I continued perfecting my disguise. After about two months, I looked very different and felt no fear walking the streets. Each morning, I would buy a few newspapers and have coffee at a dock-workers' café. One hot early July morning, I was at the newsagent's and saw a *Daily Mirror* front-page headline, THE LONG SILENCE OF MR MYSTERY. Underneath was a photograph of me. I bought a copy. The report stated that Thames Valley Police had called off the search for me and that my disappearance had been the subject of discussion in the Houses of Parliament. Another blaze of publicity followed in the *Daily Mirror*'s wake.

'You need another name and more disguise,' said Dai. 'Everyone's talking about you on the Tube. I'm not calling you Howard any more. And I'm not calling you Mr Mystery either.'

'Call me Albi,' I said, partly in deference to my old friend Albert Hancock and partly because it was an anagram of bail.

'All right,' said Dai. 'Why don't you get yourself a pair of glasses?'

'From whom?'

'I think they're called opticians, Albi.'

'But there's nothing wrong with my eyes, Dai. They won't give me a pair.'

'You walk into a dentist; he'll say you've got bad teeth. You walk into an optician, and he'll say you need glasses. That's the way they make money. Anyway, I read the other day that the stuff you keep smoking causes long sight. Why don't you smoke a load and go to an optician?'

Dai had probably read one of those absurd scare stories of marijuana causing just above everything from sterility to nymphomania. But there might be something to it. I knew marijuana had some effect on intraocular pressure. I smoked several joints and had my eyes tested. I needed glasses, and a special pair was made. They dramatically changed my appearance, but made things rather blurry, except when I was stoned.

Intermittent press speculation on my whereabouts continued for over a month. The FBI feared for my life. A West Country man, of whom I'd never heard, confessed to murdering me and burying me beneath a motorway bridge near Bristol.

'You'll have to go, Albi. This is driving me, Jane, and Sian nuts.'

'Okay, Dai. I'm sorry. I never thought I'd be staying here this long, and I never thought all this madness would happen.'

'Why don't you leave the country?'

'I haven't got a passport, Dai. I don't know where to start.'

'Take mine.'

Normally, Dai and I look a bit like each other. We were tall, dark, blue-eyed, clean-shaven, and heavily featured. Now, with my moustache and stoned glasses, we didn't, but the photograph could easily be changed; the Foreign and Commonwealth Office embossed stamp covered just a minute part of the corner. Its absence on the replacement photograph would not be noticed. Dai gave me his driving licence as well. He was anxious that nothing hold me up.

I decided to go to Italy. There were two main reasons. A large Winnebago motorised caravan lay in a camping site in Genova. I had bought it a year previously for Eric to use, had he landed the Lebanese in Italy rather than made it available to Greek sponge fishermen. Living in it appealed to me. Also, my sister was about to start a teaching course in Padova, so I had an easy way of keeping in touch with the family. Apart from the Winnebago, my assets were about £5,000 cash. Everything else had gone. While I was on bail, Ernie had sent someone to Amsterdam to try to get the $100,000 and the Peter Hughes passport from the safe-deposit box in Algemene Bank Nederland, but the cupboard was bare. The authorities had got there first. The guy Ernie had sent, Burton Moldese, apparently had some Los Angeles Mafia connections, and I'm sure that this is what gave rise to the *Daily Mirror*'s Mafia theory. Ernie would lend me some money, I was sure, particularly if, as seemed increasingly likely, there would be no estreatment of bail sureties. I had a mailing address for Ernie, but was unsure how he would have reacted to all the weird publicity. I'd contact him when everything was settled.

Remembering McCann's advice, I didn't fly directly to Italy. I took a ferry to Denmark and caught a flight from Copenhagen to Genova. The passport stood up. The Winnebago started first time, and I cruised around the camping sites of the Italian Riviera. I stopped wearing my glasses and began a period of debauched promiscuity, driving up and down Italian roads picking up female hitch-hikers. The Winnebago had a kitchen, sitting room, shower, loud stereo, and comfortably slept six. I would usually pick up just one hitch-hiker, but occasionally as many as fifteen or sixteen. From Como to Napoli, the autostradas became my home. I had to pay for petrol, but dope, sex, food, and drink seemed to be free.

Rosie brought out Myfanwy to see me for a couple of weeks. They had now sold the Yarnton cottage and, together with Julian Peto and his family, had bought a large house at Northleigh, outside Oxford. I kept in touch with Rosie through Fanny Hill. In September, I called Rosie at Fanny's and mentioned that my parents were hoping to come out to see me. It later emerged that this conversation had been overheard on another extension by Raymond Carr, Master of St Anthony's College, who was still having an affair with Fanny. It is not certain that Raymond Carr passed on this information to the authorities, but it is likely. My parents did come out and shared with my sister and me a two-week holiday touring Northern Italy in the Winnebago.

After they left, I hung around at a camp site in Padova. My sister came to see me in a panic. The *Daily Mirror* were trying to interview her. They knew I was in Italy and knew my parents had been to see me. I had to assume the authorities also knew. Where could I go now? I had almost no money. The police would not be looking for me in England. That would be the last place they'd expect to find me, and there I could find at least a floor to sleep on.

On October 28th, 1974, I drove the Winnebago to the Genova campsite I had collected it from three months earlier. I put yet another photograph in Dai's passport and booked a seat on a British Caledonian flight to Gatwick.

On arrival at Genova airport, I had several glasses of *grappa* before passing uneventfully through the passport check, and settled down to some serious drinking in the departure lounge. At the duty-free shop, I bought some cigarettes and a few bottles of *sambuca negra*. During the flight I ordered several more drinks and even began drinking from the *sambuca negra* bottles. Newspapers were distributed, and I took a copy of the *Daily Mirror*. On the front page was a photograph of me under a blazing headline HE'S ALIVE. The article was several pages long and stated that Mr Mystery was living as a guest of the Mafia in Padova. Mr Mystery's hideout was known only to the Mafia and my sister. Mr Mystery was living undercover as a student, shielded and protected by Mafia gangsters. The aeroplane was full of people reading this exclusive. Ably assisted by the *sambuca negra*, I was again losing touch with reality. By the time we disembarked, I was giggling uncontrollably and cannot even remember any confrontation with Immigration or Customs. I followed the passengers through to Gatwick railway station and got on a train to Victoria. I was still drinking *sambuca negra* when the train arrived. I took a Tube to Paddington and, following my drunken homing instincts, took a train to Oxford, arriving at about 9 p.m. I walked from Oxford railway station to the police station in St Aldate's. When I got there I was extremely confused. I could not bring myself to believe that the last six months had actually happened. I wanted to rewind my life back to when I was signing on for bail in Oxford. I had understood everything until then. A policeman walked out of the station. I asked him how I could get a bus to Northleigh. He said it was too late. I would have to take a taxi. I went into a telephone box to call Rosie at Northleigh. No reply. I walked to Leckford Road, where I had last been seen by the sane world. The pub around the corner, the Victoria Arms, one that I and friends of mine had frequented, was still there. I walked in. There was a deathly silence. Almost everyone recognised me. Julian Peto was there and exploded into helpless laughter. I asked where Rosie was. She and Myfanwy were at a party, to which he was now going himself. Rosie and Myfanwy had left by the time we arrived. I drank some punch and smoked some joints. Julian and I drove to Northleigh. Rosie was in a state of shock. Chief Superintendent Philip Fairweather of the Thames Valley Police, the man in charge of investigating my disappearance, had just left. Rosie put me to bed. The next morning's news reported that Mohammed Ali had regained the world heavyweight championship from George Foreman and that an Old Bailey judge had decided not to forfeit any money from those who had stood bail for me, despite the police's knowing my whereabouts in Italy. Police inquiries were at an end. It was not in the 'public interest' to disclose where I was. But I was alive. At least I had stopped being a dead spy.

Judy Lane, now all of nineteen, was paying a social visit to Northleigh. We hadn't forgotten each other, and I did not have to be persuaded to accept her kind offer of accommodation at her flat in Brighton. Judy had five brothers and sisters. At that point, I had only met Patrick, who for the last year had been living in self-imposed exile in the Dordogne, growing snails. Judy's mother had recently died from cancer, and her father had a new young girlfriend. All her brothers and sisters lived away from home or in boarding-school. The former family flat in Brighton was at Judy's disposal. Judy and I have been together ever since.

Again, the media furore died as quickly as it had begun. I felt safe in Judy's flat, and I began to contact old business friends including Johnny Martin, Anthony Woodhead, and Jarvis. With their help, I managed to sell the Winnebago and procure the release of the few thousand pounds I had deposited in the Swiss

Bank Corporation the year before. I wrote to Ernie giving him Judy's phone number. The telephone rang in the middle of the night.

'Albi, it's for you,' said Judy.

'How you doin'? I thought you'd disappeared on me for good. So what's been happening? What you been doing?'

'Sorry, Ernie. With all the reports in the press about me, I thought you wouldn't want to know.'

'I never saw any of that. You'd be small fry here. Look, my girlfriend, Patty, is coming over to see you. She'll explain what I've got together these days. You need some money for living? She'll have $10,000 for you.'

Anthony Woodhead had procured a London penthouse flat overlooking Regent's Park at an extremely low rental. I unofficially rented it from him, and Judy and I took up residence there. Patty arrived and gave me Ernie's particulars and the codes we should use when talking over the phone. Ernie had a connection in New York's John F. Kennedy Airport who could clear through US Customs any consignment from anywhere, provided it was smell-proof and came in on Alitalia. The fee was 25% of the American wholesale price. Ernie had an old Brotherhood of Eternal Love associate, Robert Crimball, who was able to export Thai sticks from Bangkok. His fee was 35% of the American wholesale price. 40% was available for middle-men. A couple of 1,000-kilo loads had already been successfully imported and sold. Did I know anyone in any dope-producing country other than Thailand who, for some money in advance and lots more afterwards, could export dope by air freight? If so, I could become extremely rich.

This was a once-in-a-lifetime offer, but I didn't know anyone who could do what was required. I had completely lost touch with Mohammed Durrani, Lebanese Sam, and Lebanese Joe. No one had any ideas except Jarvis. One of his friends had lived in Nepal for seven years. His name was John Denbigh, and he was known as Old John. Jarvis arranged a meeting for the three of us at his flat.

Old John was a very tall, mature, masculine version of Mick Jagger. He was dressed like a Hell's Angel and adorned with necklaces, chains, beads, amulets, and semi-precious stones. He was a walking bust. But Old John had never smoked a joint, and he bought and repaired stoves to make a living. His words were full of wisdom, but if one stopped concentrating on them for just one second, he seemed incoherent. Otherwise, his wisdom would seem to profoundly by-pass all forms of convention and platitude. Old John's street sense was second to none; the streets of Fulham had given him that, as well as his accent. He was a keen soccer player and cricketer. His father had been educated at Oxford University. Old John had absolute integrity and honesty. No one could wish for a better, closer, or more trusted friend.

Jarvis rolled joints and made cups of tea. Old John smoked Tom Thumb cigars and drank whisky. We discussed the Welsh and English rugby teams. Wales had just slaughtered England 20–4 at Cardiff Arms Park. After an hour, I managed to bring up Nepal.

'You must have had an interesting time there, John.'

'Interesting, yes, and they are superb people, the Nepalese, I promise you.'

'Do you get many foreigners going there these days?'

'Well, the thing is there was this Englishman who told me he had nine talents. I told him I just had one: I could throw him out of the window. And he went and painted the outside of his house with religion, and then went to live inside the house. Madness.'

I just about followed that one and took it to mean that Old John had a certain contempt for expatriate communities in the East. I had to get more to the point.

'Did Customs here give you a hard time when you came back?'

'Hard? No, not hard. I heard one of them say, "Stop that cunt. I'm going to take him apart," and he came up to me and said, "Excuse me, sir," and I said, "Sir? No. Don't call me sir. My name is Cunt. Please call me Cunt." That dealt with him. Then the other one said, "Can I see your passport?" and I said, "It's not my passport, it's yours," and gave it to him. He asked what I did in Nepal. I told him I was a barman. Vodka and lime. What would you like? He asked me if I smoked any funny tobacco. I asked if he meant Kinabis, and he said it didn't matter. Then I caught a bus to Fulham.'

I had to come straight to the point.

'Can you send stuff out from Nepal by air, John?'

'Ooh! No. No. I can't do anything like that. No. No. No. Now, I know a man. He knows a man who might know.'

'How much would it cost?'

'Well, money is the thing, and they always do things for a fair and honest price, I promise you.'

'What's a fair price, John?'

'You will tell me, I'm quite sure.'

'What will you want out of it, John?'

'If I help you do business, I'm sure you will give me a drink.'

'A drink?'

'Yes. If a man does something for you, you give him a drink. Please, if everything goes well, give me a drink.'

'Can you check that the quality will be all right?'

'I only smoke Tom Thumb, but I know a man who has a knife.'

I took this as a yes.

'Can you make it smell-proof?'

'Not if God made it smell.'

'Do you know a man who can?'

'No. But if you do, let him come and do it, or give me instructions.'

'How much can they send?'

'I should think it depends on when you want to do it by.'

'Well, John, the Americans will want to do a ton as soon as possible.'

'Now I was in America once, and the thing is that Americans will always want more, and there is no end to their madness.

Lovely people, for sure, but you have to keep them in line. When my visa ran out, the Immigration asked me why I wanted to extend it, and I said it was because I hadn't run out of money. He stamped it and said, "Have a nice day." So, if the Americans ask for a ton tomorrow, say you will do half a ton when Wales win the Triple Crown. That will deal with their madness, and everyone can get on with their lives. It saves all that tidding.'

'Tidding?'

'Talking Imaginary Deals.'

Accurately conveying the contents of my conversation with Old John to Ernie wasn't easy. I told Ernie hashish could be exported from Nepal for about the same price as Robert Crimball charged in Bangkok, but 500 kilos was the most they could do at one time, and someone would have to be sent out to ensure the consignment was smell-proof. Ernie sent his right-hand man, Tom Sunde, with money, instructions, and smell-proof know-how. Tom came to London first before going to Kathmandu to meet Old John. He had been authorised by Ernie to keep nothing from me regarding the intricacies of the New York scam.

During the 1970s, the most powerful Mafia crime family in the United States was that of Carlo Gambino, the prototype for Vito Corleone in Mario Puzo's novel, *The Godfather*. Born in Sicily at the beginning of the century, Gambino was still of the old-school belief that the Mafia should steer away from involvement in drug-trafficking. Carmine Galante, the main contender for Gambino's position as the godfather of the New York Mob, had no such scruples. The Mafia should control everything, including dope. Carmine Galante's organisation used the services of Don Brown, an Irish-American who made his money dope-dealing in Queens, New York, and spent it in Los Angeles. Don Brown knew Richard Sherman, an extremely shrewd California defence attorney retained by Ernie Combs. Unwittingly, Sherman introduced Ernie to Don Brown. A scam was born.

Large quantities of missing goods provided strong evidence of the Gambino crime family's ability to remove items from John F. Kennedy Airport without going through the usual channels. Smuggling quickly followed. The preferred method was to send a cargo of legitimate goods from a New York company to the dope-producing country. The importing company in the dope country would ostensibly return the imported goods as faulty or different from ordered. In fact, a consignment of hashish would be sent and grabbed by the Mob.

As a prelude to the Nepalese scam, an air-conditioning company called Kool-Air had been formed in New York. It was ready to export real air-conditioning equipment. On separate flights, Old John and Tom Sunde, carrying a small suitcase full of Ernie's dollars, flew to Kathmandu to take care of business. First Old John had to form a Nepalese company capable of importing air-conditioning equipment and let me know its particulars. A week later, I received a telegram from Kathmandu. The message comprised one word, 'YETI.' I knew that yeti was the Nepalese name for the abominable snowman of the Himalayas, but this didn't help. Ernie was anxious for news. I didn't know what to tell him, so I cabled Old John in Kathmandu to call me.

'John, what's this message mean?'

'That's the name of the thing you wanted.'

I wasn't happy with calling an air-conditioning company The Abominable Snowman.

'That's really not a very relevant name, John.'

'It's very relevant, I promise you. They haven't caught one yet.'

I gave up.

'Okay, John, that's the name. Is everything else all right?'

'No. They don't eat spaghetti here; they like to use chopsticks or they eat wurst or smorgasbord. We can't get the thing to go for spaghetti.'

Each day I was finding Old John easier to understand. He was unable to ensure that the load would be transferred to Alitalia before it reached New York. He could only manage to ensure the consignment's New York arrival on other European or Far East airlines. I told Ernie. He said he'd work on it.

With the money Ernie had given me, I added some luxuries to the Regent's Park penthouse: a stereo system and records. Judy's father and his girlfriend had moved into the Brighton family flat, so Judy now had the use of her father's flat, which was quite near Regent's Park. At about four o'clock on a spring afternoon, I was alone in the penthouse, idly gazing at London's skyline and listening to *Ladies Love Outlaws* by Waylon Jennings. I looked down and saw four hefty men with overcoats rushing up the street towards the entrance to my block of flats. Something told me they were coming for me, but I didn't know who they were. The ground-floor entrance doorbell buzzed in the penthouse. I asked who it was, and a muffled voice said something incomprehensible. I released the downstairs door, put on my stoned glasses, walked out of the flat, and started descending the emergency stairs, reasoning that the men would be likely to take the lift. When I got to the bottom of the emergency stairs, I noticed that the four men were still outside the glass double-doored entrance. The caretaker was holding open one of the doors and talking to them. They all saw me, and the caretaker motioned his head in my direction. I walked slowly and brazenly to the door as if to leave the building. One of the men took a flash photograph of me.

Then another said, 'That's not him.'

'We're sorry, sir. Excuse us,' said another.

I flashed them a look of irritation, walked to the street, and took a cab to Soho.

It was obviously the *Daily Mirror*, with or without the police. How did they know? I had no idea, but I couldn't go back to the penthouse again and had to consider as lost the money and valuables left there. Anthony Woodhead, who was the penthouse's official occupant, might encounter a few problems, unless it was he who had tipped them off. I was meant to be masterminding the sending to the New York Mafia of the first-ever air-freighted hashish from Kathmandu, and I had nothing in the world but a few pounds in my pocket and a pair of stoned glasses. I telephoned Judy. She picked me up in her car, and we drove to Liverpool and checked into the Holiday Inn under a false name. The next morning, the *Daily Mirror* was slid under the room door. Again I dominated the front page, which was headlined THE FACE OF A FUGITIVE. Underneath was a large picture of me wearing my stoned glasses and moustache. I shaved, put Brylcreem on my hair, and combed it straight back. Judy went out to rent the cheapest possible bed-sitter, £4 a week with shared bathroom and kitchen in an area called Sheill Park. I telephoned my parents to let them know I was okay, and telephoned Ernie to tell him what had happened. He was unperturbed. I didn't have the nerve to ask him for more money. He had some good news for Old John. The load could arrive on Japanese Air Lines (JAL); the Italians had been talking to the Japanese, and an arrangement had been made.

By far the largest organised crime network in the world is the Yakuza, with a membership of several hundred thousand. Originating in the early seventeenth century as a group of young Robin Hood-type rebels defying samurai overlords, the Yakuza emerged after World War II as a more typically Western collection of gangsters with dark suits and sun-glasses. By the end of the 1960s, the Yakuza had forged important links with the Chinese Triads in Hong Kong, Malaysia, Taiwan, and Thailand; and an unprecedently powerful Chinese–Japanese syndicate was beginning to send large shipments of heroin to the United States. Some of these went through Kennedy Airport. Now the Yakuza and the Mafia were waiting for Old John's Yeti to do its stuff.

I gave Ernie the number of the telephone box at the end of the road and told him I would be there between 8 and 8.15 every Tuesday night. I cabled Old John in Kathmandu with the same information and the good news about JAL, and I began to live the life of a Liverpool dosser about to be a rich man. A few hundred pounds was scrounged from some long-suffering friends and family.

My lack of identity documents began to worry me. A 21-year-old policeman had been shot dead by the IRA, and the Birmingham Black Panther and the Cambridge hooded rapist were at large. One could be stopped by the police at any time, and it would be embarrassing for me to be unable to palm them off with a piece of paper showing some false identity. The Driver and Vehicle Licence Centre in Swansea required no proof of identity when applying for a provisional driving licence. I ordered one in the name of Albert Lane, and it was delivered to the Liverpool bedsit. I applied to sit a driving test and passed. A full licence was issued. I joined the local library and opened a Post Office Savings Account, using the name Albert Lane. A bone-shaker of a Bedford van was purchased for next to nothing, and Judy and I set off on week-long vacations to a variety of campsites. We loved this perpetual holiday lifestyle, but Judy would often complain about my insistence that the tent was pitched adjacent to the public telephone box, whose number had been handed out everywhere from Los Angeles to the Himalayas. I had to make and accept telephone calls at all hours and did not want to be traipsing across moonlit fields in my pyjamas. The telephone box was almost invariably next to the campsite's bathrooms and toilets. Ours would be the only tent in the vicinity. During the day, we would either take advantage of the campsite's recreation facilities or join a local library under a couple of silly names. During the evening, we would attempt innovative ways of acquiring further false identities.

Our favourite method was through fortune-telling. Judy dressed up as a sexy clairvoyant and sat alone in a pub. I sat some distance away. Sooner or later, a man of about my age would initiate a conversation with her and find out she was an astrologer, palmist, and numerologist, capable of telling his fortune. She needed a few details, of course: date and place of birth, mother's maiden name, and his travels or travel plans. Some of them had no intention of going abroad because they didn't trust foreign beer. We ended up with enough information to procure several birth certificates from St Catherine's House, London.

On Independence Day, July 4th, 1975, 500 kilos of hand-pressed Nepalese temple balls, some of the best hashish in the world, was flown from Kathmandu via Bangkok and Tokyo to New York. It was being smoked in Greenwich Village the next day. I was very rich again, and I was still in my twenties.

PART FOUR

EXTRACTS OF OPIUM

Young Asia no longer smokes because 'grandfather smoked.' Young Europe smokes because 'grandfather did not smoke.' Since, alas, young Asia imitates young Europe, it is through us that opium will return to its starting point.

From *Opium: Diary of a Cure* by Jean Cocteau (1929)

All the hallucinogenic drugs are considered sacred by those who use them – there are Peyote Cults and Bannisteria Cults, Hashish Cults and Mushroom Cults . . . but no one ever suggested that junk is sacred. There are no opium cults. Opium is profane and quantitative like money.

From *Naked Lunch* by William S. Burroughs (1959)

Like cannabis, opium was cultivated by Stone Age farmers. By 6,000 BC. it was already being harvested in the western Mediterranean region, the interzone between Europe and Asia. Opium cults surfaced in certain areas of both continents including Cyprus, Crete, Greece and Central Asia. The commercial potential of the narcotic poppy was not lost on ancient man; the Bronze Age Cypriots ran an opium trade that supplied the Egyptian market.

In Asia at least aspects of an opium cult still live on, among the Lahu people of northern Thailand, for example. In *Lahu*

Prayers for a Bountiful Opium Crop, the spirit of the fields is
called upon to aid the growth of the poppy. Yet these rituals
are anything but innocent exhortations. In the second of the
prayers the farmer offers the spirit a fifty-fifty split of the
opium crop. As Anthony R. Walker, the translator of these
prayers, points out, this kind of lying to the spirits is common
practice among the Lahu who clearly have no intention of
sticking to their end of the bargain.

The elevation of the spirit by means of opium is one of the
themes of *Confessions of an English Opium-Eater* by Thomas De
Quincey (1785–1859). In the extract, *The Pleasures of Opium*,
De Quincey describes his first forays into opium use,
beginning on a rainy Sunday in London in 1804. In *Ligeia* by
Edgar Allan Poe (1809–1849), mystery and imagination
combine in a classic tale of morbid hallucination and
melancholic narcosis precipitated by grief and fuelled by
opium. A lighter note is struck by Errol Flynn (1909–1959) in
his own account of his dabbling with opium from his
autobiography *My Wicked, Wicked Ways*. The Tasmanian Devil
fancied his chances at producing his own version of De
Quincey's *Confessions*. Soon realising the task was hopeless he
snapped out of his nascent addiction after a punch-up with his
friend Freddie McEvoy.

First published in 1959 by the Olympia Press in Paris,
Naked Lunch by William S. Burroughs (1914–1998) went on
to become one of the most influential novels since the
Second World War. The book was certainly novel,
introducing to the literary world his now famous 'cut-up'
style. Burroughs had already written a more conventional
novel (in style if not in subject matter) entitled *Junkie* in
which he tipped his hat to the hard-boiled style of detective
writing typical of forties America. In the extract *Hauser and
O'Brien* from *Naked Lunch* the brusque prose style of *Junkie* is
infiltrated by the corrosive nature of his more radical
experiments. In Will Self's *Junking the Image*, we return to the
two themes with which we began – opium and cults, and

East and West. He compares the cultural revolutions of East and West during the 1960s and their figureheads (Mao and Burroughs respectively), and despite his great admiration for the writings of the 'Great Junksman' he calls for an end to the cult of Burroughs.

Lahu Prayers for a Bountiful Opium Crop (1)

Anthony R. Walker

Oh, today, in exchange for this poppy field, I bring for you today two pairs of beeswax candles, Prince of this place, Ruler of this place.

Grant this blessing to the members of my household that from one day's work in this my poppy field, we may obtain enough to eat for ten days.

Let others talk of our good fortune, let us enjoy *G'ui sha's*[1] great wealth, let us obtain ten thousand *caweh*[1] of opium.

Hereafter, when we fell the trees, may the members of my household all work together in the fields united by the same pure thoughts.

Oh Spirit of this place, carefully separate and protect us from iron and copper, from sharp points of wood, from blades of wood; separate and protect us from blades of wood; Spirit of this place, here at this place your children will farm the land.

Oh, today and hereafter may I obtain ten thousand *caweh* of opium; do not conquer me, do not conquer all my children, but let other people talk of our good fortune.

Oh, let there be no sickness in this household; let the household members delight in working in the fields, let there be no

[1] *G'ui sha* is the name of the supernatural creator of the Lahu people; *caweh* is a Lahu unit of measurement equivalent to 1.6 kg.

fighting amongst them, and when we work together in the fields let us all be joined by the same pure thoughts, let there be no fighting amongst the members of this household.

Carefully give us sufficient food to eat, let others talk of our good fortune; we will prepare this poppy field, let us obtain more than ten thousand *caweh* of opium.

Lahu Prayers for a Bountiful Opium Crop (2)

Anthony R. Walker

Oh, in exchange for this opium field, I bring for you this beautiful rice made by my own hand, and these beautiful beeswax candles made by my own hand, all-knowing Ruler, all-true Ruler, under your feet and under your hands I ask your permission to prepare this field.

Oh, I bring for you these beeswax candles made by my own hand, I bring for you this beautiful rice made by my own hand, I bring for you these beautiful beeswax candles made by my own hand, Ruler who sits at the bends in the hills, ruler who sits at the bends of the dales.

If this is your dwelling place, please move to the bottom or to the top of this field; this field I buy from you, I exchange these offerings for it.

Oh, if this is your dwelling place, please move to the bottom of the field or to the top of the field; please move to the top of the hill or the bottom of the hill.

We people cannot know all things, you who know all, so please move away a little.

Oh, with one half of the yield from my labours, I wish to follow the custom of the elders, the custom of the men and women; one half I will give to you, I will offer to you.

Please move your dwelling place to the bottom of the field or the top of the field; this field I buy from you, I exchange with you.

Oh, please grant a little of this blessing, that if we work for one day in the fields, the food will not be exhausted in ten days, if we work for one year in the fields, the food may not be exhausted in ten years; bestow upon us and cover us with this blessing.

Extract from *Opium: Diary of a Cure*

Jean Cocteau

It is hard to feel oneself dismissed by opium after several failures: it is hard to know that this magic carpet exists and that one will no longer fly on it; it was pleasant to buy it, as in the Baghdad of the Caliphs, from the Chinese in a sordid street hung with washing; pleasant to return home quickly to try it out in one's hotel, in the room between the columns where George Sand and Chopin lived, to unroll it, stretch out on it, open the window on to the port, and take off. Undoubtedly too pleasant.

The Pleasures of Opium

Thomas De Quincey

It is very long since I first took opium; *so* long that if it had been a trifling incident in my life, I might have forgotten its date: but cardinal events are not to be forgotten; and, from circumstances connected with it, I remember that this inauguration into the use of opium must be referred to the spring or to the autumn of 1804; during which seasons I was in London, having come thither for the first time since my entrance at Oxford. And this event arose in the following way: – From an early age I had been accustomed to wash my head in cold water at least once a-day. Being suddenly seized with toothache, I attributed it to some relaxation caused by a casual intermission of that practice, jumped out of bed, plunged my head into a basin of cold water, and with hair thus wetted went to sleep. The next morning, as I need hardly say, I awoke with excruciating rheumatic pains of the head and face, from which I had hardly any respite for about twenty days. On the twenty-first day I think it was, and on a Sunday, that I went out into the streets; rather to run away, if possible, from my torments, than with any distinct purpose of relief. By accident, I met a college acquaintance, who recommended opium. Opium! dread agent of unimaginable pleasure and pain! I had heard of it as I had heard of manna or of ambrosia, but no further. How unmeaning a sound was opium at that time! what solemn chords does it now strike upon my heart! what heart-quaking vibrations of sad and happy remembrances! Reverting for a moment to these, I feel a mystic importance attached to the minutest circumstances connected with the place, and the time, and the man (if man he was), that first laid open to me the paradise of opium-eaters. It was a Sunday afternoon, wet and cheerless; and a duller spectacle this earth of ours has not to show than a rainy Sunday in London. My road homewards lay through Oxford Street; and near 'the *stately* Pantheon' (as Mr. Wordsworth has obligingly called it[1]) I saw a druggist's shop. The druggist (unconscious minister of celestial pleasures!), as if in sympathy with the rainy Sunday, looked dull and stupid, just as any mortal druggist might be expected to look on a rainy London Sunday; and, when I asked for the tincture of opium, he gave it to me as any other man might do; and, furthermore, out of my shilling returned to me what seemed to be real copper halfpence, taken out of a real wooden drawer. Nevertheless, and notwithstanding all such indications of humanity, he has ever since figured in my mind as a beatific vision of an immortal druggist, sent down to earth on a special mission to myself. And it confirms me in this way of considering him that, when I next came up to London, I sought him near the stately Pantheon, and found him not; and thus to me, who knew not his name (if, indeed, he had one), he seemed rather to have vanished from Oxford Street than to have flitted into any other locality, or (which some abominable man suggested) to have absconded from the rent. The reader may choose to think of him as, possibly, no more than a sublunary druggist; it may be so, but my faith is better. I believe him to have evanesced.[2] So unwillingly would I connect any mortal

---

[1] '*Stately*': – It is but fair to say that Wordsworth meant to speak of the *interior*, which could very little be inferred from the mean, undistinguished outside, as seen presenting itself endways in Oxford Street.

[2] '*Evanesced*': – This way of going off from the stage of life appears to have been well known in the seventeenth century, but at that time to have been considered a peculiar privilege of royalty, and by no means open to the use of druggists. For, about the year 1686, a poet of rather ominous name (and

remembrances with that hour, and place, and creature that first brought me acquainted with the celestial drug.

Arrived at my lodgings, it may be supposed that I lost not a moment in taking the quantity prescribed. I was necessarily ignorant of the whole art and mystery of opium-taking; and what I took I took under every disadvantage. But I took it; and in an hour, O heavens! what a revulsion! what a resurrection, from its lowest depths, of the inner spirit! what an apocalypse of the world within me! That my pains had vanished was now a trifle in my eyes; this negative effect was swallowed up in the immensity of those positive effects which had opened before me, in the abyss of divine enjoyment thus suddenly revealed. Here was a panacea, a *Φάρμακον νηπενθές* for all human woes; here was the secret of happiness, about which philosophers had disputed for so many ages, at once discovered; happiness might now be bought for a penny, and carried in the waistcoat-pocket; portable ecstasies might be had corked up in a pint-bottle; and peace of mind could be sent down by the mail.

And, first, one word with respect to its bodily effects; for upon all that has been hitherto written on the subject of opium, whether by travellers in Turkey (who may plead their privilege of lying as an old immemorial right), or by professors of medicine writing *ex cathedra*, I have but one emphatic criticism to pronounce – Nonsense! I remember once, in passing a book-stall, to have caught these words from a page of some satiric author – 'By this time I became convinced that the London newspapers spoke truth at least twice a-week – viz. on Tuesday and Saturday[1] – and might safely be depended upon for – the list of bankrupts.' In like manner, I do by no means deny that some truths have been delivered to the world in regard to

who, apparently, did justice to his name) – viz. Mr. FLATMAN – in speaking of the death of Charles II., expresses his surprise that any prince should commit so vulgar an act as dying; because, says he,

'Kings should disdain to die, and only *disappear*.'

[1] '*Tuesday and Saturday*': – viz. the two days on which the 'Gazette' is (or used to be) published.

opium: thus, it has been repeatedly affirmed by the learned that opium is a tawny brown in colour – and this, take notice, I grant; secondly, that it is rather dear – which also I grant, for in my time East India opium has been three guineas a-pound, and Turkey eight; and, thirdly, that, if you eat a good deal of it, most probably you must do what is disagreeable to any man of regular habits – viz. die.[1] These weighty propositions are, all and singular, true; I cannot gainsay them; and truth ever was, and will be, commendable. But in these three theorems I believe we have exhausted the stock of knowledge as yet accumulated by man on the subject of opium. And therefore, worthy doctors, as there seems to be room for further discoveries, stand aside, and allow me to come forward and lecture on this matter.

First, then, it is not so much affirmed as taken for granted by all who ever mention opium, formally or incidentally, that it does or can produce intoxication. Now, reader, assure yourself, *meo periculo*, that no quantity of opium ever did, or could, intoxicate. As to the tincture of opium (commonly called laudanum), *that* might certainly intoxicate, if a man could bear to take enough of it; but why? Because it contains so much proof spirits of wine, and not because it contains so much opium. But crude opium, I affirm peremptorily, is incapable of producing any state of body at all resembling that which is produced by alcohol; and not in *degree* only incapable, but even in *kind*; it is not in the quantity of its effects merely, but in the quality, that it differs altogether. The pleasure given by wine is always rapidly mounting, and tending to a crisis, after which as rapidly it

---

[1] Of this, however, the learned appear latterly to have doubted; for, in a pirated edition of Buchan's 'Domestic Medicine,' which I once saw in the hands of a farmer's wife, who was studying it for the benefit of her health, the doctor was made to caution his readers against taking more than 'twenty-five *ounces*' of laudanum at one dose. The true reading had doubtless been twenty-five *drops* or minims, which in a gross equation is held equivalent to one grain of average opium; but opium itself – crude opium – varies enormously in purity and strength; consequently the tincture prepared from it. And most of the medical connoisseurs whom I have known boiled their opium, so as to cleanse it from gross impurities.

declines; that from opium, when once generated, is stationary for eight or ten hours: the first, to borrow a technical distinction from medicine, is a case of acute, the second a chronic, pleasure; the one is a flickering flame, the other a steady and equable glow. But the main distinction lies in this – that, whereas wine disorders the mental faculties, opium, on the contrary (if taken in a proper manner), introduces amongst them the most exquisite order, legislation, and harmony. Wine robs a man of his self-possession; opium sustains and reinforces it. Wine unsettles the judgment, and gives a preternatural brightness and a vivid exaltation to the contempts and the admirations, to the loves and the hatreds, of the drinker; opium, on the contrary, communicates serenity and equipoise to all the faculties, active or passive; and, with respect to the temper and moral feelings in general, it gives simply that sort of vital warmth which is approved by the judgment, and which would probably always accompany a bodily constitution of primeval or antediluvian health. Thus, for instance, opium, like wine, gives an expansion to the heart and the benevolent affections; but, then, with this remarkable difference, that, in the sudden development of kindheartedness which accompanies inebriation, there is always more or less of a maudlin and a transitory character, which exposes it to the contempt of the bystander. Men shake hands, swear eternal friendship, and shed tears – no mortal knows why; and the animal nature is clearly uppermost. But the expansion of the benigner feelings incident to opium is no febrile access, no fugitive paroxysm; it is a healthy restoration to that state which the mind would naturally recover upon the removal of any deep-seated irritation from pain that had disturbed and quarrelled with the impulses of a heart originally just and good. True it is that even wine up to a certain point, and with certain men, rather tends to exalt and to steady the intellect; I myself, who have never been a great wine-drinker, used to find that half-a-dozen glasses of wine advantageously affected the faculties, brightened and intensified the consciousness, and gave to the mind a feeling of being 'ponderibus librata suis'; and certainly it is most absurdly said, in popular language, of any man, that he is *disguised* in liquor; for, on the contrary, most men are disguised by sobriety, and exceedingly disguised; and it is when they are drinking that men display themselves in their true complexion of character; which surely is not disguising themselves. But still, wine constantly leads a man to the brink of absurdity and extravagance; and, beyond a certain point, it is sure to volatilise and to disperse the intellectual energies; whereas opium always seems to compose what had been agitated, and to concentrate what had been distracted. In short, to sum up all in one word, a man who is inebriated, or tending to inebriation, is, and feels that he is, in a condition which calls up into supremacy the merely human, too often the brutal, part of his nature; but the opium-eater (I speak of him *as* such, and assume that he is in a normal state of health) feels that the diviner part of his nature is paramount – that is, the moral affections are in a state of cloudless serenity, and high over all the great light of the majestic intellect.

This is the doctrine of the true church on the subject of opium: of which church I acknowledge myself to be the Pope (consequently infallible), and self-appointed *legate a latere* to all degrees of latitude and longitude. But then it is to be recollected that I speak from the ground of a large and profound personal experience, whereas most of the unscientific[1] authors who have all treated of opium, and even of those who have

---

[1] Amongst the great herd of travellers, &c., who show sufficiently by their thoughtlessness that they never held any intercourse with opium, I must caution my readers specially against the brilliant author of 'Anastasius' [Thomas Hope, 1770–1831, merchant-prince, oriental traveller, novelist, &c.]. This gentleman, whose wit would lead one to presume him an opium-eater, has made it impossible to consider him in that character, from the grievous misrepresentation which he has given of its effects at pages 215–217 of Vol. I. Upon consideration, it must appear such to the author himself; for, waiving the errors I have insisted on in the text, which (and others) are adopted in the fullest manner, he will himself admit that an old gentleman, 'with a snow-white beard,' who eats 'ample doses of opium,' and is yet able to deliver what is meant and received as very weighty counsel on

written professionally on the *materia medica*, make it evident, by the horror they express of it, that their experimental knowledge of its actions is none at all. I will, however, candidly acknowledge that I have met with one person who bore evidence to its intoxicating power, such as staggered my own incredulity; for he was a surgeon, and had himself taken opium largely for a most miserable affection (past all hope of cure) seated in one particular organ. This affection was a subtle inflammation, not acute, but chronic; and with this he fought for more (I believe) than twenty years; fought victoriously, if victory it were, to make life supportable for himself, and during all that time to maintain in respectability a wife and a family of children altogether dependent on him.[1] I happened to say to him, that his enemies (as I

the bad effects of that practice, is but an indifferent evidence that opium either kills people prematurely, or sends them into a madhouse. But, for my part, I see into this old gentleman and his motives; the fact is, he was enamoured of 'the little golden receptacle of the pernicious drug' which Anastasius carried about him; and no way of obtaining it so safe and so feasible occurred as that of frightening its owner out of his wits. This commentary throws a new light upon the case, and greatly improves it as a story; for the old gentleman's speech, as a lecture on pharmacy, is absurd; but, considered as a hoax on Anastasius, it reads excellently.

[1] This surgeon it was who first made me aware of the dangerous variability in opium as to strength under the shifting proportions of its combination with alien impurities. Naturally, as a man professionally alive to the danger of creating any artificial need of opium beyond what the anguish of his malady at any rate demanded, trembling every hour on behalf of his poor children, lest, by any indiscretion of his own, he should precipitate the crisis of his disorder, he saw the necessity of reducing the daily dose to a *minimum*. But to do this he must first obtain the means of measuring the quantities of opium; not the apparent quantities as determined by weighing, but the *virtual* quantities after allowing for the alloy or varying amounts of impurity. This, however, was a visionary problem. To allow for it was simply impossible. The problem, therefore, changed its character. Not to measure the impurities was the object; for, whilst entangled with the operative and efficient parts of the opium, they could not be measured. To separate and eliminate the impure (or inert) parts, this was now the object. And this was effected finally by a particular mode of boiling the opium. That done, the residuum became equable in strength; and the daily doses could be nicely adjusted. About 18 grains formed his daily ration for many years. This, upon

had heard) charged him with talking nonsense on politics, and that his friends apologised for him, by suggesting that he was constantly in a state of intoxication from opium. Now, the accusation, said I, is not *prima facie* an absurd one; but the defence *is*. To my surprise, however, he insisted that both his enemies and his friends were in the right. 'I will maintain,' said he, 'that I *do* talk nonsense; and, secondly, I will maintain that I do not talk nonsense upon principle, or with any view to profit, but solely and simply,' said he – 'solely and simply – solely and simply (repeating it three times over) because I am drunk with opium; and that daily.' I replied that, as to the allegation of his enemies, as it seemed to be established upon such respectable testimony, seeing that the three parties concerned all agreed so far, it did not become me to question it; but the defence set up I must demur to. He proceeded to discuss the matter, and to lay down his reasons; but it seemed to me so impolite to pursue an argument which must have presumed a man mistaken in a point belonging to his own profession, that I did not press him, even when his course of argument seemed open to objection; not to mention that a man who talks nonsense, even though 'with no view to profit,' is not altogether the most agreeable respondent in a dispute. I confess, however, that the authority of a surgeon, and one who was reputed a good one, may seem a weighty one to my prejudice; but still I must plead my experience, which was greater than his greatest by more than seven thousand drops a-day; and, though it was not possible to suppose a medical man unacquainted with the characteristic symptoms of vinous intoxication, yet it struck me that he might proceed on a logical error

the common hospital evaluation, expresses 18 times 25 drops of laudanum. But, since 25 is = $\frac{100}{4}$, therefore 18 times one quarter of a hundred is = one quarter of 1800, and that, I suppose, is 450. So much this surgeon averaged upon each day for about twenty years. Then suddenly began a fiercer stage of the anguish from his disease. But then, also, the fight was finished, and the victory was won. All duties were fulfilled: his children prosperously launched in life; and death, which to himself was becoming daily more necessary as a relief from torment, now fell injuriously upon nobody.

of using the word intoxication with too careless a latitude, extending it generically to all modes of nervous excitement, instead of restricting it to one special quality of pleasurable elevation, distinguished by well-known symptoms, and connected with tendencies not to be evaded. Two of these tendencies I will mention as diagnostic, or characteristic and inseparable marks of ordinary alcoholic intoxication, but which no excess in the use of opium ever develops. One is the loss of self-command, in relation to all one's acts and purposes, which steals gradually (though with varying degrees of speed) over *all* persons indiscriminately when indulging in wine or distilled liquors beyond a certain limit. The tongue and other organs become unmanageable: the intoxicated man speaks inarticulately; and, with regard to certain words, makes efforts ludicrously earnest, yet oftentimes unavailing, to utter them. The eyes are bewildered, and see double; grasping too little, and too much. The hand aims awry. The legs stumble, and lose their power of *concurrent* action. To this result *all* people tend, though by varying rates of acceleration. Secondly, as another characteristic, it may be noticed that in alcoholic intoxication the movement is always along a kind of arch; the drinker rises through continual ascents to a summit or *apex*, from which he descends through corresponding steps of declension. There is a crowning point in the movement upwards, which once attained cannot be renewed: and it is the blind, unconscious, but always unsuccessful effort of the obstinate drinker to restore this supreme altitude of enjoyment which tempts him into excesses that become dangerous. After reaching this *acme* of genial pleasure, it is a mere necessity of the case to sink through corresponding stages of collapse. Some people have maintained, in my hearing, that they had been drunk upon green tea; and a medical student in London, for whose knowledge in his profession I have reason to feel great respect, assured me, the other day, that a patient, in recovering from an illness, had got drunk on a beef-steak. All turns, in fact, upon a rigorous definition of intoxication.

Having dwelt so much on this first and leading error in

respect to opium, I shall notice briefly a second and a third; which are, that the elevation of spirits produced by opium is necessarily followed by a proportionate depression, and that the natural and even immediate consequence of opium is torpor and stagnation, animal as well as mental. The first of these errors I shall content myself with simply denying; assuring my reader that, for ten years during which I took opium not regularly but intermittingly, the day succeeding to that on which I allowed myself this luxury was always a day of unusually good spirits.

With respect to the torpor supposed to follow, or rather (if we were to credit the numerous pictures of Turkish opium-eaters) to accompany, the practice of opium-eating, I deny that also. Certainly, opium is classed under the head of narcotics, and some such effect it may produce in the end; but the primary effects of opium are always, and in the highest degree, to excite and stimulate the system. This first stage of its action always lasted with me, during my novitiate, for upwards of eight hours; so that it must be the fault of the opium-eater himself if he does not so time his exhibition of the dose as that the whole weight of its narcotic influence may descend upon his sleep.

Ligeia

Edgar Allan Poe

And the will therein lieth, which dieth not. Who knoweth the mysteries of the will, with its vigor? For God is but a great will pervading all things by nature of its intentness. Man doth not yield himself to the angels, nor unto death utterly, save only through the weakness of his feeble will.

Joseph Glanvill

I cannot for my soul, remember how, when, or even precisely where, I first became acquainted with the lady Ligeia. Long years have since elapsed, and my memory is feeble through much suffering. Or, perhaps, I cannot *now* bring these points to mind, because, in truth, the character of my beloved, her rare learning, her singular yet placid caste of beauty, and the thrilling and enthralling eloquence of her low musical language, made their way into my heart by paces so steadily and stealthily progressive, that they have been unnoticed and unknown. Yet I believe that I met her first and most frequently in some large, old, decaying city near the Rhine. Of her family – I have surely heard her speak. That it is of a remotely ancient date cannot be doubted. Ligeia! Ligeia! Buried in studies of a nature more than all else adapted to deaden impressions of the outward world, it is by that sweet word alone – by Ligeia – that I bring before mine eyes in fancy the image of her who is no more. And now, while I write, a recollection flashes upon me that I have *never known* the paternal name of her who was my friend and my betrothed, and who became the partner of my studies, and finally the wife of my bosom. Was it a playful charge on the part of my Ligeia? or was it a test of my strength of affection, that I should institute no inquiries upon this point? or was it rather a caprice of my own – a wildly romantic offering on the shrine of the most passionate devotion? I but indistinctly recall the fact itself – what wonder that I have utterly forgotten the circumstances which originated or attended it? And, indeed, if ever that spirit which is entitled *Romance* – if ever she, the wan and the misty-winged *Ashtophet* of idolatrous Egypt, presided, as they tell, over marriages illomened, then most surely she presided over mine.

There is one dear topic, however, on which my memory fails me not. It is the *person* of Ligeia. In stature she was tall, somewhat slender, and, in her latter days, even emaciated. I would in vain attempt to portray the majesty, the quiet ease, of her demeanor, or the incomprehensible lightness and elasticity of her footfall. She came and departed as a shadow. I was never made aware of her entrance into my closed study, save by the dear music of her low sweet voice, as she placed her marble hand upon my shoulder. In beauty of face no maiden ever equalled her. It was the radiance of an opium-dream – an airy and spirit-lifting vision more wildly divine than the phantasies which hovered about the slumbering souls of the daughters of Delos. Yet her features were not of that regular mould which we have been falsely taught to worship in the classical labors of the heathen. 'There is no exquisite beauty,' says Bacon, Lord Verulam, speaking truly of all the forms and *genera* of beauty, 'without some *strangeness* in the proportion.' Yet, although I saw that the features of Ligeia were not of a classical regularity – although I perceived that her loveliness was indeed 'exquisite,' and felt that there was much of 'strangeness' pervading it, yet I have tried in vain to detect the irregularity and to trace home my own perception of 'the strange.' I examined the contour of the lofty and pale forehead – it was faultless – how cold indeed that word when applied to a majesty so divine! – the skin rivalling the purest ivory, the commanding extent and repose, the gentle prominence of the regions above the temples; and then the raven-black, the glossy, the luxuriant, and naturally-curling tresses, setting forth the full force of the Homeric epithet, 'hyacinthine!' I looked at the delicate outlines of the nose – and nowhere but in the graceful medallions of the Hebrews had I beheld a similar perfection. There were the same luxurious smoothness of surface, the same scarcely perceptible tendency to the aquiline, the same harmoniously curved nostrils speaking the free spirit. I regarded the sweet mouth. Here was indeed the triumph of all things heavenly – the magnificent turn of the short upper lip – the soft, voluptuous slumber of the under – the dimples which sported, and the color which spoke – the teeth glancing back, with a brilliancy almost startling, every ray of the holy light which fell upon them in her serene and placid, yet most exultingly radiant of all smiles. I scrutinized the formation of the chin – and here, too, I found the gentleness of breadth, the softness and the majesty, the fulness and the spirituality, of the Greek – the contour which the god Apollo revealed but in a dream, to Cleomenes, the son of the Athenian. And then I peered into the large eyes of Ligeia.

For eyes we have no models in the remotely antique. It might have been, too, that in these eyes of my beloved lay the secret to which Lord Verulam alludes. They were, I must believe, far larger than the ordinary eyes of our own race. They were even fuller than the fullest of the gazelle eyes of the tribe of the valley of Nourjahad. Yet it was only at intervals – in moments of intense excitement – that this peculiarity became more than slightly noticeable in Ligeia. And at such moments was her beauty – in my heated fancy thus it appeared perhaps – the beauty of beings either above or apart from the earth – the beauty of the fabulous Houri of the Turk. The hue of the orbs was the most brilliant of black, and, far over them, hung jetty lashes of great length. The brows, slightly irregular in outline, had the same tint. The 'strangeness,' however, which I found in the eyes, was of a nature distinct from the formation, or the color, or the brilliancy of the features, and must, after all, be referred to the *expression*. Ah, word of no meaning! behind whose vast latitude of mere sound we intrench our ignorance of so much of the spiritual. The expression of the eyes of Ligeia! How for long hours have I pondered upon it! How have I, through the whole of a midsummer night, struggled to fathom it! What was it – that something more profound than the well of Democritus – which lay far within the pupils of my beloved? What *was* it? I was possessed with a passion to discover. Those eyes! those large, those shining, those divine orbs! they became to me twin stars of Leda, and I to them devoutest of astrologers.

There is no point, among the many incomprehensible anomalies of the science of mind, more thrillingly exciting than the fact – never, I believe, noticed in the schools – that, in our endeavors to recall to memory something long forgotten, we often find ourselves *upon the very verge* of remembrance, without being able, in the end, to remember. And thus, how frequently, in my intense scrutiny of Ligeia's eyes, have I felt approaching the full knowledge of their expression – felt it approaching – yet not quite be mine – and so at length entirely depart! And (strange, oh strangest mystery of all!) I found, in the commonest objects of the universe, a circle of analogies to that expression. I mean to say that, subsequently to the period when Ligeia's beauty passed into my spirit, there dwelling as in a shrine, I derived, from many existences in the material world, a sentiment such as I felt always around, within me, by her large and luminous orbs. Yet not the more could I define that sentiment, or analyze, or even steadily view it. I recognised it, let me repeat, sometimes in the survey of a rapidly-growing vine – in the contemplation of a moth, a butterfly, a chrysalis, a stream of running water. I have felt it in the ocean; in the falling of a meteor. I have felt it in the glances of unusually aged people. And there are one or two stars in heaven – (one especially, a star of the sixth magnitude, double and changeable, to be found near the large star in *Lyra*) in a telescopic scrutiny of which I have been made aware of the feeling. I have been filled with it by certain sounds from stringed instruments, and not unfrequently by passages from books. Among innumerable other instances, I well remember something in a volume of Joseph Glanvill, which (perhaps merely from its quaintness – who shall say?) never failed to inspire me with the sentiment: 'And the will therein lieth, which dieth not. Who knoweth the mysteries of the will, with its vigor? For God is but a great will pervading all things by nature of its intentness. Man doth not yield him to the angels, not unto death utterly, save only through the weakness of his feeble will.'

Length of years, and subsequent reflection, have enabled me to trace, indeed, some remote connection between this passage in the English moralist and a portion of the character of Ligeia. An *intensity* in thought, action, or speech, was possibly, in her, a result, or at least an index, of that gigantic volition which, during our long intercourse, failed to give other and more immediate evidence of its existence. Of all the women whom I have ever known, she, the outwardly calm, the ever-placid Ligeia, was the most violently a prey to the tumultuous vultures of stern passion. And of such passion I could form no estimate, save by the miraculous expansion of those eyes which at once so delighted and appalled me – by the almost magical melody, modulation, distinctness, and placidity of her very low voice – and by the fierce energy (rendered doubly effective by contrast with her manner of utterance), of the wild words which she habitually uttered.

I have spoken of the learning of Ligeia: it was immense – such as I have never known in woman. In the classical tongues was she deeply proficient, and as far as my own acquaintance extended in regard to the modern dialects of Europe, I have never known her at fault. Indeed upon any theme of the most

admired, because simply the most abstruse of the boasted cru-
dition of the academy, have I *ever* found Ligeia at fault? How
singularly – how thrillingly, this one point in the nature of my
wife has forced itself, at this late period only, upon my attention! I said her knowledge was such as I have never known in
woman – but where breathes the man who has traversed, and
successfully, *all* the wide areas of moral, physical, and mathe-
matical science? I saw not then what I now clearly perceive,
that the acquisitions of Ligeia were gigantic, were astounding;
yet I was sufficiently aware of her infinite supremacy to resign
myself, with a child-like confidence, to her guidance through
the chaotic world of metaphysical investigation at which I was
most busily occupied during earlier years of our marriage. With
how vast a triumph – with how vivid a delight – with how
much of all that is ethereal in hope – did I *feel*, as she bent over
me in studies but little sought – but less known – that delicious
vista by slow degrees expanding before me, down whose long,
gorgeous, and all untrodden path, I might at length pass
onward to the goal of a wisdom too divinely precious not to be
forbidden!

How poignant, then, must have been the grief with which,
after some years, I beheld my well-grounded expectations take
wings to themselves and fly away! Without Ligeia I was but as
a child groping benighted. Her presence, her readings alone,
rendered vividly luminous the many mysteries of the transcen-
dentalism in which we were immersed. Wanting the radiant
lustre of her eyes, letters, lambent and golden, grew duller than
Saturnian lead. And now those eyes shone less and less frequently upon the pages over which I pored. Ligeia grew ill. The
wild eyes blazed with a too – too glorious effulgence; the pale
fingers became of the transparent waxen hue of the grave; and
the blue veins upon the lofty forehead swelled and sank
impetuously with the tides of the most gentle emotion. I saw
that she must die – and I struggled desperately in spirit with the
grim Azrael. And the struggles of the passionate wife were, to
my astonishment, even more energetic than my own. There

had been much in her stern nature to impress me with the belief that, to her, death would have come without its terrors; but not so. Words are impotent to convey any just idea of the fierceness of resistance with which she wrestled with the Shadow. I groaned in anguish at the pitiable spectacle. I would have soothed – I would have reasoned; but, in the intensity of her wild desire for life – for life – *but* for life – solace and reason were alike the uttermost of folly. Yet not until the last instance, amid the most convulsive writhings of her fierce spirit, was shaken the external placidity of her demeanor. Her voice grew more gentle – grew more low – yet I would not wish to dwell upon the wild meaning of the quietly uttered words. My brain reeled as I hearkened, entranced, to a melody more than mortal – to assumptions and aspirations which mortality had never before known.

That she loved me I should not have doubted; and I might have been easily aware that, in a bosom such as hers, love would have reigned no ordinary passion. But in death only, was I fully impressed with the strength of her affection. For long hours, detaining my hand, would she pour out before me the overflowing of a heart whose more than passionate devotion amounted to idolatry. How had I deserved to be so blessed by such confessions? – how had I deserved to be so cursed with the removal of my beloved in the hour of her making them? But upon this subject I cannot bear to dilate. Let me say only, that in Ligeia's more than womanly abandonment to a love, alas! all unmerited, all unworthily bestowed, I at length recognised the principle of her longing, with so wildly earnest a desire, for the life which was now fleeing so rapidly away. It is this wild longing – it is this eager vehemence of desire for life – *but* for life – that I have no power to portray – no utterance capable of expressing.

At high noon of the night in which she departed, beckoning me, peremptorily, to her side, she bade me repeat certain verses composed by herself not many days before. I obeyed her. They were these:–

Lo! 'tis a gala night
  Within the lonesome latter years!
An angel throng, bewinged, bedight
  In veils, and drowned in tears,
Sit in a theatre, to see
  A play of hopes and fears,
While the orchestra breathes fitfully
  The music of the spheres.

Mimes, in the form of God on high,
  Mutter and mumble low,
And hither and thither fly;
  Mere puppets they, who come and go
At bidding of vast formless things
  That shift the scenery to and fro,
Flapping from out their condor wings
  Invisible Wo!

That motley drama! – oh, be sure
  It shall not be forgot!
With its Phantom chased for evermore,
  By a crowd that seize it not,
Through a circle that ever returneth in
  To the self-same spot;
And much of Madness, and more of Sin
  And horror, the soul of the plot!

But see, amid the mimic rout
  A crawling shape intrude!
A blood-red thing that writhes from out
  The scenic solitude!
It writhes – it writhes! – with mortal pangs
  The mimes become its food,
and the seraphs sob at vermin fangs
  In human gore imbued.

> *Out – out are the lights – out all!*
> *And over each quivering form,*
> *The curtain, a funeral pall,*
> *Comes down with the rush of a storm –*
> *And the angels, all pallid and wan,*
> *Uprising, unveiling, affirm*
> *That the play is the tragedy, 'Man,'*
> *And its hero, the conqueror Worm.*

'O God!' half shrieked Ligeia, leaping to her feet and extending her arms aloft with a spasmodic movement, as I made an end of these lines – 'O God! O Divine Father! – shall these things be undeviatingly so? – shall this conqueror be not once conquered? Are we not part and parcel in Thee? Who – who knoweth the mysteries of the will with its vigor? Man doth not yield him to the angels, *nor unto death utterly*, save only through the weakness of his feeble will.'

And now, as if exhausted with emotion, she suffered her white arms to fall, and returned solemnly to her bed of death. And as she breathed her last sighs, there came mingled with them a low murmur from her lips. I bent to them my ear, and distinguished, again, the concluding words of the passage in Glanvill: – '*Man doth not yield him to the angels, nor unto death utterly, save only through the weakness of his feeble will.*'

She died: and I, crushed into the very dust with sorrow, could no longer endure the lonely desolation of my dwelling in the dim and decaying city by the Rhine. I had no lack of what the world calls wealth. Ligeia had brought me far more, very far more, than ordinarily falls to the lot of mortals. After a few months, therefore, of weary and aimless wandering, I purchased, and put in some repair, an abbey, which I shall not name, in one of the wildest and least frequented portions of fair England. The gloomy and dreary grandeur of the building, the almost savage aspect of the domain, the many melancholy and time-honored memories connected with both, had much in unison with the feelings of utter abandonment which had driven me into that remote and unsocial region of the country. Yet although the external abbey, with its verdant decay hanging about it, suffered but little alteration, I gave way, with a child-like perversity, and perchance with a faint hope of alleviating my sorrows, to a display of more than regal magnificence within. For such follies, even in childhood, I had imbibed a taste, and now they came back to me as if in the dotage of grief. Alas, I feel how much even of incipient madness might have been discovered in the gorgeous and fantastic draperies, in the solemn carvings of Egypt, in the wild cornices and furniture, in the Bedlam patterns of the carpets of tufted gold! I had become a bounden slave in the trammels of opium, and my labors and my orders had taken a coloring from my dreams. But these absurdities I must not pause to detail. Let me speak only of that one chamber, ever accursed, whither in a moment of mental alienation, I led from the altar as my bride – as the successor of the unforgotten Ligeia – the fair-haired and blue-eyed Lady Rowena Trevanion, of Tremaine.

There is no individual portion of the architecture and deco-ration of that bridal chamber which is not now visibly before me. Where were the souls of the haughty family of the bride, when, through thirst of gold, they permitted to pass the thresh-old of an apartment *so* bedecked, a maiden and a daughter so beloved? I have said, that I minutely remember the details of the chamber – yet I am sadly forgetful on topics of deep moment; and here there was no system, no keeping, in the fan-tastic display, to take hold upon the memory. The room lay in a high turret of the castellated abbey, was pentagonal in shape, and of capacious size. Occupying the whole southern face of the pentagon was the sole window – an immense sheet of unbroken glass from Venice – a single pane, and tinted of a leaden hue, so that the rays of either the sun or moon passing through it, fell with a ghastly lustre on the objects within. Over the upper por-tion of this huge window, extended the trellis-work of an aged vine, which clambered up the massy walls of the turret. The ceiling, of gloomy-looking oak, was excessively lofty, vaulted, and elaborately fretted with the wildest and most grotesque specimens of a semi-gothic, semi-Druidical device. From out the most central recess of this melancholy vaulting, depended, by a single chain of gold with long links, a huge censer of the same metal, Saracenic in pattern, and with many perforations so contrived that there writhed in and out of them, as if endued with a serpent vitality, a continual succession of parti-colored fires.

Some few ottomans and golden candelabra, of Eastern figure, were in various stations about; and there was the couch, too – the bridal couch – of an Indian model, and low, and sculptured of solid ebony, with a pall-like canopy above. In each of the angles of the chamber stood on end a gigantic sarcophagus of black granite, from the tombs of the kings over against Luxor, with their aged lids full of immemorial sculpture. But in the draping of the apartment lay, alas! the chief phantasy of all. The lofty walls, gigantic in height – even unproportionately so – were hung from summit to foot, in vast folds, with a heavy and massive-looking tapestry – tapestry of a material which was found alike as a carpet on the floor, as a covering for the ottomans and the ebony bed, as a canopy for the bed, and as the gorgeous volutes of the curtains which partially shaded the window. The material was the richest cloth of gold. It was spotted all over, at irregular intervals, with arabesque figures, about a foot in diameter, and wrought upon the cloth in patterns of the most jetty black. But these figures partook of the true character of the arabesque only when regarded from a single point of view. By a contrivance now common, and indeed traceable to a very remote period of antiquity, they were made changeable in aspect. To one entering the room, they bore the appearance of simple monstrosities; but upon a farther advance, this appearance gradually departed; and, step by step, as the visitor moved his station in the chamber, he saw himself surrounded by an endless succession of the ghastly forms which belong to the superstition of the Norman, or arise in the guilty slumbers of the monk. The phantasmagoric effect was vastly heightened by the artificial introduction of a strong continual current of wind behind the draperies – giving a hideous and uneasy animation to the whole.

In halls such as these – in a bridal chamber such as this – I passed, with the Lady of Tremaine, the unhallowed hours of the first month of our marriage – passed them with but little disquietude. That my wife dreaded the fierce moodiness of my temper – that she shunned me, and loved me but little – I could not help perceiving; but it gave me rather pleasure than otherwise. I loathed her with a hatred belonging more to demon than to man. My memory flew back, (oh, with what intensity of regret!) to Ligeia, the beloved, the august, the beautiful, the entombed. I revelled in recollections of her purity, of her wisdom, of her lofty, her ethereal nature, of her passionate, her idolatrous love. Now, then, did my spirit fully and freely burn with more than all the fires of her own. In the excitement of my opium dreams, (for I was habitually fettered in the shackles of the drug,) I would call aloud upon her name, during the silence of the night, or among the sheltered recesses of the glens by day, as if, through the wild eagerness, the solemn passion, the consuming ardor of my longing for the departed, I could restore her to the pathway she had abandoned – ah, *could* it be for ever? – upon the earth.

About the commencement of the second month of the marriage, the Lady Rowena was attacked with sudden illness, from which her recovery was slow. The fever which consumed her, rendered her nights uneasy; and in her perturbed state of half-slumber, she spoke of sounds, and of motions, in and about the chamber of the turret, which I concluded had no origin save in the distemper of her fancy, or perhaps in the phantasmagoric influences of the chamber itself. She became at length convalescent – finally, well. Yet but a brief period elapsed, ere a second more violent disorder again threw her upon a bed of suffering; and from this attack her frame, at all times feeble, never altogether recovered. Her illnesses were, after this epoch, of alarming character, and of more alarming recurrence, defying alike the knowledge and the great exertions of her physicians. With the increase of the chronic disease, which had thus, apparently taken too sure hold upon her constitution to be eradicated by human means, I could not fail to observe a similar increase in the nervous irritation of her temperament, and in her excitability by trivial causes of fear. She spoke again, and now more frequently and pertinaciously, of the sounds – of the slight sounds – and of the unusual motions among the tapestries, to which she had formerly alluded.

One night, near the closing in of September, she pressed this distressing subject with more than usual emphasis upon my attention. She had just awakened from an unquiet slumber, and I had been watching, with feelings half of anxiety, half of vague terror, the workings of her emaciated countenance. I sat by the side of her ebony bed, upon one of the ottomans of India. She partly arose, and spoke, in an earnest low whisper, of sounds which she *then* heard, but which I could not hear – of motions which she *then* saw, but which I could not perceive. The wind was rushing hurriedly behind the tapestries and I wished to show her (what, let me confess it, I could not *all* believe) that those almost inarticulate breathings, and those very gentle variations of the figures upon the wall, were but the natural effects of that customary rushing of the wind. But a deadly pallor, overspreading her face, had proved to me that my exertions to reassure her would be fruitless. She appeared to be fainting, and no attendants were within call. I remembered where was deposited a decanter of light wine which had been ordered by her physicians, and hastened across the chamber to procure it. But, as I stepped beneath the light of the censer, two circumstances of a startling nature attracted my attention. I had felt that some palpable although invisible object had passed lightly by my person; and I saw that there lay upon the golden carpet, in the very middle of the rich lustre thrown from the censer, a shadow – a faint, indefinite shadow of angelic aspect – such as might be fancied for the shadow of a shade. But I was wild with the excitement of an immoderate dose of opium, and heeded these things but little, nor spoke of them to Rowena. Having found the wine, I recrossed the chamber, and poured out a goblet-ful, which I held to the lips of the fainting lady. She had now partially recovered, however, and took the vessel herself, while I sank upon an ottoman near me, with my eyes fastened upon her person. It was then that I became distinctly aware of a gentle footfall upon the carpet, and near the couch; and in a second thereafter, as Rowena was in the act of raising the wine to her lips, I saw, or may have dreamed that I saw, fall within the goblet, as if from some invisible spring in the atmosphere of the room, three or four large drops of a brilliant and ruby colored fluid. If this I saw – not so Rowena. She swallowed the wine unhesitatingly, and I forbore to speak to her of a circumstance which must, after all, I considered, have been but the suggestion of a vivid imagination, rendered morbidly active by the terror of the lady, by the opium, and by the hour.

Yet I cannot conceal it from my own perception that, immediately subsequent to the fall of the ruby-drops, a rapid change for the worse took place in the disorder of my wife; so that, on the third subsequent night, the hands of her menials prepared her for the tomb, and on the fourth, I sat alone, with her shrouded body, in that fantastic chamber which had received her as my bride. – Wild visions, opium-engendered, flitted, shadow-like before me. I gazed with unquiet eye upon the sarcophagi in the angles of the room, upon the varying figures of the drapery, and upon the writhing of the parti-colored fires in the censer overhead. My eyes then fell, as I called to mind the circumstances of a former night, to the spot beneath the glare of the censer where I had seen the faint traces of the shadow. It was there, however, no longer; and breathing with greater freedom, I turned my glances to the pallid and rigid figure upon the bed. Then rushed upon me a thousand memories of Ligeia – and then came back upon my heart, with the turbulent violence of a flood, the whole of that unutterable wo with which I had regarded *her* thus enshrouded. The night waned; and still, with a bosom full of bitter thoughts of the one only and supremely beloved, I remained gazing upon the body of Rowena.

It might have been midnight, or perhaps earlier, or later, for I had taken no note of time, when a sob, low, gentle, but very distinct, startled me from my revery. I *felt* that it came from the bed of ebony – the bed of death. I listened in an agony of superstitious terror – but there was no repetition of the sound. I strained my vision to detect any motion in the corpse – but there was not the slightest perceptible. Yet I could not have been deceived. I *had* heard the noise, however faint, and my soul was awakened within me. I resolutely and perseveringly kept my attention riveted upon the body. Many minutes elapsed before any circumstances occurred tending to throw light upon the mystery. At length it became evident that a slight, a very feeble, and barely noticeable tinge of color had flushed up within the cheeks, and along the sunken small veins of the eyelids. Through a species of unutterable horror and awe, for which the language of mortality has no sufficiently energetic expression, I felt my heart cease to beat, my limbs grow rigid where I sat. Yet a sense of duty finally operated to restore my self-possession. I could no longer doubt that we had been precipitate in our preparations – that Rowena still lived. It was necessary that some immediate exertion be made; yet the turret was altogether apart from the portion of the abbey tenanted by the servants – there were none within call – I had no means of summoning them to my aid without leaving the room for many minutes – and this I could not venture to do. I therefore struggled alone in my endeavors to call back the spirit still hovering. In a short period it was certain, however, that a relapse had taken place; the color disappeared from both eyelid and cheek, leaving a wanness even more than that of marble; the lips became doubly shrivelled and pinched up in the ghastly expression of death; a repulsive clamminess and coldness overspread rapidly the surface of the body; and all the usual rigorous stiffness immediately supervened. I fell back with a shudder upon the couch from which I had been so startingly aroused, and again gave up myself to passionate waking visions of Ligeia.

An hour thus elapsed, when (could it be possible?) I was a second time aware of some vague sound issuing from the region of the bed. I listened – in extremity of horror. The sound came again – it was a sigh. Rushing to the corpse, I saw – distinctly saw – a tremor upon the lips. In a minute afterwards they relaxed, disclosing a bright line of the pearly teeth. Amazement now struggled in my bosom with a profound awe which had hitherto reigned there alone. I felt that my vision grew dim, that my reason wandered; and it was only by a violent effort that I at length succeeded in nerving myself to the task which duty thus once more had pointed out. There was now a partial glow upon the forehead and upon the cheek and throat; a perceptible warmth pervaded the whole frame; there was even a slight pulsation at the heart. The lady *lived*; and with redoubled ardor I betook myself to the task of restoration. I chafed and bathed the temples and the hands, and used every exertion which experience, and no little medical reading, could suggest. But in vain. Suddenly, the color fled, the pulsation ceased, the lips resumed the expression of the dead, and, in an instant afterward, the whole body took upon itself the icy chilliness, the livid hue, the intense rigidity, the sunken outline, and all the loathsome peculiarities of that which has been, for many days, a tenant of the tomb.

And again I sunk into visions of Ligeia – and again (what marvel that I shudder while I write?) *again* there reached my ears a low sob from the region of the ebony bed. But why shall I minutely detail the unspeakable horrors of that night? Why shall I pause to relate how, time after time, until near the period of the gray dawn, this hideous drama of revivication was repeated; how each terrific relapse was only into a sterner and apparently more irredeemable death; how each agony wore the aspect of a struggle with some invisible foe; and how each struggle was succeeded by I know not what of wild change in the personal appearance of the corpse? Let me hurry to a conclusion.

The greater part of the fearful night had worn away, and she who had been dead, once again stirred – and now more vigorously than hitherto, although arousing from a dissolution more appalling in its utter hopelessness than any. I had long ceased to struggle or to move, and remained sitting rigidly upon the ottoman, a helpless prey to a whirl of violent emotions, of which extreme awe was perhaps the least terrible, the least consuming. The corpse, I repeat, stirred, and now more vigorously than before. The hues of life flushed up with unwonted energy into the countenance – the limbs relaxed – and, save that the eyelids were yet pressed heavily together, and that the bandages and draperies of the grave still imparted their charnel character to the figure, I might have dreamed that Rowena had indeed shaken off, utterly, the fetters of Death. But, if this idea was not, even then, altogether adopted, I could at least doubt no longer, when, arising from the bed, tottering, with feeble steps, with closed eyes, and with the manner of one bewildered in a dream, the thing that was enshrouded advanced boldly and palpably into the middle of the apartment.

I trembled not – I stirred not – for a crowd of unutterable fancies connected with the air, the stature, the demeanor of the figure, rushed hurriedly through my brain, had paralyzed – had chilled me into stone. I stirred not – but gazed upon the apparition. There was a mad disorder in my thoughts – a tumult unappeasable. Could it indeed, be the *living* Rowena who confronted me? Could it indeed be Rowena *at all* – the fair-haired, blue-eyed Lady Rowena Trevanion of Tremaine? Why, *why*, should I doubt it? The bandage lay heavily about the mouth – but then might it not be the mouth of the breathing Lady of Tremaine? And the cheeks – there were the roses as in her noon of life – yes, these might indeed be the fair cheeks of the living Lady of Tremaine. And the chin, with its dimples, as in health, might it not be hers? – but *had she then grown taller since her malady?* What inexpressible madness seized me with that thought? One bound, and I had reached her feet! Shrinking from my touch, she let fall from her head, unloosened, the ghastly cerements which had confined it, and there streamed forth, into the rushing atmosphere of the chamber, huge masses of long and dishevelled hair; *it was blacker than the raven wings of midnight*! And now slowly opened *the eyes* of the figure which stood before me. 'Here then, at least,' I shrieked aloud, 'can I never – can I never be mistaken – these are the full, and the black, and the wild eyes – of my lost love – of the Lady – of the Lady Ligeia.'

Errol on Opium
Errol Flynn

Freddie McEvoy didn't know how to box, but he was about twice as strong as any man I knew, including me. He had a grip of Australian steel. My only chance in a row with him was to hit him on the nose, which pictorially looked strong and aquiline. Actually his nose couldn't take it. Quite unexpectedly, between his nose and my current ambition to do some writing, I discovered how much he had my interest at heart.

I had just read Thomas De Quincey's *Confessions of an Opium Eater*. I was so impressed with it that I decided I must go through the same thing – subject myself to opium, write about it. I asked a friend if he could get me some opium. He said, 'My plane carries a lot of that junk.'

He came up with enough to dope half a studio.

I started to take it. Then I tried to write. At first I think I did pretty well. I didn't know my face was growing greyer and greyer by the day. Others noticed my change of complexion. The more I experimented – that's what I called it – the less I wrote. I began to wonder how De Quincey had done it. What I wrote made no sense at all. Maybe this was because I tried to write while taking the stuff. Others wrote afterwards.

I didn't tell Freddie about this. I kept the supply of opium syrettes on a window-sill over the bathroom sink.

Each day I worked at the studio. Each evening home for a syrette of opium.

One night I came home, reached into my cache for the daily

dose and found nothing. I scrabbled around frantically, wondering if I had, in some stupor, misplaced it.

Freddie opened the door. 'What are you looking for?'

'Oh, nothing.'

'You stupid son-of-a-bitch. Have you seen yourself lately?'

'What are you talking about?'

'If you want to know where that dope is I'll show you.'

He led me into the study, where there was a big fire going in the fireplace. 'There they are. Now, what are you going to make of that?'

'You bastard. You are a guest in my house. Do you mean to say—'

'Sure, I burned them. All of them!'

I let fly. He caught one right on the nose. I knew just where to tab him. We rolled and rolled around my study. The furniture began to crack up. We almost fell into the fireplace.

'You son-of-a-bitch,' I said, 'come on outside. I'm not going to soil my place with your blood.'

We went outside.

There it was a little better. He would come and try to grab me and I would try to knock him down. If he had got his hands around me he would have finished me, but I was faster.

Finally we were both lying on the ground, mutually knocked out. He was panting. 'I'm not going to get up again,' he said. 'Why should I be knocked down by you? If you are stupid enough to go on with this, nobody can stop you.'

Freddie snapped me out of it – the hard way, and I dropped the opium before it became a habit. I withdrew in the next few days. I did have something to write about: withdrawal symptoms. These are horrible, and worth writing about. You feel that every single nerve in your body is popping out. There is nothing very new or scientific in pointing that out.

Subsequently I have taken a narcotic now and then, but only on a doctor's advice, administration or prescription.

The only real thing that came of it was my realisation of what a good friend Freddie really was.

Extract from *Opium: Diary of a Cure*

Jean Cocteau

Raw opium. If you do not shut it up in a metal chest but content your-self with a box, the black serpent will soon have crept out. Be warned! It hugs the walls, goes down the stairs and the floors, turns, crosses the hall and the courtyard, passes through the archway and will soon coil itself round the policeman's neck.

Hauser and O'Brien
William S. Burroughs

When they walked in on me that morning at 8 o'clock, I knew that it was my last chance, my only chance. But they didn't know. How could they? Just a routine pick-up. But not quite routine.

Hauser had been eating breakfast when the Lieutenant called: 'I want you and your partner to pick up a man named Lee, William Lee, on your way downtown. He's in the Hotel Lamprey. 103 just off B way.'

'Yeah I know where it is. I remember him too.'

'Good. Room 606. Just pick him up. Don't take time to shake the place down. Except bring in all books, letters, manuscripts. *Anything* printed, typed or written. Ketch?'

'Ketch. But what's the angle . . . Books . . .'

'Just do it.' The Lieutenant hung up.

Hauser and O'Brien. They had been on the City Narcotic Squad for 20 years. Oldtimers like me. I been on the junk for 16 years. They weren't bad as laws go. At least O'Brien wasn't. O'Brien was the conman, and Hauser the tough guy. A vaudeville team. Hauser had a way of hitting you before he said anything just to break the ice. Then O'Brien gives you an Old Gold – just like a cop to smoke Old Golds somehow . . . and starts putting down a cop con that was really bottled in bond. Not a bad guy, and I didn't want to do it. But it was my only chance.

I was just tying up for my morning shot when they walked in with a pass key. It was a special kind you can use even when the door is locked from the inside with a key in the lock. On the table in front of me was a packet of junk, spike, syringe – I got the habit of using a regular syringe in Mexico and never went back to using a dropper – alcohol, cotton and a glass of water.

'Well well,' says O'Brien . . . 'Long time no see eh?'

'Put on your coat Lee,' says Hauser. He had his gun out. He always has it out when he makes a pinch for the psychological effect and to forestall a rush for toilet sink or window.

'Can I take a bang first, boys?' I asked . . . 'There's plenty here for evidence . . .'

I was wondering how I could get to my suitcase if they said no. The case wasn't locked, but Hauser had the gun in his hand.

'He wants a shot,' said Hauser.

'Now you know we can't do that, Bill,' said O'Brien in his sweet con voice, dragging out the name with an oily, insinuating familiarity, brutal and obscene.

He meant, of course, 'What can you do for *us*, Bill?' He looked at me and smiled. The smile stayed there too long, hideous and naked, the smile of an old painted pervert, gathering all the negative evil of O'Brien's ambiguous function.

'I might could set up Marty Steel for you,' I said.

I knew they wanted Marty bad. He'd been pushing for five years, and they couldn't hang one on him. Marty was an old-timer, and very careful about who he served. He had to know a man and know him well before he would pick up his money. No one can say they ever did time because of me. My rep is perfect, but still Marty wouldn't serve me because he didn't know me long enough. That's how skeptical Marty was.

'Marty!' said O'Brien. 'Can you score from him?'

'Sure I can.'

They were suspicious. A man can't be a cop all his life without developing a special set of intuititions.

'O.K.,' said Hauser finally. 'But you'd better deliver, Lee.'

'I'll deliver all right. Believe me I appreciate this.'

I tied up for a shot, my hand trembling with eagerness, an archetype dope fiend.

'Just an old junky, boys, a harmless old shaking wreck of a junky.' That's the way I put it down. As I had hoped, Hauser looked away when I started probing for a vein. It's a wildly unpretty spectacle.

O'Brien was sitting on the arm of a chair smoking an Old Gold, looking out the window with that dreamy what I'll do when I get my pension look.

I hit a vein right away. A column of blood shot up into the syringe for an instant sharp and solid as a red cord. I pressed the plunger down with my thumb, feeling the junk pound through my veins to feed a million junk-hungry cells, to bring strength and alertness to every nerve and muscle. They were not watching me. I filled the syringe with alcohol.

Hauser was juggling his snub-nosed detective special, a Colt, and looking around the room. He could smell danger like an animal. With his left hand he pushed the closet door open and glanced inside. My stomach contracted. I thought, 'If he looks in the suitcase now I'm done.'

Hauser turned to me abruptly. 'You through yet?' he snarled. 'You'd better not try to shit us on Marty.' The words came out so ugly he surprised and shocked himself.

I picked up the syringe full of alcohol, twisting the needle to make sure it was tight.

'Just two seconds,' I said.

I squirted a thin jet of alcohol, whipping it across his eyes with a sideways shake of the syringe. He let out a bellow of pain. I could see him pawing at his eyes with the left hand like he was tearing off an invisible bandage as I dropped to the floor on one knee, reaching for my suitcase. I pushed the suitcase open, and my left hand closed over the gun butt – I am righthanded but I shoot with my left hand. I felt the concussion of Hauser's shot before I heard it. His slug slammed into the wall behind me. Shooting from the floor, I snapped two quick shots into Hauser's belly where his vest had pulled up showing an inch of white shirt. He grunted in a way I could feel and doubled forward. Stiff with panic, O'Brien's hand was tearing at the gun in his shoulder holster. I clamped my other hand around my gun wrist to steady it for the long pull – this gun has the hammer filed off round so you can only use it double action – and shot him in the middle of his red forehead about two inches below the silver hairline. His hair had been grey the last time I saw him. That was about 15 years ago. My first arrest. His eyes went out. He fell off the chair onto his face. My hands were already reaching for what I needed, sweeping my notebooks into a briefcase with my works, junk, and a box of shells. I stuck the gun into my belt, and stepped out into the corridor putting on my coat.

I could hear the desk clerk and the bell boy pounding up the stairs. I took the self-service elevator down, walked through the empty lobby into the street.

It was a beautiful Indian Summer day. I knew I didn't have much chance, but any chance is better than none, better than being a subject for experiments with ST(6) or whatever the initials are.

I had to stock up on junk fast. Along with airports, R.R. stations and bus terminals they would cover all junk areas and connections. I took a taxi to Washington Square, got out and walked along 4th Street till I spotted Nick on a corner. You can always find the pusher. Your need conjures him up like a ghost. 'Listen, Nick,' I said, 'I'm leaving town. I want to pick up a piece of H. Can you make it right now?'

We were walking along 4th Street. Nick's voice seemed to drift into my consciousness from no particular place. An eerie, disembodied voice. 'Yes, I think I can make it. I'll have to make a run uptown.'

'We can take a cab.'

'O.K., but I can't take you in to the guy, you understand.'

'I understand. Let's go.'

We were in the cab heading North. Nick was talking in his flat, dead voice.

'Some funny stuff we're getting lately. It's not weak

exactly . . . I don't know . . . It's different. Maybe they're putting some synthetic shit in it . . . Dollies or something . . .'

'What!!!? Already?'

'Huh? . . . But this I'm taking you to now is O.K. In fact it's about the best deal around that I know of . . . Stop here.'

'Please make it fast,' I said.

'It should be a matter of ten minutes unless he's out of stuff and has to make a run . . . Better sit down over there and have a cup of coffee . . . This is a hot neighborhood.'

I sat down at a counter and ordered coffee, and pointed to a piece of Danish pastry under a plastic cover. I washed down the stale rubbery cake with coffee, praying that just this once, please God, let him make it now, and not come back to say the man is all out and has to make a run to East Orange or Greenpoint.

Well here he was back, standing behind me. I looked at him, afraid to ask. Funny, I thought, here I sit with perhaps one chance in a hundred to live out the next 24 hours – I had made up my mind not to surrender and spend the next three or four months in death's waiting room. And here I was worrying about a junk score. But I only had about five shots left, and without junk I would be immobilized . . . Nick nodded his head.

'Don't give it to me here,' I said. 'Let's take a cab.'

We took a cab and started downtown. I held out my hand and copped the package, then I slipped a fifty-dollar bill into Nick's palm. He glanced at it and showed his gums in a toothless smile. 'Thanks a lot . . . This will put me in the clear . . .'

I sat back letting my mind work without pushing it. Push your mind too hard, and it will fuck up like an overloaded switch-board, or turn on you with sabotage . . . And I had no margin for error. Americans have a special horror of giving up control, of letting things happen in their own way without interference. They would like to jump down into their stomachs and digest the food and shovel the shit out.

Your mind will answer most questions if you learn to relax and wait for the answer. Like one of those thinking machines, you feed in your question, sit back, and wait . . .

I was looking for a name. My mind was sorting through names, discarding at once F.L. – Fuzz Lover, B.W. – Born Wrong, N.C.B.C. – Nice Cat But Chicken: putting aside to reconsider, narrowing, sifting, feeling for the name, the answer.

'Sometimes, you know, he'll keep me waiting three hours. Sometimes I make it right away like this.' Nick had a deprecating little laugh that he used for punctuation. Sort of an apology for talking at all in the telepathizing world of the addict where only the quantity factor – How much $? How much junk? – requires verbal expression. He knew and I knew all about waiting. At all levels the drug trade operates without schedule. Nobody delivers on time except by accident. The addict runs on junk time. His body is his clock, and junk runs through it like an hour-glass. Time has meaning for him only with reference to his need. Then he makes his abrupt intrusion into the time of others, and, like all Outsiders, all Petitioners, he must wait, unless he happens to mesh with non-junk time.

'What can I say to him? He knows I'll wait,' Nick laughed.

I spent the night in the Ever Hard Baths – (homosexuality is the best all-around cover story an agent can use) – where a snarling Italian attendant creates such an unnerving atmosphere sweeping the dormitory with infra red see in the dark fieldglasses.

('All right in the North East corner! I see you!' switching on floodlights, sticking his head through trapdoors in the floor and wall of the private rooms, that many a queen has been carried out in a strait-jacket . . .)

I lay there in my open top cubicle room looking at the ceiling . . . listened to the grunts and squeals and snarls in the nightmare halflight of random, broken lust . . .

'Fuck off you!'

'Put on two pairs of glasses and maybe you can see something!'

Walked out in the precise morning and bought a paper . . . Nothing . . . I called from a drugstore phone booth . . . and asked for Narcotics:

'Lieutenant Gonzales . . . who's calling?'

'I want to speak to O'Brien.' A moment of static, dangling wires, broken connections . . .

'Nobody of that name in this department . . . Who are *you*?'

'Well let me speak to Hauser.'

'Look, Mister, no O'Brien no Hauser in this bureau. Now what do you want?'

'Look, this is important . . . I've got info on a big shipment of H coming in . . . I want to talk to Hauser or O'Brien . . . I don't do business with anybody else . . .'

'Hold on . . . I'll connect you with Alcibiades.'

I began to wonder if there was an Anglo-Saxon name left in the Department . . .

'I want to speak to Hauser or O'Brien.'

'How many times I have to tell you no Hauser no O'Brien in this department . . . Now who is this calling?'

I hung up and took a taxi out of the area . . . In the cab I realized what had happened . . . I had been occluded from space-time like an eel's ass occludes when he stops eating on the way to Sargasso . . . Locked out . . . Never again would I have a Key, a Point of Intersection . . . The Heat was off me from here on out . . . relegated with Hauser and O'Brien to a landlocked junk past where heroin is always twenty-eight dollars an ounce and you can score for yen pox on the Chink Laundry of Sioux Falls . . . Far side of the world's mirror, moving into the past with Hauser and O'Brien . . . clawing at a not-yet of Telepathic Bureaucracies, Time Monopolies, Control Drugs, Heavy Fluid Addicts:

'I thought of that three hundred years ago.'

'Your plan was unworkable then and useless now . . . Like Da Vinci's flying machine plans . . .'

Junking the Image
Will Self

There were two cultural revolutions in the sixties. Both appeared to involve the overthrow of established orthodoxies, both were spearheaded by almost mythic figures, and both of them had undertaken long marches. But whereas the Orient had a Great Helmsman, we in the Occident merely had a Great Junksman.

The Great Helmsman has been in his grave for over a decade, but defying the exigencies of the toxified body, the Great Junksman is still with us, and celebrates his eightieth birthday today.

During *his* long march William Burroughs went south from New York City, fleeing a federal rap for forging morphine prescriptions. In New Orleans in the late forties he marshalled his revolutionary cadres – Jack Kerouac, Neal Cassady and Allen Ginsberg – before fleeing still further south to Mexico City, this time on the run from a marijuana possession rap. In Mexico City Burroughs accidentally shot dead his common-law wife, Joan Vollmer Burroughs, and while on bail once more skipped the country, this time headed for South America.

From South America to Tangier, from Tangier to Paris, from Paris to London, and then eventually back to New York in the early eighties. In his absence Burroughs's *magnum opus*, *Naked Lunch*, the arcane text which became the little red book of our spurious cultural revolution, had been published. Initially it was only available in a samizdat form, courtesy of a Chicago-based alternative magazine, *Big Table*, which, appropriately enough, self-destructed after the issues that carried *Naked Lunch*. But subsequently the Olympia Press in Paris brought this explosive text out in book form. The rest, of course, is history.

These are the bare bones of Burroughs's long march. Put down in this fashion they already take on the lineaments of some biblical tale. Burroughs's mark of Cain was homosexuality and drug addiction. And his 'sin' was both destructive and creative. He himself has written (in the foreword to his autobiographical novel *Queer*) that were it not for the accidental shooting of his wife, he doesn't believe he would have become a writer.

Why did the Great Junksman survive, while so many of his confrères fell by the wayside? What specific qualities have allowed him to become that rarest of things: a legend in his own lifetime? But perhaps more pertinently, what does the Burroughs myth have to tell us about our attitudes towards the creative writer in the late twentieth century?

I think it tells us this: that ours is an era in which the idea and practice of decadence – in the Nietzschean sense – has never been more clearly realized. And that far from representing a dissolution of nineteenth-century romanticism, the high modernism of the mid-twentieth century, of which Burroughs is one of the last surviving avatars, has both compounded and enhanced the public image of the creative artist as deeply self-destructive, highly egotistic, plangently amoral and, of course, the nadir of anomie.

This is why the cultural revolution of the sixties has been shown up to be so spurious. This is why the avant-garde has never been deader than now. This is why there is no meaningful input from youth into the cultural mainstream.

A friend of mine once said: 'When I was fifteen I read *Junky*, when I was sixteen I was a junkie.' I could say the same of myself. My form prize in the lower sixth at Christ's College,

Finchley, was *Naked Lunch*. As far as I was concerned, Burroughs demonstrated that you could have it all: live outside the law, get stoned the whole time, and still be hailed by Norman Mailer as 'the only living American writer conceivably possessed of genius'. When I awoke from this delusion, aged twenty, diagnosed by a psychiatrist as a 'borderline personality', and with a heroin habit, I was appalled to discover that I wasn't a famous underground writer. Indeed, far from being a writer at all, I was simply underground.

Of course, it would be simplistic to regard this as a causal relationship. No responsibility for my delusion can be laid at the feet of Burroughs. He is blameless. He never claimed any suzerainty over the burgeoning cultural revolution of the sixties. In fact, he was appalled by the sloppiness and lack of tone displayed by the counter-culture as early as 1952, when he was resident in Mexico City and saw the first wave of Beats follow in his wake.

The idea of the pernicious druggy writer spawning a generation of emulators far antedates Burroughs. De Quincey was accused of having just such a dangerous influence after the publication of *The Confessions of an English Opium-Eater* in 1822. In the years that followed there were a number of deaths of young men from opium overdoses that were laid at his feet.

The truth is that books like *Junky* and De Quincey's *Confessions* no more create drug addicts than video nasties engender pre-pubescent murderers. Rather, culture, in this wider sense, is a hall of mirrors in which cause and effect endlessly reciprocate one another in a diminuendo that tends ineluctably towards the trivial.

Thus it is that in the heroin subculture – a crepuscular zone which I feel some authority to talk about – the Great Junksman is known of, and talismanically invoked, as a guarantor of the validity of the addict lifestyle, even by those who have never read a single line of Burroughs's works. By the same token, the image of the artist that the Great Junksman represents has now pullulated into the realm of popular culture. His true heirs are not junkie writers at all, but pop musicians who fry their brains with LSD and cocaine, ecstatic teenagers who gibber at acid-house raves, and urban crack-heads who dance to a different drum machine.

The status of 'drugs' as panapathanogenic – inherently evil or nasty – is something that artists such as Burroughs and the law enforcement agencies he would affect to despise, have conspired to create. One man's creative meat is another's social poison, but both parties in some strange way wish to keep it that way. It was Burroughs himself who in the preface to *Naked Lunch* drew his readers' attention to the fact that there was something inherently 'profane' about opiates, in contrast to other kinds of drugs.

But this is false. The fact of the matter is that the self-destructive image of the artist, and the failure of occidental culture to develop meaningful and valid drug rituals, are two sides of the same coin. It always puzzles me that I was unable to sort cause and effect out in this fashion. The reason was that, while I understood the above intuitively, I was still in a very important way an *apparatchik* of the Great Junksman. I, like him, came to believe – as many addicts do – in the reality of a magical world of hidden forces. I, like him, came to writing as a function of a dialectic of illness and recovery. The heightened sensitivity of heroin withdrawal produces a ghastly reactive sensitivity, which in turn calls forth a stream of grossly sentimental imagery, an imaginative correlative to the spontaneous and joyless orgasms experienced by the kicking addict. This is the origin of De Quincey's *Suspira de Profundis* and Coleridge's 'The Pains of Sleep', just as much as it is of Burroughs's *Nova Express* and Cocteau's *Opium*. It follows that the nineteenth and twentieth centuries form a dyad. And in both, some of the finest creative minds have traded the coin of their own self-realization for the noxious draught of notoriety. The Great Junksman's perverse and – given his own femicide – macabre obsession with the 'right to bear arms', his afffected, militant homosexuality and consequent misogynism, his – and our – confabulation of an image that owes as much to the facts of his fiction as it does to the fictions of his fact – all of these reach a peculiar apogee in this one perverse fact: he is eighty and alive whereas by all rights he should be long gone.

By saying this I mean no disrespect. I merely wish to point up the paradox of this anti-establishment establishmentarian: this sometime junkie with a ribbon in his buttonhole that shows he is a member of the American Academy of Arts and Letters; this bohemian exile who lives in Andy Hardy, small-town America; this 'Hombre Invisible' who has become so terribly visible.

If the Burroughs story tells us anything, it is that we are in a pretty pass. We desperately need a new image of the creative artist with which to replace this tired old *pas de deux*. At the moment we circle round creative genius like hicks visiting a freak show. And this is, of course, the attitude that has spawned an industry of literary biography which threatens to overtopple the production of fiction itself.

So, let us use this anniversary, not to celebrate and further garnish the legend of the Great Junksman, but instead to re-examine the continuing relevance of his alter ego's great fictions: his satirical visions of cancerous capitalism and addictive consumerism; his elegiac and poetic invocations of sadness and dislocation; his enormous fertility of ideas and imagery. And let us say: rest in peace, Bill Burroughs; may you live to celebrate many more birthdays, but a pox on the Great Junksman, let's topple his monumental statues and move forward on our own long march towards some more spiritually valid conception of the writer's role.

PART FIVE

LIQUID, GAS, SMOKE AND POWDER

Part five of the anthology contains a number of disparate texts concerning the uses and effects of stimulants such as tobacco and cocaine, and inebriants such as ether, nitrous oxide (laughing gas) and chloroform. Tobacco use originated in South America and was thought by the Indians to be intimately connected to the spiritual world. According to the shamans, tobacco is the food of spirits. Often the plant itself was thought to be in possession of a spirit, and with the introduction of tobacco to Europe such notions were also imported. In 1602 Sir John Beaumont wrote of tobacco as a bounteous gift from God, whilst, as we have seen, a mere two years later King James denounced it as an infernal offering.

Belief in the spirit of tobacco lived on under poetic licence for some time. J. M. Barrie (1860–1937), best known for his embodiment of the spirit of eternal youth, Peter Pan, himself long served another spirit, the spirit of the tobacco pipe, which he termed *My Lady Nicotine*. He saw tobacco as a mistress that he must give up for the sake of his marriage. Barrie's account of his ridding himself of the habit has a curious twist in its tail, for having forsaken the sensual allures of Lady Nicotine, he cannot resist listening through the wall to his neighbour tapping his pipe. Barrie's remarkable deductions concerning his neighbour's smoking habits could only have been attained by a Sherlock Holmes or by one addicted to the aural version of voyeurism. According to Sir Arthur Conan Doyle (1859–1930) in *The Sign of Four*, Sherlock Holmes himself, when bored between cases, would inject himself with cocaine or morphine. His justification for his indulgences left Dr Watson singularly unimpressed.

Sir Humphry Davy (1778–1829), chemist and inventor of the miner's safety lamp, wasn't one to let the spirit of Christmas interfere with his scientific experiments. Instead he had his own literal rendition of Boxing Day, and on 26 December 1799 he decided to place himself in an air-tight box along with twenty quarts of nitrous oxide! In a story entitled *Under the Knife*, H. G. Wells (1866–1946) describes how a man fearing his life is nearly over undergoes a surgical operation under the influence of the anaesthetic chloroform. He is suddenly propelled into an inner journey through the solar system and beyond, not knowing whether he is dead or alive. Ether abuse is the subject of an extract from *Phantastica: Narcotic and Stimulating Drugs* by the pioneer psychopharmacologist Louis Lewin (1850–1929). He puts forward a strong case for its popularity being caused by attempts to suppress the use of alcohol.

In *The Drug Bag* from Hunter S. Thompson's masterpiece of black comedy *Fear and Loathing in Las Vegas: A Savage Journey to the Heart of the American Dream*, no such motive can be found. In Thompson's writing inebriants such as nitrous oxide and ether are merely part of a vast psychoactive panorama. But was Thompson true to his art? All the indications are that he was. His biographer E. Jean Carroll reports how a typical day in the life of her subject consisted of the consumption of a mind-bending menu of cocaine, grass, acid, alcohol and cigarettes, with brief respites to eat junk food, watch pornographic movies and, of course, to write. Thompson was a regular contributor to *Rolling Stone* during the 1970s, and *Cocaine Consciousness: The Gourmet Trip* by Jerry

Hopkins originally appeared in the same magazine in 1971. The revised version of this article included here takes a look at cocaine chic during the first half of the seventies, long before the emergence of crack stripped the drug of its glamorous image.

My Lady Nicotine
J. M. Barrie

Matrimony and Smoking Compared

The circumstances in which I gave up smoking were these.

I was a mere bachelor, drifting toward what I now see to be a tragic middle age. I had become so accustomed to smoke issuing from my mouth that I felt incomplete without it; indeed the time came when I could refrain from smoking if doing nothing else, but hardly during the hours of toil. To lay aside my pipe was to find myself soon afterwards wandering restlessly round my table. No blind beggar was ever more abjectly led by his dog, or more loth to cut the string.

I am much better without tobacco, and already have difficulty in sympathizing with the man I used to be. Even to call him up, as it were, and regard him without prejudice is a difficult task, for we forget the old selves on whom we have turned our backs as we forget a street that has been reconstructed. Does the freed slave always shiver at the crack of a whip? I fancy not, for I recall but dimly, and without acute suffering, the horrors of my smoking days. There were nights when I woke with a pain at my heart that made me hold my breath. I did not dare move. After perhaps ten minutes of dread, I would shift my position an inch at a time. Less frequently I felt this sting in the daytime, and believed I was dying while my friends were talking to me. I never mentioned these experiences to a human being; indeed, though a medical man was among my companions, I cunningly deceived him on the rare occasions when he questioned me about the amount of tobacco I was consuming weekly. Often in the dark I not only vowed to give up smoking, but wondered why I cared for it. Next morning I went straight from breakfast to my pipe, without the smallest struggle with myself. Latterly I knew, while resolving to break myself of the habit, that I would be better employed trying to sleep. I had elaborate ways of cheating myself, for it became disagreeable to me to know how many ounces of tobacco I was smoking weekly. Often I smoked cigarettes to reduce the number of my cigars.

On the other hand, if these sharp pains be excepted, I felt quite well. My appetite was as good as it is now, and I worked as cheerfully and certainly harder. To some slight extent, I believe, I experienced the same pains in my boyhood, before I smoked, and I am not an absolute stranger to them yet. They were most frequent in my smoking days, but I have no other reason for charging them to tobacco. Possibly a doctor who smoked himself would have pooh-poohed them. Nevertheless, I have lit my pipe, and then, as I may say, hearkened for them. At the first intimation that they were coming I laid the pipe down and ceased to smoke – until they had passed.

I will not admit that, once sure it was doing me harm, I could not, unaided, have given up tobacco. But I was reluctant to make sure. I should like to say that I left off smoking because I considered it a mean form of slavery, to be condemned for moral as well as physical reasons; but though I see the folly of smoking clearly now, I was blind to it for some months after I had smoked my last pipe. I gave up my most delightful solace, as I regarded it, for no other reason than that the lady who was willing to fling herself away on me said that I must choose between it and her. This deferred our marriage for six months.

I have now come, as those who read will see, to look upon smoking with my wife's eyes. My old bachelor friends complain because I do not allow smoking in the house, but I am always ready to explain my position, and I have not an atom of pity for them. If I cannot smoke here neither shall they. When I visit them in the old Inn they take a poor revenge by blowing rings of smoke almost in my face. This ambition to blow rings is the most ignoble known to man. Once I was a member of a club for smokers, where we practised blowing rings. The most successful got a box of cigars as a prize at the end of the year. Those were days. Often I think wistfully of them. We met in a cosy room off the Strand. How well I can picture it still; time-tables lying everywhere, with which we could light our pipes. Some smoked clays, but for the Arcadia Mixture give me a briar. My briar was the sweetest ever known. It is strange now to recall a time when a pipe seemed to be my best friend.

My present state is so happy that I can only look back with wonder at my hesitation to enter upon it. Our house was taken while I was still arguing that it would be dangerous to break myself of smoking all at once. At that time my ideal of married life was not what it is now, and I remember Jimmy's persuading me to fix on this house because the large room upstairs with the three windows was a smoker's dream. He pictured himself and me there in the summer-time blowing rings, with our coats off and our feet out at the windows; and he said that the closet at the back, looking on to a blank wall, would make a charming drawing-room for my wife. For the moment his enthusiasm carried me away, but I see now how selfish it was, and I have before me the face of Jimmy when he paid us his first visit and found that the closet was not the drawing-room. Jimmy is a fair specimen of a man, not without parts, destroyed by devotion to his pipe. To this day he thinks that mantelpiece vases are meant for holding pipe-lights in. We are almost certain that when he stays with us he smokes in his bedroom – a detestable practice that I cannot permit.

Two cigars a day at ninepence apiece come to £27 7s. 6d. yearly, and four ounces of tobacco a week at nine shillings a pound come to £5 17s. yearly. That makes £33 4s. 6d. When we calculate the yearly expense of tobacco in this way we are naturally taken aback, and our extravagance shocks us the more after we have considered how much more satisfactorily the money might have been spent. With £33 4s. 6d. you can buy new Oriental rugs for the drawing-room, as well as a spring bonnet and a nice dress. These are things that give permanent pleasure, whereas you have no interest in a cigar after flinging away the stump. Judging by myself, I should say that it is want of thought rather than selfishness that makes heavy smokers of so many bachelors. Once a man marries his eyes are opened to many things that he was quite unaware of previously, among them being the delight of adding an article of furniture to the drawing-room every month and having a bedroom in pink and gold, the door of which is always kept locked. If men would only consider that every cigar they smoke would buy part of a new piano-stool in terra-cotta plush, and that for every pound tin of tobacco purchased away goes a vase for growing dead geraniums in, they would surely hesitate. They do not consider, however, until they marry, and then they are forced to it. For my own part, I fail to see why bachelors should be allowed to smoke as much as they like when we are debarred from it.

The very smell of tobacco is abominable, for one cannot get it out of the curtains, and there is little pleasure in existence unless the curtains are all right. As for a cigar after dinner, it only makes you dull and sleepy and disinclined for ladies' society. A far more delightful way of spending the evening is to go straight from dinner to the drawing-room and have a little music. It calms the mind to listen to your wife's niece singing 'Oh, that we two were maying.' Even if you are not musical as is the case with me, there is a great deal in the drawing-room to refresh you. There are the Japanese fans on the wall, which are things of beauty, though your artistic taste may not be sufficiently educated to let you know it except by hearsay; and it is pleasant to feel that they were bought with money which, in the foolish old days, would have been squandered on a box of cigars. In like manner every pretty trifle in the room reminds you how much wiser you are now than you used to be. It is even gratifying to stand in summer at the drawing-room window and watch the very cabbies passing with cigars in their mouths. At the same time, if I had the making of the laws I would prohibit people's smoking in the street. If they are married men, they are smoking drawing-room fire-screens and mantelpiece borders for the pink and gold room. If they are bachelors, it is a scandal that bachelors should get the best of everything.

Nothing is more pitiable than the way some men of my acquaintance enslave themselves to tobacco. Nay, worse, they make an idol of some one particular tobacco. I know a man who considers a certain mixture so superior to all others that he will walk three miles for it. Surely every one will admit that this is lamentable. It is not even a good mixture, for I used to try it occasionally; and if there is one man in London who knows tobaccos, it is myself. There is only one mixture in London deserving the adjective superb. I will not say where it is to be got, for the result would certainly be that many foolish men would smoke more than ever; but I never knew anything to compare to it. It is deliciously mild yet of full fragrance, and it never burns the tongue. If you try it once you smoke it ever afterwards. It clears the brain and soothes the temper. When I went away for a holiday anywhere I took as much of that exquisite health-giving mixture as I thought would last me the whole time, but I always ran out of it. Then I telegraphed to London for more, and was miserable until it arrived. How I tore the lid off the canister. That is a tobacco to live for. But I am better without it.

Occasionally I feel a little depressed after dinner still, without being able to say why, and if my wife has left me I wander about the room restlessly, like one who misses something. Usually, however, she takes me with her to the drawing-room, and reads aloud her delightfully long home letters or plays soft music to me. If the music be sweet and sad it takes me away to a stair in an Inn, which I climb gaily and shake open a heavy door on the top floor, and turn up the gas. It is a little room I am in once again, and very dusty. A pile of papers and magazines stands as high as a table in the corner furthest from the door. The cane-chair shows the exact shape of Marriot's back. What is left (after lighting the fire) of a framed picture lies on the hearthrug. Gilray walks in uninvited. He has left word that his visitors are to be sent on to me. The room fills. My hand feels along the mantelpiece for a brown jar. The jar is between my knees, I fill my pipe . . .

After a time the music ceases, and my wife puts her hand on my shoulder. Perhaps I start a little, and then she says I have been asleep. This is the book of my dreams.

When My Wife is Asleep and all the House is Still

Perhaps the heading of this chapter will deceive some readers into thinking that I smoke nowadays in camera. It is, I know, a common jest among smokers that such a promise as mine is seldom kept, and I allow that the Arcadians tempt me still. But never shall it be said of me with truth that I have broken my word. I smoke no more, and, indeed, though the scenes of my bachelorhood frequently rise before me in dreams, painted as Scrymgeour could not paint them, I am glad, when I wake up, that they are only dreams. Those selfish days are done, and I see that though they were happy days, the happiness was a mistake. As for the struggle that is supposed to take place between a man and tobacco after he sees smoking in its true colours, I never experienced it. I have not even any craving for the Arcadia now, though it is a tobacco that should only be smoked by our greatest men. Were we to present a tin of it to our national heroes, instead of the freedom of the city, they would probably thank us more. Jimmy and the others are quite unworthy to smoke it; indeed, if I had my way they would give up smoking altogether. Nothing, perhaps, shows more completely how I have severed my bonds than this: that my wife is willing to let our friends smoke in the study, but I will not hear of it. There shall be no smoking in my house; and I have determined to speak to Jimmy about smoking out at our spare bedroom window. It is a mere contemptible pretence to say that none of the smoke comes back into the room. The curtains positively reek of it, and we must have them washed at once. I shall speak plainly to Jimmy because I want him to tell the others. They must understand clearly on what terms they are received in this house, and if they prefer making chimneys of themselves to listening to music, by all means let them stay at home.

But when my wife is asleep and all the house is still, I listen to the man through the wall. At such times I have my briar in my mouth, but there is no harm in that, for it is empty. I did not like to give away my briar, knowing no one who understood it, and I always carry it about with me now to remind me of my dark past. When the man through the wall lights up I put my cold pipe in my mouth and we have a quiet hour together.

I have never to my knowledge seen the man through the wall, for his door is round the corner, and, besides, I have no interest in him until half-past eleven p.m. We begin then. I know him chiefly by his pipes, and them I know by his taps on the wall as he knocks the ashes out of them. He does not smoke the Arcadia, for his temper is hasty, and he breaks the coals with his foot. Though I am compelled to say that I do not consider his character very lovable he has his good points, and I like his attachment to his briar. He scrapes it, on the whole, a little roughly, but that is because he is so anxious to light up again, and I discovered long ago that he has signed an agreement with his wife to go to bed at half-past twelve. For some time I could not understand why he had a silver rim put on the bowl. I noticed the change in the tap at once, and the natural conclusion would have been that the bowl had cracked. But it never had the tap of a cracked bowl. I was reluctant to believe that the man through the wall was merely some vulgar fellow, and I felt that he could not be so or else he would have smoked his meerschaum more. At last I understood. The bowl had worn away on one side, and the silver rim had been needed to keep the tobacco in. Undoubtedly this was the explanation, for even before the rim came I was a little puzzled by the taps of the briar. He never seemed to hit the wall with the whole mouth of the bowl, but of course the reason was that he could not. At the same time I do not exonerate him from blame. He is a clumsy smoker to burn his bowl at one side, and I am afraid he lets the stem slip round in his teeth. Of course I see that the mouthpiece is loose, but a piece of blotting-paper would remedy that.

His meerschaum is not such a good one as Jimmy's. Though Jimmy's boastfulness about his meerschaum was hard to bear, none of us ever denied the pipe's worth. The man through the wall has not a cherry-wood stem to his meerschaum, and consequently it is too light. A ring has been worn into the palm of his left hand owing to his tapping the meerschaum there, and it is as marked as Jimmy's ring, for, though Jimmy tapped more strongly, the man through the wall has to tap oftener.

What I chiefly dislike about the man through the wall is his treatment of his clay. A clay, I need scarcely say, has an entirely different tap from a meerschaum, but the man through the wall does not treat these two pipes as if they were on an equality. He ought to tap his clay on the palm of his hand, but he seldom does so, and I am strongly of opinion that when he does, it is only because he has forgotten that this is not the meerschaum. Were he to tap the clay on the wall or on the ribs of the fire he would smash it, so he taps it on a coal. About this there is something contemptible. I am not complaining because he has little affection for his clay. In face of all that has been said in honour of clays, and knowing that this statement will occasion an outcry against me, I admit that I never cared for clays myself. A rank tobacco is less rank through a churchwarden, but to smoke the Arcadia through a clay is to incur my contempt, and even my resentment. But to disbelieve in clays is one thing and to treat them badly is another. If the man through the wall has decided after reflection and experiment that his clay is a mistake, I say let him smoke it no more; but so long as he does smoke it I would have it receive consideration from him. I very much question whether, if he read his heart, he could learn from it that he loves his meerschaum more than his clay, yet because the meerschaum costs more he taps it on his palm. This is a serious charge to bring against any man, but I do not make it lightly.

The man through the wall smokes each of these three pipes nightly, beginning with the briar. Thus he does not like a hot pipe. Some will hold that he ought to finish with the briar, as it is his favourite, but I am not of that opinion. Undoubtedly, I think, the first pipe is the sweetest; indeed, I feel bound to make a statement here. I have an uneasy feeling that I never did justice to meerschaums, and for this reason: I only smoked them after my briar was hot, so that I never gave them a fair chance. If I had begun the day with a meerschaum, might it not have shown itself in a new light? That is a point I shall never be able to decide now, but I often think of it, and I leave the verdict to others.

Even though I did not know that the man through the wall must retire at half-past twelve, his taps at that hour would announce it. He then gives each of his pipes a final tap, not briskly as before, but slowly, as if he was thinking between each tap. I have sometimes decided to send him a tin of the only tobacco to smoke, but on the whole I could not undertake the responsibility of giving a man, whom I have only studied for a few months, such a testimonial. Therefore when his last tap says good-night to me I take my cold briar out of my mouth, tap it on the mantelpiece, smile sadly, and so to bed.

Sherlock on Cocaine
Sir Arthur Conan Doyle

Sherlock Holmes took his bottle from the corner of the mantel-piece, and his hypodermic syringe from its neat morocco case. With his long, white, nervous fingers he adjusted the delicate needle, and rolled back his left shirt-cuff. For some little time his eyes rested thoughtfully upon the sinewy forearm and wrist, all dotted and scarred with innumerable puncture-marks. Finally, he thrust the sharp point home, pressed down the tiny piston, and sank back into the velvet-lined arm-chair with a long sigh of satisfaction.

Three times a day for many months I had witnessed this performance, but custom had not reconciled my mind to it. On the contrary, from day to day I had become more irritable at the sight, and my conscience swelled nightly within me at the thought that I had lacked the courage to protest. Again and again I had registered a vow that I should deliver my soul upon the subject; but there was that in the cool, nonchalant air of my companion which made him the last man with whom one would care to take anything approaching to a liberty. His great powers, his masterly manner, and the experience which I had had of his many extraordinary qualities, all made me diffident and backward in crossing him.

Yet upon that afternoon, whether it was the Beaune which I had taken with my lunch, or the additional exasperation produced by the extreme deliberation of his manner, I suddenly felt that I could hold out no longer.

'Which is it to-day,' I asked, 'morphine or cocaine?'

He raised his eyes languidly from the old black-letter volume which he had opened.

'It is cocaine,' he said, 'a seven-per-cent solution. Would you care to try it?'

'No, indeed,' I answered brusquely. 'My constitution has not got over the Afghan campaign yet. I cannot afford to throw any extra strain upon it.'

He smiled at my vehemence. 'Perhaps you are right, Watson,' he said. 'I suppose that its influence is physically a bad one. I find it, however, so transcendently stimulating and clarifying to the mind that its secondary action is a matter of small moment.'

'But consider!' I said earnestly. 'Count the cost! Your brain may, as you say, be roused and excited, but it is a pathological and morbid process, which involves increased tissue-change and may at least leave a permanent weakness. You know, too, what a black reaction comes upon you. Surely the game is hardly worth the candle. Why should you, for a mere passing pleasure, risk the loss of those great powers with which you have been endowed? Remember that I speak not only as one comrade to another, but as a medical man to one for whose constitution he is to some extent answerable.'

He did not seem offended. On the contrary, he put his finger-tips together, and leaned his elbows on the arms of his chair, like one who has a relish for conversation.

'My mind,' he said, 'rebels at stagnation. Give me problems, give me work, give me the most abstruse cryptogram or the most intricate analysis, and I am in my own proper atmosphere. I can dispense then with artificial stimulants. But I abhor the dull routine of existence. I crave for mental exaltation. That is why I have chosen my own particular profession, or rather created it, for I am the only one in the world.'

Laughing Gas on Boxing Day

Sir Humphry Davy

On December 26th, I was inclosed in an air-tight breathing-box, of the capacity of about 9 cubic feet and half, in the presence of Dr. Kinglake.

After I had taken a situation in which I could by means of a curved thermometer inserted under the arm, and a stop-watch, ascertain the alterations in my pulse and animal heat, 20 quarts of nitrous oxide were thrown into the box.

For three minutes I experienced no alteration in my sensations, though immediately after the introduction of the nitrous oxide the smell and taste of it were very evident.

In four minutes I began to feel a slight glow in the cheeks, and a generally diffused warmth over the chest, though the temperature of the box was not quite 50°. I had neglected to feel my pulse before I went in; at this time it was 104 and hard, the animal heat was 98°. In ten minutes the animal heat was near 99°, in a quarter of an hour 99.5°, when the pulse was 102, and fuller than before.

At this period 20 quarts more of nitrous oxide were thrown into the box, and well-mingled with the mass of air by agitation.

In 25 minutes the animal heat was 100°, pulse 124. In 30 minutes, 20 quarts more of gas were introduced.

My sensations were now pleasant; I had a generally diffused warmth without the slightest moisture of the skin, a sense of exhilaration similar to that produced by a small dose of wine, and a disposition to muscular motion and to merriment.

In three quarters of an hour the pulse was 104, and animal heat not 99.5°, the temperature of the chamber was 64°. The pleasurable feelings continued to increase, the pulse became fuller and slower, till in about an hour it was 88°, when the animal heat was 99°.

20 quarts more of air were admitted. I had now a great disposition to laugh, luminous points seemed frequently to pass before my eyes, my hearing was certainly more acute and I felt a pleasant lightness and power of exertion in my muscles. In a short time the symptoms became stationary; breathing was rather oppressed, and on account of the great desire of action, rest was painful.

I now came out of the box, having been in precisely an hour and a quarter.

The moment after, I began to respire 20 quarts of unmingled nitrous oxide. A thrilling extending from the chest to the extremities was almost immediately produced. I felt a sense of tangible extension highly pleasurable in every limb; my visible impressions were dazzling and apparently magnified, I heard distinctly every sound in the room and was perfectly aware of my situation.[1] By degrees as the pleasurable sensations increased, I lost all connection with external things; trains of vivid visible images rapidly passed through my mind and were connected with words in such a manner, as to produce perceptions perfectly novel. I existed in a world of newly connected and newly modified ideas. I theorised; I imagined that I made discoveries. When I was awakened from this semi-delirious trance by Dr. Kinglake, who took the bag from my mouth, indignation and pride were the first feelings produced by the sight of the persons about me. My emotions were enthusiastic and sublime; and for a minute I walked round the room perfectly regardless of what was said to me. As I recovered my former state of mind, I felt an inclination

---

[1] In all these experiments after the first minutes, my cheeks became purple.

to communicate the discoveries I had made during the experiment. I endeavoured to recall the ideas, they were feeble and indistinct; one collection of terms, however, presented itself: and with the most intense belief and prophetic manner, I exclaimed to Dr. Kinglake, *'Nothing exists but thoughts! – the universe is composed of impressions, ideas, pleasures and pains!'*

About three minutes and half only, had elapsed during this experiment, though the time as measured by the relative vividness of the recollected ideas, appeared to me much longer.

Not more than half of the nitrous oxide was consumed. After a minute, before the thrilling of the extremities had disappeared, I breathed the remainder. Similar sensations were again produced; I was quickly thrown into the pleasurable trance, and continued in it longer than before. For many minutes after the experiment, I experienced the thrilling in the extremities, the exhilaration continued nearly two hours. For a much longer time I experienced the mild enjoyment before described connected with indolence; no depression or feebleness followed. I ate my dinner with great appetite and found myself lively and disposed to action immediately after. I passed the evening in executing experiments. At night I found myself unusually cheerful and active; and the hours between eleven and two, were spent in copying the foregoing detail from the commonplace book and in arranging the experiments. In bed I enjoyed profound repose. When I awoke in the morning, it was with consciousness of pleasurable existence, and this consciousness more or less, continued through the day.

Under the Knife

H. G. Wells

'What if I die under it?' The thought recurred again and again, as I walked home from Haddon's. It was a purely personal question. I was spared the deep anxieties of a married man, and I knew there were few of my intimate friends but would find my death troublesome chiefly on account of their duty of regret. I was surprised indeed, and perhaps a little humiliated, as I turned the matter over, to think how few could possibly exceed the conventional requirement. Things came before me stripped of glamour, in a clear dry light, during that walk from Haddon's house over Primrose Hill. There were the friends of my youth: I perceived now that our affection was a tradition, which we foregathered rather laboriously to maintain. There were the rivals and helpers of my later career: I suppose I had been cold-blooded or undemonstrative – one perhaps implies the other. It may be that even the capacity for friendship is a question of physique. There had been a time in my own life when I had grieved bitterly enough at the loss of a friend; but as I walked home that afternoon the emotional side of my imagination was dormant. I could not pity myself, nor feel sorry for my friends, nor conceive of them as grieving for me.

I was interested in this deadness of my emotional nature – no doubt a concomitant of my stagnating physiology; and my thoughts wandered off along the line it suggested. Once before, in my hot youth, I had suffered a sudden loss of blood, and had been within an ace of death. I remembered now that my affections as well as my passions had drained out of me, leaving scarce anything but a tranquil resignation, a dreg of self-pity. It had been weeks before the old ambitions, and tendernesses, and all the complex moral interplay of a man, had reasserted themselves. It occurred to me that the real meaning of this numbness might be a gradual slipping away from the pleasure-pain guidance of the animal man. It has been proven, I take it, as thoroughly as anything can be proven in this world, that the higher emotions, the moral feelings, even the subtle tendernesses of love, are evolved from the elemental desires and fears of the simple animal: they are the harness in which man's mental freedom goes. And it may be that, as death overshadows us, as our possibility of acting diminishes, this complex growth of balanced impulse, propensity, and aversion, whose interplay inspires our acts, goes with it. Leaving what?

I was suddenly brought back to reality by an imminent collision with a butcher-boy's tray. I found that I was crossing the bridge over the Regent's Park Canal, which runs parallel with that in the Zoological Gardens. The boy in blue had been looking over his shoulder at a black barge advancing slowly, towed by a gaunt white horse. In the Gardens a nurse was leading three happy little children over the bridge. The trees were bright green; the spring hopefulness was still unstained by the dusts of summer; the sky in the water was bright and clear, but broken by long waves, by quivering bands of black, as the barge drove through. The breeze was stirring; but it did not stir me as the spring breeze used to do.

Was this dullness of feeling in itself an anticipation? It was curious that I could reason and follow out a network of suggestion as clearly as ever: so, at least, it seemed to me. It was calmness rather than dullness that was coming upon me. Was there any ground for the belief in the presentiment of death? Did a man near to death begin instinctively to withdraw himself from the meshes of matter and sense, even before the cold hand was laid upon his? I felt strangely isolated – isolated without regret – from the life and existence about me. The children playing in the sun and gathering strength and experience for the business of life, the park-keeper gossiping with a nursemaid, the nursing mother, the young couple intent upon each other as they passed me, the trees by the wayside spreading new pleading leaves to the sunlight, the stir in their branches – I had been part of it all, but I had nearly done with it now.

Some way down the Broad Walk I perceived that I was tired, and that my feet were heavy. It was hot that afternoon, and I turned aside and sat down on one of the green chairs that line the way. In a minute I had dozed into a dream, and the tide of my thoughts washed up a vision of the resurrection. I was still sitting in the chair, but I thought myself actually dead, withered, tattered, dried, one eye (I saw) pecked out by birds. 'Awake!' cried a voice; and incontinently the dust of the path and the mould under the grass became insurgent. I had never before thought of Regent's Park as a cemetery, but now, through the trees, stretching as far as eye could see, I beheld a flat plain of writhing graves and heeling tombstones. There seemed to be some trouble: the rising dead appeared to stifle as they struggled upward, they bled in their struggles, the red flesh was tattered away from the white bones. 'Awake!' cried a voice; but I determined I would not rise to such horrors. 'Awake!' They would not let me alone. 'Wike up!' said an angry voice. A cockney angel! The man who sells the tickets was shaking me, demanding my penny.

I paid my penny, pocketed my ticket, yawned, stretched my legs, and, feeling now rather less torpid, got up and walked on towards Langham Place. I speedily lost myself again in a shifting maze of thoughts about death. Going across Marylebone Road into that crescent at the end of Langham Place, I had the narrowest escape from the shaft of a cab, and went on my way with a palpitating heart and a bruised shoulder. It struck me that it would have been curious if my meditations on my death on the morrow had led to my death that day.

But I will not weary you with more of my experiences that day and the next. I knew more and more certainly that I should die under the operation; at times I think I was inclined to pose to myself. The doctors were coming at eleven, and I did not get up. It seemed scarce worth while to trouble about washing and dressing, and though I read my newspapers and the letters that came by the first post, I did not find them very interesting. There was a friendly note from Addison, my old school friend, calling my attention to two discrepancies and a printer's error in my new book, with one from Langridge venting some vexation over Minton. The rest were business communications. I breakfasted in bed. The glow of pain at my side seemed more massive. I knew it was pain, and yet, if you can understand, I did not find it very painful. I had been awake and hot and thirsty in the night, but in the morning bed felt comfortable. In the night-time I had lain thinking of things that were past; in the morning I dozed over the question of immortality. Haddon came, punctual to the minute, with a neat black bag; and Mowbray soon followed. Their arrival stirred me up a little. I began to take a more personal interest in the proceedings. Haddon moved the little octagonal table close to the bedside, and, with his broad black back to me, began taking things out of his bag. I heard the light click of steel upon steel. My imagination, I found, was not altogether stagnant. 'Will you hurt me much?' I said in an off-hand tone.

'Not a bit!' Haddon answered over his shoulder. 'We shall chloroform you. Your heart's as sound as a bell.' And as he spoke, I had a whiff of the pungent sweetness of the anæsthetic.

They stretched me out, with a convenient exposure of my side, and, almost before I realised what was happening, the chloroform was being administered. It stings the nostrils, and there is a suffocating sensation, at first. I knew I should die – that this was the end of consciousness for me. And suddenly I felt that I was not prepared for death: I had a vague sense of a duty overlooked – I knew not what. What was it I had not done? I could think of nothing more to do, nothing desirable left in life; and yet I had the strangest disinclination to death. And the physical sensation was painfully oppressive. Of course the doctors did not know they were going to kill me. Possibly I struggled. Then I fell motionless, and a great silence, a monstrous silence, and an impenetrable blackness came upon me.

There must have been an interval of absolute unconsciousness, seconds or minutes. Then, with a chilly, unemotional clearness, I perceived that I was not yet dead. I was still in my body; but all the multitudinous sensations that come sweeping from it to make up the background of consciousness had gone, leaving me free of it all. No, not free of it all; for as yet something still held me to the poor stark flesh upon the bed – held me, yet not so closely that I did not feel myself external to it, independent of it, straining away from it. I do not think I saw, I do not think I heard; but I perceived all that was going on, and it was as if I both heard and saw. Haddon was bending over me, Mowbray behind me; the scalpel – it was a large scalpel – was cutting my flesh at the side under the flying ribs. It was interesting to see myself cut like cheese, without a pang, without even a qualm. The interest was much of a quality with that one might feel in a game of chess between strangers. Haddon's face was firm and his hand steady; but I was surprised to perceive (*how* I know not) that he was feeling the gravest doubt as to his own wisdom in the conduct of the operation.

Mowbray's thoughts, too, I could see. He was thinking that Haddon's manner showed too much of the specialist. New suggestions came up like bubbles through a stream of frothing meditation, and burst one after another in the little bright spot of his consciousness. He could not help noticing and admiring Haddon's swift dexterity, in spite of his envious quality and his disposition to detract. I saw my liver exposed. I was puzzled at my own condition. I did not feel that I was dead, but I was different in some way from my living self. The grey depression, that had weighted on me for a year or more and coloured all my thoughts, was gone. I perceived and thought without any emotional tint at all. I wondered if everyone perceived things in this way under chloroform, and forgot it again when he came out of it. It would be inconvenient to look into some heads, and not forget.

Although I did not think that I was dead, I still perceived quite clearly that I was soon to die. This brought me back to the consideration of Haddon's proceedings. I looked into his mind, and saw that he was afraid of cutting a branch of the portal vein. My attention was distracted from details by the curious changes going on in his mind. His consciousness was like the quivering little spot of light which is thrown by the mirror of a galvanometer. His thoughts ran under it like a stream, some through the focus bright and distinct, some shadowy in the highlight of the edge. Just now the little glow was steady; but the least movement on Mowbray's part, the slightest sound from outside, even a faint difference in the slow movement of the living flesh he was cutting, set the light-spot shivering and spinning. A new sense-impression came rushing up through the flow of thoughts; and lo! the light-spot jerked away towards it, swifter than a frightened fish. It was wonderful to think that upon that unstable, fitful thing depended all the complex motions of the man; that for the next five minutes, therefore, my life hung upon its movements. And he was growing more and more nervous in his work. It was as if a little picture of a cut vein grew brighter, and struggled to oust from his brain another picture of a cut falling short of the mark. He was afraid: his dread of cutting too little was battling with his dread of cutting too far.

Then, suddenly, like an escape of water from under a lock-gate, a great uprush of horrible realisation set all his thoughts swirling, and simultaneously I perceived that the vein was cut. He started back with a hoarse exclamation, and I saw the brown-purple blood gather in a swift bead, and run trickling. He was horrified. He pitched the red-stained scalpel on to the octagonal table; and instantly both doctors flung themselves upon me, making hasty and ill-conceived efforts to remedy the disaster. 'Ice!' said Mowbray, gasping. But I knew that I was killed, though my body still clung to me.

I will not describe their belated endeavours to save me, though I perceived every detail. My perceptions were sharper and swifter than they had ever been in life; my thoughts rushed through my mind with incredible swiftness, but with perfect definition. I can only compare their crowded clarity to the effects of a reasonable dose of opium. In a moment it would all be over, and I should be free. I knew I was immortal, but what would happen I did not know. Should I drift off presently, like a puff of smoke from a gun, in some kind of half-material body, an attenuated version of my material self? Should I find myself suddenly among the innumerable hosts of the dead, and know the world about me for the phantasmagoria it had always seemed? Should I drift to some spiritualistic *séance*, and there make foolish, incomprehensible attempts to affect a purblind medium? It was a state of unemotional curiosity, of colourless expectation. And then I realised a growing stress upon me, a feeling as though some huge human magnet was drawing me upward out of my body. The stress grew and grew. I seemed an atom for which monstrous forces were fighting. For one brief, terrible moment sensation came back to me. That feeling of falling headlong which comes in nightmares, that feeling a thousand times intensified, that and a black-horror swept across my thoughts in a torrent. Then the two doctors, the naked body with its cut side, the little room, swept away from under me and vanished, as a speck of foam vanishes down an eddy.

I was in mid-air. Far below was the West End of London, receding rapidly, – for I seemed to be flying swiftly upward, – and, as it receded, passing westward, like a panorama. I could see, through the faint haze of smoke, the innumerable roofs chimney-set, the narrow roadways, stippled with people and conveyances, the little specks of squares, and the church steeples like thorns sticking out of the fabric. But it spun away as the earth rotated on its axis, and in a few seconds (as it seemed) I was over the scattered clumps of town about Ealing, the little Thames a thread of blue to the south, and the Chiltern Hills and the North Downs coming up like the rim of a basin, far away and faint with haze. Up I rushed. And at first I had not the faintest conception what this headlong rush upward could mean.

Every moment the circle of scenery beneath me grew wider and wider, and the details of town and field, of hill and valley, got more and more hazy and pale and indistinct, a luminous grey was mingled more and more with the blue of the hills and the green of the open meadows; and a little patch of cloud, low and far to the west, shone ever more dazzlingly white. Above, as the veil of atmosphere between myself and outer space grew thinner, the sky, which had been a fair springtime blue at first, grew deeper and richer in colour, passing steadily through the intervening shades, until presently it was as dark as the blue sky of midnight, and presently as black as the blackness of a frosty starlight, and at last as black as no blackness I had ever beheld. And first one star, and then many, and at last an innumerable host broke out upon the sky: more stars than anyone has ever seen from the face of the earth. For the blueness of the sky is the light of the sun and stars sifted and spread abroad blindingly: there is diffused light even in the darkest skies of winter, and we do not see the stars by day only because of the dazzling irradiation of the sun. But now I saw things – I know not how; assuredly with no mortal eyes – and that defect of bedazzlement blinded me no longer. The sun was incredibly strange and wonderful. The body of it was a disc of blinding white light: not yellowish, as it seems to those who live upon the earth, but livid white, all streaked with scarlet streaks and rimmed about with a fringe of writhing tongues of red fire. And, shooting half-way across the heavens from either side of it, and brighter than the Milky Way, were two pinions of silver-white, making it look more like those winged globes I have seen in Egyptian sculpture, than anything else I can remember upon earth. These I knew for the solar corona, though I had never seen anything of it but a picture during the days of my earthly life.

When my attention came back to the earth again, I saw that it had fallen very far away from me. Field and town were long since indistinguishable, and all the varied hues of the country were merging into a uniform bright grey, broken only by the brilliant white of the clouds that lay scattered in flocculent masses over Ireland and the west of England. For now I could see the outlines of the north of France and Ireland, and all this island of Britain, save where Scotland passed over the horizon to the north, or where the coast was blurred or obliterated by cloud. The sea was a dull grey, and darker than the land; and the whole panorama was rotating slowly towards the east.

All this had happened so swiftly that, until I was some thousand miles or so from the earth, I had no thought for myself. But now I perceived I had neither hands nor feet, neither parts nor organs, and that I felt neither alarm nor pain. All about me I perceived that the vacancy (for I had already left the air behind) was cold beyond the imagination of man; but it troubled me not. The sun's rays shot through the void, powerless to light or heat until they should strike on matter in their course. I saw things with a serene self-forgetfulness, even as if I were God. And down below there, rushing away from me, – countless miles in a second, – where a little dark spot on the grey marked the position of London, two doctors were struggling to restore life to the poor hacked and outworn shell I had abandoned. I felt then such release, such serenity as I can compare to no mortal delight I have ever known.

It was only after I had perceived all these things that the meaning of that headlong rush of the earth grew into comprehension. Yet it was so simple, so obvious, that I was amazed at my never anticipating the thing that was happening to me. I had suddenly been cut adrift from matter: all that was material of me was there upon earth, whirling away through space, held to the earth by gravitation, partaking of the earth-inertia, moving in its wreath of epicycles round the sun, and with the sun and the planets on their vast march through space. But the immaterial has no inertia, feels nothing of the pull of matter for matter: where it parts from its garment of flesh, there it remains (so far as space concerns it any longer) immovable in space. *I* was not leaving the earth: the earth was leaving *me*, and not only the earth, but the whole solar system was streaming past. And about me in space, invisible to me, scattered in the wake of the earth upon its journey, there must be an innumerable multitude of souls, stripped like myself of the material, stripped like myself of the passions of the individual and the generous emotions of the gregarious brute, naked intelligences, things of newborn wonder and thought, marvelling at the strange release that had suddenly come on them!

As I receded faster and faster from the strange white sun in the black heavens, and from the broad and shining earth upon which my being had begun, I seemed to grow, in some incredible manner, vast: vast as regards this world I had left, vast as regards the moments and periods of a human life. Very soon I saw the full circle of the earth, slightly gibbous, like the moon when she nears her full, but very large; and the silvery shape of America was now in the noonday blaze wherein (as it seemed) little England had been basking but a few minutes ago. At first the earth was large, and shone in the heavens, filling a great part of them; but every moment she grew smaller and more distant. As she shrunk, the broad moon in its third quarter crept into view over the rim of her disc. I looked for the constellations. Only that part of Aries directly behind the sun and the Lion, which the earth covered, were hidden. I recognised the tortuous, tattered band of the Milky Way, with Vega very bright between sun and earth; and Sirius and Orion shone splendid against the unfathomable blackness in the opposite quarter of the heavens. The Pole Star was overhead, and the Great Bear hung over the circle of the earth. And away beneath and beyond the shining corona of the sun were strange groupings of stars I had never seen in my life – notably, a dagger-shaped group that I knew for the Southern Cross. All these were no larger than when they had shone on earth; but the little stars that one scarce sees shone now against the setting of black vacancy as brightly as the first-magnitudes had done, while the larger worlds were points of indescribable glory and colour. Aldebaran was a spot of blood-red fire, and Sirius condensed to one point of light of a world of sapphires. And they shone steadily: they did not scintillate, they were calmly glorious. My impressions had an adamantine hardness and brightness; there was no blurring softness, no atmosphere, nothing but infinite darkness set with the myriads of these acute and brilliant points and specks of light. Presently, when I looked again, the little earth seemed no bigger than the sun, and it dwindled and turned as I looked, until, in a second's space (as it seemed to me), it was halved; and so it went on swiftly dwindling. Far away in the opposite direction, a little pinkish pin's head of light, shining steadily, was the planet Mars. I swam motionless in vacancy, and, without a trace of terror or astonishment, watched the speck of cosmic dust we call the world fall away from me.

Presently it dawned upon me that my sense of duration had changed: that my mind was moving not faster but infinitely slower, that between each separate impression there was a period of many days. The moon spun once round the earth as I noted this; and I perceived clearly the motion of Mars in his orbit. Moreover, it appeared as if the time between thought and thought grew steadily greater, until at last a thousand years was but a moment in my perceptions.

At first the constellations had shone motionless against the black background of infinite space; but presently it seemed as though the group of stars about Hercules and the Scorpion was contracting, while Orion and Aldebaran and their neighbours were scattering apart. Flashing suddenly out of the darkness there came a flying multitude of particles of rock, glittering like dust-specks in a sunbeam, and encompassed in a faintly luminous haze. They swirled all about me, and vanished again in a twinkling far behind. And then I saw that a bright spot of light, that shone a little to one side of my path, was growing very rapidly larger, and perceived that it was the planet Saturn rushing towards me. Larger and larger it grew, swallowing up the heavens behind it, and hiding every moment a fresh multitude of stars. I perceived its flattened, whirling body, its disc-like belt, and seven of its little satellites. It grew and grew, till it towered enormous; and then I plunged amid a streaming multitude of clashing stones and dancing dust-particles and gas-eddies, and saw for a moment the mighty triple belt like three concentric arches of moonlight above me, its shadow black on the boiling tumult below. These things happened in one-tenth of the time it takes to tell of them. The planet went by like a flash of lightning; for a few seconds it blotted out the sun, and there and then became a mere black, dwindling, winged patch against the light. The earth, the mother mote of my being, I could no longer see.

So, with a stately swiftness, in the profoundest silence, the solar system fell from me, as it had been a garment, until the sun was a mere star amid the multitude of stars, with its eddy of planet-specks, lost in the confused glittering of the remoter light. I was no longer a denizen of the solar system: I had come to the Outer Universe, I seemed to grasp and comprehend the whole world of matter. Ever more swiftly the stars closed in about the spot where Antares and Vega had vanished in a luminous haze, until that part of the sky had the semblance of a whirling mass of nebulæ, and ever before me yawned vaster gaps of vacant blackness, and the stars shone fewer and fewer. It seemed as if I moved towards a point between Orion's belt and sword; and the void about that region opened vaster and vaster every second, an incredible gulf of nothingness, into which I was falling. Faster and ever faster the universe rushed by, a hurry of whirling motes at last, speeding silently into the void. Stars glowing brighter and brighter, with their circling planets catching the light in a ghostly fashion as I neared them, shone out and vanished again into inexistence; faint comets, clusters of meteorites, winking specks of matter, eddying light points, whizzed past, some perhaps a hundred millions of miles or so from me at most, few nearer, travelling with unimaginable rapidity, shooting constellations, momentary darts of fire, through that black, enormous night. More than anything else it was like a dusty draught, sunbeam-lit. Broader and wider and deeper grew the starless space, the vacant Beyond, into which I was being drawn. At last a quarter of the heavens was black and blank, and the whole headlong rush of stellar universe closed in behind me like a veil of light that is gathered together. It drove away from me like a monstrous jack-o'lantern driven by the wind. I had come out into the wilderness of space. Ever the vacant blackness grew broader, until the hosts of the stars seemed only like a swarm of fiery specks hurrying away from me, inconceivably remote, and the darkness, the nothingness and emptiness, was about me on every side. Soon the little universe of matter, the cage of points in which I had begun to be, was dwindling, now to a whirling disc of luminous glittering, and now to one minute disc of hazy light. In a little while it would shrink to a point, and at last would vanish altogether.

Suddenly feeling came back to me – feeling in the shape of overwhelming terror: such a dread of those dark vastitudes as no words can describe, a passionate resurgence of sympathy and social desire. Were there other souls, invisible to me as I to them, about me in the blackness? or was I indeed, even as I felt, alone? Had I passed out of being into something that was neither being nor not-being? The covering of the body, the covering of matter, had been torn from me, and the hallucinations of companionship and security. Everything was black and silent. I had ceased to be. I was nothing. There was nothing, save only that infinitesimal dot of light that dwindled in the gulf. I strained myself to hear and see, and for a while there was naught but infinite silence, intolerable darkness, horror, and despair.

Then I saw that about the spot of light into which the whole world of matter had shrunk there was a faint glow. And in a band on either side of that the darkness was not absolute. I watched it for ages, as it seemed to me, and through the long waiting the haze grew imperceptibly more distinct. And then about the band appeared an irregular cloud of the faintest, palest brown. I felt a passionate impatience; but the thing grew brighter so slowly that they scarce seemed to change. What was unfolding itself? What was this strange reddish dawn in the interminable night of space?

The cloud's shape was grotesque. It seemed to be looped along its lower side into four projecting masses, and, above, it ended in a straight line. What phantom was it? I felt assured I had seen that figure before; but I could not think what, nor where, nor when it was. Then the realisation rushed upon me. *It was a clenched Hand.* I was alone in space, alone with this huge, shadowy Hand, upon which the whole Universe of Matter lay like an unconsidered speck of dust. It seemed as though I watched it through vast periods of time. On the forefinger glittered a ring; and the universe from which I had come was but a spot of light upon the ring's curvature. And the thing that the hand gripped had the likeness of a black rod. Through a long eternity I watched this Hand, with the ring and the rod, marvelling and fearing and waiting helplessly on what might follow. It seemed as though nothing could follow: that I should watch for ever, seeing only the Hand and the thing it held, and understanding nothing of its import. Was the whole universe but a refracting speck upon some greater Being? Were our worlds but the atoms of another universe, and those again of another, and so on through an endless progression? And what was I? Was I indeed immaterial? A vague persuasion of a body gathering about me came into my suspense. The abysmal darkness about the Hand filled with impalpable suggestions, with uncertain, fluctuating shapes.

Then, suddenly, came a sound, like the sound of a tolling bell: faint, as if infinitely far; muffled, as though heard through thick swathings of darkness: a deep, vibrating resonance, with vast gulfs of silence between each stroke. And the Hand appeared to tighten on the rod. And I saw far above the Hand, towards the apex of the darkness, a circle of dim phosphorescence, a ghostly sphere whence these sounds came throbbing; and at the last stroke the Hand vanished, for the hour had come, and I heard a noise of many waters. But the black rod remained as a great band across the sky. And then a voice, which seemed to run to the uttermost parts of space, spoke, saying, 'There will be no more pain.'

At that an almost intolerable gladness and radiance rushed in upon me, and I saw the circle shining white and bright, and the rod black and shining, and many things else distinct and clear. And the circle was the face of the clock, and the rod the rail of my bed. Haddon was standing at the foot, against the rail, with a small pair of scissors on his fingers; and the hands of my clock on the mantel over his shoulder were clasped together over the hour of twelve. Mowbray was washing something in a basin at the octagonal table, and at my side I felt a subdued feeling that could scarce be spoken of as pain.

The operation had not killed me. And I perceived, suddenly, that the dull melancholy of half a year was lifted from my mind.

Etheromania
Louis Lewin

The habit of drinking ether seems to be comparatively common. It is easy to understand that in those countries where anti-alcoholism has succeeded in attaining an outward victory, the craving for another inebriating substance leads to the discovery of substitutes. Ether is one of these succedanea. Not a drop of alcohol is taken, but ether and spirit of ether is used in increasing quantities. It is not considered as becoming in the female sex to consume large quantities of concentrated alcohol habitually, and for this reason women contribute a large contingent to etheromania. A small phial of ether is an indispensable vade-mecum for such women. Many drinkers of ether take excessive daily doses. For instance, the chemist Bucquet consumed over half a litre and Rouelle one litre daily.

The organic disturbances generally begin with disorders of the functions of the stomach. Dyspepsia, gastric pains, and vomiting set in. Trembling, muscular weakness, and glycosuria are less frequent. In the case of a woman who had consumed ether poured on sugar every day before meals and had in the course of two and a half months taken in all 180 gr., weakness and trembling of the hands and feet, morbid contraction of certain muscles of the legs when walking, pains in the thorax and between the shoulder-blades, vomiting, tinnitus aurium, headache, palpitation of the heart and cramps in the calves appeared and the patient had no appetite. In the morning vomiting occurs as in the case of heavy drinkers. The activity of the heart soon becomes irregular and weak, the skin assumes a pallid hue. The character also soon changes. Irritability, sudden changes of temper, capriciousness and concurrent loss of willpower can be observed. The subjects are negligent and lazy. It has on the other hand been pointed out that delirium does not occur as with alcoholists, nor cachexia as with morphinists. It is said that among the Irish ether-drinkers, now to be described, there are some cases in which mental modification alone occurs and the physical state is not affected. It has even been considered a blessing that the Catholic clergy have persuaded the Irish to abandon alcohol in favour of the harmless ether.

For some time attention has been drawn to the fact that in Ireland the drinking of ether seems to be becoming very popular. The origin of this abuse has not been ascertained. It is stated on the one hand that the Irish peasants began ether-drinking in the year 1840, at the time of Father Mathew's preaching against alcohol, and on the other that medical men prescribed ether too liberally. The reason for this mischief has also been sought, however, in the limitation of the alcohol distilleries. The inhabitants of Northern Ireland drink the cheap ether manufactured in England mixed with alcohol. In Northern Ireland more ether is used than in the whole of England. On market days in Draperstown and Cookstown the air used to be filled with the vapour of ether, and the same odour impregnated the carriages of the local railway. In this part of the country, men, women, and children drink ether, the former in doses of 8 to 15 gr. repeatedly one after the other. In order to alleviate the burning sensation which the drug produces and to reduce the loss by belching, the addicts drink water after the doses of the narcotic. Some of them can tolerate 150 to 500 gr. of ether in several portions. Intoxication sets in rapidly and disappears with the same speed. The initial symptoms consist in violent excitation, profuse salivation and eructation. Occasionally, convulsions similar to those of epilepsy occur. A state of stupor is evoked after the consumption of very large doses. Ether-drinkers of this kind are quarrelsome, tend to become liars and suffer from gastric disorders and nervous prostration.

In consequence of these facts the retail sale of ether has been regulated. The drug is now included in the list of poisons, and is only supplied in pharmacies on production of a written authority.

In Norway the use of ether seems to have assumed large proportions. On holidays old and young, men and women consume the drug.

In some German districts, especially in the neighbourhood of Memel an Heydekrug, the drinking of ether has assumed the form of an epidemic among the Lithuanian inhabitants. In 1897 in the town of Memel alone 69 carboys of 60 litres, and in the district of Memel 74 carboys of 70 litres, 8,580 litres in all, were sold for drinking purposes. On market days the smell of ether exhaled by the drinkers is noticeable at every turn. When, on the road between Heydekrug and the neighbouring villages, a carriage with noisy inmates drawn by a madly galloping horse which the intoxicated driver is unmercifully beating, passes the wayfarer, a strong smell of ether can be ascertained in the rush of air.

When the market is closed many men and women intoxicated with ether can be seen reeling about. Even children are habituated to ether at a very delicate age. School children have suffered mentally to a large extent in consequence. Whole families have been ruined by habitual consumption of ether. I cannot say how far the state of affairs has changed since the war.

In Russia, and especially in Galicia, country doctors observed a similar epidemic. The poorer inhabitants of the country are particularly addicted to ether. Mixed with a small amount of alcohol it is consumed in inconceivable quantities. In these people a kind of morbid stupidity develops which in serious cases renders thought impossible. Cardiac disorders usually terminate their lives.

Particular cases prove that ether also has its victims in high society. In one case an English baronet used morphia and ether concurrently for three years and succumbed to his passion. In another case an etheromaniac earl committed extravagances which, from a moral point of view, classified him among mental deficients.

I have no doubt that anatomical investigation of ether-drinkers would shew modifications similar to those of alcoholists.

The Drug Bag
Hunter S. Thompson

About 20 miles east of Baker I stopped to check the drug bag. The sun was hot and I felt like killing something. Anything. Even a big lizard. Drill the fucker. I got my attorney's .357 Magnum out of the trunk and spun the cylinder. It was loaded all the way around: Long, nasty little slugs – 158 grains with a fine flat trajectory and painted aztec gold on the tips. I blew the horn a few times, hoping to call up an iguana. Get the buggers moving. They were out there, I knew, in that goddamn sea of cactus – hunkered down, barely breathing, and every one of the stinking little bastards was loaded with deadly poison.

Three fast explosions knocked me off balance. Three deafening, double-action blasts from the .357 in my right hand. Jesus! Firing at nothing, for no reason at all. Bad craziness. I tossed the gun into the front seat of the Shark and stared nervously at the highway. No cars either way; the road was empty for two or three miles in both directions.

Fine luck. It would not *do* to be found in the desert under these circumstances: firing wildly into the cactus from a car full of drugs. And especially not now, on the lam from the Highway Patrol.

Awkward questions would arise: 'Well now, Mister . . . ah . . . Duke; you understand, of course, that it *is* illegal to discharge a firearm of any kind while standing on a federal highway?'

'What? Even in self-defense? This goddamn gun has a *hair trigger*, officer. The truth is I only meant to fire *once* – just to scare the little bastards.'

A heavy stare, then speaking very slowly: 'Are you saying, Mister Duke . . . that you were *attacked* out here?'

'Well . . . no . . . not literally attacked, officer, but seriously *menaced*. I stopped to piss, and the minute I stepped out of the car these filthy little bags of poison were all around me. They moved like *greased lightning*!'

Would this story hold up?

No. They would place me under arrest, then routinely search the car – and when that happened all kinds of savage hell would break loose. They would never believe all these drugs were necessary to my work; that in truth I was a professional journalist on my way to Las Vegas to cover the National District Attorneys' Conference of Narcotics and Dangerous Drugs.

'Just samples, officer. I got this stuff off a road man for the Neo-American Church back in Barstow. He started acting funny, so I worked him over.'

Would they buy this?

No. They would lock me in some hellhole of a jail and beat me on the kidneys with big branches – causing me to piss blood for years to come . . .

Luckily, nobody bothered me while I ran a quick inventory on the kit-bag. The stash was a hopeless mess, all churned together and half-crushed. Some of the mescaline pellets had disintegrated into a reddish-brown powder, but I counted about thirty-five or forty still intact. My attorney had eaten all the reds, but there was quite a bit of speed left . . . no more grass, the coke bottle was empty, one acid blotter, a nice brown lump of opium hash and six loose amyls . . . Not enough for anything serious, but a careful rationing of the mescaline would probably get us through the four-day Drug Conference.

On the outskirts of Vegas I stopped at a neighborhood pharmacy and bought two quarts of Gold tequila, two fifths of

Chivas Regal and a pint of ether. I was tempted to ask for some amyls. My angina pectoris was starting to act up. But the druggist had the eyes of a mean Baptist hysteric. I told him I needed the ether to get the tape off my legs, but by that time he'd already rung the stuff up and bagged it. He didn't give a fuck about ether.

I wondered what he would say if I asked him for $22 worth of Romilar and a tank of nitrous oxide. Probably he would have sold it to me. Why not? Free enterprise . . . Give the public what it needs – especially this bad-sweaty, nervous-talkin' fella with tape all over his legs and this terrible cough, along with angina pectoris and these godawful Aneuristic flashes every time he gets in the sun. *I mean this fella was in bad shape, officer. How the hell was I to know he'd walk straight out to his car and start abusing those drugs?*

How indeed? I lingered a moment at the magazine rack, then got a grip on myself and hurried outside to the car. The idea of going completely crazy on laughing gas in the middle of a DAs' drug conference had a definite warped appeal. But not on the *first day*, I thought. Save that for later. No point getting busted and committed before the conference even starts.

Cocaine Consciousness:
The Gourmet Trip

Jerry Hopkins

Not since Sherlock Holmes was taking it to improve his mental acuity back around 1900 and the original recipe for Coca-Cola actually contained some extract of coca leaf had cocaine been so avidly accepted by a large public. Not since LSD swept through the popular marketplace a decade earlier had an illegal drug been so massively exploited. And *never* before had a 'hard drug' (an epithet usually reserved for opium derivatives) been so widely bought and sold, in successful song and cinema (affecting wardrobe, slang, etc., just as LSD had done) as well as on the street.

In the early 1970's, along with bisexuality, platform heels and *Deep Throat*, cocaine snorting became chic, was in some subcultures *de rigeur*, crossing all generation gaps and reaching into Bel Air mansions, Harlem tenements, Berkeley crash pads and split-level rancheros in Middle America with equal facility and dispatch.

There is a story told by Gary Stromberg, who was the Rolling Stones' personal publicist when they toured the U.S. in 1972 and still goes on the road regularly with bands, thus is exposed to a large slice of the popular marketplace. 'Do you know how many coke spoons I see and do you know who's wearing them around their necks?' he asks. 'Fourteen-year-olds! In Cleveland, man. In Cleveland and Houston and Minneapolis.'

Gary says he was startled at first, because as anyone 'into it' knows, most people who use it don't wear paraphernalia where every cop in town can see it. More important, in 1974 cocaine was selling for between $1,000 and $2,000 an ounce, $50 to $80 for a 'spoon' (or gram) – the latter being about enough to get two people high for about half an hour.

'Those kids couldn't have known from cocaine,' the publicist says. 'But they bought the image, they bought the symbol, they bought the coke spoon, and hung it on a chain with a roach clip, a cross, a Star of David.'

A registered pharmacist chuckles when he hears this story. He buys cocaine from the Mallinkrodt Chemical Works in St. Louis, or possibly from the Merck Chemical Company in West Germany, for $22.40 an ounce. And it's pure, while what is sold illegally on the street has been 'stepped on,' or cut, an unknown number of times with such variant substances as Vitamin B_{12} (popular in 1974), methamphetamne (generally agreed to be a bummer) and (the old standby, used for its innocuous taste) a baby laxative called Minite.

Worse, much of the coke being sold is not even cocaine at all, but a mix of procaine and methedrine – procaine being one of several chemical combinations that are more anesthetic than stimulant: thus, the blend with speed. And when it *is* coke, because the drug passes through so many hands on the way to the consumer, the actual cocaine may be reduced to only 6 to 30 per cent of the snort.

Why would anyone pay up to 10,000 per cent mark-up on a product he knows has been brutally adulterated? In the glittery, shattered early '70's, cocaine offered more than chemical euphoria – it also offered a higher station in life. In a word, Status. In a drug-oriented society, coke had become the gourmet trip.

Ted is one of the top dealers in New York. He is twenty-four and black. 'Consider the accessories,' he says. 'Now you can buy a little brass coke spoon tucked inside a 30-caliber bullet for $2.95, add a dollar for a neck chain, but if you're really into coke, man, you're into fine accessories. You don't put something that expensive in brass. You carry it around in a silver vial – maybe it's even monogrammed. And you snort from a silver spoon. That's my marketplace. I don't sell to the musicians any more. It was far-out being on that scene in a way, but only a few of the musicians have any re-finement, if you know what I mean. My man has to have class. Now I sell on Park Avenue.'

Still, gourmet drug or not, much of the traffic of the early '70's has been in the low-income or no-income 'hip' community. At first it may seem puzzling. Then it becomes clear that many of the coke-heads are dealing, as in the marijuana market, just enough to keep themselves in coke.

'Look,' says a small-time pusher, 'I can buy a fairly clean ounce for 1,500 bucks, step on it once and double my money, or sell half after I cut it, get my money back and still have half an ounce for myself.'

He pulls a small glass vial of white powder from the pocket of his faded, embroidered, patchwork jeans, carefully sprinkles two thin rows of the powder on a pocket mirror, tightly rolls a new $20 bill, places one end next to one row, the other end in his right nostril. He presses his left nostril closed and inhales through his right, vacuuming the powder in a swift movement along the row. *Sniffff.* He breathes deeply, then repeats the procedure with the other row and the other nostril. *Sniffff.*

(Coke can also be dropped, rubbed on the gums, or shoved as a suppository, although these techniques are rarely used, and shot, which is popular largely amongst ghetto blacks and 'needle freaks,' and usually thought to be outside the circle of status-heads. Even sprinkling it on an open cut will get the user high. Coke is that readily absorbed.)

Almost immediately the pusher's heartbeat accelerates, his body temperature rises slightly, his pupils dilate, his face flushes a little, his nose numbs. In minutes he will become garrulous, restless, excited. He will feel confident, larger than life.

'Dynamite!' he says, holding the vial aloft. 'Wanna little taste? The first snort's on me.'

Of course the pusher would like his snorting partner to buy a gram or two. But that does not mean the offer of a free nose-full was necessarily made merely in the interest of salesmanship. The coke may have been offered for other reasons entirely. 'Some people,' says one Los Angeles user, 'don't even do it to get high. It's social now. It's like: "I've got so much money I can afford to give you some."'

Naturally cocaine is not the only drug to have found a gourmet status-seeking audience. In the 1840's, some of Paris's most respectable physicians and artists and writers (including Théophile Gautier and Charles Baudelaire) were ritualistically sharing a drug recently brought back as spoils from Algiers; they called themselves members of 'The Hashish Club.' More recently, when an entire marijuana subculture developed, a status-conscious pecking order was given the lowly weed according to geographic origins: *i.e.*, Panama Red, Acapulco Gold and Michoacan in North America, and in Europe the imports from Africa, Durban Poison, Swazi Gold and Malawi Laughing Grass; to the dealers and smokers who had them went a sort of elitist respect.

Nor has cocaine gone unappreciated. By 1880 – eighteen years after its first distillation from the coca plant – it was widely prescribed in the U.S. for alcoholism and four years after that the young Viennese physician Sigmund Freud was recommending it for everything from morphine addiction to digestive disorders and melancholia.

By the turn of the century the image was changing and the audience was broadening. That was when Sherlock Holmes became popular literature's first coke-head . . . when coca cigarettes, cocaine cordials, 'tonics' and other patent medicines, including popular 'catarrh cures,' were available . . . when one American firm even promised in its ads that the wonder drug would 'supply the place of food, make the coward brave, the silent eloquent . . .'

All this came to an end with the Pure Food and Drug Act of 1906 and the Harrison Narcotic Act of 1914, which made the gift, sale, and possession of cocaine subject to the same dire federal penalties as those regarding morphine and heroin. Most states also mistakenly identified cocaine as a narcotic and similar laws were passed everywhere. That was when coke went underground.

It wasn't too long before the drug made its first come-back, however. That was in the 1920's and 1930's, when cocaine was popularized simultaneously by singers in the rigidly limited rhythm and blues (or 'race') and country and western markets, and the faraway chic of the Broadway set.

There were, for example, several songs called 'Cocaine Blues.' One had as its key line, 'I'm simply wild about my good cocaine,' but also contained a warning: 'Coke's good for horses/Not for women or men/The doctor said it'd kill you/But he didn't say when.'

Another song with the same title told the story of a man who shoots his woman down (while high on coke) and closed with a more direct admonition: 'Lay off that liquor and let that cocaine be.'

Then, in 1930, the Memphis Jug Band recorded 'Cocaine Habit Blues.' The first two lines told the tale: 'Cocaine habit's mighty bad/It's the worst ol' habit that I ever had.'

Not all songwriters agreed. In 1927, Victoria Spivey's 'Dope Head Blues' openly praised the drug for its superman qualities: 'Just give me one more sniffle/Another sniffle of that dope/I'll catch a cow like a cowboy/Throw a bull without a rope.'

While Champion Jack Dupree, one of the great New Orleans blues pianists, recorded two versions of 'Junker's Blues,' in the first saying his sister used coke, in the second saying, 'Some people say I use the needle/And some say I sniff cocaine/But that's the best ol' feeling/In the world that I've ever seen.'

Meantime, in the glamorous world of the Great White Way, Cole Porter, who was known to try anything at least once, wrote in his appropriately titled Broadway show *Anything Goes* (staged in 1934): 'I get no kick from cocaine/I'm sure that if/I took even one sniff/It would bore me terrifi-ically too/But I get a kick out of you.'

Lillian Hellman in her 1974 best seller *Pentimento* told a story about a lunch she had with her friend Tallulah Bankhead in 1939: 'Tallulah, Herman [Shumlin, the producer] and I were having dinner in the old Artists and Writers Club, a hangout for newspapermen. Tallulah took two small bottles from her pocketbook, put them on the table, and seemed to forget about them. As we were about to go back to rehearsal, she picked up one bottle and tipped it to put drops in her eyes. She rose from the table, repacked the bottles, led the way to the door, and let out a shriek that brought the restaurant to its feet.

'Herman rushed to her, she pushed him aside, other people pushed towards her, she turned for the door, changed her mind, and whispered to nobody, "I have put the wrong drops in my eyes."

'Herman ran to a phone booth, she shouted after him, he called out that he was getting a doctor, she said he was to mind his own business, and suddenly, in the shouting and running, she grabbed my arm, pulled me into the toilet and said, "Get Herman off that phone. I put the cocaine in my eyes and I don't tell that to doctors or to anybody else. Tell him to shut up about it or I won't go back to the theatre."'

Tallulah's appreciation notwithstanding, cocaine use was waning in the late 1930's and although it remained a special and occasional treat among some segments of society – notably jazz musicians who sometimes mixed it with heroin to increase the 'bang' or 'rush' (this was called a 'speedball'), and doctors, to whom the drug was most available – by the 1950's the drug was essentially forgotten, or pushed into a position of general disrespect. This was the period when Raymond Chandler, in 1942 in his novel *High Window*, talked sneeringly of 'coke peddlers,' while another writer said of Sherlock Holmes: 'People get put in jail by a coke fiend. How could you trust this bum?' It was also during this time that the phrase 'coke-head' became a synonym for any dull or slow-reacting person, and the drug was given so many of its colorful nicknames, usually associated with the criminal world: Bernice, big bloke, bouncing powder, C, Charlie, C.K., Corrine, cubes, flake, girl (an antonym for heroin, or 'boy'), gold dust, happy dust, her, the leaf, sea snow, star dust, white drugs and white stuff.[1]

There is a responsible body of research and belief that supports the theory that the black market for coke dried up and was replaced by a cluster of synthetic drugs, the amphetamines. It is further believed that cocaine made its big comeback in the 1960's when the narcotics agencies began coming down on the amphetamine black markets.

This is only part of the story, for it was in the 1960's that the concept of 'drug gourmet' was developed and adopted by such large numbers. This was when it wasn't enough that you dropped acid, it was also important what *kind* of acid it was; did Owsley make it? was it called 'sunshine' or 'window pane'? or was it imported from the Sandoz labs in Switzerland? Marijuana was being rated simultaneously and as that happened the top price of grass went through the roof; whereas in 1968, southern Californians could buy a kilo (which usually was under the 2.2 pounds that it was supposed to be) for $125, a few years later the same short kilo was selling for $300 to $1,400. With the higher priced stuff nearly always going to those few in the youth subculture who could afford it, the rock stars.

In the 1960's, and now in the 1970's, the rock stars set the social pace, succeeding the fading heroes and heroines of cinema as the prime shapers of popular society. (There were obvious exceptions, such as Peter Fonda and Dennis Hopper, about whom more in a minute.) As it happened, one of the things the singers, songwriters and musicians were into was drugs, and some of these were into coke. So they sang about it.

---

[1] From *The Underground Dictionary*, Eugene E. Landy, Simon & Schuster, 1971.

This was when Fred Neil, Hoyt Axton, and Dave Van Ronk, all folksingers, contributed to a song best identified by the line 'Cocaine . . . running around my heart and my brain.' From Neil's version: 'I said, "Come here, mama/come here quick/Cocaine makin' your poor boy so sick/Ah, bitter sweet."'

At the same approximate time in New York, a column from the underground *East Village Other* called 'Kokaine Karma' became a radio show at a college station in East Orange, New Jersey, then made the move to the bigger audience of New York's hip, listener-sponsored station, WBAI-FM. And not long after that, Wavy Gravy was talking to the *Realist*: 'I like to think of it as the thinking man's Dristan.' And *Esquire* put a gold coke spoon on the cover of an issue that paid noble and reverent homage to 'soul.'

In California, much of the hip white establishment was aboard the cocaine train by 1969, when coke made its first important, contemporary film appearance, as record producer Phil Spector made a buy from actors Dennis Hopper and Peter Fonda in *Easy Rider*. At the time, many of the viewers thought the drug Phil was snorting was heroin; never in the film was the drug identified. But neither was the act of snorting *any drug* ever challenged; *no moral judgments were made*. The attitude seemed to be that which Spector himself took the following December when he used a photograph from the film as his Christmas card. There was Phil, one finger held firm against one nostril, snorting a white powder from a tiny spoon through his other nostril. With the message: 'A Little Snow at Christmas Time Never Hurt Anyone!'

(Actually, nearly a year ahead of *Easy Rider* came *The Night of the Following Day*, a kidnap thriller starring Marlon Brando, Richard Boone, and Rita Moreno, the latter of whom seemed to spend most of the film snorting coke through a tightly rolled $100 bill. The film was not successful and can be said to have contributed little if anything to 'cocaine consciousness.')

By late 1969 the rock and roll rush was on, as dozens of the top stars were known to be using coke regularly. In San

Francisco, many of these stars also were including coke references in their new songs. Paul Kantner of Jefferson Airplane, for example, released his first solo album, in it a song called 'Hijack,' which opened with a simile: 'The summer was dry like your nose when you've been behind coke for a day and a season.' A year later Paul was back with Grace Slick in another album, *Sunfighter*, which came with a booklet carrying the message, 'Those of you who are serious about this whole thing, oozing along like a Cadillac, need some good solid hospital wacco in the nose.' While the Grateful Dead (in the summer of 1970) released an album that included a song they played at most concerts, 'Casey Jones': 'Drivin' that train/High on cocaine/Casey Jones, you better watch your speed.' The following year (1971) the Dead returned with a best-selling single, singing about 'living on reds, Vitamin C and cocaine' in another concert favorite, 'Truckin'.'

In Los Angeles, meantime, another rock band, Steppenwolf, had a minor hit the same summer (1971) with a song written by Hoyt Axton, 'Snowblind Friend': 'He said he wanted Heaven/But prayin' was too slow/So he bought a one-way ticket/On an airline made of snow.' Suddenly the word 'Cocaine!' made an emphatic appearance between the third and fourth verses of John Lennon's 'Hold On John.' And then came a blues with a Cole Porter-ish lyric from Taj Mahal: 'Champagne don't drive me crazy/Cocaine don't make me lazy/Ain't nobody's business what I do.'

The big push came in the late summer of 1972. This was when a Los Angeles band called the Eagles went onto the singles charts with a song called 'Witchy Woman.' Part of the lyric was coke-inspired – 'Crazy laughter in another room/And she drove herself to madness with a silver spoon' – and the record went to No. 9, remaining on the charts for thirteen weeks.

This was also when a film called *Superfly* was released, which, accompanied by a superb soundtrack album and two hit singles from Curtis Mayfield, further saturated a large segment of the popular marketplace. Cocaine consciousness was peaking.

The opening scene set the style and philosophy of the film, as Priest, a big-time Manhattan coke dealer, won a street fight against impossible odds and escaped to his rat-infested Harlem tenement building, where he traveled the garbage-choked hallways and then unlocked his apartment. Zap! It looked like a Playboy Pad designed by Wilt Chamberlain. It was thus quickly established that Priest was a hero, a man of physical daring and prowess who, in the great American tradition of Horatio Alger, overcame the vast and oppressive forces of his environment to become an enviable success. That he was a criminal – and black! – was not important because Priest wanted to get out of the business and even if he wanted to make one last big score ($1,000,000 split two ways), the bottom line read 'pusher-gone-good,' and that alone gave him heroic stature, made him acceptable to an otherwise closed Christian community. That he was a hedonist who wore flashy clothing, drove expensive cars, and had a white woman as well as a black, satisfied other American traditions (and fantasies), and that 'the man' he eventually met in the film, from whom he was going to buy thirty kilos for $300,000, turned out to be a deputy commissioner of police, made him a counterculture hero, too. For some of the same reasons, Priest (played by Ron O'Neal) remained a black hero, as well, and was not co-opted by a predominantly white audience (as was, say, Jimi Hendrix), satisfying instead a number of black dreams (the life style, the shoulder-length straightened hair, the Caucasian nose) while personifying the epitome of black *machismo*, becoming what the reviewer in *Rolling Stone* called 'Supernigger.' *Superfly* appealed to nearly everyone.

(Of course, the story had a happy ending. Anticipating a double-cross, Priest switched briefcases with his girlfriend – the black one – and drove away to freedom and retirement . . . thereby satisfying the cinematic tradition of riding off into the setting sun.)

Black *machismo* was all the rage in the next two years as *Superfly* became the progenitor and archetype of a new genre:

the black exploitation film, which by 1974 seemed destined to outnumber the beach party and motorcycle exploitation flicks of American-International a decade earlier. So many were there that Walter Burrell, movie reviewer for the black Los Angeles *Star*, when asked couldn't remember the titles of more than two. What he did remember was that 'just about every so-called black movie I've seen has a coke scene in it.' Another reviewer, *Daily Variety*'s Arthur Murphy, agreed, saying, 'Coke scenes are as *de rigeur* as explicit fuck scenes, so numerous these days they are sleep-inducing.'

As in the case of most song lyrics, most of the black drug films carried an antidrug message. In Universal Studios' *Willie Dynamite* coke was snorted in a scene that portrayed the users unflatteringly. In *Gordon's War*, from Twentieth Century-Fox, a returning Vietnam vet's 'old lady' overdosed and he and some friends set out to clean all the coke and heroin from the neighborhood. Even in *Superfly* it was clear how hollow a life Priest led as a dealer and criminal; it was, after all, a life style he wanted to end. The film also showed the process that kept coke illegal yet available in quantity in the ghetto.[1] It didn't matter. The audience accepted the medium, not the message – perhaps believing that something that was *that* illegal (twenty years for possession in some states) and *that* expensive couldn't be all bad.

The success of the music of *Superfly* paralleled the success of the film most precisely. Just as the weekly grosses pushed the movie into the late summer and autumn Big Boxoffice lists, so did record sales account for an impressive record-buying audience. The title theme, 'Freddie's Dead,' first appeared on the singles charts in mid-August and remained there for sixteen weeks, going as high as No. 4. A follow-up single, 'Superfly,'

[1] Not all the films dramatically using cocaine have been American. Spanish director Luis Buñuel won a Cannes prize in 1975 for *The Discreet Charm of the Bourgeoisie*, and *Turkish Delight*, from Holland, was nominated for an Academy Award.

entered the same charts in November, stayed for fifteen weeks and went to No. 8. While the soundtrack album was a best seller for nearly a year and went to No. 1: 'I'm your mother/I'm your father/I'm that nigger in the alley/I'm the doctor when you need/Want some coke? Have some weed/You know me/ I'm your friend/Your main boy/You contend/I'm your pusher-man . . .'

By 1973 there was a degree of market satiation that was astonishing. Whirling almost dervishly in its continuing quest for new life styles to exploit, the hungry media settled briefly on that of the black pimp and suddenly there were dozens of magazine articles and books and television reports – most of them featuring cocaine and its use and sale quite prominently. In head shops, bookstores, and boutiques in all major cities and most smaller ones there was a rash of cocaine posters. One had the word 'cocaine' emblazoned across a large red circle in Coca-Cola script. (This reverse rip-off also appeared on T shirts.) Another was a reproduction of one of the soft drink's vintage serving trays, showing the Coca-Cola girl lifting a spoon to her nose. (Coca-Cola, ever diligent in the protection of registered trade marks – and fragile sensitivities – sued to halt distribution, and won.) Cocaine paraphernalia in stores – spoons, vials, dispensers, and snorters – began crowding some of the more traditional marijuana roach clips and hash pipes.

As the popularity of the drug increased, the product proliferated, and, as the product proliferated, the popularity of the drug increased.

There was also by now a rapidly developing cocaine 'mythology,' the storytelling that made certain dealers, smugglers, events, and rituals 'legend in their time.' There was a dealer from Minnesota, for example, who successfully crossed customs in Los Angeles (coming from Peru) with two kilos of coke taped to his legs and torso by placing a note inside his passport that read: 'I'm a federal narcotics officer and am traveling without identification. I'm following the brunette with the big purse. Please expedite my crossing and hers. There could be violence.'

Another story told often in the rock circuit had the singer of a No. 1 novelty dance record investing the $40,000 he made from his hit in cocaine, then living for four years off the profit of that.

On a recent tour of the English group, the Who, a dealer called 'Mr. Peru' appeared backstage in Atlanta and Montreal, and was replaced by 'Mr. Bolivia' in Dallas, Detroit, Boston, and Philadelphia. In New York there were small devices that looked like a large fat silver bullet with a rodlike handle – hold the rod and turn the bullet and exactly one snort's worth is expelled from the bullet's nose: a steal at $250. While in another area of ritual, it became known that if the user rubbed cocaine onto the glans penis, numbing it, he could prolong his sexual performance indefinitely – or, at least, until the coke ran out.

Before 1974, rock bands had to stock up before leaving their East Coast or West Coast homes to go on tour, but by then coke was available everywhere. Perhaps a little less so in New York, where new laws made dealing so perilous, but according to publicist Gary Stromberg, 'it didn't mean coke wasn't available – it only meant it was somewhat harder to find and considerably more expensive.' The rapidly swelling staffs of the U.S. Bureau of Narcotics and Dangerous Drugs in New Orleans, Atlanta, and Miami, major ports of entry for illegal cocaine, add further testimony to increased volume. And whereas police in dozens of cities reported few arrests for possession or sale of the drug a few years earlier, by 1974 the arrests and charges were numerous. It was quite clear that the black market for coke was greater than ever before in the drug's 110-year-old history.

But if popularity was up, abuse seemed to be down. A few years earlier there *was* abuse – as was chronicled (in 1971) by a doctor in Los Angeles who wanted to remain anonymous lest he develop a reputation as someone who treated only Hollywood's coke-heads. At the time, he said, a significant part of his practice came from the rock community.

'Coke is an easy drug to abuse,' he said, 'because it is so rapidly metabolized. But it also leaves the body rapidly, so the user, if he can afford it, does some more coke, and when that detox-ifies, he does some more. The next thing you know he's in my office complaining of congestion, saying nasal sprays don't help. Sales of these sprays, and drops, have rocketed, by the way, and I directly attribute that increase to the widely extended use of cocaine.'

The doctor reached for *The Pharmacological Basics of Therapeutics*, the recognized authority on pharmacology (the science of drugs), and turned to the section on cocaine.

'Listen to this,' he said. 'Nobody's going to argue with Goodman and Gilman [the authors] and this book was pub-lished in 1970, but listen to this and see how fast these things get outdated. This is a quote: "Cocaine abuse is uncommon in Western countries." You know what I got to say to that? Bullshit.'

He dropped the heavy volume on the desk. 'When a musician comes in with nasal congestion, the first thing I ask is how much coke is he sniffing. It's so rampant now. I see coke spoons and roach holders on neck chains every day. Coke spoons, roach holders, and nose drops.'

The doctor said there wasn't much he could do for the visit-ing stars, but he did give them some advice. 'These people were experiencing "chronic poisoning" from their habitual use. Their friends might have noticed a mental deterioration, weight loss, a definite change of character. I told them that prolonged sniff-ing could cause chronic nasal congestion and – this is the part that got home – perforation of the septum, the nasal wall. Cocaine causes the blood vessels to constrict and with insuffi-cient blood reaching the area, the partition between the nostrils atrophies. I also told them that because the drug attacks the mucous membranes, it also invited infection from bacteria and that although it was not physiologically addictive, there was a high potential for psychological addiction. My advice was to spend their money on something else.'

Three years passed and, in 1974, most of the doctor's old patients had long ago stopped seeing him. Nor was he seeing

many *new* patients. In fact, many of the original cocaine gourmets had got off the train. They had seen friends burn
themselves out, snorting themselves into a state of acute paranoia, which was often accompanied by a loss of critical
judgment. One San Francisco musician, who had been importing his cocaine from Merck in West Germany, says he woke up
one morning and couldn't breathe, so quit. Others did much the
same. Or cut down.

'The price is the other thing,' said a thirtyish record-company
executive. 'Who can afford enough to abuse it? If you don't
deal, and you aren't independently wealthy, it's practically
impossible to afford a big coke habit. It all depends upon what
kind of expense account you have.'

Thus, in 1974, cocaine was socially canonized. One could
imagine a magazine advertisement with the headline: 'What
kind of man snorts coke? The man with an expense account . . .'

Or the man who lived like he had one.

PART SIX

HALLUCINATING HISTORY

The psychologist Havelock Ellis (1859–1939) is perhaps best remembered for his writings on sexology, yet he also wrote about his personal experiences with the peyote cactus (*Lophophora williamsii* previously known as *Anhalonium lewinii*) long before Aldous Huxley published his account of the effects of mescaline in *The Doors of Perception* in 1954. Mescaline is the main psychoactive agent of this cactus that grows in Mexico and Texas, and archaeological evidence indicates that it has been used for attaining visions for at least 4,000 years. Since the latter part of the nineteenth century its use spread from its homeland and it was taken as a sacrament by many native American peoples as far north as Canada. The mescaline alkaloid was isolated from the cactus by the German chemist Arthur Heffter in the 1890s. In *Mescal: A New Artificial Paradise* (a reference to the writings of Baudelaire), Ellis describes how, on his own on Good Friday 1896, he drank a decoction of three 'mescal buttons' (the then current term for the heads of the peyote cactus) and went about recording his brilliantly colourful visions. He later introduced others to this hallucinogen including the poet W. B. Yeats.

Henri Michaux (1899–1984), poet, painter and psychonaut, writes in *Hallucinogenic Drugs and the Problem of Eros* (1964) of the ritual use of peyote among the Indians, including the

Tarahumara whom Artaud describes in *Peyote Dance*. Michaux
then considers the fall from grace when the alkaloid mescaline
is isolated from its botanical home and abruptly placed in the
limited minds of Western experimenters. He explores the
possibilities of transcending the ego with the aid of mescaline
and the pitfalls inherent in its manichean nature. He then
contrasts its effects with those of the 'Luciferian' and 'sensual'
hashish.

The Poet's Paradise by Robert Graves (1895–1985) is a written
version of an address given whilst he was a visiting professor of
poetry at the University of Oxford. In it he explores the
possibility that there was a common drug experience behind
the notion of paradise as described in the Bible, the Epic of
Gilgamesh, and the various mythologies of Greece, Polynesia
and pre-Columbian Mexico. He pays particular attention to the
cultural role of magic mushrooms (*Psilocybe, Panaeolus* spp.)
and the fly-agaric toadstool (*Amanita muscaria*) and describes
his own experiences with the *Psilocybe*. In 1960 he took the
mushroom in the company of R. Gordon Wasson, a New York
banker who was also an expert on hallucinogenic fungi. As
they partook of the mushroom they listened to a tape-
recording of the chants of Maria Sabina, the Mexican-Indian
medicine woman who had initiated Wasson into its mysteries.
Graves goes on to consider society's acceptance of the
'mundane' drugs such as alcohol, tobacco and tranquillisers,
and its suppression of the hallucinogens. He concludes by
contrasting the 'passive' trance induced by the mushroom with
the 'active' poetic trance and states his preference for the latter.
In *Drugs that Shape Men's Minds* Aldous Huxley (1894–1963)
explores some of the same themes as Graves, for example the
contrast between alcohol and tranquillisers on the one hand
and hallucinogens like mescaline and LSD on the other. He
speculates with remarkable lucidity on the possible drugs of the
future and puts forward his belief that a religious revival is
more likely to come about through the use of mind-expanding
drugs than through TV evangelism.

Twentieth-century history of hallucinogen use entered a new era with the rise to fame of Timothy Leary, the 'High Priest of LSD'. *Timothy Leary, LSD and Harvard* is taken from Stewart Tendler's and David May's definitive account of the so-called hippie Mafia, the LSD-dealing organisation *The Brotherhood of Eternal Love*. In this extract they describe Leary's encounter with the magic mushroom and his subsequent Harvard research project on psilocybin produced by Sandoz laboratories in Switzerland (where Albert Hofmann had discovered LSD). Among the volunteers were William Burroughs, Allen Ginsberg, Alan Watts, Aldous Huxley and Arthur Koestler. The authors then follow the trail to Leary's Boston commune, his subsequent expulsion from Harvard and his flight from the authorities. Whilst Leary was busy in the States, Terence McKenna, another explorer of the world of hallucinogens, was experimenting 'in the head nests of hippie Asia'. *Kathmandu Interlude*, from Terence McKenna's Amazonian drug odyssey *True Hallucinations*, is a literary flashback by the author to Nepal in 1969 and some seminal experiences with hashish, LSD and *Datura metel*, culminating in a sexual crescendo on DMT which involved the creation of an ectoplasmic obsidian fluid. In *The Other Cary Grant*, interviewer Warren Hoge talks to the actor about his use of LSD under medical supervision. Grant's frank and positive views about his experiences give an insight into the drug from a decidedly unexpected source.

Mescal: A New Artificial Paradise
Havelock Ellis

It has been known for some years that the Kiowa Indians of New Mexico are accustomed to eat, in their religious ceremonies, a certain cactus called Anhalonium Lewinii, or mescal button. Mescal – which must not be confounded with the intoxicating drink of the same name made from an agave – is found in the Mexican valley of the Rio Grande, the ancestral home of the Kiowa Indians, as well as in Texas, and is a brown and brittle substance, nauseous and bitter to the taste, composed mainly of the blunt dried leaves of the plant. Yet, as we shall see, it has every claim to rank with haschisch and the other famous drugs which have procured for men the joys of an artificial paradise. Upon the Kiowa Indians, who first discovered its rare and potent virtues, it has had so strong a fascination that the missionaries among these Indians, finding here a rival to Christianity not yielding to moral suasion, have appealed to the secular arm, and the buying and selling of the drug has been prohibited by Government under severe penalties. Yet the use of mescal prevails among the Kiowas to this day.

It has indeed spread, and the mescal rite may be said to be today the chief religion of all the tribes of the Southern plains of the United States. The rite usually takes place on Saturday night; the men then sit in a circle within the tent round a large campfire, which is kept burning brightly all the time. After prayer the leader hands each man four buttons, which are slowly chewed and swallowed, and altogether about ten or twelve buttons are consumed by each man between sundown and daybreak. Throughout the night the men sit quietly round the fire in a state of reverie – amid continual singing and the beating of drums by attendants – absorbed in the colour visions and other manifestations of mescal intoxication, and about noon on the following day, when the effects have passed off, they get up and go about their business, without any depression or other unpleasant after-effect.

There are five or six allied species of cacti which the Indians also use and treat with great reverence. Thus Mr. Carl Lumholtz has found that the Tarahumari, a tribe of Mexican Indians, worship various cacti as gods, only to be approached with uncovered heads. When they wish to obtain these cacti, the Tarahumari cense themselves with copal incense, and with profound respect dig up the god, careful lest they should hurt him, while women and children are warned from the spot. Even Christian Indians regard Hikori, the cactus god, as co-equal with their own divinity, and make the sign of the cross in its presence. At all great festivals, Hikori is made into a drink and consumed by the medicine man, or certain selected Indians, who sing as they partake of it, invoking Hikori to grant a 'beautiful intoxication;' at the same time a rasping noise is made with sticks, and men and women dance a fantastic and picturesque dance – the women by themselves in white petticoats and tunics – before those who are under the influence of the god.

In 1891 Mr. James Mooney, of the United States Bureau of Ethnology, having frequently observed the mescal rites of the Kiowa Indians and assisted at them, called the attention of the Anthropological Society at Washington to the subject, and three years later he brought to Washington a supply of mescal, which was handed over for examination to Drs. Prentiss and Morgan. These investigators experimented on several young men, and demonstrated, for the first time, the precise character of mescal intoxication and the remarkable visions to which it gives rise. A little later Dr. Weir Mitchell, who, in addition to his eminence as a physician, is a man of marked æsthetic temperament, experimented on himself, and published a very interesting record of the brilliant visions by which he was visited under the influence of the plant. In the spring of the past year I was able to obtain a small sample of mescal in London, and as my first experiment with mescal was also, apparently, the first attempt to investigate its vision-producing properties outside America,[1] I will describe it in some detail, in preference to drawing on the previously published descriptions of the American observers.

On Good Friday I found myself entirely alone in the quiet rooms in the Temple which I occupy when in London, and judged the occasion a fitting one for a personal experiment. I made a decoction (a different method from that adopted in America) of three buttons, the full physiological dose, and drank this at intervals between 2.30 and 4.30 P.M. The first symptom observed during the afternoon was a certain consciousness of energy and intellectual power.[2] This passed off, and about an hour after the final dose I felt faint and unsteady; the pulse was low, and I found it pleasanter to lie down. I was still able to read, and I noticed that a pale violet shadow floated over the page around the point at which my eyes were fixed. I had already noticed that objects not in the direct line of vision, such as my hands holding the book, showed a tendency to look obtrusive, heightened in colour, almost monstrous, while, on closing my eyes, after-images were vivid and prolonged. The appearance of visions with closed eyes was very gradual. At first there was

[1] Lewin, of Berlin, indeed, experimented with Anhalonium Lewinii, to which he gave its name, as early as 1888, and as he found that even a small portion produced dangerous symptoms, he classed it amongst the extremely poisonous drugs, like strychnia. He failed to discover its vision-producing properties, and it seems, in fact, highly probable that he was really experimenting with a different cactus from that now known by the same name.
[2] I pass lightly over the purely physiological symptoms which I have described in some detail in a paper on 'The Phenomena of Mescal Intoxication' (*Lancet*, June 5, 1897), which, however, contains no description of the visions.

merely a vague play of light and shade, which suggested pictures, but never made them. Then the pictures became more definite, but too confused and crowded to be described, beyond saying that they were of the same character as the images of the kaleidoscope, symmetrical groupings of spiked objects. Then, in the course of the evening, they became distinct, but still indescribable – mostly a vast field of golden jewels, studded with red and green stones, ever changing. This moment was, perhaps, the most delightful of the experience, for at the same time the air around me seemed to be flushed with vague perfume – producing with the visions a delicious effect – and all discomfort had vanished, except a slight faintness and tremor of the hands, which, later on, made it almost impossible to guide a pen as I made notes of the experiment; it was, however, with an effort, always possible to write with a pencil. The visions never resembled familiar objects; they were extremely definite, but yet always novel; they were constantly approaching, and yet constantly eluding, the semblance of known things. I would see thick glorious fields of jewels, solitary or clustered, sometimes brilliant and sparkling, sometimes with a dull rich glow. Then they would spring up into flower-like shapes beneath my gaze, and then seem to turn into gorgeous butterfly forms or endless folds of glistening, iridescent, fibrous wings of wonderful insects; while sometimes I seemed to be gazing into a vast hollow revolving vessel, on whose polished concave mother-of-pearl surface the hues were swiftly changing. I was surprised, not only by the enormous profusion of the imagery presented to my gaze, but still more by its variety. Perpetually some totally new kind of effect would appear in the field of vision; sometimes there was swift movement, sometimes dull, sombre richness of colour, sometimes glitter and sparkle, once a startling rain of gold, which seemed to approach me. Most usually there was a combination of rich sober colour, with jewel-like points of brilliant hue. Every colour and tone conceivable to me appeared at some time or another. Sometimes all the different varieties of one colour, as of red – with scarlets, crimsons, pinks – would spring up together, or in quick succession. But in spite of this immense profusion, there was always a certain parsimony and æsthetic value in the colours presented. They were usually associated with form, and never appeared in large masses, or, if so, the tone was very delicate. I was further impressed, not only by the brilliance, delicacy, and variety of the colours, but even more by their lovely and various texture – fibrous, woven, polished, glowing, dull, veined, semi-transparent – the glowing effects, as of jewels, and the fibrous, as of insects' wings, being perhaps the most prevalent. Although the effects were novel, it frequently happened, as I have already mentioned, that they vaguely recalled known objects. Thus, once the objects presented to me seemed to be made of exquisite porcelain, again they were like elaborate sweetmeats, again of a somewhat Maori style or architecture, and the background of the pictures frequently recalled, both in form and tone, the delicate architectural effects, as of lace carved in wood, which we associate with the *mouchrabieh* work of Cairo. But always the visions grew and changed without any reference to the characteristics of those real objects of which they vaguely reminded me, and when I tried to influence their course it was with very little success. On the whole, I should say that the images were most usually what might be called living arabesques. There was often a certain incomplete tendency to symmetry, as though the underlying mechanism was associated with a large number of polished facets. The same image was in this way frequently repeated over a large part of the field; but this refers more to form than to colour, in respect to which there would still be all sorts of delightful varieties, so that if, with a certain uniformity, jewel-like flowers were springing up and expanding all over the field of vision, they would still show every variety of delicate tone and tint.

Weir Mitchell found that he could only see the visions with closed eyes and in a perfectly dark room. I could see them in the dark with almost equal facility, though they were not of equal brilliancy, when my eyes were wide open. I saw them best, however, when my eyes were closed, in a room lighted only by flickering firelight. This evidently accords with the experience of the Indians, who keep a fire burning brightly throughout their mescal rites.

The visions continued with undiminished brilliance for many hours, and, as I felt somewhat faint and muscularly weak, I went to bed, as I undressed being greatly impressed by the red, scaly, bronzed, and pigmented appearance of my limbs whenever I was not directly gazing at them. I had not the faintest desire for sleep; there was a general hyperæsthesia of all the senses as well as muscular irritability, and every slightest sound seemed magnified to startling dimensions. I may also have been kept awake by a vague alarm at the novelty of my condition, and the possibility of further developments.

After watching the visions in the dark for some hours I became a little tired of them and turned on the gas. Then I found that I was able to study a new series of visual phenomena, to which previous observers had made no reference. The gas jet (an ordinary flickering burner) seemed to burn with great brilliance, sending out waves of light, which expanded and contracted in an enormously exaggerated manner. I was even more impressed by the shadows, which were in all directions heightened by flushes of red, green, and especially violet. The whole room, with its white-washed but not very white ceiling, thus became vivid and beautiful. The difference between the room as I saw it then and the appearance it usually presents to me was the difference one may often observe between the picture of a room and the actual room. The shadows I saw were the shadows which the artist puts in, but which are not visible in the actual sense under normal conditions of casual inspection. I was reminded of the paintings of Claude Monet, and as I gazed at the scene it occurred to me that mescal perhaps produces exactly the same conditions of visual hyperæsthesia, or rather exhaustion, as may be produced on the artist by the influence of prolonged visual attention. I wished to ascertain how the subdued and steady electric light would influence vision, and passed into the next room; but here the shadows were little marked, although walls and floor seemed tremulous and insubstantial, and the texture of everything was heightened and enriched.

About 3.30 A.M. I felt that the phenomena were distinctly diminishing – though the visions, now chiefly of human figures, fantastic and Chinese in character, still continued – and I was able to settle myself to sleep, which proved peaceful and dreamless. I awoke at the usual hour and experienced no sense of fatigue, nor other unpleasant reminiscence of the experience I had undergone. Only my eyes seemed unusually sensitive to colour, especially blue and violet; I can, indeed, say that ever since this experience I have been more æsthetically sensitive than I was before to the more delicate phenomena of light and shade and colour.

It occurred to me that it would be interesting to have the experiences of an artist under the influence of mescal, and I induced an artist friend to make a similar experiment. Unfortunately no effects whatever were produced at the first attempt, owing, as I have since discovered, to the fact that the buttons had only been simply infused and their virtues not extracted. To make sure of success the experiment was repeated with four buttons, which proved to be an excessive and unpleasant dose. There were paroxysmal attacks of pain at the heart and a sense of imminent death, which naturally alarmed the subject, while so great was the dread of light and dilation of the pupils that the eyelids had to be kept more or less closed, though it was evident that a certain amount of vision was still possible. The symptoms came on very suddenly, and when I arrived they were already at their height. As the experiences of this subject were in many respects very unlike mine, I will give them in his own words: 'I noticed first that as I happened to turn my eyes away from a blue enamel kettle at which I had been unconsciously looking, and which was standing in the fender of the fireplace, with no fire in it, it seemed to me that I saw a spot of the same blue in the black coals of the grate, and that this spot appeared again, further off, a little brighter in hue. But I was in doubt whether I had not imagined these blue spots. When, however, I lifted my eyes to the mantelpiece, on which were scattered all sorts of odds and ends, all doubt was over. I saw an intensely vivid blue light begin to play around every object. A square cigarette-box, violet in colour, shone like an amethyst. I turned my eyes away, and beheld this time, on the back of a polished chair, a bar of colour glowing like a ruby. Although I was expecting some such manifestation as one of the first symptoms of the intoxication, I was nevertheless somewhat alarmed when this phenomenon took place. Such a silent and sudden illumination of all things around, where a moment before I had seen nothing uncommon, seemed like a kind of madness beginning from outside me, and its strangeness affected me more than its beauty. A desire to escape from it led me to the door, and the act of moving had, I noticed, the effect of dispelling the colours. But a sudden difficulty in breathing and a sensation of numbness at the heart brought me back to the arm-chair from which I had risen. From this moment I had a series of attacks or paroxysms, which I can only describe by saying that I felt as though I were dying. It was impossible to move, and it seemed almost impossible to breathe. My speedy dissolution, I half imagined, was about to take place, and the power of making any resistance to the violent sensations that were arising within was going, I felt, with every second.

'The first paroxysms were the most violent. They would come on with tinglings in the lower limbs, and with the sensation of a nauseous and suffocating gas mounting up into my head. Two or three times this was accompanied by a colour vision of the gas bursting into flame as it passed up my throat. But I seldom had visions during the paroxysms; these would appear in the intervals. They began with a spurting up of colours; once, of a flood of brightly illuminated green water covering the field of vision, and effervescing in parts, just as when fresh water with all the air-bubbles is pumped into a swimming bath. At another time my eye seemed to be turning into a vast drop of dirty water in which millions of minute creatures resembling tadpoles were in motion. But the early visions consisted mostly of a furious succession of coloured arabesques, arising and descending or sliding at every possible angle into the field of view. It would be as difficult as to give a description of the whirl of water at the bottom of a waterfall as to describe the chaos of colour and design which marked this period.

'Now also began another series of extraordinary sensations. They set in with bewildering suddenness and followed one another in rapid succession. These I now record as they occur to my mind at haphazard: (1) My right leg became suddenly heavy and solid; it seemed indeed as if the entire weight of my body had shifted into one part, about the thigh and knee, and that the rest of my body had lost all substantiality. (2) With the suddenness of a neuralgic pang, the back of my head seemed to open and emit streams of bright colour; this was immediately followed by the feeling as of a draught blowing like a gale through the hair in the same region. (3) At one moment the colour, green, acquired a taste in my mouth; it was sweetish and somewhat metallic. Blue, again, would have a taste that seemed to recall phosphorus. These are the only colours that seemed to be connected with taste. (4) A feeling of delightful relief and preternatural lightness about my forehead, succeeded by a growing sensation of contraction. (5) Singing in one of my ears. (6) A sensation of burning heat in the palm of my left hand. (7) Heat about both eyes. The last continued throughout the whole period, except for a moment when I had a sensation of cold upon the eyelids, accompanied with a colour vision of the wrinkled lid, of the skin disappearing from the brow, of dead flesh, and finally of a skull.

'Throughout these sensations and visions my mind remained not only perfectly clear, but enjoyed, I believe, an unusual lucidity. Certainly I was conscious of an odd contrast in hearing myself talk rationally with H. E., who had entered the room a short time before, and experiencing at the same moment the wild and extraordinary pranks that were taking place in my body. My reason appeared to be the sole survivor of my being. At times I felt that this, too, would go, but the sound of my own voice would establish again the communication with the outer world of reality.

'Tremors were more or less constant in my lower limbs. Persistent, also, was the feeling of nausea. This, when attended by a feeling of suffocation and a pain at the heart, was relieved by taking brandy, coffee, or biscuit. For muscular exertion I felt neither the wish nor the power. My hands, however, retained their full strength.

'It was painful for me to keep my eyes open above a few seconds; the light of day seemed to fill the room with a blinding glare. Yet every object, in the brief glimpse I caught, appeared normal in colour and shape. With my eyes closed, most of the visions, after the first chaotic display, represented parts or the whole of my body undergoing a variety of marvellous changes, of metamorphoses or illumination. They were more often than not comic and grotesque in character, though often beautiful in colour. At one time I saw my right leg filling up with a delicate heliotrope; at another the sleeve of my coat changed into a dark green material in which was worked a pattern in red braid, and the whole bordered at the cuff with sable. Scarcely had my new sleeve taken shape than I found myself attired in a complete costume of the same fashion, mediæval in character, but I could not say to what precise period it belonged. I noted that a chance movement – of my hand, for instance – would immediately call up a colour vision of the part exerted, and that this again would pass, by a seemingly natural transition, into another wholly dissimilar. Thus, pressing my fingers accidentally against my temples, the finger-tips became elongated, and then grew into the ribs of a vaulting or of a dome-shaped roof. But most of the visions were of a more personal nature. I happened once to lift a spoonful of coffee to my lips, and as I was in the act of raising my arm for that purpose, a vision flashed before my closed (or nearly closed) eyes, in all the hues of the rainbow, of my arm separated from my body, and serving me with coffee from out of dark and indefinite space. On another occasion, as I was seeking to relieve slight nausea by taking a piece of biscuit, passed to me by H. E., it suddenly streamed out into blue flame. For an instant I held the biscuit close to my leg. Immediately my trouser caught alight, and then the whole of the right side of my body, from the foot to the shoulder, was enveloped in waving blue flame. It was a sight of wonderful beauty. But this was not all. As I placed the biscuit in my mouth it burst out again into the same coloured fire and illuminated the interior of my mouth, casting a blue reflection on the roof. The light of the Blue Grotto at Capri, I am able to affirm, is not nearly as blue as seemed for a short space of time the interior of my mouth. There were many visions of which I could not trace the origin. There were spirals and arabesques and flowers, and sometimes objects more trivial and prosaic in character. In one vision I saw a row of small white flowers, one against the other like pearls of a necklace, begin to revolve in the form of a spiral. Every flower, I observed, had the texture of porcelain. It was at a moment when I had the sensation of my cheeks growing hot and fever-ish that I experienced the strangest of all the colour visions. It began with feeling that the skin of my face was becoming quite thin and of no stouter consistency than tissue paper, and the feeling was suddenly enhanced by a vision of my face, paper-like and semi-transparent and somewhat reddish in colour. To my amazement I saw myself as though I were inside a Chinese lantern, looking *out through my cheek* into the room. Not long after this I became conscious of a change in the visions. Their *tempo* was more moderate, they were less frequent, and they were losing somewhat in distinctness. At the same time the feeling of nausea and of numbness was departing. A short period followed in which I had no visions at all, and experi-enced merely a sensation of heaviness and torpor. I found that I was able to open my eyes again and keep them fixed on any object in the room without observing the faintest blue halo or prism, or bar of glowing colour, and that, moreover, no visions appeared on closing them. It was now twilight, but beyond the fact of not seeing light or colour either without or within, I had a distinct feeling that the action of the drug was at an end and that my body had become sober, suddenly. I had no more visions, though I was not wholly free from abnormal sensations, and I retired to rest. I lay awake till the morning, and with the exception of the following night, I scarcely slept for the next three days, but I cannot say that I felt any signs of fatigue, unless perhaps, on one of the days when my eyes, I noticed, became very susceptible to any indications of blue in an object. Of colour visions, or of any approach to colour visions, there was no further trace; but all sorts of odd and grotesque images passed in succession through my mind during part of the first night. They might have been the dreams of a Baudelaire or of an Aubrey Beardsley. I would see figures with prodigious limbs, or strangely dwarfed and curtailed, or impossible combinations such as five or six fish, the colour of canaries, floating about in air in a gold wire cage. But these were purely mental images, like the visions seen in a dream by a distempered brain.

'Of the many sensations of which my body had been the theatre during three hours, not the least strange was the feeling I experienced on coming back into a normal condition. The recovery did not proceed gradually, but the whole outer and inner world of reality came back, as it were, with a bound. And for a moment it seemed strange. It was the sensation – only much intensified – which every one has known on coming out into the light of day from an afternoon performance at a theatre, where one has sat in an artificial light of gas and lamps, the spectator of a fictitious world of action. As one pours out with the crowd into the street, the ordinary world, by force of contrast with the sensational scenes just witnessed, breaks in upon one with almost a sense of unreality. The house, the aspect of the street, even the light of day appear a little foreign for a few moments. During these moments everything strikes the mind as odd and unfamiliar, or at least with a greater degree of objectivity. Such was my feeling with regard to my old and habitual self. During the period of intoxication, the connection between the

normal condition of my body and my intelligence had broken –
my body had become in a manner a stranger to my reason – so
that now on reasserting itself it seemed, with reference to my
reason, which had remained perfectly sane and alert, for a
moment sufficiently unfamiliar for me to become conscious of its
individual and peculiar character. It was as if I had unexpectedly
attained an objective knowledge of my own personality. I saw, as
it were, my normal state of being with the eyes of a person who
sees the street on coming out of the theatre in broad day.

'This sensation also brought out the independence of the
mind during the period of intoxication. It alone appeared to
have escaped the ravages of the drug; it alone remained sane
during a general delirium, vindicating, so it seemed, the majesty
of its own impersonal nature. It had reigned for a while, I now
felt, as an autocrat, without ministers and their officiousness.
Henceforth I should be more or less conscious of the interde-
pendence of the body and brain; a slight headache, a touch of
indigestion, or what not, would be able to effect what a general
intoxication of my senses and nerves could not touch.'

I next made experiments on two poets, whose names are
both well known. One is interested in mystical matters, an
excellent subject for visions, and very familiar with various
vision-producing drugs and processes. His heart, however, is
not very strong. While he obtained the visions, he found the
effects of mescal on his breathing somewhat unpleasant; he
much prefers haschisch, though recognising that its effects are
much more difficult to obtain. The other enjoys admirable
health, and under the influence of mescal he experienced
scarcely the slightest unpleasant reaction, but, on the contrary,
a very marked state of well-being and beatitude. He took somewhat less than three buttons, so that the results were rather less
marked than in my case, but they were perfectly definite. He
writes: 'I have never seen a succession of absolutely pictorial
visions with such precision and such unaccountability. It seemed
as if a series of dissolving views were carried swiftly before me,
all going from right to left, none corresponding with any seen

reality. For instance, I saw the most delightful dragons, puffing out their breath straight in front of them like rigid lines of steam, and balancing white balls at the end of their breath! When I tried to fix my mind on real things, I could generally call them up, but always with some inexplicable change. Thus, I called up a particular monument in Westminster Abbey, but in front of it, to the left, knelt a figure in Florentine costume, like some one out of a picture of Botticelli; and I *could not* see the tomb without also seeing this figure. Late in the evening I went out on the Embankment, and was absolutely fascinated by an advertisement of "Bovril," which went and came in letters of light on the other side of the river; I cannot tell you the intense pleasure this moving light gave me, and how dazzling it seemed to me. Two girls and a man passed me, laughing loudly, and lolling about as they walked. I realised, intellectually, their coarseness, but visually I saw them, as they came under a tree, fall into the lines of a delicate picture; it might have been an Albert Moore. After coming in I played the piano with closed eyes, and got waves and lines of pure colour, almost always without form, though I saw one or two appearances which might have been shields or breastplates – pure gold, studded with small jewels in intricate patterns. All the time I had no unpleasant feelings whatever, except a very slight headache, which came and went. I slept soundly and without dreams.'

The results of music in the case just quoted – together with the habit of the Indians to combine the drum with mescal rites, and my own observation that very slight jarring or stimulation of the scalp would affect the visions – suggested to me to test the influence of music on myself. I therefore once more put myself under the influence of mescal (taking a somewhat smaller dose than on the first occasion), and lay for some hours on a couch with my head more or less in contact with the piano, and with closed eyes directed towards a subdued light, while a friend played, making various tests, of his own devising, which were not explained to me until afterwards. I was to watch the visions in a purely passive manner, without seeking to direct them, nor was I to think about the music, which, so far as possible, was unknown to me. The music stimulated the visions and added greatly to my enjoyment of them. It seemed to harmonise with them, and, as it were, support and bear them up. A certain persistence and monotony of character in the music was required in order to affect the visions, which then seemed to fall into harmony with it, and any sudden change in the character of the music would blur the visions, as though clouds passed between them and me. The chief object of the tests was to ascertain how far a desire on the composer's part to suggest definite imagery would affect my visions. In about half the cases there was no resemblance, in the other half there was a distinct resemblance which was sometimes very remarkable. This was especially the case with Schumann's music, for example with his *Waldscenen* and *Kinderscenen*; thus 'The Prophet Bird' called up vividly a sense of atmosphere and of brilliant feathery bird-like forms passing to and fro; 'A Flower Piece' provoked constant and persistent images of vegetation; while 'Scheherazade' produced an effect of floating white raiment, covered by glittering spangles and jewels. In every case my description was, of course, given before I knew the name of the piece. I do not pretend that this single series of experiments proves much, but it would certainly be worth while to follow up this indication and to ascertain if any light is hereby thrown on the power of a composer to suggest definite imagery, or the power of a listener to perceive it.

It would be out of place here to discuss the obscure question as to the underlying mechanism by which mescal exerts its magic powers. It is clear from the foregoing descriptions that mescal intoxication may be described as chiefly a saturnalia of the specific senses, and, above all, an orgy of vision. It reveals an optical fairyland, where all the senses now and again join the play, but the mind itself remains a self-possessed spectator. Mescal intoxication thus differs from the other artificial paradises which drugs procure. Under the influence of alcohol, for instance, as in normal dreaming, the intellect is impaired, although there may be a consciousness of unusual brilliance; haschisch, again, produces an uncontrollable tendency to movement and bathes its victim in a sea of emotion. The mescal drinker remains calm and collected amid the sensory turmoil around him; his judgment is as clear as in the normal state; he falls into no oriental condition of vague and voluptuous reverie. The reason why mescal is of all this class of drugs the most purely intellectual in its appeal is evidently because it affects mainly the most intellectual of the senses. On this ground it is not probable that its use will easily develop into a habit. Moreover, unlike most other intoxicants, it seems to have no special affinity for a disordered and unbalanced nervous system; on the contrary, it demands organic soundness and good health for the complete manifestation of its virtues.[1] Further, unlike the other chief substances to which it may be compared, mescal does not wholly carry us away from the actual world, or plunge us into oblivion; a large part of its charm lies in the halo of beauty which it casts around the simplest and commonest things. It is the most democratic of the plants which lead man to an artificial paradise. If it should ever chance that the consumption of mescal becomes a habit, the favourite poet of the mescal drinker will certainly be Wordsworth. Not only the general attitude of Wordsworth, but many of his most memorable poems and phrases cannot – one is almost tempted to say – be appreciated in their full significance by one who has never been under the influence of mescal. On all these grounds it may be claimed that the artificial paradise of mescal, though less seductive, is safe and dignified beyond its peers.

At the same time it must be remembered that at present we are able to speak on a basis of but very small experience, so far as civilised men are concerned. The few observations recorded

---

[1] It is true, as many persons do not need to be reminded, that in neurasthenia and states of over-fatigue, symptoms closely resembling the slight and earlier phenomena of mescal intoxication are not uncommon; but in such cases there is rarely any sense of well-being and enjoyment.

in America and my own experiments in England do not enable us to say anything regarding the habitual consumption of mescal in large amounts. That such consumption would be gravely injurious I cannot doubt. Its safeguard seems to lie in the fact that a certain degree of robust health is required to obtain any real enjoyment from its visionary gifts. It may at least be claimed that for a healthy person to be once or twice admitted to the rites of mescal is not only an unforgettable delight but an educational influence of no mean value.

Hallucinogenic Drugs and the Problem of Eros

Henri Michaux

Peyote, when it was rediscovered in Mexico at the end of the last century, along with the cult surrounding it, had a restricted, exclusive and religious function.

Rare were the tribes that still used it: the Huichols, the Tarahumaras.

Once a year the Huichols would journey to the remote and bare desert plateaux where it is to be found. They went there in order to come face to face with the divine.

Plant for the ignorant, *Echinoccactus Williamsii* for the botanist, peyote for him who knows, is god, a god who portions out his divinity. Indeed, it is eaten, imbibed, consumed and then the deifying god appears shortly after, in supernatural lights . . . in a kind of promise and foretaste of immortality, of everlastingness, and also in colours of every shade, possessing a brilliance and a subtlety that man, left merely to his imagination, is patently incapable of.

> *After eating of a cactus, the Mexicans received a god as their apportionment.*
>
> *Peyote the divinising divine.*

Such was the use for which peyote was destined at that time:

it was religious, mystical (the practice of a people for whom most things are linked and significant); it was, above all, naturally appropriate that a plant which makes it possible for the divine[1] to be attained, and which is almost the bearer of the divine, should be so used.

Indeed, all that constitutes religious emotion is combined in the effect of the plant: the profound impression of being mysteriously linked to everything, the profound impression of beyondness, of for-ever-ness, the profound impression of living a life outside the body, and outside time, of participating in the absolute, in the Perpetual.

God, and meeting-place of the gods, peyote, for the Huichol, 'the cup from which the god of fire drinks[2]', is brought by 'our elder brother, Fat Hicouri, who goes in all places[3]', god of air, that is to say, the wind. In relation to the rain and to the corn, peyote is still a stag or a deer.

In a more remote yesteryear, before occupation by the oppressors come from the West, peyote was used on the morning of battles, when war amongst them was still something sacred. The impression of immortality, of invulnerability, made them go off to fight with an incomparable fearlessness, and if it nevertheless happened that they died on the battlefield, it was that they might become, more certainly than any other warrior, 'companions of the eagle', that is to say, 'companions of the sun'.

---

the impression of immortality

the impression of invulnerability in battle

impression of unceasing, unstoppable prolongation.

---

[1] A *luminous* divine which was bound to have repercussions in a country which had always had a cult of the sun and of numerous stellar divinities (the luminous ones, the *devi*, was also the first name that the Hindus gave to the gods).

[2] and [3] ROUHIER. *Le peyotl: la plante qui fait les yeux émerveilles.*

For some, peyote uncovered things which were hidden or remote, or it opened up time to them, making it possible to see events yet to come. Was there any other kind of intoxication? We do not know. Perhaps. Was it sometimes mixed with certain substances? Surely not (or if so, only recently) with alcohol[1]. Intoxication caused by alcohol, far from being considered 'divine' by the Aztec emperors (they did not make such a mistake), was severely punished by them as being extremely harmful.

According to Lhumoltz[2] who, around 1890, was able to accompany a group of Huichols and observe them on the spot, when the 'religious' effect of peyote on the pilgrim was not obtained, owing, so it was thought then, to its being badly prepared, this was hardly to be noticed except by untimely fits of laughter, confused agitation, cries and mad sprints.

Rites so as to be pure to consume the spiritualizing plant.

The women had been left behind in the village and, even before setting out, continence was observed. The pilgrims had been purified and several of them had confessed their sins (by way of the great Mexican confession which gave absolution from everything but which could only be made once in the

---

[1] According to SAHAGUN (*Histoire générale de las Casas de Nueva Espana*, vol. 1, p. 185 and vol. 11, p. 99 *sqq*, quoted by Jacques SOUSTELLE, *La vie quotidienne des Azteques*, 1955), alcohol was held in abomination.

'This drink, declared the Emperor, addressing the people on the day of his enthronement, this drink which is called "octli" (now *pulque*, fermented agave sap) is the root and origin of all evil and all perdition. From drunkenness proceed rape, the corruption of maidens, incest, theft, crimes, curses and the bearing of false witness, culumnies and brawling.'

The punishments were terrible. Examples: '. . . a drunken man walking along singing or in the company of other drunken men, if he was a plebian he was punished by being thrashed until he died, or else he was strangled in front of the young people of the neighbourhood, to serve as an example. If the drunken man was a noble he was secretly strangled.'

[2] Carl LHUMOLTZ, *Indians of Mexico*, 1890.

course of a lifetime). Most foods were abstained from, in order to be 'pure in body and spirit[1]'.

As for Soma in India, there was a guiding ritual which, without being anywhere near so meticulously constructed, served to provide a certain spiritual setting. Moreover, the believer was always himself surrounded by other members of the faithful who often bore the insignia of officiants.

Everything impeded any form of personal distraction.

Western Man appeared. Reappeared. Western man is of a completely different type. Without arms this time, but still an adventurer, greedy no longer for gold or the propagation of his religion, but for knowledge now, his new big thing. Still excited, still profanatory, but in a different way: a stranger to piety who drags impiety along with him, an outsider who, no longer expecting anything other than the profane, remains an outsider, seeing everything profanely.

Immediately become deconsecrated, peyote still had a part to play.

Fallen from its high estate, the midget nopal was still to reveal worlds to them. It had not finished. It refused to be made mediocre. Shortly after, however, not finding it strong enough, despite its being a god, they experimented on it to such an extent that a much stronger one was extracted from it.

Condensed, peyote becomes mescaline.

Changed into mescaline, peyote, its cult abandoned, yet still the purest of divinogenics, no longer revealed its divine nature[2]

---

[1] In the words of Rouhier.

[2] Recently in America hundreds of religious experiments have been carried out, based on the use of mescaline and lysergic acid.

After a process of questioning – and even of investigation – a selection is made from amongst the candidates, and those who have been chosen are prepared for the great liberation.

And yet, there is something funny about all this. When one reads of any quite so readily. Nevertheless, it never abandoned completely its power of infinitization, revealing it clearly to those who know how to see, and revealing it indirectly and, as it were, treacherously, to those taking it in order to have a good time.

Indeed, it is not to everything that the infinite can be imparted, just like that, nor is everything an interesting object of infinitization. Suddenly, by surprise, in the midst of an inoffensive sequence, the confident and idle spectator was all at once mysteriously 'thrown into gear' and found himself dragged off at an insane speed, incapable of extricating himself from the maddening process tormenting him, incapable of getting out of the infernal, invisible vehicle carrying him away.

Let me repeat that it is only through the state of trance that peyote and mescaline have any real value. The rest is imagery, distraction, division, movement that makes no headway, the raking over of the same territory, transports, fits of impatience, disharmonies, skids, reversals, scatterings, samplings, infernal concatenations which finally add up to destruction. Destruction on account of not reaching the state of trance, that state which is the only viable one to be found under drugs and which makes drugs superior and not of shattering effect, not infinitely disconcerting.

What is ecstasy? It is an exceptional oneness in the soul to a degree where it appears miraculous, a uniformity without the tiniest or most minute deviation. If there appear images or a sequence of ideas, if any of these become conscious, they will

of the neophytes' accounts of their experiences (which have even appeared on a book), one is often dumbfounded before the flagrant lack of elevation, of interiority, of exigency, and by the lack of consciousness involved in speaking like salesmen or M.C.s in the name of infinite Love, the ego-less Life and Illumination.

Like journalists invited to the Crucifixion.

This new object of scandal and disgust in the matter of religion provides some food for thought.

To be consulted: *Psychedelic Review* (Cambridge, Mass.), a useful source of critical information, and *Joyous Cosmology*, one of the valid books on this subject, written by the philosopher Alan Watts.

pass into a univocal harmony whence all ambivalence, opposition, censure and heterogeneity is totaly banished, where even the most banal relationship with otherness is completely imperceptible, a state which sets everything at the same level, beyond measurement, beyond appreciation or depreciation, a oneness unthinkable to him who has not known it, even if it were to be described one hundred times, for all description is bound to fall short. Here is a concentrate unparalleled, autonomous, possessed of its own momentum, which cannot be stopped.

The ecstatic trance

Overwhelmed by a perfect oneness

This ecstasy is only possible on condition that fervour and expansive feeling are vast, that the object of ecstasy is transformed from that which is limited to that which is unlimited, becomes no longer personal but impersonal, and that one of the major paths is followed, those paths that lead to the great human exaltations; and in this way the fervour and expansiveness become either the impulse of love with the self given up, or the heroic impulse, fearlessness, with all care and self-preservation forgotten, or lastly, the impulse towards total comprehension and illumination (by way of vacuity, being purged of the ego).

In these fundamental and primitive exaltations I have never encountered[1] the impulse of hatred, nor has anyone of my acquaintance. It must be unusual, rarely felt in its full force, less

[1] It seems more than unlikely that plentitude through hatred should still not be revealed. I am thinking of certain of the mentally deranged who are possessed by a destructive frenzy and of one in particular whom I saw tied in such a way as to be completely powerless and in whom there dwelt such a concentration of hatred that his gaze, unsullied by any other feeling, was, in the strictest meaning of the word, unbearable. Bullets seemed fired from his eyes of flint. It was a pure hatred, horrible to see, and to which nothing could be fruitfully opposed, a hatred in all likelihood corresponding to a totalitarian state of mind.

overwhelming by its nature than I would have thought, and more fragmentary, provisional and transitory than it appears in life and even than it appears in the subconscious. The drug might, however, be suitably tried out, in massive quantities, upon any of those unruly ones who devote their lives to maleficence and who never give up revenging themselves upon others and upon society. There would perhaps be some surprises.

It is (curiously enough) fear rather than hatred which lies in wait for those whom love has not satisfied and which slyly takes up position deep within them and which will be brought into the open one day by an accident or a drug or some serious misadventure, surprising everyone by its appearance. Fear will become strangely present in the form of persecution mania and phobias, bringing back the impression of helplessness experienced in childhood.

But then why, under the influence of drugs, does one not encounter – constantly – the trance of fear, utter terror? Reply: Who aspires to be overwhelmed by fear? Who does not flee before absolute abject fear? Under mescaline, one flees from it to the best of one's ability as soon as it is perceived. Sometimes, when things are going badly, fear is there, in every corner, lying in wait for you, and continually, endlessly, you steal away from it or you deploy yourself in combat with it, now in front-line and now in rearguard action, and the sole purpose of all this is to 'get out of there', to get out of the abyss of terror that opens up all around you.

It is therefore with particular relief that, arriving in calmer waters, one finds again the beneficent (in the form of beings, objects and places which can be loved and which inspire love), the beneficient which is here almost indispensable. Is it then so vital, is it born of such real necessity? Apparently. Love goes with bliss (and confidence) as fear goes with that which terrifies. In the state of mescalinean intoxication, fear almost unfailingly causes terrorizing scenes to appear to the imagination. So one has to take one's bearings, extremely quickly, for the incoercible manicheism of the drug no longer allows indifference and distraction, makes

it impossible to come and go from the agreeable to the disagreeable without taking up a definite position. No more strolling
around; one can no longer go where one pleases. In terms of an
idea that occurs one is suddenly magnetized and almost invinci-
bly snatched away by one of two poles, the beneficient or the
maleficent. Fear cannot be indulged in with impunity; one cannot
simply let oneself go as one can in life and, even more so, when
one reads spine-chilling accounts of highway-robberies, of wars,
of pillages, when one reads dramas and melodramas or detective
novels, when one plays at being afraid for a certain amount of
time, held, up to a certain point, 'in suspense'. Here, there is no
suspense, one is thrown headlong. One places one's mind in jeop-
ardy by accepting fear, which immediately becomes terror, and
one is hurled into it, one falls.

Accordingly, the beneficient is urgent, necessary and fundamental, as is love, which is itself thirst for the beneficient.

It does not follow that love, although present in everyone,
even in those who thought they could do without it, or who
had, so they thought, become indifferent to it – for love, as is
confirmed by the drug, the feeling of love, present in some like
an obsession, is basic and is linked to the aspiration towards
happiness – it does not follow that any form of love produces a
trance of love, just like that. Far from it.

A beyond of love

What occurs if this is not achieved

In order for the extraordinary, exalted oneness to be realized
in one's being, it is necessary that, with the agreement and
secret desire of the subject, love be de-substantialized, going on
to become a beyond of love. If this does not happen, mescaline
wards it off, brushes it aside with one movement, passing by
without seeing it, without being allowed to set love in motion
except, sometimes, by way of short-lived squalls of images, like
bursts of grape-shot and tauntings.

Mescaline creates many unpleasant surprises for those who, whilst in the throes of dispossession are called back by their possessive natures. Even with all resistance imperiously broken down, they still refuse to give themselves absolutely, as they should, in such a way as no longer to be there, for that which is stands in the way. Here, universal love, despite its being unexpected for many, is more fully, more truly experienced than anything else, whilst *transcendental* love is very, very rarely attained, but is not absent, being 'anticipated'.

As for the trance of erotic love, it scarcely occurs. In almost all those who tried their hand at it, love remained inconstant, imperfect, incomplete. There was no veritable transport then, only the force of its allurement. Even so, there is no question of mescaline coming to ground. It is impossible for mescaline to be weighed down. It is protected from this by its infinitization, and by its impersonalization. It is erotism about to change as an electric current flows through it, a fluid erotism which will no longer have any of the indulgences of libidinous nature. Another force has taken hold of it, a supreme force which in several ways is going to mark it, make it change its course. When mescaline at its highest point of intensity throws itself upon one who is naturally voluptuous, who was hoping to play the game of love with the drug, when it abruptly releases its galvanizing tremor, its amazing multiplied quiverings, into the stream of languishments, into the cradle of the gentle current, which immediately becomes like a torrent, like a cataract, where it interpenetrates through thousands of pinpoints, and which it crosses, which it divides and atomizes, then it is really no longer a question of sensuality, but of something quite different.

---

erotism charged with electricity

*when suddenly the electrical charge passes through the
fluvial lasciviousness*

> *interpenetrates interpenetrates*
>
> *jagged-teethed erotism seismic erotism an impossible crumbling*

The subject, divided, also feels multiplied. He is a crossroads where a hundred savage currents intersect, he is pulled at in opposing directions, in lightning states of alienation, and he also has to contend with a gigantic surging thrust which would seem to be leading to an assumption, a horizontal, median assumption. An indefinable something surrounds him with its majestic gait, its swagger and promenadings, which has banished all mediocrity and feelings of unease. To such an extent that he will have the impression that the whole world might be present in this, to such an extent is the event of the utmost, solemn importance.

> *Travesties superseded. Assumption, solemnization of the erotic*

Although doubtless every feature of erotism is present, when it is called to account it escapes him, having been transmuted, altered beyond recognition.

More than anything else, the extraordinary, mescalinean version of time is adept at achieving this transformation. Time is so different that, as he watches the dial of a chronometer, he at first thinks that the second hand has stopped, it takes so long to move, it takes so long to cover a distance that mentally he covers twenty times, there and back, there and back, during which interval countless ideas occur to him, whilst this clock-face time still lags inexplicably behind.

> *Constellation of delights*

Even this unique moment of abandon, this oasis where physical love comes to an end, and whose distinctive quality is that it causes all to disappear as though by magic, undergoes an amazing transformation. The expected eclipse of consciousness does not appear.

> *No abandon*
> *No more abandon*
>
> *Riddled orgasm, stair-case ridges*

Mescaline which would instil awareness into a paving-stone, mescaline, through the medium of the exemplary pause which it converts into hundreds of moments as it pursues its insane and insanely vigilant course without releasing its grip on the phenomenon – but noting all the details of it, be it orgasm itself, as it comes under the hammer of its maddening micro-second meter – mescaline detaches, reveals and enumerates the innumerable or at least the multiple here-and-now's contained in the terminal moment. The subject, astounded as well as uplifted, witnesses the prolongation of that which has always been considered impossible, which is repeated. He no longer understands. He seeks to locate his error, his delirium. But the instant supreme is repeated and repeated, no doubt about it, is repeated like the pulsation of another heart magically installed in him, another heart purely for pleasure, a prodigious phenomenon which all the same ends up by surely becoming non-organic, but which still throbs and continues to beat with a metaphysical pulsation in the deepest depths of his being.

> *repeated*
> *repeated*
> *unutterable mental jerks*
>
> *paraphysical event*
>
> *in ricochets in pulsations a heart for spasms*

This is only one of the travesties that mescaline with its extremely slender particles of time ushers in and brings to effect, merely by its presence, creating accumulation of existences in one existence, accumulation of minutes in one minute, accumulation of seconds in one second, disaggregating the compact, reducing the unique to rubble.

Such is the strange, petrifying disfiguration known by some of those who in the midst of the transubstantiatory and infinitizing movement wanted to hold on to the carnal, but were not really able to, perhaps did not dare[1], so much so that even the sexually obsessed frequently showed hesitation. It is possible that, before the abyss of eros, they started back, were held by a feeling of remorse, a memory of purity (a super-ego at variance), or that simply they saw that there are better things to do. Perhaps they were also disgusted by this unexpected, incomparable revelation of their 'inner world'.

This spectacular psychorepresentation, this profligate display of self is unique, and they are witness to it. Never otherwise would they have been able to see it thus, fully revealed[2], in all its living reality. It is for them to learn from this, to understand what brought them to this[3], to judge whether it is really in their way of thinking.

Mescaline reveals the subject's temper and, being by nature mechanical and jerky, also, thanks to its extremely rapid alternations, discloses and illustrates in its own particular and particularly disagreeable way his ambivalence, his desires and his hesitations.

Infinitization, of this kind especially, is something one never

[1] Without, however, making a clean break with erotism, that refuge against fear: erotism as a precaution, erotism through cowardice.

[2] No one can know what there *is* in the subconscious, but only what *passes* through it at a given moment, passes through it again and again, frequently, or rather which comes from it. It is for this reason that, under drugs, each moment is always a surprise.

[3] For the importance of the *biological traces of habits*, see *La morale dans son rapport avec les faits biologiques*, Dr Henri SAMSON, of Montreal, *Limites de l'humain* (Editions carmélitaines).

gets used to. A young woman, M.S., communicates the following to me, subsequent to an experience:

'I was at the edge of an unknown sea. The last waves of this sea on the shore came right up to me. Each one of the waves rolled me up, enveloped me and plunged me in delight, no, stopped short just before delight, before the boundary of delight, and then, abruptly, receded, the waves had receded, and I remained there alone, unsatisfied, then the sea came back as regular as breathing, the waves came rolling towards me, knocking me down, almost plunging me in delight, and it would have been the most unparalleled, fantastic delight, and it came and it was there, when the ebb of the tide abruptly took it back again; and I remained there, unsatisfied, in agony, and then the sea returned, impetuously, flinging its waves back at me, rolling me up so that now I was saved, bringing me back, tearing me away, and then, at the very moment of my surrender, the wave departed and was gone; then the waves returned, kept on returning . . . and I was there with my thoughts and dreams in the wave which now entwined me, which was about to overwhelm me, when the sea which was moving more and more quickly and which was becoming less and less a real sea, less and less the salt sea of our shores, but an immaterial, extremely rapid, rapid sea, almost rolled me up until I was no more, flinging me back just before the end, taking me up again amorously, flinging me back . . .'

---

caught up in the infernal back-and-forth

It is true that in this case it was hashish that had been taken, which also had infinitizing effects, but weaker ones, usually concealed by others, which are of greater interest to those who do not mean to cut themselves off too much from the terrestrial.

Moreover, it is usual for the Luciferian Hashish to show little religion and much irreligion, little that is celestial and much that is paradisiacal, little elevation and many levitations, and generally to be in this matter as in so many others for 'the other side of things', so that, even in the matter of love, it holds up to ridicule, is often blasphemous and desecratory.

---

the disrespectful Hashish and love

Certainly to eros it is not indifferent. It goes on the prowl around it. It is not difficult to tempt it and it has been tempted and to a far greater extent and much more successfully than published writings reveal[1] . . . But it has its own ways of responding which are very different from those that the hashishate expects.

Doubtless barriers do come down. A certain reserve is even apparently conjured away. There is nothing more to give concern. The body has been liberated, but it is no longer the same. Something has slipped out of it, and not only from one's own body. The bodies around it have become strangely 'disembodied'.

Inversely, signs and traces of someone who is absent are 'bodied forth'. From an obscure painting, from a poor snapshot the person portrayed emanates, comes to life and presents himself, more real than to any of his family circle, but without the heaviness of the real, transformed in such a way as to resemble the sudden delightful expansiveness which has overtaken the hashishate, the happiness which makes him light-headed, or light-headedness which makes him happy, delivering him, into the state (but far better)[2] of 'one who has just learned something which overwhelms him with joy'.

He no longer feels any restraint, he feels uplifted, would fly away almost, and, if he kept his eyes closed, it would perhaps be possible for him to see, through the eyes of his imagination,

---

[1] In hashisheen literature there are scarcely any valid erotic descriptions. In the famous collection of oriental tales, despite some audaciousness and exaggeration, the erotic night of hashish is one of the most boring of the boring *Thousand and One Nights*. No diffuse sensuality. Sensuality of the mind only, and the inexpressive account of a quantitative phenomenon.

[2] MOREAU DE TOURS, *Le haschich et le'aliénation mentale*.

men drifting effortlessly through the air, borne on carpets or divans. Everything is experienced in the domain of the air. Once weight and heaviness have been taken away, what is there that does not become different? The naked form is no longer a naked form but an illumination of being. Mass no longer has any importance. Body is a translation of spirit and character is a place wherein electrical currents are harnessed. Breast or belly, it is always the spirit that he touches, that he gains access to, or rather, and more often, fluids of surprising density.

Meanwhile the real persons who surround him are a source of discomfort rather than assistance in this general transubstantiation. Drug of the impoverished one, of him who is deprived, hashish easily makes do without people; out of almost nothing it creates a presence, it has the gift of life. To provide it with something real would be like taking water to the ocean.

No, it is in signs, in paintings and photographs, which almost instantly it brings to life, that hashish excels. (Although without any kind of prop, in inner visions, eyes closed, it is even more extraordinary, certainly more strange and bewildering, but contradictory, fickle, ungovernable.) With signs hashish is tamed and held. It is therefore advisable to take care in choosing the rallying-point, in proposing the place of encounter. The Orient, it appears was learned in these things, and there were organizers of the spectacle. (Even for inner visions there were directors, counsellors, who knew how to avert from the subject visions of horror, illusions of death, of falling from precipices, of imprisonment, or who were able to get him free if he found himself thus ensnared.)

But the hashishate needs hardly anything in the way of scenery. The slightest, most slender of props is the best. If he requires a helping-hand, it should be provided by the poorest image. Hashish will take care of the rest, imparting depth and beauty to it, linking it up, providing atmosphere, charm, the palpitations of life. It will 'create an illusion'.

From the shape of a girl traced in the sand it is able to make the spell-binding dancer who smiles at him, from a rough, crudely coloured sketch of a few flowers and two or three birds it is able to make an enchanting garden where, among the harmoniously coloured flowers, birds fly, full of life, turtle-doves coo and peacocks spread their tails. At the sound of musical instruments, so full of harmony that it hurts, the tatterdemalion who has taken the inebriating paste finds himself in a royal palace of which he had only been shown the outline, or a drawing of it, or merely been told its history. But who still wants to see a palace? Present-day man desires only to recover the marvellous, the marvellous of true strangeness. Thousands and thousands of 'reproductions' of all kinds and from every country accessible to him provide an opportunity previously unknown. In each one of them he can meet up with an unreal reality. The forays that the hashishate makes into a painting or a photo are totally new. Images possess a new power, a linking power. Especially faces in paintings and photographs. The miracle, for him who looks at them in this state, the miracle in being with them, instantaneously, in being immediately in the company of these immediately familiar ones, this is the inexhaustible miracle, an impression which never ceases to fascinate.

The hasishate swings over into the other (although he only has the other's image) and the other streams into him, in a vast, delicate organic complicity.

---

multiform mental touch

The mental adaptation of the hashishate and of the person who 'emerges' from the photo is perfect, it leaves nothing to be desired, and it occurs at every moment. It is also incredibly varied, possessed of a concordance which is established every fraction of a second, and which is resumed and re-established by means of a subtle modification which will prevent even the most infinitesimal 'detachment' (whence derives its hypnotic power). You proceed at the same pace, exactly. Finally the hashishate is able to abandon himself completely, for the image that has been roused to life is not at all capable of any great initiative. There is no fear of it being heavy-handed or at cross-purposes; it is essentially harmonising, vibratory. (Certain dangerous faces reveal themselves to be repulsive. To be averted at once.)

> *He sees he touches human effulgence*
>
> *perfect imaginary communion wherein you advance*
> *at the same pace*

Although faces are infinitely more expressive than the rest of the body, there is a temptation, one that has been recognized, to use images of naked forms to find oneself amongst naked forms, amongst desirable naked bodies[1]. They too awake to life, become present, and the hashishate partakes of the same life, and there is not the slightest embarassment at their being

---

[1] Am I dwelling too much on sexuality? No, not here. The subject has been thrown off balance by the drug. He refers his body to sensuality which acts in such a way as to help him find his balance again. It drowns all feelings of discomfort. Sometimes a voluptuous atmosphere is all that is necessary. At other times he will not stop there, but afterwards, without reference to the sensual, he will no longer get through the trials to which he is submitted by the drug. From this there arises a relationship, a conditioning, which may change his life. Often in cases of mental discomfort, as in mental illness, but less compellingly, erotism has a new *raison d'étre*.

In lunatic asylums, at every period in time, patients have been observed who ceaselessly stimulate their genital organs until, having used up all their strength, they become limp like rags. Might one not conclude, especially when one considers the dejected appearance of some of them, in which there is not the slightest suggestion of an explosive and exciting sexuality, that they seek in this simple way, by means of that which is immediately to hand and by appealing to a function whose value has been proven, to dominate and go beyond, or merely put up with, the intense impression of misery and the atrocious lack of satisfaction which they feel, to which – so it seems to them – there must be set in opposition, urgently, a genuine satisfaction which sweeps everything else aside. But it comes to nothing, for the ailment of alienation is greater, more constant, more powerful, and, unlike the body, cannot be exhausted.

together. Even here, the subconscious, having been roused by the vexatious and liberating[1] hashish, sometimes provides interesting revelations. Having become more himself than he is, liberated without yet knowing it, borne by an extraordinary momentum which he perhaps does not even feel (later, in retrospect, he will be astounded, but for the moment he finds it quite natural) the subject undergoes a sudden transformation and makes to one of these people who really did not deserve it (but can one really be sure?), the gift of himself, the gift without reservation.

Perhaps she is a prostitute, the girl whose photo he has found, or a dancer who has murdered for gain. No matter! With a pure gaze, possessing the power to purify, purified by surprise, having gone beyond this body which should have aroused him to desire (which he already felt), he contemplates her. Even naked, woman needs to be 'discovered', revealed from under the cover of her day-to-day existence, the mediocrity of her habits, the daily round that she pursues, resulting from her compromises. Having disentangled her from all that, he sees her, her being, her unique, almost holy character, holy with a virtual, possible holiness which, in spite of her life, dwells with its small light within her – and which is linked to a deep-seated aspiration – too deep-seated to be seen by an ordinary gaze, too deep-seated even in her for her to perceive it, not without a miraculous shock, but which he, momentarily gifted with double sight, perceives and receives like the light of day following upon the night, he sees her being that awaits transfiguring grace. To this person, seen in her essence, whose future, in spite of appearances, is not yet entirely played out, not completely ruined, he wants to give himself, as an uncontrollable wave rises within him and he feels a sudden, exorbitant need, to which he can set no bounds, a need to *devote himself,* or even more, a need for a *veritable devotion.*

---

[1] Libertine because of its liberating effect, but also capable of liberating from libertinism.

> *from desirable to holy*
>
> *from love to devotion*

Stupidity? Lucidity?

Is there not something in her, as in every woman which awaits transfiguration? A human being is always extremely below what he could be.

Despite the apparent error, he perhaps sees better than in the normal, mediocre state, for mediocrity records but mediocrity. He sees the woman beyond herself, he sees her being, he sees that it is totally above her present condition, he sees her whom a reception like that which he extends her, but greater, more absolute, more saintly, more persevering, revealing her to herself, would transfigure *really*.

Doubtless the gift of himself without restriction, now experienced in its plenitude, perhaps he had desired it all his life, without being able to satisfy it, there was always something preventing it, something had frustrated this immense desire which merely required a perfect abandon, this heart to which simple love affords no contentment. Ridiculous . . . that such a thing should happen just when he was hoping to live amidst naked forms! But he can neither recover himself nor recover the gift that he has made[1]. The pull of allurement remains sovereign.

The treacherous hashish, so skilled in deception, has acted here in a certain way, although the opposite way is more usual for it. Hashish has only too often displayed perversity and the perverse know how to assist it. The fearsome faculty of imparting life, under the influence of hashish, has caused certain people who have taken the drug to bring together images of the most disparate personalities in order for them to live together in

---

[1] Careful! Sacher Masoch isn't far. Here is humility become erotic. Here is Beauty in devoting oneself even to that which is base. Crossroads. Crossroads with new deviations possible. Snares all around.

a state of shameful encounter. (Before experiencing them in conjunction with each other, it will sometimes be necessary first to experience them one by one.)

Between him who is looked at and him who looks, relations are woven to infinity, all with great subtlety, as vast as the natural divergence may be between the two. Taking advantage of the miracle that hashish achieves in linking him who looks and him who is looked at (both of them mutually understanding each other in a fantastically multiple and complex manner), and also in linking amongst themselves those who are looked at, the hashishate possesses, thanks to some simple photographs, the power of bringing individuals face to face whom life could never bring together, of combining in such a way as to produce the most scandalous assembly, which immediately comes to life and *takes root*. An unforgettable shock, which jolts the mind and affects it almost traumatically. Enough about that.

---

strangers set face to face come into contact

shameful confrontation

Hashish, the true 'polymorphous perverse'

When the mind has been worked over by so many imaginings, resistance to the marvellous, presented in the form of a real person, grows weaker. There are presences everywhere, clouds lighter than mist. Everything responds to everything else. The hashishate discovers a wild extravagance of harmony and of all kinds of correspondence, between people, impressions, ideas, and between odours, sounds, words, vowels, colours, responding each to the other, substituting themselves amongst each other, at every pitch and scale, suddenly interchanging and being exchanged one for the other.

Then they can sometimes know, those lovers who are extremely suited to each other, a fusion such as had never been glimpsed, a baffling symbiosis. They experience the illusion of being in contact not so much with a body as with fluids, fluids which require to be followed, to be accompanied. The other's rhythm is felt, but as though it had not just been inaugurated . . . the heart which beats in the breast of the beloved assumes an august and magnificent character. But without losing its driving power, its steady beat, its reign over the body. The beloved now is above all else a heart, a heart surrounded by a body. A heart to which one's own heart seeks to respond, directly, in a language of palpitations and pulsations. Breathing has also assumed an unfamiliar grandeur, becoming so extraordinary that on each breath that fills the lungs a world seems borne. What beauty in the life of breath.

> *physically hearts to each other respond*

But surrounded by snares, ready at each moment to change direction, to find its way into something quite different, to lose its very nature, even the most carnal love may be decomposed, may betray itself in something vast and undefined, and may sometimes be *diverted* into a feeling that turns up for no reason, a feeling of immeasurable indulgence, or kindness, or forgiveness accorded . . . to everyone. It will happen that abruptly and completely he will forget her with whom but a moment before he was so perfectly united. The feeling and sudden need of a vast communion of all beings throughout the world will have taken her place. Hashish cannot be trusted: it is unfamiliar with the straight line, it deals in discontinuities, it uproots without a word of warning, it overrides all sense of 'seriousness', all that is noble, or eminent, or respectable, or simply that which forms a 'whole'. It is against all that forms a 'whole', against coherence and above all against the attitude and conviction that goes with it, which it pursues relentlessly until it is destroyed.

> *Starting to swerve again*

More often than impressions of harmony, impressions of dis-
cord appear, fantastically multiplied, with scandalous visions in
the imagination, clownish antics in which the hashishate sees
himself or feels himself making love to a headless woman, or to
a woman with a sow's head, or who has ten heads, or who top-
ples over and comes tumbling down, a trunk woman, down
endless stairs, or who is carried away into the air, or a grimacing
monkey in the fork of a tree. Still she changes, into a grotesque
machine whose pistons charge to and fro with a madly acceler-
ated and burlesque movement. And all may finish up in an
immense and blasphemous bric-a-brac. The explosion that love
is, usually more or less contained, now overtakes love on every
side and, far from limiting itself to love, goes on exploding in
every direction, being tempted to go in every direction, degrading, demystifying, spilling over, desire that itches for deliverance
along every channel, desire seized with frenzy, eruptive, hack-
ing out its paths of insults, ravages, destruction, savagery and
even cannibalism whose archetypal thrustings take the form of
exaggerated images in the shaken being of him who insanely
seeks release, who frantically rebels against all obstruction or
limitation.

These few pages are intended to serve as the beginnings of an
attempt to shed some light on a subject which required eluci-
dation, but which I leave to others to investigate properly. They
will perhaps suffice to explain how, generally speaking, the hallucinogenic drugs, whilst not leading away from love in the
manner of heroin or morphine, are not conductive to it either,
and cause one in many ways and through multiple deviations,
to be present at its dethronement. After which, it becomes difficult to return to love in all its simplicity[1]. It is perhaps for this
reason, suspected vaguely, that there is a certain, instinctive,

---

[1] Although at other times, rarer it is true, they have the opposite effect and
act like electro-shocks, bringing back to normal one who was previously hindered or prevented.

unanimity against those who use drugs. For once in agreement, lovers along with puritans, young and old, men and women, workers and middle-class, all spontaneously experience bad temper, hostility and indignation when mention is made of these scandalous heretics of sensation.

The Poet's Paradise
Robert Graves

We have narrowed our minds by a neglect of the physical senses: relying on reason, we no longer see, hear, taste, smell or feel anything like so acutely as our primitive ancestors did, or as most little children still do before their education hardens. Henry Vaughan's *The Retreat*, imitated by Wordsworth in his better known *Intimations of Immortality*, begins:

> *Happy those early days when I*
> *Shin'd in my angel-infancy,*
> *Before I understood this place*
> *Appointed for my second race*
> *Or taught my soul to fancy aught*
> *But a while celestial thought,*
> *When yet I had not walked above*
> *A mile or two from my first love*
> *And looking back (at that short space),*
> *Could see a glimpse of his bright face*
> *When on some gilded cloud or flower*
> *My gazing soul would dwell an hour . . .*

Civilized man notices a gilded cloud and, at best, mutters 'cumulus' or 'cirrus' or 'mare's tale', speculating on the weather it portends; notices a flower and dismisses it with a

casual recognition of the variety. To gaze at a wild rose or but-
tercup for even a minute and find illumination in the sight,
would never occur to him; if only because all his senses are
blunted by a persistent disregard of the ugly smells, ugly
sounds, ugly sights and unpalatable tastes which the struggle
for existence entails. His spirit, also, has lost touch with the
ideas of mystery, grace and love that originally informed it:
intellect and habit starve out imagination. How to awaken
these dormant capacities is a problem seldom raised, except by
mystics, who usually suggest a daunting formula of spiritual
exercises designed to tame bodily lusts. Some claim to have
themselves visited Paradise in a state of trance so induced, and
to have found it the seat of true felicity and perfect wisdom.
Here is a typical passage from Thomas Traherne's *Centuries of
Meditation* (he was a contemporary of Vaughan's):

> *The corn was orient and immortal wheat, which never should
> be reaped nor ever was sown. I thought it had stood from
> everlasting to everlasting. The dust and stones of the street were
> as precious gold: the gates were at first the end of the world. The
> green trees when I first saw them through one of the gates
> transported and ravished me: their sweetness and unusual
> beauty made my heart to leap, and almost mad with ecstasy,
> they were such strange and beautiful things . . . all things
> abided eternally as they were in their proper place. Eternity was
> manifest in the light of the day and something infinite behind
> everything appeared, which talked with my expectation and
> moved my desire.*

Today, the main alleviations for the stress of commercial and
industrial life are organized religion, organized entertainment,
drink. Organized religion may sober the spirit, but except
among the more ecstatic sects, rarely purges it. Organized entertainment distracts, but does not illuminate, the mind. Though
some poems, melodies, works of art, love-affairs and fever
dreams may give glimpses of a lost magical reality, their spell is

short-lasting: it does not create such a permanent nostalgia for the fairyland of childhood as possessed, say, John Clare in Northampton Asylum. The hard, dirty, loveless, synthetic world re-asserts itself as the sole factual truth. Yet a superstitious dream that, somehow, happiness, love, glory, magic lie hidden close at hand, protects the world from the nervous breakdown of which recent wars have been symptomatic; a dream that, when fostered by films and family magazines, becomes optimistically attached to personal success in a career or in marriage and, when fostered by the Church, optimistically attached to a Paradisal afterworld.

In ancient times, 'Paradise' was strictly reserved for an illuminated aristocracy, until the Church at last threw open the gates to all converts, however brutish or feeble-minded, who would accept baptism. Priests then preached Heaven's glories (attainable only by a belief in Christ) as the reward of patience and humility after traversing this vale of tears. Yet St John's Apocalyptic Paradise is borrowed from chapters of the pre-Christian *Book of Enoch*, which are themselves based on the 'Eden' chapters of *Ezekiel* and *Genesis*; and these, again, on the Babylonian Paradise described in the Gilgamesh Epic and elsewhere. The Persians knew a similar Paradise; and their name for it, *paridaeza*, yields the Syrian-Greek word *paradeisos* and the Hebrew *pardess*. Those middle-Eastern Paradises, so far back as the Sumerian, are reported as being delightful mountain-top gardens watered by a four-headed crystal river, their fruit-trees laden with flashing jewels; and a wise serpent always haunts them. Rare humans who enter Paradise while in a state of grace are granted 'perfect wisdom' by the Serpent – 'knowledge of good and evil' means knowledge of 'all things that exist' – and only the herb of immortality is denied them. Thus Gilgamesh, having visited the jewelled Babylonian Paradise, dived to the sea-bottom and drew up the herb of immortality; but the Serpent took it from him, and he meekly resigned himself to death. Adam and Eve were driven out of Eden ('pleasure') by God lest they might discover and eat the fruit of immortality;

the Cherub, on guard at the gate thereafter with a flaming sword, is the very Serpent who gave them the fruit of knowledge. The King of Tyre, though perfect in beauty and wisdom, is figuratively expelled from Eden (*Ezekiel* xxviii) for claiming to be an immortal god with a seat in the heart of the sea. *Enoch* mentions both the tree of wisdom and the tree of life; and *the Secrets of Enoch* places the latter in the Third Heaven, a paradise to which St Paul claimed that he had been caught up.

Greek mythographers told of a Paradise on Mount Atlas, the 'Garden of the Hesperides', guarded by a hundred-headed Serpent; but made Heracles shoot the Serpent, take away some of the jewelled fruit, and become immortal. This Paradise, like the Sumerian one that antedates Gilgamesh's 'Garden of Delights', belonged to a Mother-goddess – it was Hera's before she married Zeus – not to a male god. Christians chose to identify the Serpent in Eden with Satan; they preached that Jesus Christ, a 'Second Adam', lives permanently in Paradise, having expelled the Serpent, and is ready there to welcome all believers when it has finally been destroyed on the Day of Judgment.

Why do paradises follow a traditional pattern, wide-spread and persistent enough to be shared even by Polynesians and pre-Columbian Mexicans? The evidence suggests that, originally, a common drug causes the paradisal visions and provides the remarkable mental illumination described as 'perfect wisdom'. One such drug, a hallucigenic mushroom, was certainly used in Central America before the Spanish conquest. Professor Roger Heim and R. G. Wasson's massive work *Les Champignons Hallucigènes de Mexique* (Paris, 1958), contains a coloured reproduction of a fresco from the Aztec city of Tepantitla, dated between 300 and 600 A.D., which shows a soul visiting Paradise. The usual elements are there: a river (stocked with fish), bordered with flowers and bejewelled trees, haunted by bright-coloured butterflies and a spectacular serpent. The soul stands open-mouthed, weeping tears of joy and wonder, his body connected to the river by a blue thread. This river is shaped like a mushroom and, at its source – the centre of the mushroom head – lurks Tlalóc, God of Mysteries, in toad form, the water issuing from his mouth. Tlalóc, who often wore a serpent head-dress, was a god of lightning. He used a sea-shell as another emblem, and 'had his seat in the midst of the seas': at the bottom of the fresco an underwater grotto appears, marked with a cross, the four heads of which are mushrooms. Nobody who has been admitted to the rite thus pictured will find much difficulty in deciphering the symbolism.

R. G. Wasson's ritual experience came as the culmination of a study on which he and his wife had been engaged for years: that of mycophobia. Mycophobia, the unreasoning fear of mushrooms, affects whole populations in Europe, Asia and Africa, being total in some regions, in other modified by certain exceptions (such as the white field mushroom among the English), elsewhere non-existent. Now, a few mushrooms, easily distinguished from edible varieties, do contain mortal poison; but most are palatable, if not delicious. Why, the Wassons asked, when wholesome fruit and vegetables are eaten freely, with a disregard for the poisonous or the inedible, should this selectivity be denied the mushroom? Why should horrible and obscene names be applied to edible mushrooms? Perhaps mycophobia pointed to an ancient taboo, like that which has given Jews and Moslems a disgust of pork, and Northern Europeans a disgust of horse-flesh – nutritious and tasty meat – both pig and horse having once been holy animals. And, since mushrooms figured alongside toads, snakes and devils in numerous late mediaeval paintings, and still bear popular names connected with toads, snakes and devils, it looked as if they might have been sacred food in a pagan rite, preserved by witches of Western Europe who kept toads and snakes as diabolic 'familiars'.

A particular variety of mushroom, the *amanita muscaria*, in Britain called 'fly-cap', grows under birch-trees in Northern countries, where it is scarlet with white spots; but under conifers to the southward, where its scarlet becomes fox-colour. Fly-cap induces in the Korjaks, a Palaeo-Siberian tribe of Kamchatka, and among the Mongol Hazaras of Afghanistan, a boisterous ecstasy which helps them to consult ancestral spirits and utter prophecies. R. G. Wasson guessed that the mushroom had been similarly used in Europe, though reserved for the priesthood; that, for security reasons, the taboo had been extended to cover the eating of all mushrooms, on pain of death; and that this taboo hung on long after the rites came to an end – except in countries where famine forced the common people to defy it and become positive mycophiles, as all Slavonic peoples now are. The name 'toadstool', particularly applied to fly-cap, is apt; because it contains a poison, *bufotenine*, which is also exuded by toads from their 'warts' when frightened.

Moreover, early Spanish archives mentioned Mexican mushroom-oracles that, though officially extinct, were still rumoured to operate in secret far from civilization. A certain mushroom was known as 'God's Body' by the Mazateks of Oaxaca Province, because sacramentally eaten. The Wassons, learning of this, visited Oaxaca during the June mushroom season, and were able to attend an oracular meeting at which the *curandero* ('healer') who took charge, ceremoniously ate certain small ill-tasting mushrooms and, speaking for the god, gave an unexpected, surprising and accurate answer to the question they had asked him. Later, when invited by a *curandera* to eat the mushrooms themselves, they understood the solemn local tradition about the feast: 'One knows all; one even sees where God dwells.' Their visions recalled the heaven shown on the Tepantitla fresco, and it became clear that they had been symbolically eating the body not of Christ, but of the god Tlalóc.

In the different regions of Mexico where the cult survives, certain religious rules are common to all. Devotees, before partaking of a mushroom feast, must fast, abstain from sexual intercourse, and be at peace with the world and themselves. Whoever disregards these rules (the *curanderos* and *curanderas* agreed) may see such demonic visions as to wish they had never been born. The Christian, Jewish, Greek and Babylonian

Heavens, it should be recalled, have a Hell which complements Paradise; and the usual vision is of innumerable demon faces grinning from lurid caverns. But those who attend such a feast while in a state of grace, report that the mushrooms not only sharpen their intelligence, so that they seem to possess 'perfect wisdom', but shower on them what Christians call 'the peace and love that passes all understanding' – a strong, non-erotic sense of spiritual comradeship.

The Roman Catholic Church teaches that Paradise cannot be attained except by repentance; and prepares every sinner for the journey with the *viaticum*, a symbolic consumption of Jesus Christ's body and blood, after asking him to purge his soul by a sincere confession. From what religion, it should be asked, did St Paul borrow this rite, since it is not attested in the Gospels and is an infringement of the Hebrew law against the drinking of blood? A question that leads to another: in what pre-Christian cult did a god deliver oracles when his flesh was symbolically eaten – as the Mazateks now believe that Tlalóc-Christ does? Tlalóc, we know, was the Spirit of lightning-engendered toadstool. More questions arise. What European god claimed this nativity? Or had associations with the serpent or the toad? Or possessed an underwater retreat? Or assisted at mysteries where ineffable visions were witnessed?

The sole European deity known to have matched Tlalóc in these respects was Dionysus. Born as a serpent-crowned child from the Earth-goddess Semele, whom a flash of lightning had impregnated, he went through a variety of transformations, was then torn to shreds and eaten by the Titans, but restored to life by his grandmother, the Goddess Rhea, Creatrix of the world; possessed an underwater retreat in the grottoes of the Seagoddess Thetis; and assisted at the chief Greek Mysteries, under the protection of goddesses.

The Greek poets tell how when Dionysus' Maenads tore off Orpheus' head, it continued to prophesy. The head of Pentheus, another figure in the Dionysus myth, was torn off by his own mother Agave; both incidents could refer to the practice of tearing the mushroom-head from its stalk – heads alone are used at Mexican oracles. The Eleusinian Mysteries, sacred to the goddesses Demeter and Persephone, and also to Dionysus, were preceded by fasting and a ritual bathe in the sea, where devotees transferred their sins to scape-pigs. They then entered a temple, drank mint-water and ate pastries baked in magical shapes and carried in baskets. As a result, they saw celestial visions which could never afterwards be forgotten. The meaning of the Greek word *mysterion* ('mystery') is disputed, but since the mysteries were an autumnal festival complementary to the spring *anthesterion*, and since this means 'flower-springing', *mysterion* may well mean *myko-sterion*, or 'mushroom-springing'.

A distinction should here be drawn between the wild Dionysian orgies of Maenads who went raging over the hills, often in the company of Satyrs (a pre-Hellenic mountain tribe), and the decently conducted temple-mysteries, where no violence occurred. Pliny's remark that an awed hush 'descends on people if a toad is placed among them' suggests that Dionysus, like Tlalóc, had a toad epiphany. But the celestial visions of the mysteries are unlikely to have been produced by fly-cap, which loses its toxic quality when cooked, and could not well be introduced raw into food and drink. However, the toxic qualities of *panaeolus papilionaceus*, a hallucigenic toadstool shown on an early Greek vase and now known to have figured in the European witch cult, resist cooking; its liquor may have been mixed in the mint-water, and its flesh baked in the magical pastries. I believe, but cannot prove, that fly-cap, which appears on a carved Etruscan mirror at the feet of the criminal Ixion, was the original mushroom sacred to the universal Toad-god, and that the more tranquil and equally delightful properties of *panaeolus papilionaceus* and *psilocybe*, were discovered by later experiment and also placed under the Toad-god's charge. Fly-cap grows in both hemispheres, and the ancient mushroom-stones of Guatemala show Tlalóc in toad shape, seated underneath a mushroom which appears to be a fly-cap, not a *psilocybe*.

Some of the Eleusinian pastries had phallic shapes and, indeed, *mykes* ('mushroom') also means 'phallus' in Greek; others were baked like piglings (a widespread term for mushrooms); some perhaps like toads and serpents. A common name for the toad in European folklore is 'the cripple', because of his clumsy feet; and 'Dionysus' means 'the lame god'. One Greek hero who, according to the myths, at first resisted Dionysus, but presently saw the light, was Perseus, King of Argos and founder of Mycenae. Punished for his obduracy with an outbreak of madness among the Argive women – they began eating their own babies raw, as also happened at Thebes when Pentheus resisted the cult – Perseus dedicated a temple to Dionysus at Mycenae. Argos had a toad as its badge, and Perseus is said to have named Mycenae after a mushroom found on the site, 'from which proceeded a stream of water'. He also made visionary flights through the air, paid a visit to the 'Stygian nymphs' on the slopes of Mount Atlas – presumably with Hesperides, who were later kind to his descendant Heracles – and claimed the same sort of nativity as Dionysus, having been engendered by Zeus in a shower of gold. Phryneus, the Toadstool-Dionysus to which these myths point, lay securely hidden behind the Wine-Dionysus and the Grain-Dionysus. Apart from a menacing Greek proverb 'Mushrooms are the food of the gods', nobody mentioned the subject. Greek peasants are mycophobes.

Baby-eating, a practice not associated with any Greek cult except that of Dionysus, also figured (according to Catholic missionaries) in the Aztec rain-making rites of Tlalóc. This god's name meant 'Pulp of the Earth' (i.e. mushroom?), and he lived at Tlalócan, a mountain paradise, with certain Grain-goddesses and his gentle sister-spouse Chalchiuthlicue, patroness of streams and family-life. Some centuries before the Spanish conquest, matriarchy and clan-totemism had been superseded among the Aztecs by patriarchy and individual totemism. Tlalóc thus officially escaped from the tutelage of goddesses, just as Dionysus did in Classical Greece when he was raised to the Olympic council of Twelve and took over the Barley-goddess

Demeter's winnowing festival, the Haloa. Yet in the Mysteries, Dionysus seems still to have been subservient to Demeter and Persephone. Similarly, the Mazatec *curandera* who initiated the Wassons addressed the Christianized Tlalóc as if he were her wayward son, and she a goddess. It is possible that, alike in Greece and Mexico, the 'babies' eaten in sacred pictures were really mushrooms.

The Christian sacrament of bread and wine was a love-feast in Hellenistic style. Initiates of the Lesser Eleusinian Mysteries, who had to undergo a period of probation before being admitted to the Greater Mysteries, saw no celestial visions. Presumably, the mystagogues withheld the sacred hallucigenic agent until sure of a candidate's worthiness; he received bread and wine only, symbols of the Grain-Dionysus and the Wine-Dionysus. The Church has indeed banished the Serpent from Paradise. Her sacramental elements give the communicant no visionary foretaste of the new Jerusalem. The disappointment often felt by Protestant adolescents at their first communion is a natural one – the priest promises more than they are able to experience. I learned only last week, from an Arabic scholar, that the root-word F.T.R. means, in Arabic, first 'toadstool', then 'divine rapture', then 'sacred pellets of bread'. This points to a pre-Islamic hallucigenic practice of immense age.

Granted, many Christian mystics and Jewish mystics have undoubtedly seen Paradisal sights, but always after a life of intense spiritual struggle; and these often alternate with terrifying visions of Hell. It is now therefore usual to treat mystics as schizophrenics, arresting them and prescribing electric-shock treatment if their enthusiasm has caused a breach of the peace. The Church herself is apt to discourage a mystic who claims to have seen sights denied to his ecclesiastical superiors; suspecting him, at best, of spiritual pride. This type of schizophrenia is chronic, uncontrollable, and what is called 'anti-social'. Only when mystics have written poems, or painted pictures, in which the illumination cannot be denied, and only when they have been dead some years – for example St John of the Cross, El

Greco, Blake, van Gogh – are they likely to be valued as great souls.

The use of hallucigenic mushrooms, on the other hand, induces a temporary, controllable schizophrenia within the Mazatek social scheme, and the sole religious demand on participants is that they shall enter the circle fasting, with a clear conscience and a quiet mind. When I ate *psilocybe* on 31 January 1960, a recording of the *curandera*'s invocation to Tlalóc as Christ gave the rite a decent solemnity. *Psilocybe* must be eaten in complete darkness – because the least light, even strained through the eyelids, becomes painful as soon as the drug takes effect. The visions last for some four and a half hours. According to the Mazateks, a novice seldom sees persons or historical scenes: he finds it enough to enter the 'Garden of Delights'. The second and third feast may widen his experiences. Adepts learn to direct their mind wherever they please, visit the past, foretell the future.

Here is the account I wrote of my experience:

That evening, four of us gathered in Gordon Wasson's apartment overlooking the East River, prepared to set out for Paradise under his guidance. He had advised us to fast beforehand, drink no liquor, and try to achieve a state of grace. At seven-thirty he gave us the mushrooms in crystalline form washed down with water and, at eight, began turning out the lights one by one, while we settled down in easy chairs. Soon no sound was heard except the swish-swish of cars passing in an endless stream along the Drive between us and the river: a noise not unlike the sound of waves on a beach.

By eight o'clock I felt a numbness in my arms, and a pricking at the nape of my neck. In the half-light that filtered through the shutters, coloured dots appeared on the ceiling; they shone brighter when I closed my eyes. We all began to shiver, our pulses slowed down, and Masha Wasson brought in blankets. Since she is a trained nurse and had twice made this journey herself, we welcomed the reassuring pressure of her hand. I remembered a

*warning quotation: 'You are going where God dwells; and will
be granted all knowledge . . . Whoever nurses evil in his heart
sees hideous demons and nameless horrors, more proper to Hell
than to Paradise, and wishes he had never been born.' I
anxiously considered my own motives. How honest were they?
Would I see demons? Though not a saint, I was at least a
dedicated historian and poet; with luck I might be spared
punishment.*

*Since even the half-light had become uncomfortably strong for
my eyes, I kept them closed. I knew that the road to Paradise
often begins under the sea, or from a lake-bottom; so the
greenish water now lapping around me came as no surprise. I
entered a marble grotto, passing a pile of massive sunken
statuary, and found myself in a high-roofed tunnel lit by
brilliantly coloured lamps. The sea lay behind.*

*This was perfect schizophrenia. My corporeal self reclined in a
chair, fully conscious, exchanging occasional confidences with
friends: but another 'I' had entered the tunnel – perhaps the
same tunnel through which, four thousand years before, the epic
hero Gilgamesh made his approach to the Babylonian Paradise?*

*Still worrying about the demons, I glanced up at the roof.
Thousands of pink, green or yellow faces, like carnival masks,
grimaced horribly down; but I dismissed them with a wave of
my hand, and they obediently vanished . . . A turn in the tunnel
brought me to the domed Treasury, without which no Paradise
is complete, whether Hindu, Babylonian, Hebrew, Icelandic,
Irish, Greek or Chinese. As the prophet Ezekiel wrote:*

Every precious stone was thy covering: the sardius,
topaz, and the diamond; the beryl, the onyx and the
jasper; the sapphire, the emerald, the carbuncle and
gold.

*Her Majesty's Crown Jewels at the Tower of London would
have looked tawdry by comparison with the fantastic treasure
now heaped before me: diadems, tiaras, necklaces, crosses,*

breast-plates, goblets, ephods, cups, platters, sceptres, blazing or twinkling. But, even richer than these jewels, were the royal silks spread out for my inspection in blue, mulberry and white: vast lengths, miraculously brocaded with birds, beasts, flowers . . . My closest experience to this had been in early childhood when, after waiting endlessly in the cold, dark hall, my sisters and I saw the drawing-room door suddenly flung open, and there blazed the Christmas tree: all its candles lighted, its branches glistening with many-coloured tinsel.

I reached for a notebook and wrote: '9 p.m. Visions of . . .' but got no further: things were happening too fast. Besides, the pen felt strange in my hand, and its scratch on paper sounded offensively loud. I remember saying after awhile: 'I have seen enough treasure for a lifetime. Is there no human beauty in Paradise?' At once the diadems, tiaras, necklaces, crosses and sceptres vanished, as the demons had done. Instead, a row of lovely, live, naked Caryatids appeared, lined along the wall, as if supporting the dome. Their faces were shrouded. Yet I hesitated to indulge in erotic fancies, lest the Caryatids turned into filthy, deformed devilkins like the ones in Flemish pictures of St Anthony's Temptations. Blushing, I dismissed them too, and came out from the tunnel into daylight. What I had been taught at school and in church proved true enough, though the truth enormously transcended the account. Around me lay a mountain-top Eden, with its jewel-bright trees, its flowers and its pellucid streams. And I experienced not only the bliss of innocence, but also the 'knowledge of good and evil'. Most Christians understand this phrase as meaning the power to distinguish right from wrong; in Hebrew, however, it signifies a universal understanding of all things, whether good or evil. Indeed, my mind suddenly became so agile and unfettered that I felt capable of solving any problem in the world; it was as if I had immediate access to all knowledge everywhere. But the sensation of wisdom sufficed – why should I trouble to exploit it?

Gordon Wasson had switched on the tape-recorder and the curandera*'s voice was now invoking Tlalóc as 'Christo'. She*

*chanted, scolded, entreated, commanded, coaxed him to do what
she required; it might have been the Goddess Aphrodite
addressing her froward son Eros . . . Every now and then she
would change her mood and song; would mourn, triumph, or
laugh. I fell wholly under her spell, and presently enjoyed the
curious experience of* seeing *sound. The song-notes became
intricate links of a round golden chain that coiled and looped in
serpentine fashion among jade-green bushes; the only serpent I
met in Eden . . . Each song was followed by a pause, and always
I waited in a lover's agony for her to begin again, tears pricking
at my eyelids. Once the* curandera *seemed to sing off-key.
Perhaps this was quarter-tone music; at any rate, my ear was
not offended: I knew what she meant when I saw one edge of the
golden chain band now formed by the sound spread out into a
spectrum; and laughed for pleasure. Towards the end came a
quick, breathless, cheerful song of creation and growth. The
notes fell to earth but rose once more in green shots which soared
swiftly up, putting on branches, leaves, flowers – until it
dominated the sky like the beanstalk in the fairytale.*

*My spirit followed after into the clear blue air, gazing down
on cornfields, fields of poppies, and the spires of a heavenly city,
and Thomas Traherne's orient and immortal wheat, 'which
never should be reaped nor ever was sown'.*

*At last the music ended. The visions were fading now. My
corporeal self sighed, stretched luxuriously, and looked around.
Most of the company had left the room. Only one friend
remained. I asked him: 'So the journey seems to be over?'*

*'Ah, but close your eyes, and you can get back at once,' he
said.*

'How do you feel?'

*'My mind has never been so clear! Did you hear such music
in all your life?'*

*We joined the others in the kitchen, ate cold turkey sandwiches
and compared notes . . . 'I saw huge slow-moving fish in the sea;
did you?' – '. . . The demons scared me nearly to death! I wept*

*and sobbed; maybe I wasn't in a state of grace. And when I
looked at my hand, O God!' – '. . . Weren't those buildings
enormous? But I couldn't place their architectural style.' –
'. . . Me, I'd take the journey all over again – this minute, if I
could!'*

*A curious bond of affection had been established between us:
so strong that I felt nothing could ever break it. At two o'clock in
the morning we said good-bye. By eight I was on my way to
Idlewild, headed for Europe: profoundly refreshed, and (in
Wordsworth's phrase) 'trailing clouds of glory' – wisps of
celestial memory which persisted nearly a month.*

Civilized consciences revolt against the abuse of hallucigenic
drugs – most of them habit-forming, dangerous, and unobtainable except by prescription, or in the black market. Spirits,
tobacco, tranquillizers – all harmful if habitually taken – are
however on unrestricted sale and, because they provide no
visions (apart from the fearful hell of *delirium tremens*), the
Churches condone their use; for hard liquor merely depresses
the senses, tobacco and tranquillizers merely dull them.

Psilocybin, the active principle of *psilocybe*, is now synthetically
made in Switzerland. At present, the medical profession controls
the supply, and uses it for the diagnosis of mental illness. But,
since the formula has been published, not even severe legislation will prevent the general public from access to the product.
It seems likely, therefore, that what was for thousands of years
a sacred and secret element, entrusted only to persons chosen
for their good conduct and integrity, will soon be snatched at by
jaded sensation-seekers. They will be disappointed. The word
'drug', originally applied to all ingredients used in chemistry,
pharmacy, dyeing and so on, has acquired a particular connota-
tion in modern English, which cannot apply to *psilocybin*: 'to
drug' is to stupefy, rather than to quicken, the senses. *Psilocybin*
provides no welcome semi-death in drunken stupor: though
the body is relaxed, the mind is conscious throughout, indeed,
supra-conscious. Psychiatrists at the Lexington Addiction

Centre, Kentucky, who gave *psilocybin* to alcoholics as a means of discovering why they are trying to escape from reality by drink, find that it intensifies and lays bare mental conflict. Experimentalists are therefore likely to see visions evoked by their own uneasy consciences: weeping for grief, not joy; or even shuddering aghast.

Good and evil alternate in most people's hearts. Few are habitually at peace with themselves; and whoever prepares to eat hallucigenic mushrooms should take as careful stock of his mental and moral well-being as initiates took before attending the Eleusinian Mysteries. The friend who ate mushrooms with us while not in a state of peace watched his hand turn corpse-like and slowly disintegrate into a dusty skeleton. This peculiar virtue of *psilocybin*, the power to enhance personal reality, turns 'Know thyself!' into a practical precept; and may commend it as the sacramental food of some new religion. *Peyotl*, made from cactus buds, another sacred hallucigenic agent – but, it seems, not in such early religious use among the Mexicans as mush-rooms – has already been sanctified by a 'Christian Church' of two hundred thousand members, extending from Central America to Canada. The Catholic and main Protestant churches can never, of course, accept visions that either *peyotl* or *psilocybin* excites as anything but diabolical and illusory. They may even put pressure on public-health authorities to outlaw *psilocybin*, arguing that, although the *psilocybe* mushroom does not make for addiction among the Mazateks, and seems to have no harm-ful effect on their minds and bodies, this may be due to its short season and a loss of virtue when dried; whereas the virtue is stable in *psilocybin*, and the results of long-term dosing are unknown – a permanent schizophrenia might occur. Liquor and tobacco interests would, no doubt, wholeheartedly support the Churches' plea.

My single experience of *psilocybe* was wholly good: an illumi-nation of the mind, a re-education of sight and hearing, and even of touch, as I handled small objects beside me. The perfect sensory control which I could enjoy, confirmed, by analogy, my lifelong faith in the poetic trance: a world where words come to life and combine, under the poet's supra-conscious guidance, into inevitable and true rhythmic statements. But I find one main difference between the two conditions: a mushroom trance is relatively passive; a poetic trance, active – the pen running briskly across paper.

Research should show how far the similarity of most people's visits to Eden or Tlalócan depends on the mushrooms' toxic properties, and how far on suggestion. I think it unnecessary, here, to cite Jung's theory of the Collective Unconscious, since a common tradition of Paradise may be attributed to ancient cultural contact even between distant civilizations, especially if these experiences can be shown to correspond with the physical action of a common toxin. A distinct lowering of body-temperature occurs an hour after eating *psilocybe*, which would explain both the cool sea-grottoes and Gilgamesh's search for the herb of immortality at the sea bottom; it is also followed by a considerable heightening of colour sensitivity, which would account for the jewels. After all, such writhing and creeping things as torment sufferers from *delirium tremens* are clearly not products of the Collective Unconscious, but due to a characteristic tremor of the optic nerve and an irritation of the skin, caused by alcohol.

Paradise, in fact, seems to be a subjective vision. As Jesus himself said: 'The Kingdom of Heaven is within you.' He might have added: 'So is the Kingdom of Hell.' The jewelled 'Garden' can be attained by the pure of heart without undergoing so austere a regimen as to become alienated from their friends; many young women have a secret garden which they frequently visit. The love-feast, for all who attend it in a state of grace and with complete mutual trust – by no means a simple condition – strengthens human friendship and at the same time bestows spiritual enlightenment: which are the twin purposes of most religions. Whether the soul visits a non-subjective Paradise or Hell on quitting its body, let theologians dispute.

The natural poetic trance, however, as I have experienced it on different levels – sometimes light, sometimes so deep that the slightest disturbance causes acute distress – means a good deal more to me than any trance induced by artificial means. I understand Coleridge's depreciation of *Kubla Khan*, which he wrote almost automatically after stupefying his mind with laudanum. It was, as it were, a demon's gift; not earned (like his other poems) by active poetic thought. True, I have survived enough operations to know the difference in kind between an opiate dream, where one is the dazed victim, and a mushroom vision that can, I know, be consciously assessed and even controlled. Since I found myself capable of dismissing that vision of Crown Jewels and Caryatids, and since one or two of my companions found it possible to visit particular places when under the influence of *psilocybe*, I hesitate to challenge the claim that Tlalóc's adepts can use their liberation of mental forces for oracular research. Nevertheless, it seems established that Tlalócan, for all its sensory marvels, contains no palace of words presided over by the Living Muse, and no small white-washed cell (furnished with only a table, a chair, pen, ink and paper) to which a poet may retire and actively write poems in her honour – rather than bask sensuously under her spell.

Drugs that Shape Men's Minds
Aldous Huxley

In the course of history many more people have died for their drink and their dope than have died for their religion or their country. The craving for ethyl alcohol and the opiates has been stronger, in these millions, than the love of God, of home, of children; even of life. Their cry was not for liberty or death; it was for death preceded by enslavement. There is a paradox here, and a mystery. Why should such multitudes of men and women be so ready to sacrifice themselves for a cause so utterly hopeless and in ways so painful and so profoundly humiliating?

To this riddle there is, of course, no simple or single answer. Human beings are immensely complicated creatures, living simultaneously in a half-dozen different worlds. Each individual is unique and, in a number of respects, unlike all the other members of the species. None of our motives is unmixed, none of our actions can be traced back to a single source and, in any group we care to study, behaviour patterns that are observably similar may be the result of many constellations of dissimilar causes.

Thus, there are some alcoholics who seem to have been bio-chemically predestined to alcoholism. (Among rats, as Prof. Roger Williams, of the University of Texas, has shown, some are born drunkards: some are born teetotallers and will never touch the stuff.) Other alcoholics have been foredoomed not by some inherited defect in their biochemical make-up, but by their neurotic reactions to distressing events in their childhood or adolescence. Again, others embark upon their course of slow suicide as a result of mere imitation and good fellowship because they have made such an 'excellent adjustment to their group' – a process which, if the group happens to be criminal, idiotic or merely ignorant, can bring only disaster to the well-adjusted individual. Nor must we forget that large class of addicts who have taken to drugs or drink in order to escape from physical pain. Aspirin, let us remember, is a very recent invention. Until late in the Victorian era, 'poppy and mandragora', along with henbane and ethyl alcohol, were the only pain relievers available to civilized man. Toothache, arthritis and neuralgia could, and frequently did, drive men and women to become opium addicts.

De Quincey, for example, first resorted to opium[1] in order to relieve 'excruciating rheumatic pains of the head'. He swallowed his poppy and, an hour later, 'What a resurrection from the lowest depths of the inner spirit! What an apocalypse!' And it was not merely that he felt no more pain. 'This negative effect was swallowed up in the immensity of those positive effects which had opened up before me, in the abyss of divine enjoyment thus suddenly revealed . . . Here was the secret of happiness, about which the philosophers had disputed for so many ages, at once discovered.'

'Resurrection, apocalypse, divine enjoyment, happiness . . .' De Quincey's words lead us to the very heart of our paradoxical mystery. The problem of drug addiction and excessive drinking is not merely a matter of chemistry and psychopathology, of relief from pain and conformity with a bad society. It is also a problem in metaphysics – a problem, one might almost say, in theology. In *The Varieties of Religious Experience* (1902), William James has touched on these metaphysical aspects of addiction:

---

[1] De Quincey's *Confessions of an English Opium-Eater* (London, 1922) was the first drug confessional and case history in literature.

The sway of alcohol over mankind is unquestionably due to its power to stimulate the mystical faculties in human nature, usually crushed to earth by the cold facts and dry criticisms of the sober hour. Sobriety diminishes, discriminates and says no. Drunkenness expands, unites and says yes. It is in fact the great exciter of the Yes function in man. It brings its votary from the chill periphery of things into the radiant core. It makes him for the moment one with truth. Not through mere perversity do men run after it. To the poor and unlettered it stands in the place of symphony concerts and literature and it is part of the deeper mystery and tragedy of life that whiffs and gleams of something that we immediately recognize as excellent should be vouchsafed to so many of us only through the fleeting earlier phases of what, in its totality, is so degrading a poison. The drunken consciousness is one bit of the mystic consciousness, and our total opinion of it must find its place in our opinion of that larger world.

William James was not the first to detect a likeness between drunkenness and the mystical and premystical states. On that day of Pentecost there were people who explained the strange behaviour of the disciples by saying, 'These men are full of new wine.'

Peter soon undeceived them: 'These are not drunken, as ye suppose, seeing it is but the third hour of the day. But this is that which was spoken by the prophet Joel. And it shall come to pass in the last days, saith God, I will pour out of my Spirit upon all flesh.'

And it is not only by 'the dry critics of the sober hour' that the state of God-intoxication has been likened to drunkenness. In their efforts to express the inexpressible, the great mystics themselves have done the same. Thus, St Theresa of Avila tells us that she 'regards the centre of our soul as a cellar, into which God admits us as and when it pleases Him, so as to intoxicate us with the delicious wine of His Grace.'

Every fully developed religion exists simultaneously on several different levels. It exists as a set of abstract concepts about the world and its governance. It exists as a set of rites and sacraments, as a traditional method for manipulating the symbols, by means of which beliefs about the cosmic order are expressed. It exists as the feelings of love, fear and devotion evoked by this manipulation of symbols.

And finally it exists as a special kind of feeling or intuition – a sense of the oneness of all things to their divine principle, a realization (to use the language of Hindu theology) that 'thou art That', a mystical experience of what seems self-evidently to be union with God.

The ordinary waking consciousness is a very useful and, on most occasions, an indispensable state of mind; but it is by no means the only form of consciousness, nor in all circumstances the best. Insofar as he transcends his ordinary self and his ordinary mode of awareness, the mystic is able to enlarge his vision, to look more deeply into the unfathomable miracle of existence.

The mystical experience is doubly valuable; it is valuable because it gives the experiencer a better understanding of himself and the world and because it may help him to lead a less self-centred and more creative life.

In hell, a great religious poet has written, the punishment of the lost is to be 'their sweating selves, but worse'. On earth we are not worse than we are, we are merely our sweating selves, period.

Alas, that is quite bad enough. We love ourselves to the point of idolatry; but we also intensely dislike ourselves – we find ourselves unutterably boring. Correlated with this distaste for the idolatrously worshipped self, there is in all of us a desire, sometimes latent, sometimes conscious and passionately expressed, to escape from the prison of our individuality, an urge to self-transcendence. It is to this urge that we owe mystical theology, spiritual exercises and yoga – to this, too, that we owe alcoholism and drug addiction.

Modern pharmacology has given us a host of new synthetics,

but in the field of the naturally occurring mind changers it has made no radical discoveries. All the botanical sedatives, stimulants, vision revealers, happiness promoters and cosmic-consciousness arousers were found out thousands of years ago, before the dawn of history.

In many societies at many levels of civilization attempts have been made to fuse drug intoxication with God-intoxication. In ancient Greece, for example, ethyl alcohol had its place in the established religion. Dionysus, or Bacchus, as he was often called, was a true divinity. His worshippers addressed him as *Lusios*, 'Liberator', or as *Theoinos*, 'Godwine'. The latter name telescopes fermented grape juice and the supernatural into a single pentecostal experience. 'Born a god,' writes Euripides, 'Bacchus is poured out as a libation to the gods, and through him men receive good.' Unfortunately they also receive harm. The blissful experience of self-transcendence which alcohol makes possible has to be paid for, and the price is exorbitantly high.

Complete prohibition of all chemical mind changers can be decreed, but cannot be enforced, and tends to create more evils than it cures. Even more unsatisfactory has been the policy of complete toleration and unrestricted availability. In England, during the first years of the eighteenth century, cheap untaxed gin – 'drunk for a penny, dead drunk for two-pence' – threatened society with complete demoralization. A century later, opium, in the form of laudanum, was reconciling the victims of the Industrial Revolution to their lot – but at an appalling cost in terms of addiction, illness and early death. Today most civilized societies follow a course between the two extremes of total prohibition and total toleration. Certain mind-changing drugs, such as alcohol, are permitted and made available to the public on payment of a very high tax, which tends to restrict their consumption. Other mind changers are unobtainable except under doctors' orders – or illegally from a dope pusher. In this way the problem is kept within manageable bounds. It is most certainly not solved. In their ceaseless search for self-transcendence, million of would-be mystics become addicts, commit scores of thousands of crimes and are involved in hundreds of thousands of avoidable accidents.

Do we have to go on in this dismal way indefinitely? Up until a few years ago, the answer to such a question would have been a rueful 'Yes, we do.' Today, thanks to recent developments in biochemistry and pharmacology, we are offered a workable alternative. We see that it may soon be possible for us to do something better in the way of chemical self-transcendence than what we have been doing so ineptly for the last seventy or eighty centuries.

Is it possible for a powerful drug to be completely harmless? Perhaps not. But the physiological cost can certainly be reduced to the point where it becomes negligible. There are powerful mind changers which do their work without damaging the taker's psychophysical organism and without inciting him to behave like a criminal or a lunatic. Biochemistry and pharmacology are just getting into their stride. Within a few years there will probably be dozens of powerful but – physiologically and socially speaking – very inexpensive mind changers on the market.

In view of what we already have in the way of powerful but nearly harmless drugs; in view, above all, of what unquestionably we are very soon going to have – we ought to start immediately to give some serious thought to the problem of the new mind changers. How ought they to be used? How can they be abused? Will human beings be better and happier for their discovery? Or worse and more miserable?

The matter requires to be examined from many points of view. It is simultaneously a question for biochemists and physicians, for psychologists and social anthropologists, for legislators and law-enforcement officers. And finally it is an ethical question and a religious question. Sooner or later – and the sooner, the better – the various specialists concerned will have to meet, discuss and then decide, in the light of the best available evidence and the most imaginative kind of foresight, what should be done. Meanwhile let us take a preliminary look at this many-faceted problem.

Last year American physicians wrote 48,000,000 prescriptions for tranquillizing drugs, many of which have been refilled, probably more than once. The tranquillizers are the best known of the new, nearly harmless mind changers. They can be used by most people, not indeed with complete impunity, but at a reasonably low physiological cost. Their enormous popularity bears witness to the fact that a great many people dislike both their environment and 'their sweating selves'. Under tranquillizers the degree of their self-transcendence is not very great; but it is enough to make all the difference, in many cases, between misery and contentment.

In theory, tranquillizers should be given only to persons suffering from rather severe forms of neurosis or psychosis. In practice, unfortunately, many physicians have been carried away by the current pharmacological fashion and are prescribing tranquillizers to all and sundry. The history of medical fashions, it may be remarked, is at least as grotesque as the history of fashions in women's hats – at least as grotesque and, since human lives are at stake, considerably more tragic. In the present case, millions of patients who had no real need of tranquillizers have been given the pills by their doctors and have learned to resort to them in every predicament, however triflingly uncomfortable. This is very bad medicine and, from the pill taker's point of view, dubious morality and poor sense.

There are circumstances in which even the healthy are justified in resorting to the chemical control of negative emotions. If you really can't keep your temper, let a tranquillizer keep it for you. But for healthy people to resort to a chemical mind changer every time they feel annoyed or anxious or tense is neither sensible nor right. Too much tension and anxiety can reduce a man's efficiency – but so can too little. There are many occasions when it is entirely proper for us to feel concerned, when an excess of placidity might reduce our chances of dealing effectively with a ticklish situation. On these occasions, tension mitigated and directed from within by the psychological methods of self-control is preferable from every point of view to complacency imposed from without by the methods of chemical control.

And now let us consider the case – not, alas, a hypothetical case – of two societies competing with each other. In Society A, tranquillizers are available by prescription and at a rather stiff price – which means, in practice, that their use is confined to that rich and influential minority which provides the society with its leadership. This minority of leading citizens consumes several billions of the complacency-producing pills every year. In Society B, on the other hand, the tranquillizers are not so freely available, and the members of the influential minority do not resort, on the slightest provocation, to the chemical control of what may be necessary and productive tension. Which of these two competing societies is likely to win the race? A society whose leaders make an excessive use of soothing syrups is in danger of falling behind a society whose leaders are not over-tranquillized.

Now let us consider another kind of drug – still undiscovered, but probably just around the corner – a drug capable of making people feel happy in situations where they would normally feel miserable. Such a drug would be a blessing, but a blessing fraught with grave political dangers. By making harmless chemical euphoria freely available, a dictator could reconcile an entire population to a state of affairs to which self-respecting human beings ought not to be reconciled. Despots have always found it necessary to supplement force by political or religious propaganda. In this sense the pen is mightier than the sword. But mightier than either the pen or the sword is the pill. In mental hospitals it has been found that chemical restraint is far more effective than strait jackets or psychiatry. The dictatorships of tomorrow will deprive men of their freedom, but will give them in exchange a happiness none the less real, as a subjective experience, for being chemically induced. The pursuit of happiness is one of the traditional rights of man; unfortunately, the achievement of happiness may turn out to be incompatible with another of man's rights – namely, liberty.

It is quite possible, however, that pharmacology will restore with one hand what it takes away with the other. Chemically induced euphoria could easily become a threat to individual liberty; but chemically induced vigour and chemically heightened intelligence could easily be liberty's strongest bulwark. Most of us function at about 15 per cent of capacity. How can we step up our lamentably low efficiency?

Two methods are available – the educational and the biochemical. We can take adults and children as they are and give them a much better training than we are giving them now. Or, by appropriate biochemical methods, we can transform them into superior individuals. If these superior individuals are given a superior education, the results will be revolutionary. They will be startling even if we continue to subject them to the rather poor educational methods at present in vogue.

Will it in fact be possible to produce superior individuals by biochemical means? The Russians certainly believe it. They are now halfway through a Five Year Plan to produce 'pharmacological substances that normalize higher nervous activity and heighten human capacity for work'. Precursors of these future mind improvers are already being experimented with. It has been found, for example, that when given in massive doses some of the vitamins – nicotinic acid and ascorbic acid are examples – sometimes produce a certain heightening of psychic energy. A combination of two enzymes – ethylene disulphonate and adenosine triphosphate, which, when injected together, improve carbohydrate metabolism in nervous tissue – may also turn out to be effective.

Meanwhile good results are being claimed for various new synthetic, nearly harmless stimulants. There is iproniazid, which, according to some authorities, 'appears to increase the total amount of psychic energy'. Unfortunately, iproniazid in large doses has side effects which in some cases may be extremely serious! Another psychic energizer is an amino alcohol which is thought to increase the body's production of acetylcholine, a substance of prime importance in the functioning of the nervous system. In view of what has already been achieved, it seems quite possible that, within a few years, we may be able to lift ourselves up by our own biochemical bootstraps.

In the meantime let us all fervently wish the Russians every success in their current pharmacological venture. The discovery of a drug capable of increasing the average individual's psychic energy, and its wide distribution throughout the U.S.S.R., would probably mean the end of Russia's present form of government. Generalized intelligence and mental alertness are the most powerful enemies of dictatorship and at the same time the basic conditions of effective democracy. Even in the democratic West we could do with a bit of psychic energizing. Between them, education and pharmacology may do something to offset the effects of that deterioration of our biological material to which geneticists have frequently called attention.

From these political and ethical considerations let us now pass to the strictly religious problems that will be posed by some of the new mind changers. We can foresee the nature of these future problems by studying the effects of a natural mind changer, which has been used for centuries past in religious worship; I refer to the Peyote cactus of Northern Mexico and the South-western United States. Peyote contains mescalin – which can now be produced synthetically – and mescalin, in William James's phrase, 'stimulates the mystical faculties in human nature' far more powerfully and in a far more enlightening way than alcohol and, what is more, it does so at a physiological and social cost that is negligibly low. Peyote produces self-transcendence in two ways – it introduces the taker into the Other World of visionary experience, and it gives him a sense of solidarity with his fellow worshippers, with human beings at large and with the divine nature of things.

The effects of peyote can be duplicated by synthetic mescalin and by LSD (lysergic acid diethylamide), a derivative of ergot. Effective in incredibly small doses, LSD is now being used experimentally by psychotherapists in Europe, in South America, in Canada and the United States. It lowers the barrier between conscious and subconscious and permits the patient to look more deeply and understandingly into the recesses of his own mind. The deepening of self-knowledge takes place against a background of visionary and even mystical experience.

When administered in the right kind of psychological environment, these chemical mind changers make possible a genuine religious experience. Thus a person who takes LSD or mescalin may suddenly understand – not only intellectually but organically, experientially – the meaning of such tremendous religious affirmations as 'God is love,' or 'Though He slay me, yet I will trust in Him.'

It goes without saying that this kind of temporary self-transcendence is no guarantee of permanent enlightenment or a lasting improvement of conduct. It is a 'gratuitous grace', which is neither necessary nor sufficient for salvation, but which, if properly used, can be enormously helpful to those who have received it. And this is true of all such experiences, whether occurring spontaneously, or as the result of swallowing the right kind of chemical mind changer, or after undertaking a course of 'spiritual exercises' or bodily mortification.

Those who are offended by the idea that the swallowing of a pill may contribute to a genuinely religious experience should remember that all the standard mortifications – fasting, voluntary sleeplessness and self-torture – inflicted upon themselves by the ascetics of every religion for the purpose of acquiring merit, are also, like the mind-changing drugs, powerful devices for altering the chemistry of the body in general and the nervous system in particular. Or consider the procedures generally known as spiritual exercises. The breathing techniques taught by the yogi of India result in prolonged suspensions of respiration. These in turn result in an increased concentration of carbon dioxide in the blood; and the psychological consequence of this is a change in the quality of consciousness. Again, meditations involving long, intense concentration upon a single idea or image may also result – for neurological reasons which I do not profess to understand – in a slowing down of respiration and even in prolonged suspensions of breathing.

Many ascetics and mystics have practised their chemistry-changing mortifications and spiritual exercises while living, for longer or shorter periods, as hermits. Now, the life of a hermit, such as Saint Anthony, is a life in which there are very few external stimuli. But as Hebb, John Lilly and other experimental psychologists have recently shown in the laboratory, a person in a limited environment, which provides very few external stimuli, soon undergoes a change in the quality of his consciousness and may transcend his normal self to the point of hearing voices or seeing visions, often extremely unpleasant, like so many of Saint Anthony's visions, but sometimes beatific.

That men and women can, by physical and chemical means, transcend themselves in a genuinely spiritual way is something which, to the squeamish idealist, seems rather shocking. But, after all, the drug or the physical exercise is not the cause of the spiritual experience; it is only its occasion.

Writing of William James's experiments with nitrous oxide, Bergson has summed up the whole matter in a few lucid sentences. 'The psychic disposition was there, potentially, only waiting a signal to express itself in action. It might have been evoked spiritually by an effort made on his own spiritual level. But it could just as well be brought about materially, by an inhibition of what inhibited it, by the removing of an obstacle; and this effect was the wholly negative one produced by the drug.'[1] Where, for any reason, physical or moral, the psychological dispositions are unsatisfactory, the removal of obstacles by a drug or by ascetic practices will result in a negative rather than a positive spiritual experience. Such an infernal experience is extremely distressing, but may also be extremely salutary. There are plenty of people to whom a few hours in hell – the hell that

---

[1] *Two Sources of Religion and Morality* (1935).

they themselves have done so much to create – could do a world of good.

Physiologically costless, or nearly costless, stimulators of the mystical faculties are now making their appearance, and many kinds of them will soon be on the market. We can be quite sure that, as and when they become available, they will be extensively used. The urge to self-transcendence is so strong and so general that it cannot be otherwise. In the past, very few people have had spontaneous experiences of a pre-mystical or fully mystical nature; still fewer have been willing to undergo the psychophysical disciplines which prepare an insulated individual for this kind of self-transcendence. The powerful but nearly costless mind changers of the future will change all this completely. Instead of being rare, premystical and mystical experiences will become common. What was once the spiritual privilege of the few will be made available to the many. For the ministers of the world's organized religions, this will raise a number of unprecedented problems. For most people, religion has always been a matter of traditional symbols and of their own emotional, intellectual and ethical response to those symbols. To men and women who have had direct experience of self-transcendence into the mind's Other World of vision and union with the nature of things, a religion of mere symbols is not likely to be very satisfying. The perusal of a page from even the most beautifully written cookbook is no substitute for the eating of dinner. We are exhorted to '*taste* and see that the Lord is good'.

In one way or another, the world's ecclesiastical authorities will have to come to terms with the new mind changers. They may come to terms with them negatively, by refusing to have anything to do with them. In that case a psychological phenomenon, potentially of great spiritual value, will manifest itself outside the pale of organized religion. On the other hand, they may choose to come to terms with the mind changers in some positive way – exactly how, I am not prepared to guess.

My own belief is that, though they may start by being

something of an embarrassment, these new mind changers will tend in the long run to deepen the spiritual life of the communities in which they are available. That famous 'revival of religion', about which so many people have been talking for so long, will not come about as the result of evangelistic mass meetings or the television appearances of photogenic clergymen. It will come about as the result of biochemical discoveries that will make it possible for large numbers of men and women to achieve a radical self-transcendence and a deeper understanding of the nature of things. And this revival of religion will be at the same time a revolution. From being an activity mainly concerned with symbols, religion will be transformed into an activity concerned mainly with experience and intuition – an everyday mysticism underlying and giving significance to everyday rationality, everyday tasks and duties, everyday human relationships.

Timothy Leary, LSD and Harvard
Stewart Tendler and David May

The tall, lean figure seen crossing Harvard Square in autumn 1960 seemed everything the New England campus might expect of its staff. Dressed in a Harris tweed jacket and grey slacks, Dr Timothy Leary was a psychologist with a reputation for stimulating, original thinking. At the age of forty he was a recent recruit to the university's Center for Research in Personality, to which he brought experience gleaned from hospital work and research projects elsewhere in America. There were those who called him 'Theory Leary', but his self-confidence was boundless. In his own words he was 'handsome, clean-cut, witty, confident, charismatic and in that inert culture unusually creative . . .'

At the start of a new decade Leary walked with the inner knowledge of his psychedelic experience. Here was a man with a strong sense of rebelliousness which more than once in his life had pulled him away from the safety of convention: a sense of mischief. Leary was an iconoclast who regarded his chosen profession as a 'piddling science'.

A few months before in Mexico, Leary had taken a fistful of mushrooms – *psilocybe Mexicana*. Within minutes he was 'swept over the edge of a sensory Niagara'. Five hours later he decided that his life would be dedicated to this 'new instrument' for psychology, a science badly in need of new directions.

He fired the enthusiasm of a young colleague at Harvard, Richard Alpert, an assistant professor of education and psychology. At first sight they made an unlikely partnership for they came from such different backgrounds. Alpert, son of a wealthy New England lawyer, was ten years younger and obsessed with 'success'. With his thick, black-rimmed glasses and neat hair, Alpert was a man aggressively determined to get on in life, even though he already had many of the trappings of attainment – an aircraft, a boat, a motorcycle, and both a sports car and a foreign limousine. Alpert's climb was going to be by the book, a brilliant frontal assault.

Leary, on the other hand, seemed to have spent his life fighting guerrilla campaigns against the establishment. His mother wanted him to become a priest and his father cherished visions of him in uniform. Neither got their way. Leary gave up his place at a Catholic seminary and then resigned from West Point after an infraction of the rules which led to his being ostracized by the other cadets for nine months (Leary used the time to study Eastern philosophy). He enrolled at Alabama University to read psychology, only to be thrown out after being caught in the girls' dormitories. After an undistinguished war career as clerk and hospital aide – he was partially deaf – he returned to finish his degree and went on to take a doctorate at the University of California, Berkeley. He joined the Kaiser Foundation Hospital in Oakland as director of psychology research and it was here that *Interpersonal Diagnosis of Personality: A Functional Theory and Methodology for Personality Evaluation*, all 518 pages of it, was born and completed in 1956. It was described as 'Best Book on Psychotherapy of the Year' by the *Annual Review of Psychology*. In the midst of public success his private life came under attack and collapsed. His two marriages failed; his first wife eventually killed herself. Leary, also disillusioned with his work, went off to Europe with his two children. In Florence he met David McClelland who was director of the Center, a division of Harvard's Laboratory of Social Relations, and who persuaded him to join the university.

Now Leary, aided by Alpert, was about to do battle again. The two men plotted the outline of a psilocybin experiment, and for reference Leary turned to Huxley's two works, *The Doors of Perception* and *Heaven and Hell*. The man who used West Point as a yoga monastery was immediately in tune with Huxley, understanding both the psychedelic and the oriental strains in the books. Even as Leary was reading them, Huxley was at MIT delivering his lectures.

The two men first met over lunch in Harvard's faculty club. In the course of a meal starting (appropriately enough) with mushroom soup, they began to discuss the Harvard project. Amid the hubbub of the dining room Huxley was charmed by the psychologist and Leary was spellbound by the writer's erudition. According to Leary, he and Alpert listened as Huxley 'advised and counselled and joked and told stories . . . and our research programme was shaped accordingly. Huxley offered to sit in on our planning meetings and was ready to take mushrooms with us when the research was under way.'

At first the Harvard psilocybin research project was small, comprising Leary, Alpert and six graduate students. Leary and Alpert wanted to study the mental and emotional effects of the drug on artists and intellectuals. Using psilocybin, ordered from Sandoz, the thirty-eight subjects were allowed to control their own dosage (within reasonable limits), taking the drug in pleasant, spacious surroundings. Huxley was among the volunteers, as were Allen Ginsberg and William Burroughs, two of the leading Beat artists; Alan Watts, noted expert on Zen Buddhism; and Arthur Koestler, writer and philosopher.

The project took a fresh direction with a series of experiments at the nearby Concord men's prison, to discover if psilocybin could cure recidivism. In the short term the drug seemed to work since only a quarter of the thirty-five who took part got into fresh trouble, against the normal rate of 80 per cent.

Huxley remained in touch with Leary, corresponding on aspects of visionary art useful to psychedelic research. It was through Huxley that he graduated on to LSD.

The man who made it possible was Michael Hollingshead, denizen of Greenwich Village and British expatriate. Hollingshead had been working as the executive secretary of a foundation established to promote Anglo-American cultural relations through student exchanges. The demands of the foundation left Hollingshead free time to investigate the wilder side of the cultures he was cross-fertilizing, in Greenwich Village coffee bars among the Beats. Impressed by Huxley's writings on mescaline and LSD, Hollingshead persuaded a fellow countryman working at a New York hospital to place an order with Sandoz's New Jersey office using hospital notepaper.

When the gram of LSD arrived, Hollingshead diluted it with water and poured it into an empty mayonnaise jar. His first taste astonished him – and left him eager to learn more. Huxley advised him to approach Leary.

Although Leary gave Hollingshead a job within his team and a room in his home, he at first could not be persuaded to dip into the mayonnaise jar. 'His view might be summarized,' said Hollingshead, 'as "when you've had one psychedelic, you've had them all".'

Leary was finally won over by the enthusiasm of those who had taken the drug. LSD became the basis of the most dramatic of the Harvard experiments – 'the miracle of Marsh Chapel'. On Good Friday 1963, twenty students from Andover Theological Seminary filed into Marsh Chapel at Boston University to test the religious and mystic possibilities of LSD. Ten were given LSD and the other ten a mild amphetamine, but none knew what they were taking. Nine of the ten who took the LSD reported mystical experience – one began to read out passages from Donne's poetry, ripped the buttons off his clothes and claimed he was a fish. Another wandered out into the Boston traffic, believing he was Christ: nothing, he thought, could harm him. Confusion reigned in the chapel as the untouched students watched their colleagues gyrating like snakes or stretched out rigid on the pews.

The 'miracle' was the climax of Leary's formal academic programme of experiments, coming in the middle of a year which proved to be a watershed for the Harvard psychologist. As the experiments extended their scope, Leary could not resist prose-lytization through less organized experimentation; 400 writers, artists, priests and students between them took 3,000 doses of the hallucinogenic. With such work came a stream of intellec-tual hyperbole which rapidly turned into a torrent of assertions and claims for the significance of LSD and its lesser brethren.

Harvard's initial response to the early psilocybin experiment was expressed as little more than academic doubt about the methodology of the work, mingled with sarcastic murmurs that the experiments were hallucinogenic cocktail parties. But by 1962 Leary's psychedelic research was alarming both the uni-versity authorities and the Massachusetts Public Health Department. When the *Boston Herald* picked up the story, the university found itself the focus for unwelcome publicity. The university decided that the contracts given to Alpert and Leary would not be renewed when they expired in the summer of 1963.

Tired of academic in-fighting and the unwelcome attention of state investigators, the researchers retreated into exile. Leary, Alpert and a dozen followers rented a hotel in Zihuatanejo, a small Mexican fishing port on the Pacific coast, to conduct per-sonal experiments without interruption. When they returned to Harvard for the start of the new academic year, the exile had restored their vigour and enforced a new militancy.

Opposition welded Leary and his disciples more tightly together. The psychedelics were not only an artistic and medical tool; they held the promise of changing the world, changing Man, heralding a new millennium.

To the group round Leary and Alpert the situation seemed simple. The creators of many great movements and intellectual developments in history have had to fight an entrenched estab-lishment in their early days, only to see themselves eventually vindicated. Could this not be the case with psychedelics? Those who had taken it were convinced of the rightness of their cause and of Leary, their leader. Even Alpert, apparently joint organizer of the experiments, was moved to say of Leary: 'I've never met a great man before and this is one of them and it is enough for my life merely to serve such a being.'

Back at Harvard, they created 'a colony for transcendental living' in a spacious house in Newton, a sedate Boston suburb. Based on Huxley's *Island*, the commune was made up of Leary, his children, another Harvard man and his family, Alpert and a number of friends. This 'multi-family' existence was invented to 'maintain a level of experience which cuts beyond routine ego and social games'. A meditation room was specially built, accessible only by ladder and furnished with cushions, mattresses and curtains. Illuminated by one small light stood a small statue of Buddha, and the fragrance of incense hung in the air. Soon, a second 'multi-family' centre was opened nearby.

Within the university, Alpert continued to lecture on motivation while Leary took his graduate seminars in research methods. Outside it they launched IFIF, the International Federation for Internal Freedom, dedicated to the new fifth freedom – freedom to expand one's consciousness. Students were encouraged to join and form 'cells' through which they would later be able to obtain drugs. Alpert went fund-raising among the wealthy in Boston and New York.

At Harvard the experiments and the authorities were moving towards fresh battles. Huxley, soon to die, wondered what would happen next. He told Osmond: 'What about Tim Leary? I spent an evening with him a few weeks ago – he talked such nonsense . . . that I became quite concerned. Not about his sanity – because he is perfectly sane – but about his prospects in the world; for this nonsense talking is just another device for annoying people in authority, flouting convention, cocking snooks at the academic world; it is the reaction of the mischievous Irish boy to the headmaster of the school. One of these days the headmaster will lose patience.'

Indeed, patience was becoming scarce at Harvard. The authorities were increasingly worried about the growing black market for drugs in and around the campus. There were reports of sugar cubes coated with LSD selling in Harvard Square for a dollar a time and a student dispensing mail-ordered peyote to his friends.

John Monro, Dean of Harvard, issued a strong warning against the evils of drugs: the psychedelics 'may result in serious hazard to the mental health and stability of even an apparently normal person'. Leary and Alpert replied that 'the control and expansion of consciousness would be a major civil liberty in the next decade'. In February 1963, IFIF sent its literature to Harvard students, graduate students and faculty members.

As matters came to a head at Harvard – Leary was facing dismissal for failing to turn up on campus, and the authorities began an investigation into both him and Alpert – IFIF, with branches in Los Angeles and other American cities, opened its most grandiose extension back at Zihuatanejo. This was intended to be an extension of the early Harvard communities and a training centre for missionaries. Leary announced he would gamble his reputation on the centre. He hired a public relations firm to stimulate interest. It opened on 1 May 1963, and lasted six weeks.

Dr Joseph Downing, a Los Angeles psychologist, reported on the Mexican centre in a 1964 survey of LSD. The group he watched was drawn from Boston, Los Angeles, San Francisco and New York. They were aged between twenty and sixty and included clinical psychologists, engineers and businessmen. Dr Downing described the IFIF philosophy as 'a mixture of modern psychology, New England mysticism and modified Mahayana Buddhism . . . The urbane and skilful writings of Aldous Huxley and Alan Watts, the Tibetan Buddhist emphasis on mystic preparation for death-rebirth experience and the stern no-nonsense pragmatism of Chinese and Japanese Zen Buddhist philosophy with its emphasis on *satori* (transcendental enlightenment) have been adapted to order and rationalize the other-worldly experiences which this school of thought attributes to the psychedelic drugs.'

The philosophic cocktail was not to the taste of the Mexican authorities, who watched the community with growing alarm. Three days after the community opened its doors Alpert was fired from Harvard; investigations revealed that he had broken a promise not to give drugs to students.

The sacking aroused further Mexican anxiety and the antipathy of at least one prominent Mexican newspaper. Public opinion gathered momentum. Eventually the government decreed that the IFIF people had entered Mexico under false pretences: they claimed to be tourists when they were in fact researchers and students. The expulsion was courteous – even friendly – but final.

Kathmandu Interlude

Terence McKenna

During the spring and summer of 1969, I had lived in Nepal and studied the Tibetan language. The wave of interest in Buddhist studies was just beginning, so those of us in Nepal with Tibetan interests were a tightly knit group. My purpose in studying Tibetan was different from that of most Westerners involved with the language in Nepal. They were nearly all interested in some aspect of Mahayana Buddhist thought, while I was interested in a religious tradition that antedated the seventh century and the introduction of Buddhism into Tibet.

This indigenous pre-Buddhist religion of Tibet was a kind of shamanism closely related to the motifs and cosmology of the classical shamanism of Siberia. Tibetan folk shamanism, called Bön, continues to be practiced today in the mountainous area of Nepal that borders Tibet. Its practitioners are generally despised by the Buddhist community, being thought of as heretics and as generally low types.

My interest in Bön and its practitioners, the Bön-po, arose out of a passion for Tibetan painting. It is common in such painting that the most fantastic, extravagant, and ferocious images are drawn from the pre-Buddhist substratum of folk imagery. The terrifying, multi-armed, and multi-headed guardians of the Buddhist teaching, called *Dharmapalas*, with their auras of flame and light, are autochthonous Bön deities

whose allegiance to the late-arriving Buddhist religion is maintained only by powerful spells and rituals that bind and secure
the loyalty of these forceful demons.

It seemed to me that the shamanic tradition that spawned
such outlandish and fantastic images must at some time have
had the knowledge of a hallucinogenic plant. Shamanic ecstasy
in Siberia was known to be attained through the use of the
mushroom *Amanita muscaria*, and Gordon Wasson has made a
good case for the use of the same mushroom in Vedic India.
Since Tibet is situated roughly between these two areas, it did
not seem impossible that, before the coming of Buddhism, hallucinogens were part of the indigenous shamanic tradition.

Amanita muscaria was only one of several candidates that
might have served as a hallucinogen in ancient Tibet. *Pegamum
harmala* of the *Zygophallaceae* family is another suspect. It, like
Banisteriopsis caapi, contains the hallucinogenic beta-carboline
alkaloid harmaline in considerable quantities and is probably
hallucinogenic by itself. Certainly in combination with a DMT-
containing plant, of which the flora of India boasts several, it
should yield a strong hallucinogen whose composition would
not differ chemically from the *ayahuasca* brews of the
Amazon.[1]

My interest in Tibetan painting and hallucinogenic shamanism led me to Nepal. I had learned there were refugee camps in
Nepal and near Simla in India whose populations were nearly
entirely outcast Bön-po, unwelcome in the camps where
Buddhist refugees were housed. I wanted to learn from the
Bön-po whatever knowledge they still retained of hallucinogens they might once have known and used. I wished, in my
naiveté, to prove my hypothesis about the influence of plant
hallucinogens on Tibetan painting and then write a monograph
about it.

[1] The giant river reed, *Arundo donax* for example, occurs in India and its roots
contain DMT. See S. Ghosal, S. K. Dutta, A. K. Sanyal, and Bhattacharya,
'Arundo donex L. (Graminae), Phytochemical and Pharmacological
Evaluation,' in the *Journal of Medical Chemistry*, vol. 12 (1969), p. 480.

As soon as I arrived in Asia, the enormity of the task and the effort that this project would require were seen more nearly in their correct proportions. My proposed plan was actually an outline for a life of scholarly research! Naturally, I found that nothing could be done at all until I was familiar with the Tibetan language, so I put aside all my research ideas and resolved to dedicate myself to learning as much Tibetan as I could in the few months that circumstances gave me in Nepal.

I moved out of Kathmandu, away from the pleasures of the hashish dens and the social swirl of the international community of travelers, smugglers, and adventurers that has made the town its own. I moved to Boudanath, a small village of great antiquity a few miles east of Kathmandu and recently flooded with Tibetans from Lhasa – people who spoke the Lhasa dialect that is understood throughout the Himalayas. The people of the village were Buddhist and I made my arrangements to study with the monks there without mentioning my interest in the Bön-po. I sought lodging and came to terms with Den Ba-do, the local miller and a Newari, one of the main ethnic groups in Nepal. He agreed to rent me a room on the third floor of his prosperous adobe house, which fronted the muddy main street of Boudanath. I struck a bargain with a local girl who agreed to bring me fresh water each day, and I settled comfortably in. I whitewashed the adobe walls of my room, commissioned a huge mosquito net in the market in Kathmandu, and arranged my books and small Tibetan writing bench inside. Finally at ease, I set about cultivating my image as a young traveler and scholar.

Tashi Gyaltsen Lama was my teacher. He was a very kind and understanding Gelugpa. In spite of his advanced age, he would arrive every morning promptly at seven for our two-hour lesson. I was like a child; we began with penmanship and the alphabet. Each morning, after the lama departed, I would study for several more hours and then the rest of the day was my own. I explored the King of Nepal's game sanctuary farther east of Boudanath and the Hindu cremation ghatts at nearby

Pashupathinath. I also made the acquaintance of a few Westerners who were living in the vicinity.

Among the latter were an English couple my own age. They were self-consciously fascinating. He was thin and blonde, with an aquiline nose and an arch manner typical of the model product of the British public school system. He was haughty and urbane, but eccentric and often hilarious. She was small and unhealthily thin – scrawny is the word I used to describe her to myself. Red-haired, wild-tempered, and cynical, she, like her companion, possessed a razor wit.

They had both been disowned by their families and were traveling hippies, as we all were then. Their relationship was bizarre – they had come together from England, but the relaxation of tension, which arrival in bucolic Nepal had brought, had been too much for their fragile liaison. Now they lived apart, he at one end of Boudanath and she, alone, at the other. They met only for the combined purpose of 'paying calls' or of abrading each other's nerves.

For some reason, in that exotic setting they managed to charm me completely. Whether they were alone or together, I was always willing to pause from my studies to pass the time with them. We became fast friends. Naturally we discussed my work, since it involved hallucinogens; they were very interested, being familiar with LSD from their days in the London scene. We also discovered that we had mutual friends in India and that we all loved the novels of Thomas Hardy. It was a very pleasant idyll.

During this time the method I had evolved for probing the shamanic dimension was to smoke DMT at the peak point of an LSD experience. I would do this whenever I took LSD, which was quite occasionally. It would allow me to enter the tryptamine dimension for a slightly extended period of time. As the summer solstice of 1969 approached, I laid plans for another such experiment.

I was going to take LSD the night of the solstice and sit up all night on my roof, smoking hashish and star-gazing. I mentioned my plan to my two English friends, who expressed a desire to join me. This was fine with me, but there was a problem; there was not enough reliable LSD to go around. My own tiny supply had arrived in Kathmandu, prophetically hidden inside a small ceramic mushroom mailed from Aspen.

Almost as a joke, I suggested that they substitute the seed of the Himalayan Datura, *Datura metel*, for the LSD. Daturas are annual bushes and the source of a number of tropane alkaloids – scopalamine, hylosciamine, and so on – compounds that produce a pseudo-hallucinogenic effect. They give an impression of flying or of confronting vague and fleeting visions, but all in a realm hard to keep control of and hard to recollect later. The seeds of *Datura metel* are used in Nepal by *saddhus* (wandering hermits and holy men), so their use was known in the area. Nevertheless my suggestion was made facetiously, since the difficulty of controlling Datura is legendary. To my surprise, my friends agreed that this was something they wanted to do, so we arranged that they would arrive at my home at six P.M. on the appointed day to make the experiment.

When the evening finally came, I moved my blankets and pipes up to the roof of the building. From there I could command a fine view of the surrounding village with its enormous *Stupa*, a conical temple with staring Buddha eyes painted on its higher portion in gold leaf. The upper golden levels of the Stupa were at that time encased in scaffolding, where repairs necessitated by a lightning strike suffered some months previously were under way. The white-domed bulk of the Stupa gave the whitewashed adobe mud village of Boudanath a saucerian and unearthly quality. Farther away, rising up many thousands of feet, I could see the great Annapurna Range; in the middle distance, the land was a patchwork of emerald paddies.

Six o'clock came and went, and my friends had not arrived. At seven they still had not been seen, and so I took my treasured tab of Orange Sunshine and settled down to wait. Ten minutes later, they arrived. I could already feel myself going, so I gestured to the two piles of Datura seeds that I had prepared.

They took them downstairs to my room and ground them with a mortar and pestle before washing them down with some tea. By the time they had returned to the roof and gotten comfortably settled, I was surging through mental space.

Hours seemed to pass. When they seated themselves, I was too distant to be aware of them. She was seated directly across from me, and he farther back and to one side, in the shadows. He played his flute. I passed the hash pipe. The moon rose full and high in the sky. I fell into long hallucinatory reveries that each lasted many minutes but felt like whole lifetimes. When I had emerged from a particularly long spell of visions, I found that my friend had stopped playing and had gone away, leaving me with his lady.

I had promised them both that I would let them try some DMT during the evening. My glass pipe and tiny stash of waxy orange DMT were before me. Slowly, and with the fluid movements of a dream, I filled the pipe and gave it to her. The stars, hard and glittering, stared down from a mighty distance on all of this. She held the pipe and took two deep inhalations, sufficient for a person so frail, then the pipe was returned to me, and I followed her into it with four huge inhalations, the fourth of which I held onto until I had broken through. For me it was an enormous amount of DMT, and I immediately had a sense of entering a high vacuum. I heard a high-pitched whine and the sound of cellophane ripping as I was transformed into the ultra-high-frequency orgasmic goblin that is a human being in DMT ecstasy. I was surrounded by the chattering of elf machines and the more-than-Arabian vaulted spaces that would shame a Bibiena. Manifestations of a power both alien and bizarrely beautiful raged around me.

At the point where I would normally have expected the visions to fade, the pretreatment with LSD synergized my state to a higher level. The cavorting hoards of DMT elf machines faded to a mere howling as the elfin mob moved on. I suddenly found myself flying hundreds of miles above the earth and in the company of silvery disks. I could not tell how many. I was fixated on the spectacle of the earth below and realized that I was moving south, apparently in polar orbit, over Siberia. Ahead of me I could see the Great Plain of Shang and the mass of the Himalayas rising up in front of the red-yellow waste of India. The sun would rise in about two hours. In a series of telescoping leaps, I went from orbit to a point where I could specifically pick out the circular depression that is the Kathmandu Valley. Then, in the next leap, the valley filled my field of vision. I seemed to be approaching it at great speed. I could see the Hindu temple and the houses of Kathmandu, the Temple of Svayambhunath to the west of the city and the Stupa at Boudanath, gleaming white and a few miles to the east. Then Boudanath was a mandala of houses and circular streets filling my vision. Among the several hundred roof tops I found my own. In the next moment I slammed into my body and was refocused on the roof top and the woman in front of me.

Incongruously, she had come to the event wearing a silver satin, full-length evening dress – an heirloom – the sort of thing one could find in an antique clothing store in Notting Hill Gate. I fell forward and thought that my hand was covered by some cool, white liquid. It was the fabric of the dress. Until that moment neither of us had considered the other a potential lover. Our relationship had functioned on quite a different level. But suddenly all the normal sets of relations were obviated. We reached out toward each other, and I had the distinct impression of passing through her, of physically reaching beyond her. She pulled her dress over her head in a single gesture. I did the same with my shirt, which ripped to pieces in my hands as I took it off over my head. I heard buttons fly, and somewhere my glasses landed and shattered.

Then we made love. Or rather we had an experience that vaguely related to making love but was a thing unto itself. We were both howling and singing in the glossolalia of DMT, rolling over the ground with everything awash in crawling, geometric hallucinations. She was transformed; words exist to describe what she became – pure anima, Kali, Leucothaea, something erotic but not human, something addressed to the species and not to the individual, glittering with the possibility of cannibalism, madness, space, and extinction. She seemed on the edge of devouring me.

Reality was shattered. This kind of fucking occurs at the very limit of what is possible. Everything had been transformed into orgasm and visible, chattering oceans of elf language. Then I saw that where our bodies were glued together there was flowing, out of her, over me, over the floor of the roof, flowing everywhere, some sort of obsidian liquid, something dark and glittering, with color and lights within it. After the DMT flash, after the seizures of orgasms, after all that, this new thing shocked me to the core. What was this fluid and what was going on? I looked at it. I looked right into it, and it was the surface of my own mind reflected in front of me. Was it translinguistic matter, the living opalescent excrescence of the alchemical abyss of hyperspace, something generated by the sex act performed under such crazy conditions? I looked into it again and now saw in it the lama who taught me Tibetan, who would have been asleep a mile away. In the fluid I saw him, in the company of a monk I had never seen; they were looking into a mirrored plate. Then I realized that they were watching me! I could not understand it. I looked away from the fluid and away from my companion, so intense was her aura of strangeness.

Then I realized that we had been singing and yodeling and uttering wild orgasmic howls for what must have been several minutes on my roof! It meant everyone in Boudanath would have been awakened and was about to open their doors and windows and demand to know what was going on. And what *was* going on? My grandfather's favorite expostulation seemed appropriate: 'Great God! said the woodcock when the hawk struck him.' This grotesquely inappropriate recollection brought uncontrollable laughter.

Then the thought of discovery sobered me enough to realize that we must get away from this exposed place. Both of us were completely naked, and the scene around us was one of total, unexplainable chaos. She was lying down, unable to rise, so I picked her up and made my way down the narrow staircase, past the grain storage bins and into my room. The whole time I remember saying over and over to her and to myself: 'I am a human being. I am a human being.' I had to reassure myself, for I was not at that moment sure.

We waited in my room many minutes. Slowly we realized that by some miracle no less strange than everything else that had occurred, no one was awake demanding to know what was going on. No one seemed even to have heard! To calm us, I made tea and, as I did this, I was able to assess my companion's state of mind. She seemed quite delirious, quite unable to discuss with me what had happened only a few moments before on the roof. It is an effect typical of Datura that whatever one experiences is very difficult, indeed usually impossible, to recollect later. It seemed that while what had transpired had involved the most intimate of acts between two people, I was nevertheless the only witness who could remember anything at all of what had happened.

Pondering all of this, I crept back to the roof and collected my glasses. Incredibly, they were unbroken, although I had distinctly heard them shatter. Obsidian liquids, the ectoplasmic excrescences of tantric hanky-panky, were nowhere to be seen. With my glasses and our clothes, I returned to my room where my companion was sleeping. I smoked a little hashish and then climbed into the mosquito net and lay down beside her. In spite of all the excitement and the stimulation of my system, I immediately went to sleep.

I have no idea how long I slept. When I awoke it was with a start and from a deep slumber. It was still dark. And there was no sign of my friend. I felt a stab of alarm; if she was delirious then it would be dangerous for her to be wandering alone around the village at night. I jumped up and threw on my *jalaba* and began to search. She was not on the roof, nor near the grain storage bins.

I found her on the ground floor of my building. She was sitting on the earthen floor staring at her reflection in the gas tank of a motorcycle, which belonged to the miller's son-in-law. Still disoriented in the way that is typical of Datura, she was hallucinating persons not present and mistaking one person for another. 'Are you my tailor?' she asked me several times as I led her back to my room. 'Are you my tailor?'

When we were once again upstairs in my quarters, I took off my *jalaba*, and we both discovered that I was wearing what she delicately described as her 'knickers.' They were too small on me and neither of us knew how they had come to be there. This little cross-dressing episode capped an amazing evening, and I roared with laughter. I returned her knickers and we went to bed, puzzled, reassured, exhausted, and amused.

As this experience passed behind us, the girl and I became even closer friends. We never made love again; it was not really the relationship that suited us. She remembered nothing of the events on the roof. About a week after all this was over, I told her my impression of what had happened. She was amazed but accepting. I did not know what had happened. I christened the obsidian fluid we had generated 'luv,' something more than love, something less than love, perhaps not love at all, but some kind of unplumbed potential human experience very little is known about.

The Other Cary Grant

From an interview with the *New York Times*

Warren Hoge

Vulnerable. The word doesn't seem to have any business asso-
ciating with Cary Grant. It is inconceivable from what we have
seen of him on the screen. The specific nature of the threat he
feels turns our judgement even more upside down – Cary
Grant, that paradigm of sex appeal, has spent most of his life
afraid of women, made positively miserable by them. It began in
his childhood with an unstable mother and has continued
through all of his relationships with women both in and out of
marriage. Moreover, Grant was wounded so deeply in these
relationships that he did something the Grant we know would
never do. He took LSD. Acting under the supervision of doctors
in this country and in England, he underwent a series of some
100 LSD sessions in an attempt to come to terms with the rejec-
tion syndrome that had repeatedly plunged him into depression.
It is hard to picture Grant as a depressive, and indeed, even as
he discusses the subject, the gleaming polish of his personality
throws up contradictory reflections. But each reflection is a sure
indication that even with Cary Grant, one of the most publicly
visible people ever, what you see is not necessarily what you
get . . .

It was when his 13-year marriage to Betsy Drake ended in
the early 1960s that he underwent the LSD sessions. Grant is
quick to say he would never recommend LSD to others, that it

simply worked for him. On no account does he want to be identified with the young people who drop acid. 'LSD is a chemical, not a drug. People who take drugs are trying to escape their lives, those who take hallucinogens are looking into it.'

Miss Drake had heard of LSD and of several doctors who believed in it, and Grant, an intensely unhappy man at that point was willing to try it. What emerged was an experience he describes as being 'reborn'.

'We come into this world with nothing on our tape,' he is saying at the outset of a conversation about it. 'We are computers, after all. The content of that tape is supplied by our mothers mainly because our fathers are off hunting or shooting or working. Now the mother can teach only what she knows, and many of these patterns of behaviour are not good, but they're still passed on to the child.' He is speaking rapidly, rushing through one sentence to the next, reciting the givens of his convictions with scarcely a pause for breath. 'I came to the conclusion that as an adult I had to be reborn, to wipe clean the tape. When I was under the LSD, at first I found myself turning on the couch, and I said to the doctor, "Why am I turning around on this sofa?" and he said, "Don't you know why?" and I said I didn't have the vaguest idea, but I wondered when it was going to stop. "When *you* stop it," he answered. Well, it was like a revelation to me, taking complete responsibility for one's own actions. I thought, "I'm unscrewing myself." That's why people use the phrase, "all screwed up."

'The first thing that happens is you don't want to look at what you are. Then the light breaks through, to use the cliché, you are enlightened. I discovered that I had created my own pattern, and I had to be responsible for it. I had to forgive my parents for what they didn't know and love them for what they did pass down – how to brush my hair, how to be polite, that sort of thing.' Grant suddenly throws his hands out in front of him as if he were splashing water. 'Things were being discharged.

'I went through rebirth. The experience was just like being born the first time, I imagined all the blood and urine, and I emerged with the flush of birth.' At this point in the story, Grant has drawn himself up straight on his chair and is looking jubilant. 'It was absolute release. You are still able to feed yourself, of course, drive your car, that kind of thing, but you've lost a lot of tension.

'It releases inhibition. You know, we are all subconsciously always holding our anus. In one LSD dream I —— all over the rug and —— all over the floor.'

PART SEVEN

CHEMISTRY SET

Of all the writings included in this anthology the following works are perhaps those that most accurately translate the actual states of body and mind experienced when under the influence of drugs. Here there is no space for the opinions of scientific bystanders nor for philosophical and ethnographic reflections; there is only room for the subjective world of personal experience and insights on the hoof. In *The Black Madness of Henbane* it is from the tranquillity of a village garden in a remote part of southern Hanover that the toxicologist Gustav Schenk rises up, like a witch on a broomstick, into the billowing clouds of henbane smoke riding on the back of a wild nightmare. Following the flight paths of a thousand witches that have gone before him, he enters the distorted and sinister world conjured up by the tropane alkaloids contained in the noxious seeds of henbane. Heart pounding, head pounding, giddy, dizzy, blurred vision, temporary loss of memory, thus far he could be drunk; then his head expands, the sun disappears, spectral herds of beasts fill the sky, he talks to his foot and his body explodes in all directions . . .

The same cluster of psychoactive and toxic alkaloids may have contributed to the states of consciousness which produced the frenzied masterpiece *Maldoror* by Isidore Ducasse, who under his poison pen name Comte de

Lautréamont wrote: 'what became of Maldoror's first lyric since his mouth, filled with leaves of belladonna, let slip in a moment of meditation across the kingdoms of wrath?' *Maldoror* was first published in its entirety in 1869 when the author was still in his twenties; the following year he was dead from unknown causes. Almost completely overlooked in his short lifetime Lautréamont was rediscovered by the surrealists who saw in his work a precocious antecedent to their own artistic and textual experiments. He was ranked by the surrealist élite amongst the very highest of their literary guides, in the august company of Arthur Rimbaud and Alfred Jarry. Whilst *Maldoror* clearly has its roots in gothic romanticism it branches out into areas of consciousness seldom explored even by the surrealists half a century later.

Alfred Jarry (1873–1907) was another precocious talent who has been described by Roger Shattuck, his English editor, as 'eccentric to the point of mania and lucid to the point of hallucination'. The diminutive Jarry, almost a midget, trained himself to control the content and direction of his dreams. He cut a strange figure in *fin-de-siècle* Paris – dressed in the garb of a cyclist, armed with pistols and living off fish he caught in the Seine. His dabbling with opium aside Jarry's chosen poison was alcohol, and in *Drink* (taken from *Exploits and Opinions of Doctor Faustroll, Pataphysician*, a work not published in its entirety until after his death) we get a taste of his unique brand of literature, a curious blend of exact scientific description and Rabelaisian humour.

Following spells in the merchant navy, the army and in the drug haunts of the Middle East and India, the writer and artist Brian Barritt found himself incarcerated for four years in Her Majesty's prison in the late sixties for possession of hashish. During this time Barritt, known as prisoner number 864, arranged for his writings to be smuggled out. Among this literary contraband was *Lune-Time*, a sketch of Walter Ralegh in the days before his eventual incarceration in the Tower of London. The collected writings became, in Barritt's words, 'fused . . . together in collage form' and were published as a book entitled *Whisper: A Timescript* in 1971. In *Drugged Spiders*, a short extract from *Miserable Miracle: Mescaline* (1956), the French poet and painter Henri Michaux contrasts the symmetry of his mescaline-inspired drawings with those made after using hashish. The latter works Michaux describes as 'cut up . . . prematurely discontinued, always showing unfinished portions'. He continues by noting that the webs of spiders that have been drugged with cannabis, benzedrine and the urine of schizophrenics remain distorted and incomplete.

Strapped for cash, the habitually nocturnal hero of Terry Southern's *The Blood of a Wig* is obliged to work as a stand-in journalist on a men's magazine. Staggering through his diurnal transformation with the help of Dexamyl (amphetamines) he finds the pusher, Trick, who can supply him with heroin, cocaine, cannabis, opium, acid, speed, mushrooms and almost anything else, including a rare psychoactive commodity known as 'red split'. The identity of this novel drug gives a new twist to the old phrase 'wigging out', as Terry Southern's hero finds himself temporarily possessed by a foreign body. Hunter S. Thompson was the self-styled founder of Gonzo journalism – if you are not familiar with this special brand of reportage then reading *Vegas Bound*, the opening chapter of *Fear and Loathing in Las Vegas: A Savage Journey to the Heart of the American Dream* should give you some idea of its form. Fuelled by a cocktail of all imaginable substances, Thompson's alter ego, along with his drug-crazed Samoan attorney, zoom off on their rip-roaring adventure, driving into the sunset of the American Dream somewhere on the road to Las Vegas. In *Toxins Discharged*, an extract from *Ecstasy: Three Tales of Chemical Romance*, Irvine Welsh injects the normally sedate world of a bowling club with a few lines of speed. The action takes place in the toilet and the bar, starting with the speed being chopped up on the cistern by one character and ending with another throwing up in the toilet bowl.

The Black Madness of Henbane

Gustav Schenk

No one can really assess the operation of plant poisons on a purely theoretical basis. One has to experience the manner in which they spread omnipotent energies through our bodies and subordinate us to their power. This is the only way to gain a proper understanding of what we are accustomed to call 'poisons', for there is indeed something mysterious about them. How is it that the contents of a plant exercise such lethal effects upon us and are capable of enslaving and transforming our minds and spirits? At the same time we must not forget that practically every vegetable poison also possesses therapeutic properties. This is the key to its strange power. Administered in carefully calculated small doses, the deadly effects of large quantities of the toxin make way for a healing and soothing action.

Research into the workings of a poison has always followed the same path. The accumulation of empirical evidence regarding the toxin's action, arising out of cases of poisoning, gives rise to a theory concerning its therapeutic use. We shall pursue this same method here. The reactions of a mind and body flooded with a spate of poison must first be described, in order thereafter and thereby to appreciate the miraculous and unfailing curative properties of this same toxin employed with restraint.

I once took the opportunity of gaining that understanding of the nature of a plant which comes only by experiencing the effects of its active principle on oneself. I was still a young man at the time and my action was a trifle reckless – nevertheless, I was on the right lines. I wanted to take a virulent poison in order to observe its effects, and thus draw closer to the plant and at the same time test my body's resistance to this alien force.

I was spending a year studying plants in a very lonely and out-of-the-way village in Southern Hanover. Directly beyond the vegetable garden belonging to the house in which I was staying rose Black Henbane, sinister-looking dark green plants. The fruit ripened and I took a handful of flat grey seeds from the seed capsules. I had learnt that the best way to liberate and absorb the hyoscyamine in them was to roast the seeds and inhale their fumes. It was a holiday; there was nobody about and I was alone in the house, undisturbed and not disturbing anyone. I placed the seeds on an iron plate and held this over a spirit flame. The seeds slowly heated, the husks burst open, and the fumes of hyoscyamine reached me, strangely penetrating, acrid and at the same time very sweet-smelling. Today I cannot recall how many seeds I strewed on the iron plate, nor can I say how long I inhaled the smoke that billowed up from the smouldering seeds.

A peculiarity of the action of Black Henbane is to obliterate the memory. All that is recollected is the general atmosphere of the experience and vivid but disconnected images, which re-enter the mind later and out of which the process of poisoning can be partially reconstructed. It is therefore very difficult for the victim of Henbane poisoning to give a clear and complete account of his experiences – quite the reverse of what happens with the Mexican cactus peyotl, which is particularly suitable for experiments on oneself because under its influence consciousness is maintained in full clarity.

But although there are wide gaps in my recollection of this black madness induced by Henbane, tremendous imaginings, powerful and sinister pictures have remained intact, as well as the sensation of my physical condition, the bodily breakdown.

The Henbane's first effect was a purely physical discomfort. My limbs lost their certainty, pains hammered in my head, and I began to feel extremely giddy. Fumes were still rising from the iron plate, so not much time can have elapsed before the onset of these initial symptoms – a quarter of an hour at most. I went to the mirror and was able to distinguish my face, but more dimly than normal. It looked flushed and must have been so – I had the feeling that my head had increased in size: it seemed to have grown broader, more solid, heavier, and I imagined that it was enveloped in firmer, thicker skin. The mirror itself was swaying and I found it difficult to keep my face within its frame. The black discs of my pupils were immensely enlarged, as though the whole iris, which was normally blue, had become black. Despite the dilation of my pupils I could see no better than usual – quite the contrary, the outlines of objects were hazy, the window and the window-frame were obscured by a thin mist.

I can still recall that as I turned away from the mirror I lost all recollection of my preceding actions. I strove to figure out what had wrought such a change in me. I saw the charred seeds on the iron plate and the still flickering flame, and I racked my brains to think what could be the cause of my strange state. I couldn't fathom it. But this dullness of mind was only the prelude to much more horrible things to come.

The effort to get to the bottom of the mystery of my confusion, drunkenness or illness was making my head ache and causing – so I firmly believed – the wretched dryness of my mouth, my giddiness and all the physical misery I suffered during those minutes. Thus I attributed my metamorphosis solely to my loss of memory. At the same time, my heart was beating loudly. I didn't hear it with my ears, for they seemed to be deaf. There was some faculty of hearing within me; some being inside me, filled with groundless panic, perceived the rapid pulsations.

To comprehend the power of Black Henbane, the reader must picture the following conditions. The ears become deaf, the eyes almost blind; they see in a haze only the bulk of objects, whose contours are blurred. The sufferer is slowly cut off from the outside world and sinks irretrievably into himself and his own inner world. The room dances; the floor, the walls and the ceiling tilt slowly to the right and then back to the left. But the victim has no sense of moving himself, although obviously he is staggering about in a stationary room.

While these terrifying signs of catastrophe accumulate the sufferer is abandoned by the familiar world. The fact that his face seems to grow larger, that heat rises into his head and brings the sweat pouring down his cheeks, that the light grows dark, the walls disappear and the rays of the sun go out – all this causes no astonishment now that he is shut up inside himself as though in a tiny room.

I still remember clearly that in the end I could no longer adjust my eyes to distance – they had lost the power of accommodation. I stared in front of me as though paralysed, and during this phase of rigid vision the first hallucinations presented themselves.

I caught a gleam of a disc of yellow metal, which assumed a terrifying significance. It was looking at me, not with eyes and with a human gaze, that would be the wrong way to describe it. A metal disc cannot see or look at us, we say. But at that instant I knew such a disc to be entirely capable of casting glances which sent a shudder through my heart. The next moment, however – and this is the extraordinary thing – this vision caused me tremendous amusement, filling me with an immoderate desire to laugh, which seemed to go on and on. Yes, everything suddenly amused me – my inability to see properly, the dancing room, the uncertainty of my hands, with which I couldn't get a grip on anything; and all the time the disc kept staring at me unwinkingly, with grim, piercing, menacing earnestness.

Now image followed upon image; they were shattered fragments of the real world. I saw them within the area of my own eyes; they were not the inventions of a passing madness. My uninhibited hilarity quickly vanished, making way for a feeling of amazement that everything I saw appeared completely topsy-turvy. A billowing, sooty cloud was a woman, or at least the essence of a woman. It was the epitome of everything female; and so demoniacal and overpowering that the impression it made upon me is beyond description.

Although I could hardly walk or even stand up, I was seized by a raging impulse to move. Since my feet seemed firmly welded to the floor, I could only clutch and grasp at things with my hands and tear them in pieces. Because my hands needed them, the things which could be moved, pulled apart and torn up were immediately there. There were animals, which looked at me keenly with contorted grimaces and staring, terrified eyes; there were flying stones and clouds of mist, all sweeping along in the same direction. They carried me irresistibly with them. Their colouring must be described – but it was not a pure hue. They were enveloped in a vague grey light which emitted a dull glow and rolled onwards and upwards into a black and smoky sky. I was flung into a flaring drunkenness, a witches' cauldron of madness. Above my head water was flowing, dark and blood-red. The sky was filled with whole herds of animals. Fluid, formless creatures emerged from the darkness. I heard words, but they were all wrong and nonsensical, and yet they possessed for me some hidden meaning. I must have spoken myself, but foolish, far-fetched nonsense. I imagined that my arm was talking, or my foot, and I answered them, uttering complete rubbish and knowing all the time that what I was saying was absurd and totally out of place.

My teeth were clenched and a dizzy rage took possession of me. I know that I trembled with horror; but I also know that I was permeated by a peculiar sense of wellbeing connected with the crazy sensation that my feet were growing lighter, expanding and breaking loose from my body. This sensation of gradual bodily dissolution is typical of Henbane poisoning. Each part of my body seemed to be going off on its own. My head was growing independently larger, and I was seized with the fear that I was falling apart. At the same time I experienced an intoxicating sensation of flying.

The frightening certainty that my end was near through the dissolution of my body was counterbalanced by an animal joy in flight. I soared where my hallucinations – the clouds, the louring sky, herds of beasts, falling leaves which were quite unlike any ordinary leaves, billowing streamers of steam and rivers of molten metal – were swirling along. All this time I was not peacefully sleeping with limbs relaxed, but in motion. The urge to move, although the capacity for movement is greatly curtailed, is the essential characteristic of *Hyoscyamus* intoxication.

Black Henbane causes a general poisoning with symptoms of illness. The sense of being seriously ill does not leave one for an instant. The first inhalation of the fumes of the roasted seeds immediately arouses a feeling of extreme discomfort and general bodily weakness, which rises to a mingled enjoyment and terror accompanied by an unparalleled wealth of visual images, to which are added unknown sensations of smell and touch.

As the delusions come to an end they are replaced by the consciousness of pain and nausea. The grey misery that fills the mind is enhanced by the precarious state of the body and the derangement of the senses. Sight, hearing, smell and touch do not obey the will and seem, still entirely under the influence of the Henbane, to be going their own ways.

This description of my subjective experience is a pointer to the objective significance of Black Henbane, which has been known and used in Europe for many thousands of years as a medicament, a narcotic, an aid to soothsaying and a bestower of visions. The dancing frenzy and witches' madness of the Middle Ages were largely induced by Black Henbane; the inhalation of *Hyoscyamus* fumes provided the stimulant for the processions of flagellants; and before this the Scythians used to burn the seeds of Black Henbane in order to put themselves in a brief state of maniac intoxication.

The Nightshades, as we see, are not purely narcotic plants like the opium poppy or hemp, from which hashish is obtained.

The Solanaceae, and particularly Henbane and Thorn Apple, stand on the borderline between the plants which intoxicate and those which cause pain. But pain predominates. Their derangement of the senses, madness and terrifyingly sombre hallucinations cannot be compared to the ephemeral bliss and euphoria induced by the well-known narcotics.

Maldoror
Comte de Lautréamont

I sought a soul that might resemble mine, and I could not find it. I scanned all the crannies of the earth: my perseverance was useless. Yet I could not remain alone. There had to be someone who would approve of my character; there had to be someone with the same ideas as myself.

It was morning. The sun in all his magnificence rose on the horizon, and behold, there also appeared before my eyes a young man whose presence made flowers grow as he passed. He approached me and held out his hand: 'I have come to you, you who seek me. Let us give thanks for this happy day.' But I replied: 'Go! I did not summon you. I do not need your friendship . . .'

It was evening. Night was beginning to spread the blackness of her veil over nature. A beautiful woman whom I could scarcely discern also exerted her bewitching sway upon me and looked at me with compassion. She did not, however, dare speak to me. I said: 'Come closer that I may discern your features clearly, for at that distance the starlight is not strong enough to illuminate them.' Then, with modest demeanour, eyes lowered, she crossed the greensward and reached my side. I said as soon as I saw her: 'I perceive that goodness and justice have dwelt in your heart: we could not live together. Now you are admiring my good looks which have bowled over more than one woman. But sooner or later you would regret having consecrated your love to me, for you do not know my soul. Not that I shall be unfaithful to you: she who devotes herself to me with so much abandon and trust – with the same trust and abandon do I devote myself to her. But get this into your head and never forget it: wolves and lambs look not on one another with gentle eyes.'

What then did I need, I who rejected with such disgust what was most beautiful in humanity! I would not have known how to formulate what I needed. I was not yet accustomed to take rigorous stock of my mind's phenomena by means of the methods philosophy recommends.

I sat on a rock near the sea. A ship had just put out from shore at full sail: an imperceptible dot had appeared on the horizon and was gradually approaching, growing rapidly, pushed on by the squall. The storm was going to begin its onslaughts and already the sky was darkening, turning into a blackness almost as hideous as a man's heart.

The vessel, which was a great warship, had dropped all her anchors to avoid being swept on to the rocks along the coast. The wind whistled furiously from all four points of the compass, and made mincemeat of the sails. Claps of thunder crashed amid the lightning but could not outdo the sound of wailing to be heard from the foundationless house – a floating sepulchre. The lurching masses of water had not managed to break the anchor chains, but had dashed open a way into the ship's sides: an enormous breach, for the pumps were quite unable to expel the vast quantities of salt water which smashed foaming over the deck like mountains.

The distressed ship fires off her alarm gun but slowly, majestically, founders.

He who has not seen a vessel founder in the midst of a hurricane, sporadic lightning, deepest darkness – while those aboard are overcome by the despair with which you are familiar – knows not life's mischances. Finally from within the ship a universal shriek of sheer woe bursts forth, while the sea redoubles its redoubtable attacks. Human strength giving way was the cause of that cry. Each man enfolds himself in the cloak of resignation and puts his fate into God's hands. They huddle at bay like a flock of sheep.

The distressed ship fires off her alarm gun but slowly, majestically, founders.

All day long they have had the pumps in action. Futile efforts. And to cap this gracious spectacle, night has fallen, dense, implacable. Each man tells himself that once in the water he will no longer be able to breathe; for no matter how far back his memory ferrets, he owns no fish as ancestor. Yet he urges himself to hold his breath as long as possible, to prolong his life by two or three seconds: that is the vengeful irony he aims at death.

The distressed ship fires off her alarm gun but slowly, majestically, founders.

He is unaware that the vessel as she sinks causes a powerful convolution of swell upon swell; that miry mud mingles with the turbid waters, and that a force coming from below – backlash of the tempest raging above – drives the element to violent jolting motions. Thus despite his reserve of composure mustered beforehand, the man marked for drowning should (on further reflection) feel glad to prolong his life amid the whirlpools of the abyss by even half a normal breath, for good measure. It will be impossible for him to defy his supreme wish, death.

The distressed ship fires off her alarm gun but slowly, majestically, founders.

An error. She fires no more shots, she does not founder. The cockle-shell has been completely engulfed. O heaven! how can one live after tasting so many delights! It has just been my lot to witness the death-throes of several of my fellow men. Minute by minute I observe the vicissitudes of their last agonies. Heard now above the market din would be the bawling of some old woman driven mad by fear; now, the solitary yelps of a suckling infant, making nautical orders hard to hear. The vessel was too far off for me clearly to distinguish the groans borne on the gale, but by an effort of will I drew nearer to them, and the optical illusion

was complete. Every quarter of an hour or so, whenever a gust
of wind stronger than the rest, keening its dismal dirge amid the
cries of startled petrels, struck and cracked the ship's length and
increased the moans of those about to be offered up to death-by-
holocaust, I would jab a sharp iron point into my cheek, secretly
thinking: 'They suffer still more!' Thus, at least, I had grounds for
comparison.

From the shore I apostrophised them, hurling imprecations
and threats at them. It seemed to me that they must have heard
me! It seemed to me that my hatred and my words, covering the
distance, destroyed the laws of acoustics and, distinctly, reached
those ears deafened by the wrathful ocean's roar! It seemed to
me that they must have thought of me and vented their
vengeance in impotent rage!

From time to time I would cast my gaze towards the cities
asleep upon terra firma, and seeing no one suspected that a
few miles offshore a ship was sinking – with a crown of birds of
prey and a pedestal of emptybellied aquatic giants – I took
courage and regained hope. I was now certain of her loss! They
could not escape! By way of extra precaution, I had been to
fetch my double-barrelled musket, so that were any survivor to
try swimming ashore from the rocks, thus escaping imminent
death, a bullet in the shoulder would shatter his arm and prevent him from effecting his purpose.

During the fiercest part of the storm I saw a forceful head, its
hair on end, cleaving the waters with desperate exertions.
Tossed about like a cork, it gulped litres of water and sank into
the gulf, but soon reappeared, hair streaming, and fixed its gaze
on the shore, seeming to defy death.

His composure was admirable. A great gory wound caused by
the outcrop of some hidden reef scarred his intrepid and noble
countenance. He could not have been more than sixteen, for by
the lightning flashes which lit the night the peachbloom on his
upper lip was barely visible. And now he was no more than two
hundred metres from the cliff and I could take a good look at
him. What courage! What indomitable spirit! How his head's

steadiness seemed to taunt destiny while vigorously ploughing through the waves whose furrows parted intractably before him! I had resolved beforehand: I owed it to myself to keep my promise: the last hour had tolled for all, none should escape it. That was my resolution. Nothing would change it . . .

There was a sharp report and the head sank at once to reappear no more.

From this murder I did not derive as much pleasure as one might think. And precisely because I was sated with perpetual killing, henceforth I would do it through sheer habit – impossible to abandon, but affording only the scantest climax. The senses were blunted, calloused. What pleasure could I feel at the death of this human being when there were more than a hundred about to present me with the spectacle of their last struggles against the waves once the ship had gone down? With this death I had not even the lure of danger, for human justice, cradled by the hurricane of this frightful night, slumbered in the houses a few steps from me.

Today when the years hang heavy on me, I sincerely state for a supreme and solemn truth: I was not as cruel as men later related; but sometimes their wickedness wreaks its enduring ravages for years on end. So my fury knew no limit; I was seized with an access of cruelty and struck awe in anyone (of my own race) who might happen to meet my haggard eyes. Were it a horse or dog, I would let it by: did you hear what I just said? Unfortunately on the night of the storm I was seized by one of my fits of wrath, my reason had flown (for as a rule I would be cruel but more discreet), and everything falling into my hands at that time had to perish. I do not intend to justify my misdeeds. The fault is not entirely with my fellow men. I simply state what *is*, while awaiting the last judgement. (Which makes me scratch my nape in anticipation . . .) What care I for the last judgement! My reason never deserts me as I claimed – to mislead you. And when I commit a crime I know what I am doing: I would not wish to do otherwise!

Standing on the rock while the hurricane lashed at my hair

and cloak, I ecstatically watched the full force of the storm hammering away at the ship, under a starless sky. In triumphant fettle I followed all the twists and turns of the drama – from the instant the vessel cast anchors until the moment she was swallowed up within that fatal garment which dragged those whom it clothed like a cloak, down into the bowels of the sea. But the time was approaching when I myself would play a part as actor in these scenes of disordered nature.

When the spot where the vessel had battled clearly showed that she had gone to spend the rest of her days in the stalls of the sea, some of those who had been borne overboard by the breakers reappeared on the surface. They clung to one another, grappling in twos and threes: this was *not* the way to save their lives, for their movements were hampered and they sank like cracked beakers . . .

What is this army of marine monsters swiftly slicing through the waves? There are six of them, with sturdy fins that cut a path through the heaving waves. The sharks soon make merely an eggless omelette of all the human beings who flail their four limbs in this unsteady continent, and share it out according to the law of the strongest. Blood mingles with the waters and the waters with blood. Their savage eyes sufficiently illumine the scene of carnage . . .

But what is this new turmoil in the water, yonder on the horizon? A waterspout approaching, perhaps. What strokes! I realise what it is. An enormous female shark is coming to partake of the duck liver pâté, to eat the cold boiled beef. She is raging, ravening. A battle ensues between her and the others to contest the few palpitating limbs that here and there bob silently on the surface of the crimson cream. To left and right her jaws slash dealing mortal wounds. But three live sharks surround her still and she is forced to thrash around in all directions to foil their manoeuvres.

With a mounting emotion hitherto unknown to him the spectator upon the shore follows this new variety of naval engagement. His eyes are fixed on this valiant female shark with her vicious teeth. He hesitates no longer. Musket to shoulder, and adroit as ever, he plants his second bullet in the gills of one of the sharks as it shows itself a moment above a wave. Two sharks remain, displaying even greater tenacity.

His mouth full of bile, the man throws himself off the rock's summit into the sea and swims towards the pleasantly-tinted carpet, gripping the steel knife he always carries. From now on each shark has one enemy to reckon with. He heads for his weary opponent and, taking his time, buries the sharp blade in its belly. Meanwhile the mobile fortress easily disposes of her last enemy . . .

Swimmer and female shark he has rescued confront each other. For some minutes they stare warily at one another, each amazed to find such ferocity in the other's stare. They swim, circling, neither losing sight of the other. Each thinking: 'Till now I was wrong – here is someone wickeder than I!' Then of one accord, in mutual admiration, they slid toward each other – the female parting the water with her fins, Maldoror smiting the surge with his arms – and held their breaths in deepest reverence, both longing to look for the first time on their living image. Three metres separated them. Effortlessly, abruptly, they fell upon each other like magnets, and embraced with dignity and recognition, in a hug as tender as a brother's or sister's.

Carnal desires soon followed this demonstration of affection. A pair of sinewy thighs clung to the monster's viscous skin, close as leeches; and arms and fins entwined about the loved one's body, surrounded it with love, while throats and breasts soon fused into a glaucous mass reeking of sea-wrack. In the midst of the tempest that continued raging. By lightning's light. The foamy wave their nuptial couch – borne on an undertow as in a cradle – they rolled over and over towards the unknown depths of the briny abyss – and came together in a long, chaste, hideous coupling! . . .

At last I had found someone who resembled me! . . . Now I would no longer be alone in life! . . . She had the same ideas as I! . . . I was facing my first love!

Drink

Alfred Jarry

Faustroll lifted with his fork toward his teeth five hams, whole, roasted, and boned, from Strasbourg, Bayonne, the Ardennes, York and Westphalia, all dripping with Johannisberger; the bishop's daughter, on her knees under the table, filled once again each unit of the ascending line of hectoliter cups in the moving belt which crossed the table in front of the doctor and passed, empty of its contents, near the raised throne of Bosse-de-Nage. I gave myself a thirst by swallowing a sheep that had been roasted alive while racing along a petrol-soaked track until done to a turn. Distinguished and Extravagant drank as thirstily as anhydrous sulphuric acid, as their names had made me suspect, and three of their jowls would have encompassed a cubic meter of firewood. However, Bishop Mendacious refreshed himself exclusively with fresh water and rat's piss.

At one time he had been in the habit of mixing this last substance with bread and Melun cheese, but had succeeded in suppressing the supererogatory vanity of these solid condiments. He sucked in water from a decanter of gold beaten as thin as the wave length of green light, served on a tray made of the fur (rather than peltry, since the bishop wanted to be fashionable), of the freshly flayed fox of a drunkard, in season, and quite equal to a twentieth of the latter's weight. Such luxury is not vouchsafed to all: the bishop kept rats at enormous expense, and also, in rooms paved with funnels, a whole seraglio of drunkards, whose conversation he imitated:

'Do you think,' he said to Faustroll, 'that a woman can ever be naked? In what do you recognize the nakedness of a wall?'

'When it is devoid of windows, doors, and other openings,' opined the doctor.

'Your reasoning is good,' continued Mendacious. 'Naked women are never naked, especially old women.'

He drank a great draught straight out of his carafe, whose point of sustentation was erect on its viscous carpet, like a root torn from its burial place. The catenulate conveyor belt of cups full of liquid or wind chanted like the incision made in a river's belly by the rosary of an illuminated towboat.

'Now,' continued the bishop, 'drink and eat. Visited, serve us with some lobster!'

'Was it not once fashionable in Paris,' I hazarded, 'to offer these animals in courtesy, like a snuff-taker proffering his snuff-box? But, from what I have heard, people were in the habit of refusing them, claiming that they were hairy pluripedes and repulsively dirty.'

'Ho-him, ho-hum,' condescended the bishop. 'If lobsters are dirty and non-depilated, it is perhaps a proof that they are free. A nobler fate than that of the can of corned beef which you carry on a ribbon round your neck, doctor navigator, like the case of a pair of salted binoculars through which you like to scrutinize people and objects.'

Lune-Time
Brian Barritt

Captain Ralegh is late. His vessel is caught in a squall off the English coast and he badly needs a joint. Staggering stiff legged across the heaving planking to the hatch he draws his blade, prises open a bale, and turns a dull grey. Rizla, the red-skinned sorceress, had turned him over for tobacco weed ('but man, I'd known her so long').

Visions of eternal disgrace haunt the captain's cabin, an iron lantern swings back and forth and the plume of his hat turns yellow-black-yellow with every other pulse of the sea. Through a hole in the sky the inter-stellar hiss of astronomical history touches the antenna of the slender masts, runs through the wet string bags of the rigging, down the plume of his hat, and sucks WR into the ink blotted pages of memory; labelled, stamped and suppressed into history as 'The Man who brought tobacco to England.' A strobe of x-films projected in cinerama onto the bowed walls feed back amplified horror at the enormity of his goof. The timbers sigh in agreement.

The Destiny pitches and rolls, a bouffant of waves claws the Dover cliffs with long hysterical fingernails, the moon rattles in the basin of night. Aloft, high in the banshee rigging, a maypole of hemp ropes flails the sodden air, the tips of the masts trace erratic ellipses on the soggy plastic sky and for an instant a star circumscribed by the point of the mast, blinks. ZOOKS, the answer strikes him right between the eyes, a blast of confidence transfigures the elements. The storm abates, the plume of his hat is yellow.

The sixteenth century daylight unfolds in a scroll across Plymouth Ho, a cold swell bobs the masts, flags and sails pasted onto the anaemic sky, and from below an indifferent horizon another irritable morning rises. From the Destiny a long-boat, its oars crawling over the green water like an insect across a leaf, points its prow towards the chests heaped along the quay, and the starched lace cameos of the Queen and her retinue anxiously waiting to score.

Playing it straight off his lace cuff, WR puts on his virile-young-gallant look, springs elegantly onto a bollard, pirouettes, spreads his ermine cloak over a puddle, sinks to one knee, and bows his head. Elizabeth knights him before it registers, and Sir Walter whispers a magic word in her ear: 'Golden Virginia – I named it after you.'

The Queen is temporarily paralysed. The Word in her own Image catalyses the high-freak-quency equipment of the Royal Brain, and turns on Her High-ness with tobacco.

Drugged Spiders
Henri Michaux

The drawings I made after taking mescaline . . . consisted of an enormous number of very fine parallel lines, very close together with an axis of symmetry and endless repetitions.

The quick vibrating lines I drew endlessly, without thinking, without hesitation, without pausing, by their very appearance gave promise of a 'visionary' drawing.

Very different my drawings after taking hashish. They were clumsy, involved, cut up, prematurely discontinued, always showing unfinished portions. The surfaces were composed of squares and polygons. A great deal was always missing.

In the same way the webs of the Zilla spider that has been drugged with atropine, and benzedrine, nembutal and marihuana (experiments made by Dr. Peter Witt of Berne University) are always incomplete, the incompleteness the same for all spiders of the same family, different for each drug used.

Similarly incomplete, as could be expected, are the webs of spiders that have been induced to take the urine of schizophrenics, another proof that the disease is first of all physical, first of all a toxicosis.

Wouldn't it be more appropriate to try the experiment on the psychiatrists, rather than on the spiders?

The Blood of a Wig

Terry Southern

My most outlandish drug experience, now that I think about it, didn't occur with beat Village or Harlem weirdos, but during a brief run with the ten-to-four Mad Ave crowd.

How it happened, this friend of mine who was working at *Lance* ('The Mag for Men') phoned me one morning – he knew I was strapped.

'One of the fiction editors is out with syph or something,' he said. 'You want to take his place for a while?'

I was still mostly asleep, so I tried to cool it by shooting a few incisive queries as to the nature of the gig – which he couldn't seem to follow.

'Well,' he said finally, 'you won't have to *do* anything, if that's what you mean.' He had a sort of blunt and sullen way about him – John Fox his name was, an ex-Yalie and would-be writer who was constantly having to 'put it back on the shelf,' as he expressed it (blunt, sullen), and take one of these hot-shot Mad Ave jobs, and always for some odd reason – like at present, paying for his mom's analysis.

Anyway, I accepted the post, and now I had been working there about three weeks. It wasn't true, of course, what he'd said about not having to do anything – I mean the way he had talked I wouldn't even have to get out of bed – but after three weeks my routine was fairly smooth: up at ten, wash face, brush teeth, fresh shirt, dex, and make it. I had this transistor-shaver I'd copped for five off a junky-booster, so I would shave with it in the cab, and walk into the office at ten-thirty or so, dapper as Dan and hip as Harry. Then into my own small office, lock the door, and start stashing the return postage from the unsolicited mss. We would get an incredible amount of mss. – about two hundred a day – and these were divided into two categories: (1) those from agents, and (2) those that came in cold, straight from the author. The ratio was about 30 to 1, in favor of the latter – which formed a gigantic heap called 'the shit pile,' or (by the girl-readers) 'the garbage dump.' These always contained a lot of return postage – so right away I was able to supplement my weekly wage by seven or eight dollars a day in postage stamps. Everyone else considered the 'shit pile' as something heinously repugnant, especially the sensitive girl ('garbage') readers, so it was a source of irritation and chagrin to my sec- retary when I first told her I wished to read '*all* unsolicited manuscripts and *no* manuscripts from agents.'

John Fox found it quite incomprehensible.

'You must be out of your nut!' he said. 'Ha! Wait until you try to read some of that crap in the shit pile!'

I explained however (and it was actually true in the begin- ning) that I had this theory about the existence of a *pure, primitive, folk-like* literature – which, if it did exist, could only turn up among the unsolicited mss. Or *weird*, something really *weird*, even insane, might turn up there – whereas I knew the stuff from the agents would be the same old predictably com- petent tripe. So, aside from stashing the stamps, I would read each of these shit-pile mss. very carefully – reading subtleties, insinuations, multilevel *entendre* into what was actually just a sort of flat, straightforward, simplemindedness. I would think each was a put-on – a fresh and curious parody of some kind, and I would read on, and on, all the way to the end, waiting for the payoff . . . but, of course, that never happened, and I grad- ually began to revise my theory and to refine my method. By the second week, I was able to reject a ms. after reading the opening sentence, and by the third I could often reject on the basis of *title* alone – the principle being if an author would allow a blatantly dumbbell title, he was incapable of writing a story worth reading. (This was thoroughly tested and proved before adopting.) Then instead of actually *reading* mss., I would spend hours, days really, just thinking, trying to refine and extend my method of blitz-rejection. I was able to take it a little farther, but not much. For example, any woman author who used 'Mrs.' in her name could be rejected out of hand – *unless* it was used with only one name, like 'by Mrs. Carter,' then it might be a weirdie. And again, any author using a middle initial or a 'Jr.' in his name, shoot it right back to him! I knew I was taking a chance with that one (because of Connell and Selby), but I figured what the hell, I could hardly afford to gear that sort of fast-moving synchro-mesh operation I had in mind to a couple of exceptions – which, after all, only went to prove the consarn rule, so to speak. Anyway, there it was, the end of the third week and the old job going smoothly enough, except that I had developed quite a little dexie habit by then – not actually a *habit*, of course, but a sort of very real dependence . . . having by nature a nocturnal metabolism whereby my day (pre-*Lance*) would ordinarily begin at three or four in the afternoon and finish at eight or nine in the morning. As a top staffer at *Lance*, however, I had to make other arrangements. Early on I had actually asked John Fox if it would be possible for me to come in at four and work until midnight.

'Are you out of your *nut*?' (That was his standard comeback.) 'Don't you know what's happening here? This is a *social* scene, man – these guys want to *see* you, they want to get to *know* you!'

'What are they, faggots?'

'No, they're not *faggots*,' he said stoutly, but then seemed hard pressed to explain, and shrugged it off. 'It's just that they don't have very much, you know, *to do*.'

It was true in a way that no one seemed to actually *do* any-thing – except for the typists, of course, always typing away. But the guys just sort of hung out, or around, buzzing each other, sounding the chicks, that sort of thing.

The point is though that I had to make in by ten, or there-abouts. One reason for this was the 'pre-lunch conference,' which Hacker, or the 'Old Man' (as, sure enough, the publisher was called), might decide to have on any given day. And so it came to pass that on this particular – Monday it was – morning, up promptly at nine-three-oh, wash face, brush teeth, fresh shirt, all as per usual, and reach for the dex . . . no dex, out of dex. This was especially inopportune because it was on top of two straight white and active nights, and it was somewhat as though an 800-pound bag, of loosely packed sand, began to settle slowly on the head. No panic, just immediate death from fatigue.

At Sheridan Square, where I usually got the taxi, I went into the drugstore. The first-shift pharmacist, naturally a guy I had never seen before, was on duty. He looked like an aging effi-ciency expert.

'Uh, I'd like to get some Dexamyl, please.'

The pharmacist didn't say anything, just raised one hand to adjust his steel-rimmed glasses, and put the other one out for the prescription.

'It's on file here,' I said, nodding toward the back.

'What name?' he wanted to know, then disappeared behind the glass partition, but very briefly indeed.

'Nope,' he said, coming back, and was already looking over my shoulder to the next customer.

'Could you call Mr. Robbins?' I asked, 'he can tell you about it.' Of course this was simply whistling in the dark, since I was pretty sure Robbins, the night-shift man, didn't know me by name, but I had to keep the ball rolling.

'I'm not gonna wake Robbins at this hour – he'd blow his stack. Who's next?'

'Well, listen, can't you just *give* me a couple – I've, uh, got a long drive ahead.'

'You can't get dexies without a script,' he said, rather

reproachfully, wrapping a box of Tampax for a teenybopper nifty behind me, '*you* know that.'

'Okay, how about if I get the doctor to phone you?'

'Phone's up front,' he said, and to the nifty: 'That's seventy-nine.'

The phone was under siege – one person using it, and about five waiting – all, for some weird reason, spade fags and prancing gay. Not that I give a damn about who uses the phone, it was just one of those absurd incongruities that seem so often to conspire to undo sanity in times of crisis. What the hell was going on? They were obviously together, very excited, chattering like magpies. Was it the Katherine Dunham contingent of male dancers? Stranded? Lost? Why out so early? One guy had a list of numbers in his hand the size of a small flag. I stood there for a moment, confused in pointless speculation, then left abruptly and hurried down West Fourth to the dinette. This was doubly to purpose, since not only is there a phone, but the place is frequented by all manner of heads, and a casual score might well be in order – though it was a bit early for the latter, granted.

And this did, in fact, prove to be the case. There was no one there whom I knew – and, worse still, halfway to the phone, I suddenly remembered my so-called doctor (Dr. Friedman, his name was) had gone to California on vacation a few days ago. Christ almighty! I sat down at the counter. This called for a quick think-through. Should I actually call him in California? Have him phone the drugstore from there? Quite a production for a couple of dex. I looked at my watch, it was just after ten. That meant just after seven in Los Angeles – Friedman would blow his stack. I decided to hell with it and ordered a cup of coffee. Then a remarkable thing happened. I had sat down next to a young man who now quite casually removed a small transparent silo-shaped vial from his pocket, and without so much as a glance in any direction, calmly tapped a couple of the belovedly familiar green-hearted darlings into his cupped hand, and tossed them off like two salted peanuts.

Deus ex machina!

'Uh, excuse me,' I said, in the friendliest sort of way, 'I just happened to notice you taking a couple of, ha ha, Dexamyl.' And I proceeded to lay my story on him – while he, after one brief look of appraisal, sat listening, his eyes straight ahead, hands still on the counter, one of them half covering the magic vial. Finally he just nodded and shook out two more on the counter. 'Have a ball,' he said.

I reached the office about five minutes late for the big pre-lunch confab. John Fox made a face of mild disgust when I came in the conference room. He always seemed to consider my flaws as his responsibility since it was he who had recommended me for the post. Now he glanced uneasily at old Hacker, who was the publisher, editor-in-chief, etc. etc. A man of about fifty-five, he bore a striking resemblance to Edward G. Robinson – an image to which he gave further credence by frequently sitting in a squatlike manner, chewing an unlit cigar butt, and mouthing coarse expressions. He liked to characterize himself as a 'tough old bastard,' one of his favorite prefaces being: 'I know most of you guys think I'm a *tough old bastard*, right? Well, maybe I am. In the quality-Lit game you *gotta* be tough!' And bla-bla-bla.

Anyway as I took my usual seat between Fox and Bert Katz, the feature editor, Old Hack looked at his watch, then back at me.

'Sorry,' I mumbled.

'We're running a *magazine* here, young man, not a *whorehouse*.'

'Right and double right,' I parried crisply. Somehow Old Hack always brought out the schoolboy in me.

'If you want to be *late*,' he continued, 'be late at the *whorehouse* – and do it on your own time!'

Part of his design in remarks of this sort was to get a reaction from the two girls present – Maxine, his cutiepie private sec, and Miss Rogers, assistant to the art director – both of whom managed, as usual, a polite blush and half-lowered eyes for his benefit.

The next ten minutes were spent talking about whether to send our own exclusive third-rate photographer to Viet Nam or to use the rejects of a second-rate one who had just come back.

'Even with the rejects we could still run our *E.L. trade*,' said Katz, referring to an italicized phrase *Exclusively Lance* which appeared under photographs and meant they were not being published elsewhere – though less through exclusivity, in my view, than general crappiness.

Without really resolving this, we went on to the subject of 'Twiggy,' the British fashion-model who had just arrived in New York and about whose boyish hair and bust-line raged a storm of controversy. What did it mean philosophically? Aesthetically? Did it signal a new trend? Should we adjust our center-spread requirements (traditionally 42–24–38) to meet current taste? Or was it simply a flash fad?

'Come next issue,' said Hack, 'we don't want to find ourselves holding the wrong end of the shit-stick, now do we?'

Everyone was quick to agree.

'Well, *I* think she's absolutely *delightful*,' exclaimed Ronnie Rondell, the art director (prancing gay and proud of it), 'she's so much more . . . sensitive-looking and . . . *delicate* than those awful . . . *milk-factories*!' He gave a little shiver of revulsion and looked around excitedly for corroboration.

Hack, who had a deep-rooted antifag streak, stared at him for a moment like he was some kind of weird lizard, and he seemed about to say something cruel and uncalled for to Ron, but then he suddenly turned on me instead.

'Well, Mister Whorehouse man, isn't it about time we heard from you? Got any ideas that might conceivably keep this operation out of the shithouse for another issue or two?'

'Yeah, well I've been thinking,' I said, winging it completely, 'I mean, Fox here and I had an idea for a series of interviews with unusual persons . . .'

'Unusual *persons*?' he growled, 'what the hell does that mean?'

'Well, you know, a whole new department, like a regular feature. Maybe call it, uh, "Lance Visits . . ."'

He was scowling, but he was also nodding vigorously. '"Lance Visits . . ." Yeh, yeh, you wantta gimme a fer instance?'

'Well, you know, like, uh . . . "Lance Visits a Typical Teenybopper" – cute teenybopper tells about cute teen-use of Saran Wrap as a contraceptive, etcetera . . . and uh, let's see . . . "Lance Visits a Giant Spade Commie Bull-Dike" . . . "Lance Visits the Author of *Masturbation Now!*", a really fun-guy.'

Now that I was getting warmed up, I was aware that Fox, on my left, had raised a hand to his face and was slowly massaging it, mouth open, eyes closed. I didn't look at Hack, but I knew he had stopped nodding. I pressed on . . . 'You see, it could become a sort of regular department, we could do a "T.L." on it . . . "*Another Exclusive Lance Visit.*" How about this one: "Lance Visits a Cute Junkie Hooker" . . . "Lance Visits a Zany Ex-Nun Nympho" . . . "Lance Visits the Fabulous Rose Chan, beautiful research and development technician for the so-called French Tickler . . ."'

'Okay,' said Hack, 'how about *this* one: "Lance Visits Lance," – know where? Up shit-creek without a paddle! Because that's where we'd be if we tried any of that stuff.' He shook his head in a lament of disgust and pity. 'Jeeze, that's some sense of humor you got, boy.' Then he turned to Fox. 'What rock you say you found him under? Jeez.'

Fox, as per usual, made no discernible effort to defend me, simply pretended to suppress a yawn, eyes averted, continuing to doodle on his 'Think Pad,' as it was called, one of which lay by each of our ashtrays.

'Okay,' said Hack, lighting a new cigar, 'suppose *I* come up with an idea? I mean, I don't wantta *surprise* you guys, cause any *heart attacks* . . . by *me* coming up with an *idea*,' he saying this with a benign serpent smile, then adding in grim significance, '*after twenty-seven years in this goddam game!*' He took a sip of water, as though trying to cool his irritation at being (as per usual) 'the only slob around here who delivers.' 'Now let's just stroke this one for a while,' he said, 'and see if it gets stiff. Okay, lemme ask you a question: what's the hottest thing in mags at this time? What's raising all the stink and hullabaloo? The *Manchester* book, right? The suppressed passages, right?' He was referring, of course, to a highly publicized account of the assassination of President Kennedy – certain passages of which had allegedly been deleted. 'Okay, now all this stink and hullabaloo – *I* don't like it, *you* don't like it. In the first place, it's infringement on freedom of the press. In the second, they've exaggerated it all out of proportion. I mean, what the hell was *in* those passages? See what I mean? All right, suppose we do a *takeoff* on those same passages?'

He gave me a slow look, eyes narrowed – ostensibly to protect them from his cigar smoke, but with a Mephistophelian effect. *He* knew that *I* knew that his 'idea' was actually an idea I had gotten from Paul Krassner, editor of *The Realist*, a few evenings earlier, and had mentioned, *en passant* so to speak, at the last prelunch confab. He seemed to be wondering if I would crack. A test, like. I avoided his eyes, doodled on the 'Think Pad.' He exhaled in my direction, and continued:

'Know what I mean? Something *light*, something *zany*, kid the pants off the guys who suppressed it in the first place. A satire like. Get the slant?'

No one at the table seemed to. Except for Hack we were all in our thirties or early forties, and each had been hurt in some way by the President's death. It was not easy to imagine any particular 'zaniness' in that regard.

Fox was the first to speak, somewhat painfully it seemed. 'I'm, uh, not quite sure I follow,' he said. 'You mean it would be done in the style of the book?'

'Right,' said Hack, 'but get this, we don't say it *is* the real thing, we say it *purports* to be the real thing. And editorially we *challenge* the *authenticity* of it! Am I getting through to you?'

'Well, uh, yeah,' said Fox, 'but I'm not sure it can be, you know, uh, *funny*.'

Hack shrugged. 'So? *You're* not sure, *I'm* not sure. Nobody's sure it can be funny. We all take a crack at it – just stroke it a while and see if we get any jism – right?'

Right.

After working that evening I picked up a new Dexamyl prescription and stopped off at Sheridan Square to get it filled. Coming out of the drugstore, I paused momentarily to take in the scene. It was a fantastic evening – late spring evening, warm breeze promise of great summer evenings imminent – and teenies in minies floating by like ballerinas, young thighs flashing. Summer, I thought, will be the acid test for minies when it gets too warm for tights, body-stockings, that sort of thing. It should be quite an interesting phenomenon. On a surge of sex-dope impulse I decided to fall by the dinette and see if anything of special import was shaking, so to speak.

Curious that the first person I should see there, hunched over his coffee, frozen saintlike, black shades around his head as though a hippy crown of thorns, should be the young man who had given me the dex that very morning. I had the feeling he hadn't moved all day. But this wasn't true because he now had on a white linen suit and was sitting in a booth. He nodded in that brief formal way it is possible to nod and mean more than just hello. I sat down opposite him.

'I see you got yourself all straightened out,' he said with a wan smile, nodding again, this time at my little paper bag with the pharmacy label on it.

I took out the vial of dex and popped a quick one, thinking to do a bit of the old creative Lit later on. Then I shook out four or five and gave them to the young man.

'Here's some interest.'

'Anytime,' he said, dropping them in his top pocket, and after a pause, 'You ever in the mood for something besides dexies?'

'Like what?'

He shrugged, 'Oh, you know,' he said, raising a vague limp hand, then added with a smile, 'I mean you know your moods better than I do.'

During the next five minutes he proved to be the most acquisitive pusher, despite his tender years, I have ever encountered. His range was extensive – beginning with New Jersey pot, and ending with something called a 'Frisco Speedball,' a concoction of heroin and cocaine, with a touch of acid ('gives it a little color'). While we were sitting there, a veritable parade of his far-flung connections commenced, sauntering over, or past the booth, pausing just long enough to inquire if he wanted to score – for sleepers, leapers, creepers . . . acid in cubes, vials, capsules, tablets, powder . . . 'hash, baby, it's black as O' . . . mushrooms, mescalin, buttons . . . cosanyl, codeine, coke . . . coke in crystals, coke in powder, coke that looked like karo syrup . . . red birds, yellow jackets, purple hearts . . . 'liquid-O, it comes straight from Indochina, stamped right on the can' . . . and from time to time the young man ('Trick' he was called) would turn to me and say: 'Got eyes?'

After committing to a modest (thirty dollars) score for crystals, and again for two ounces of what was purported to be 'Panamanian Green' ('It's "one-poke pot", baby.'), I declined further inducement. Then an extremely down-and-out type, a guy I had known before whose actual name was Rattman, but who was known with simple familiarity as 'Rat,' and even more familiarly, though somehow obscurely, as 'The Rat-Prick Man,' half staggered past the booth, clocked the acquisitive Trick, paused, moved uncertainly towards the booth, took a crumpled brown paper bag out of his coat pocket, and opened it to show.

'Trick,' he muttered, almost without moving his lips, '. . . Trick, can you use any Lights? Two-bits for the bunch.' We both looked in, on some commodity quite unrecognizable – tiny, dark cylinder-shaped capsules, sticky with a brown-black guk, flat on each end, and apparently made of plastic. There was about a handful of them. The young man made a weary face of distaste and annoyance.

'Man,' he asked softly, plaintively, looking up at Rattman, '*when* are you going to get buried?'

But the latter, impervious, gave a soundless guffaw, and shuffled on.

'What,' I wanted to know, 'were those things?' asking this of the young man half in genuine interest, half in annoyance at not knowing. He shrugged, raised a vague wave of dismissal. 'Lights they're called . . . they're used nicotine-filters. You know, those nicotine filters you put in a certain kind of cigarette holder.'

'*Used* nicotine-filters? What do you do with them?'

'Well, you know, drop two or three in a cup of coffee – gives you a little buzz.'

'A little *buzz*?' I said, 'are you kidding? How about a little *cancer*? That's all tar and nicotine in there, isn't it?'

'Yeah, well, you know . . .' he chuckled dryly, 'anything for kicks. Right?'

Right, right, right.

And it was just about then he sprung it – first giving me his look of odd appraisal, then the sigh, the tired smile, the haltering deference: 'Listen, man . . . you ever made red-split?'

'I beg your pardon?'

'Yeah, you know – *the blood of a wig*.'

'No,' I said, not really understanding, 'I don't believe I have.'

'Well, it's something else, baby, I can tell you that.'

'Uh, well, *what* did you call it – I'm not sure I understood . . .'

'"Red-split," man, it's called "red-split" – it's schizo-juice . . . *blood* . . . the blood of a wig.'

'Oh, I see.' I had, in fact, read about it in a recent article in the *Times* – how they had shot up a bunch of volunteer prisoners (very normal, healthy guys, of course) with the blood of schizophrenia patients – and the effect had been quite pronounced . . . in some cases, manic; in other cases, depressive – about 50/50 as I recalled.

'But that can be a big bring-down, can't it?'

He shook his head sombrely. 'Not with *this* juice it can't. You know who this is out of?' Then he revealed the source – Chin Lee, it was, a famous East Village resident, a Chinese symbolist poet, who was presently residing at Bellevue in a straightjacket.

'Nobody,' he said, 'and I mean *nobody*, baby, has gone anywhere but *up, up, up* on *this* taste!'

I thought that it might be an interesting experience, but using caution as my watchword (the *Times* article had been very sketchy) I had to know more about this so-called red-split, blood of a wig. 'Well, how long does it, uh, you know, *last*?'

He seemed a little vague about that – almost to the point of resenting the question. 'It's a *trip*, man – four hours, six if you're lucky. It all depends. It's a question of *combination* – how your blood makes it with his, you dig?' He paused and gave me a very straight look. 'I'll tell you this much, baby, it *cuts acid and STP . . .*' He nodded vigorously. 'That's right, cuts both them. *Back*, *down*, and *sideways*.'

'Really?'

He must have felt he was getting a bit too loquacious, a bit too much on the old hard-sell side, because then he just cooled it, and nodded. 'That's right,' he said, so soft and serious that it wasn't really audible.

'How much?' I asked, finally, uncertain of any other approach.

'I'll level with you,' he said, 'I've got this connection – a ward attendant . . . you know, a male nurse . . . has, what you might call *access* to the hospital pharmacy . . . does a little trading with the guards on the fifth floor – that's where the *monstro*-wigs are – "High Five" it's called. That's where Chin Lee's at. Anyway, he's operating at cost right now – I mean, he'll cop as much M, or whatever other hard-shit he can, from the pharmacy, then he'll go up to High Five and trade for the juice – you know, just fresh, straight, uncut wig-juice – 90 c.c.'s, that's the regular hit, about an ounce, I guess . . . I mean, that's what they hit the wigs for, a 90 c.c. syringeful, then they cap the spike and put the whole outfit in a insulated wrapper. Like it's supposed to stay at body temperature, you dig? They're very strict about that – about how much they tap the wig for, and about keeping it fresh and warm, that sort of thing. Which is okay, because that's the trip – 90 c.c.'s, "piping hot," as they say.' He gave a tired little laugh at the curious image. 'Anyway the point is, he never knows in front what the *price* will be, my friend doesn't, because he never knows what kind of M score he'll make. I mean like if he scores for half-a-bill of M, then that's what he charges for the split, you dig?'

To me, with my Mad Ave savvy, this seemed fairly illogical.

'Can't he hold out on the High Five guys?' I asked, '. . . you know, tell them he only got half what he really got, and save it for later?'

He shrugged, almost unhappily. 'He's a very ethical guy,' he said, 'I mean like he's pretty weird. He's not really interested in narcotics, just *changes*. I mean, like he lets *them* do the count on the M – they tell him how much it's worth and that's what he charges for the split.'

'That *is* weird,' I agreed.

'Yeah, well it's like a new market, you know. I mean there's no established price yet, he's trying to develop a clientele – can you make half-a-bill?'

While I pondered, he smiled his brave tired smile, and said: 'There's one thing about the cat, being so ethical and all – he'll never burn you.'

So in the end it was agreed, and he went off to complete the arrangements.

The effect of red-split was 'as advertised' so to speak – in this case, quite gleeful. Sense-derangementwise, it was unlike acid in that it was not a question of the 'Essential I' having new insights, but of becoming a different person entirely. So that in a way there was nothing very scary about it, just extremely weird, and as it turned out, somewhat mischievous (Chin Lee, incidentally, was not merely a great wig, but also a great wag). At about six in the morning I started to work on the alleged 'Manchester passages.' Krassner might be cross, I thought, but what the hell, you can't copyright an idea. Also I intended to give him full and ample credit. 'Darn good exposure for Paul' I mused benignly, taking up the old magic quill.

The first few passages were fairly innocuous, the emphasis being on a style identical to that of the work in question. Towards the end of Chapter Six, however, I really started cooking: '. . . wan, and wholly bereft, she steals away from the others, moving trancelike towards the darkened rear-compartment where the casket rests. She enters, and a whispery circle of light shrouds her bowed head as she closes the door behind her and leans against it. Slowly she raises her eyes and takes a solemn step forward. She gasps, and is literally slammed back against the door by the sheer impact of the outrageous horror confronting her: i.e., the hulking Texan silhouette at the casket, its lid half raised, and he hunching bestially, his coarse animal member thrusting into the casket, and indeed into the neck-wound itself.

'*Great God,*' she cries, 'how heinous! It must be a case of . . . of . . . *NECK-ROPHILIA!*'

I finished at about ten, dexed, and made it to the office. I went directly into Fox's cubicle (the 'Lair' it was called).

'You know,' I began, lending the inflection a childlike candor, 'I could be wrong but I think I've *got* it,' and I handed him the ms.

'Got what?' he countered dryly, 'the clap?'

'You know, that Manchester thing we discussed at the last pre-lunch confab.' While he read, I paced about, flapped my arms in a gesture of uncertainty and humble doubt. 'Oh, it may need a little tightening up, brightening up, granted, but I hope you'll agree that the *essence* is there.'

For a while he didn't speak, just sat with his head resting on one hand staring down at the last page. Finally he raised his eyes; his eyes were always somehow sad.

'You really *are* out of your nut, aren't you?'

'Sorry, John,' I said. 'Don't follow.'

He looked back at the ms., moved his hands a little away from it as though it were a poisonous thing. Then he spoke with great seriousness:

'I think you ought to have your head examined.'

'My *head* is swell,' I said, and wished to elaborate, 'my *head* . . .' but suddenly I felt very weary. I had evidently hit on a cow sacred even to the cynical Fox.

'Look,' he said, 'I'm not a *prude* or anything like that, but this . . .' – he touched the ms. with a cough which seemed to stifle a retch – . . . 'I mean, *this* is the most . . . *grotesque* . . . *obscene* . . . well, I'd rather not even discuss it. Frankly, I think you're in very real need of psychiatric attention.'

'Do you think Hack will go for it?' I asked in perfect frankness.

Fox averted his eyes and began to drum his fingers on the desk.

'Look, uh, I've got quite a bit of work to do this morning, so, you know, if you don't mind . . .'

'Gone too far, have I, Fox? Is that it? Maybe you're missing the point of the thing – ever consider that?'

'Listen,' said Fox stoutly, lips tightened, one finger raised in accusation, 'you show this . . . *this thing* to anybody else, you're liable to get a *big smack in the kisser!*' There was an unmistakable heat and resentment in his tone – a sort of controlled hysteria.

'How do you know I'm not from the C.I.A.?' I asked quietly. 'How do *you* know this isn't a *test*?' I gave him a shrewd narrow look of appraisal. 'Isn't it just possible, Fox, that this quasi-indignation of yours is, in point of fact, simply an *act*? A *farce*? A *charade*? An *act*, in short, to *save your own skin!?!*'

He had succeeded in putting me on the defensive. But now, steeped in Chink poet cunning, I had decided that an offense was the best defense, and so plunged ahead. 'Isn't it true, Fox, that in this parable you see certain underlying homosexual tendencies which you unhappily recognize in yourself? Tendencies, I say, which to confront would bring you to the very brink of, "fear and trembling," so to speak.' I was counting on the Kierkegaard allusion to bring him to his senses.

'You crazy son of a bitch,' he said flatly, rising behind his desk, hands clenching and unclenching. He actually seemed to be moving towards me in some weird menacing way. It was then I changed my tack. 'Well listen,' I said, 'what would you say if I told you that it wasn't actually *me* who did that, but a Chinese poet? Probably a Commie . . . an insane Commie-fag-spade-Chinese poet. Then we could view it objectively, right?'

Fox, now crazed with his own righteous adrenalin, and somewhat encouraged by my lolling helplessly in the chair, played his indignation to the hilt.

'Okay, Buster,' he said, towering above me, 'keep talking, but make it good.'

'Well, uh, let's see now . . .' So I begin to tell him about my experience with the red-split. And speaking in a slow, deliberate, very serious way, I managed to cool him. And then I told him about an insight I had gained into Viet Nam, Cassius Clay, Chessman, the Rosenbergs, and all sorts of interesting things. He couldn't believe it. But, of course, no one ever really does – do they?

Vegas Bound

Hunter S. Thompson

We were somewhere around Barstow on the edge of the desert when the drugs began to take hold. I remember saying something like 'I feel a bit lightheaded; maybe you should drive . . .' And suddenly there was a terrible roar all around us and the sky was full of what looked like huge bats, all swooping and screeching and diving around the car, which was going about a hundred miles an hour with the top down to Las Vegas. And a voice was screaming: 'Holy Jesus! What are these goddamn animals?'

Then it was quiet again. My attorney had taken his shirt off and was pouring beer on his chest, to facilitate the tanning process. 'What the hell are you yelling about?' he muttered, staring up at the sun with his eyes closed and covered with wraparound Spanish sunglasses. 'Never mind,' I said. 'It's your turn to drive.' I hit the brakes and aimed the Great Red Shark toward the shoulder of the highway. No point mentioning those bats, I thought. The poor bastard will see them soon enough.

It was almost noon, and we still had more than a hundred miles to go. They would be tough miles. Very soon, I knew, we would both be completely twisted. But there was no going back, and no time to rest. We would have to ride it out. Press registration for the fabulous Mint 400 was already underway, and we had to get there by four to claim our sound-proof suite. A fashionable sporting magazine in New York had taken care of the reservations, along with this huge red Chevy convertible we'd just rented off a lot on the Sunset Strip . . . and I was, after all, a professional journalist; so I had an obligation to *cover the story*, for good or ill.

The sporting editors had also given me $300 in cash, most of which was already spent on extremely dangerous drugs. The trunk of the car looked like a mobile police narcotics lab. We had two bags of grass, seventy-five pellets of mescaline, five sheets of high-powered blotter acid, a salt shaker half full of cocaine, and a whole galaxy of multi-colored uppers, downers, screamers, laughers . . . and also a quart of tequila, a quart of rum, a case of Budweiser, a pint of raw ether and two dozen amyls.

All this had been rounded up the night before, in a frenzy of high-speed driving all over Los Angeles County – from Topanga to Watts, we picked up everything we could get our hands on. Not that we *needed* all that for the trip, but once you get locked into a serious drug collection, the tendency is to push it as far as you can.

The only thing that really worried me was the ether. There is nothing in the world more helpless and irresponsible and depraved than a man in the depths of an ether binge. And I knew we'd get into that rotten stuff pretty soon. Probably at the next gas station. We had sampled almost everything else, and now – yes, it was time for a long snort of ether. And then do the next hundred miles in a horrible, slobbering sort of spastic stupor. The only way to keep alert on ether is to do up a lot of amyls – not all at once, but steadily, just enough to maintain a focus at ninety miles an hour through Barstow.

'Man, this is the way to travel,' said my attorney. He leaned over to turn the volume up on the radio, humming along with the rhythm section and kind of moaning the words: 'One toke over the line, Sweet Jesus . . . One toke over the line . . .'

One toke? You poor fool! Wait till you see those goddamn bats. I could barely hear the radio . . . slumped over on the far side of the seat, grappling with a tape recorder turned all the way up on 'Sympathy for the Devil.' That was the only tape we had, so we played it constantly, over and over, as a kind of demented counterpoint to the radio. And also to maintain our rhythm on the road. A constant speed is good for gas mileage – and for some reason that seemed important at the time. Indeed. On a trip like this one *must* be careful about gas consumption. Avoid those quick bursts of acceleration that drag blood to the back of the brain.

My attorney saw the hitchhiker long before I did. 'Let's give this boy a lift,' he said, and before I could mount any argument he was stopped and this poor Okie kid was running up to the car with a big grin on his face, saying, 'Hot damn! I never rode in a convertible before!'

'Is that right?' I said. 'Well, I guess you're about ready, eh?'

The kid nodded eagerly as we roared off.

'We're your friends,' said my attorney. 'We're not like the others.'

O Christ, I thought, he's gone around the bend. 'No more of that talk,' I said sharply. 'Or I'll put the leeches on you.' He grinned, seeming to understand. Luckily, the noise in the car was so awful – between the wind and the radio and the tape machine – that the kid in the back seat couldn't hear a word we were saying. Or could he?

How long can we *maintain*? I wondered. How long before one of us starts raving and jabbering at this boy? What will he think then? This same lonely desert was the last known home of the Manson family. Will he make that grim connection when my attorney starts screaming about bats and huge manta rays coming down on the car? If so – well, we'll just have to cut his head off and bury him somewhere. Because it goes without saying that we can't turn him loose. He'll report us at once to some kind of outback nazi law enforcement agency, and they'll run us down like dogs.

Jesus! Did I *say* that? Or just think it? Was I talking? Did they hear me? I glanced over at my attorney, but he seemed oblivious – watching the road, driving our Great Red Shark along at a hundred and ten or so. There was no sound from the back seat.

Maybe I'd better have a chat with the boy, I thought. Perhaps if I *explain* things, he'll rest easy.

Of course. I leaned around in the seat and gave him a fine big smile . . . admiring the shape of his skull.

'By the way,' I said. 'There's one thing you should probably understand.'

He stared at me, not blinking. Was he gritting his teeth?

'Can you *hear* me?' I yelled.

He nodded.

'That's good,' I said. 'Because I want you to know that we're on our way to Las Vegas to find the American Dream.' I smiled. 'That's why we rented this car. It was the only way to do it. Can you grasp that?'

He nodded again, but his eyes were nervous.

'I want you to have all the background,' I said. 'Because this is a very ominous assignment – with overtones of extreme personal danger . . . Hell, I forgot all about this beer; you want one?'

He shook his head.

'How about some ether?' I said.

'What?'

'Never mind. Let's get right to the heart of this thing. You see, about twenty-four hours ago we were sitting in the Polo Lounge of the Beverly Hills Hotel – in the patio section, of course – and we were just sitting there under a palm tree when this uniformed dwarf came up to me with a pink telephone and said, "This must be the call you've been waiting for all this time, sir."'

I laughed and ripped open a beer can that foamed all over the back seat while I kept talking. 'And you know? He was right! I'd been *expecting* that call, but I didn't know who it would come from. Do you follow me?'

The boy's face was a mask of pure fear and bewilderment.

I blundered on: 'I want you to understand that this man at the wheel is my *attorney!* He's not just some dingbat I found on the Strip. Shit, *look* at him! He doesn't look like you or me, right? That's because he's a foreigner. I think he's probably Samoan. But it doesn't matter, does it? Are you prejudiced?'

'Oh, hell *no!*' he blurted.

'I didn't think so,' I said. 'Because in spite of his race, this man is extremely valuable to me.' I glanced over at my attorney, but his mind was somewhere else.

I whacked the back of the driver's seat with my fist. 'This is *important*, goddamnit! This is a *true story!*' The car swerved sickeningly, then straightened out. 'Keep your hands off my fucking neck!' my attorney screamed. The kid in the back looked like he was ready to jump right out of the car and take his chances.

Our vibrations were getting nasty – but why? I was puzzled, frustrated. Was there no communication in this car? Had we deteriorated to the level of *dumb beasts*?

Because my story *was* true. I was certain of that. And it was extremely important, I felt, for the *meaning* of our journey to be made absolutely clear. We had actually been sitting there in the Polo Lounge – for many hours – drinking Singapore Slings with mescal on the side and beer chasers. And when the call came, I was ready.

The Dwark approached our table cautiously, as I recall, and when he handed me the pink telephone I said nothing, merely listened. And then I hung up, turning to face my attorney. 'That was headquarters,' I said. 'They want me to go to Las Vegas at once, and make contact with a Portuguese photographer named Lacerda. He'll have the details. All I have to do is check into my suite and he'll seek me out.'

My attorney said nothing for a moment, then he suddenly came alive in his chair. 'God *hell!*' he exclaimed. 'I think I see the *pattern*. This one sounds like real trouble!' He tucked his khaki undershirt into his white rayon bellbottoms and called for more drink. 'You're going to need plenty of legal advice before this thing is over,' he said. 'And my first advice is that you should rent a very fast car with no top and get the hell out of L.A. for at least forty-eight hours.' He shook his head sadly. 'This blows my weekend, because naturally I'll have to go with you – and we'll have to arm ourselves.'

'Why not?' I said. 'If a thing like this is worth doing at all, it's worth doing right. We'll need some decent equipment and plenty of cash on the line – if only for drugs and a super-sensitive tape recorder, for the sake of a permanent record.'

'What kind of a story is this?' he asked.

'The Mint 400,' I said. 'It's the richest off-the-road race for motorcycles and dune-buggies in the history of organized sport – a fantastic spectacle in honor of some fatback *grossero* named Del Webb, who owns the luxurious Mint Hotel in the heart of downtown Las Vegas . . . at least that's what the press release says; my man in New York just read it to me.'

'Well,' he said, 'as your attorney I advise you to buy a motor-cycle. How else can you cover a big thing like this righteously?'

'No way,' I said. 'Where can we get hold of a Vincent Black Shadow?'

'What's that?'

'A fantastic bike,' I said. 'The new model is something like two thousand cubic inches, developing two hundred brake-horsepower at four thousand revolutions per minute on a magnesium frame with two styrofoam seats and a total curb weight of exactly two hundred pounds.'

'That sounds about right for this gig,' he said.

'It is,' I assured him. 'The fucker's not much for turning, but it's pure hell on the straightaway. It'll outrun the F-111 until takeoff.'

'Takeoff?' he said. 'Can we handle that much torque?'

'Absolutely,' I said. 'I'll call New York for some cash.'

Toxins Discharged
Irvine Welsh

It was a pretty glorious summer's evening when ah got out in the street. Ah found myself with a strange spring in my step. Of course, it was Thursday. Last weekend's drugs had been well and truly processed by now, the toxins discharged: sweated, shat and pished out; the hangover finito; the psychological self-loathing waning as the chemistry of the brain de-fucked itself and the fatigue sinking into the past as the old adrenalin pump starts slowly getting back into gear in preparation for the next round ay abuse. This feeling, when you've cracked the depressive hangover and the body and mind is starting to fire up again, is second only to coming up on a good E.

At the club, Vaughan's playing bools with this old cunt. He nods at me, and the auld cunt looks up with a slightly tetchy stare and ah realise that I've broken his concentration by casting my shadow over his line of vision. Steeling himself, the auld codger lets the bool roll, roll, roll and I'm thinking he's gone too far out, but naw, the wily auld cunt kens the score because the bool does a Brazilian spin, that's what it does, a fuckin Brazilian spin, and it comes back like a fuckin boomerang and slips like a surreptitious queue-jumper in behind Vaughan's massed lines of defence, rolling up to the jack and sneaking it away.

Ah cheer the auld gadge for that shot. Vaughan has his last one but ah decide no tae watch it but to go in and get some drinks. Ah discover I've a wrap of speed in my pocket, left over from fuck knows when. Ah take it to the bog, and chop it out into some lines on the cistern. If I'm gaunny have to talk bools ah might as well fuckin go for it in a big way . . . Ah come out, charged up to fuck. Ah remember this gear, dabbing away at it the other week. It's much better to snort though, this stuff.

– Didnae stay for the climax, Vaughan says, looking deflated. – Could have done wi yir support fir that last shot thair.

– Sorry, Vaughan, ah wis burstin fir a tropical fish, eh. Did ye git it?

– Naw, eh wis miles oot! The auld cunt roars. The auld cunt is dressed in white slacks, a blue open-necked shirt and has a sunhat on.

Ah slap the auld cunt on the back, – Nice one there, mate! Brilliant shot by the way, that wee spinner that nicked it at the end. Ah'm Lloyd, Vaughan's brother.

– Aye Lloyd, ah'm Eric, he extends his hand and gies ays a crushing masonic grip, – ye play the bools yersel?

– Naw, Eric, naw ah dinnae, mate; it's no really ma scene, ken. Ah mean ah'm no knockin the game n that, a great game . . . ah mean ah wis chillin oot the other day watchin that Richard Corsie gadge oan the box . . . he used tae be wi the Post, did eh no? That boy kens how tae fling a bool . . .

Fuck me, this Lou Reed is hitting the mark quickstyle.

– Eh, what yis wantin? Vaughan shouts, a wee bit embarrassed at ma ranting.

– Naw, naw naw, ah'll git them. Three lager, is it no?

– Poof's pish, Eric scoffs, – make mine Special.

– A special drink for a special victory, eh, Eric, ah smile. The auld cunt gie ays one back. – Yuv goat Vaughan's puss seekint here right enough!

– Aye, right, Vaughan goes, – are you gaunnae git them in, or what?

Ah hit the bar and the guy behind says that you have to

have a tray to get served, and ah joke that I've got enough to carry as it is and he says something short like house rules, but a wee cunt in the queue hands me one anyway. I've forgotten about all the daft fuckin rules they have in places like this, the Brylcreemed cunts wi their blazers wi the club badges on them and how at closing time there's mair falling masonry than when the Luftwaffe bombed Coventry cathedral . . . and now I'm back at my seat.

– Cheers, boys! ah say, raising my pint, – Tell ye what, Eric, ah knew that you had the bools after seeing ye in action there. This gadge has bools, ah telt maself. That Brazilian spin, man! Whoa, ya cunt that ye fuckin well are!

– Aye, said Eric, smugly, – it wis a wee thing ah thought ah'd try. Ah said tae masel, Vaughan's marshalled his defences well, but, ah thought, try a wee sneaky one roond the backdoor, and it just might come off.

– Aye, it wis a good shot, Vaughan conceded.

– It wis fuckin ace, ah told him. – You've heard of total fitba, the Dutch invented it, right? Well this man here, ah nodded towards Eric, – is total bools. You could've went for the blast there, Eric, tried that Premier League style huffing and puffing but naw, a bit ay class, a bit ay art.

The pint was drained. Vaughan hit the bar.

This was always a thing with Vaughan when he met me. He had a sense of duty, of the responsibilities ay a married man and a parent, so that whenever he did have an allocated time he would try tae squeeze as many units of alcohol into it as he possibly could. And he could drink. Thank fuck it was draught Becks ah was on. Ah wouldnae touch any Scottish shite, especially McEwan's lager, the vile toxic pish that it is, for anything. The pints kept flowing and this speed was still digging in, and ah was almost hyperventilating. The thing is, it was like auld Eric got dragged in by the vibe, by the exuberance, and it was like the auld bastard had snorted a few lines n aw.

After a quick draining of the next pint he came back wi some mair beers, wi nips as chasers.

– Fuckin hell! ah said, – Expect the unexpected wi this man, eh?

– Aye, too right, Vaughan smiled. Vaughan was looking at us both with a big, indulgent those-are-mad-cunts-but-I-love-them smile. It made me feel close to him.

– Ye should go up n see Ma n Dad, Vaughan told me.

– Aye, ah guiltily conceded, – ah've been meanin tae drop by this tape ah made up for them. Motown, eh.

– Good. They'll appreciate that.

– Aye, Marvin, Smokey, Aretha n aw that, ah said, then promptly changed the subject, turnin tae Eric, – Listen, Eric, that stunt you pulled wi the bools, ah began.

– Aye, Eric cut in, – fair took the wind oot ay Vaughan here's sails, that's if ye dinnae mind ays sayin like, Vaughan! Eric laughed. – Expect the unexpected!

– Do-do-do-do, do-do-do-do, ah start the Twilight Zone theme tune, then ah think of something, – Listen, Eric, your second name isnae Cantona, by any chance, is it?

– Eh naw, Stewart, he said.

– It's just that there wis a Cantonaesque quality aboot that final shot thair, ah began giggling, a real dose ay the Flight Lieutenants, and Eric did too, – it fair blew fuckin Vaughan Ryan's Express right out the water . . .

– Aye . . . awright then, ya cunts, Vaughan sulked.

– Ooh ah, Cantona, ah started, and Eric joined in. A few groups of drinkers and auld couples looked over at us.

Encouraged, auld Eric and ah were up doing the can-can: na, na na, na na na na na na na, na, na na, na na na na na na . . .

– Hey, come oan now, that's enough. Thir's folk here tryin tae enjoy a drink, a mumpy cunt with a blazer and badge moans.

– Aye, well nae herm done! auld Eric shouts back, then says in lower voice tae us, but still enough for every cunt tae hear, – What's his fuckin problem?

– C'moan Eric . . . Vaughan goes, – Lloyd's no a member here.

– Aye, well, the laddie's been signed in. Signed in as a guest.

It's aw bona fide. Wir no daein herm. Like ah sais, nae herm done, Eric shook his head.

— Procedures have been observed, eh, Eric, ah smirk.

— The situation's completely bona fide, Eric confirms stoically.

— Ah think a certain Monsieur Vaughan Buist may be smarting over a recent sporting setback, n'est-ce pas, Monsieur Cantona? He ees, ow you say, ay leetal peesed off.

— Je suis une booler, Eric cackles.

— It's not that, Lloyd, Vaughan mumps, — Aw ah'm tryin tae say is thit you're no a member here. Yir a guest. Yir the responsibility ay the people that bring ye. That's aw ah'm tryin tae say.

— Aye . . . bit nae herm done . . . mumbles Eric.

— It's jist like that club you go tae, Lloyd. That place up at The Venue. What's that club called?

— The Pure.

— Aye, right. It's like if you're at The Pure n ah wis tae come up n you were tae sign ays in . . .

— As ma guest, ah snorted, laughing uncontrollably at the thought. Ah heard auld Eric start as well. It got soas we were gaunnae peg oot.

— As your guest . . . Vaughan had started now. Ah thought: this is me fucked. Flight Lieutenant Biggles, hovering over the grim metropolis of Cunt City . . . Auld Eric started wheezing, as Vaughan carried on, — as the guest of one's brother Lloyd at the exclusive club in town he frequents . . .

We were interrupted by a choking sound as auld Eric boaked thin beer-sick over the table. The humpty cunt with the blazer and badge was right over to him and grabbed up his pint. — That's it! Ooot, c'moan! Oot!

Vaughan grabbed the pint back. — That's no fuckin well it at aw, Tommy.

— Aye it bloody well is! That's it, the humpty cunt snapped.

— Dinnae fuckin well come ower tae this table n say that's it, Vaughan said, — cause that's no it at aw.

Ah slapped Eric on the back and helped the auld cunt to his feet and through to the lavvy. — It's a sair ficht, right enough, ah caught him gasp between mouthfuls of sick as he spewed up into the bog pan.

– Aye, Eric, yir awright, man. Nae danger, ah said encouragingly. Ah felt like ah was at Rez, talking Woodsy down when he had his freak-out, but here ah was with a daft ault cunt in a bowling club.

Acknowledgements

I would like to extend my thanks to the following authors, translators and publishers for their kind permission to quote from their works:

Excerpts from *Opium: The Diary of a Cure* by Jean Cocteau, Peter Owen, London, 1957 (translated by Margaret Crosland and Sinclair Road); David R. Slavitt, translation of *The Metamorphoses of Ovid*, pp.316–17 ©1994, Johns Hopkins University Press, Baltimore and London; 'The Ointments of Pamphile' from *The Golden Ass* by Apuleius; Clarendon Press, Oxford, 1994 (translated by P.G. Walsh), reprinted by permission of Oxford University Press; 'Inquisition in the Pigsty' from *Quaestio de Strigibus* by Bartolommeo Spina; Venice, 1523, pp.133–4 from *Hallucinogens and Shamanism*, edited by Michael J. Harner, © 1973 Oxford University Press, Inc. Used by permission of Oxford University Press, Inc.; 'Women are Made to Cast Off Their Clothes and Go Naked' and 'To Make a Man Out of His Senses for a Day' from *Natural Magick* by John Baptista Porta; London, 1658; 'The Ant Wine Aphrodisiac' from *The Holy Guide* by John Heydon; London, 1662; 'Anti-Aphrodisiacs According to the Physician Rondibilis' from *Gargantua and Pantagruel* by François Rabelais; J. M. Dent, London, 1929, 'The Powder of Marvellous Virtue' from the *Decameron* by Giovanni Boccaccio, Navarre Society Limited, London, 1921 (translated by J. M. Rigg); 'The Satanic Nun' from *The Geography of Witchcraft* by Montague Summers; Kegan Paul, Trench, Trubner & Co., London, 1927; reprinted by permission of Routledge; 'Counterblaste to Tobacco' by King James I; London, 1604; 'How They

Brought Back Tobacco' from *Myths of the Cherokee* by James Mooney, in *Nineteenth Annual Report of the Bureau of American Ethnology, Part One*, Government Printing Office, Washington, 1900; 'The Abominable Unction of the Mexican Priests' from *The Naturall and Morall Historie of the East and West Indies* . . . by José de Acosta; London, 1604; Excerpts from 'The Race of Lost Men' and 'The Peyote Rite Among the Tarahumara' from *The Peyote Dance* by Antonin Artaud, translated by Helen Weaver. Translation copyright © 1976 by Farrar, Straus & Giroux, Inc. Reprinted by permission of Farrar, Straus & Giroux, Inc. Translated from *Les Tarahumaras* by Antonin Artaud © Editions Gallimard, 1971; 'The Hallucinogenic Snuff of the Muras Indians' from *Travels in Brazil During the Years from 1817 to 1820* by J.B. von Spix and C.F.P. von Martius; M. Lindauer, Munich, 1823–31 (translated by Hedwig Schleiffer); 'Narcotic Snuff and First Origins' from *Desana Texts and Contexts* by Gerardo Reichel-Dolmatoff, *Acta Ethnologica et Linguistica, Number 62, Series Americana 12*, Wien-Föhrenau, 1989; 'Hallucinogens of the Jívaro Headhunters' from *The Jívaro: People of the Sacred Waterfalls* by Michael J. Harner; University of California Press, Berkeley © 1972 The Regents of the University of California; 'Zombie Poisons of Haiti' from *Passage of Darkness: The Ethnobiology of the Haitian Zombie* by E. Wade Davis; University of North Carolina Press, Chapel Hill, 1988 © 1988 by Edmund Wade Davis. Used by permission of the publisher; 'Mushrooms in Kamchatka' from *Soma: Divine Mushroom of Immortality* by R.G. Wasson; Ethnomycological Studies Number 1, Harcourt Brace Jovanovich, New York, 1968; Quote on hashish and mescaline, and 'Drugged Spiders' from *Miserable Miracle (Mescaline)* by Henri Michaux; City Lights Books, San Francisco, 1963, translated by Louis Varèse from *Misérable Miracle* © Editions Gallimard 1972; 'In Defense of the Pygmies' from *The Dragons of Eden: Speculations on the Evolution of Human Intelligence* by Carl Sagan; Hodder and Stoughton, London, 1978. Reprinted by permission of Ms A. Druyan and Janklow & Nesbit Associates; 'The Origin of Ganja' from *Myths of Middle India* by Verrier Elwin, Geoffrey Cumberlege; Oxford University Press, Indian Branch, New Delhi, 1949. Reprinted by permission of Oxford University Press, New Delhi; 'Nasreddin Khoja' reprinted with the kind permission of Taner Baybars; 'The Old Man of the Mountain' from *The Travels of Marco Polo*, Marsden translation edited by Manuel Komroff, Printing House of Leo Hart, Rochester, New York, 1933; 'The Poem of Hashish' from *My Heart Laid Bare and Other Prose Writings* by Charles Baudelaire (translated by Norman Cameron), Soho Book

Company, London, 1986; 'The Night Entrance' from *The Hasheesh Eater* by Fitzhugh Ludlow, Harper & Brothers, New York, 1857; 'Baluchistan Garden' from *The Road of Excess: A Psychedelic Biography* by Brian Barritt; PSI Publishing, London, 1998. Reprinted by permission of Brian Barritt, Whisper Promotions, 111 Este Road, London SW11 2TT and Barry Mason, PSI Publishing; 'Identity Crisis' from *Mr Nice* by Howard Marks; Martin Secker and Warburg, London, 1996. Reprinted by permission of Howard Marks and David Godwin Associates; 'Lahu Prayers for a Bountiful Opium Crop' from *Lahu Nyi (Red Lahu) Farming Rites (North Thailand)* by Anthony R. Walker in *Anthropos* 73, 1978. Reprinted by permission of Professor Othmar Gächter, Editor-in-Chief, *Anthropos*; 'The Pleasures of Opium' from *Confessions of an English Opium-Eater* by Thomas de Quincey; Geoffrey Cumberlege, Oxford University Press, London, n.d.; 'Ligeia' from *The Works of Edgar Allan Poe, Volume III: Tales,* Harper & Brothers, New York and London, n.d.; 'Errol on Opium' from *My Wicked, Wicked Ways* by Errol Flynn; William Heinemann, London, 1960. Reprinted by permission of William Heinemann (Random House UK); 'Hauser and O'Brien' and other excerpts from *The Naked Lunch* by William S. Burroughs, Olympia Press, Paris, 1959. Reprinted by permission of the Wylie Agency (UK) Ltd; 'Junking the Image' by Will Self; originally published in the *Guardian,* February 1994. Reprinted by permission of the Guardian Media Group plc; Excerpts from *My Lady Nicotine* by J.M. Barrie; Hodder & Stoughton, London, 1890. Reprinted by permission of Samuel French Ltd., London, on behalf of the Barrie Estate; 'Sherlock on Cocaine' from *The Sign of Four* by Arthur Conan Doyle, Copyright © 1996 The Sir Arthur Conan Doyle Copyright Holders. Reprinted by kind permission of Jonathan Clowes Ltd., London, on behalf of Andrea Plunket, Administrator of the Sir Arthur Conan Doyle Copyrights; 'Laughing Gas on Boxing Day' from *Researches, Chemical and Philosophical; Chiefly Concerning Nitrous Oxide, or Dephlogisticated Nitrous Air, and its Respiration* by Humphry Davy; J. Johnson, London, 1800; 'Under the Knife' from *The Plattner Story and Others* by H.G. Wells; Methuen & Co., London, 1897. Reprinted by permission of A.P. Watt on behalf of The Literary Executors of the Estate of H.G. Wells; 'Etheromania' from *Phantastica: Narcotic and Stimulating Drugs* by Louis Lewin; Routledge & Kegan Paul, London, 1931; 'The Drug Bag' and 'Vegas Bound' from *Fear and Loathing in Las Vegas: A Savage Journey to the Heart of the American Dream* by Hunter S. Thompson; Random House, New York, 1971. Reprinted by permission of The Wylie Agency, Inc. (USA) on behalf of the author;

'Cocaine Consciousness: The Gourmet Trip' by Jerry Hopkins; from George Andrews and David Solomon (editors) *The Coca Leaf and Cocaine Papers,* Harcourt Brace Jovanovich, New York, 1968; 'Mescal: A New Artificial Paradise' by Havelock Ellis in *The Contemporary Review* Volume 73, January–June 1898, Leonard Scott Publication Company, New York, 1898. Reprinted by kind permission of Professor Francois Lafitte; 'Hallucinogenic Drugs and the Problem of Eros' from *Infinite Turbulence* by Henri Michaux, Calder and Boyars, London, 1975, translated by Michael Fineberg. Reprinted by permission of Calder Publications Ltd., London; 'The Poet's Paradise' from *Oxford Addresses on Poetry* by Robert Graves, Cassell & Co., London, 1961. Reprinted by permission of Carcanet Press Ltd., Manchester; 'Drugs That Shape Men's Minds' from *Collected Essays* by Aldous Huxley; Chatto & Windus, London, 1960. Reprinted by permission of Random House (UK) and Mrs Laura Huxley; 'Timothy Leary, LSD and Harvard' from *The Brotherhood of Eternal Love* by Stewart Tendler and David May, Panther Books, Granada Publishing, London, 1984. Used by permission of Maria Carvainis Agency, Inc. All rights reserved; 'Kathmandu Interlude' from *True Hallucinations: Being an Account of the Author's Extraordinary Adventures in the Devil's Paradise* by Terence McKenna, Harper San Francisco, 1993. Copyright © 1993 Terence McKenna. Reprinted by permission of HarperCollins Publishers Inc. 'The Other Cary Grant' by Warren Hoge from *The New York Times Magazine* 3 July 1977. Copyright © 1977 by *The New York Times*. Reprinted by permission; 'The Black Madness of Henbane' from *The Book of Poisons* by Gustav Schenk; translated by Michael Bullock, Weidenfeld and Nicolson, London, 1956; Excerpt from *Maldoror* by Comte de Lautréamont, translated by Alexis Lykiard, Allison & Busby, London, 1970. Reprinted by permission of Allison & Busby Ltd., London; 'Drink' from *Selected Works* by Alfred Jarry, Jonathan Cape, London, 1965 (edited by Roger Shattuck and Simon Watson Taylor); 'Lune-Time' from *Whisper: A Timescript* by Brian Barritt, Whisper Promotions, London, 1971. Reprinted by permission of Brian Barritt; 'The Blood of a Wig' from *Red-Dirt Marijuana and Other Tastes* by Terry Southern; Jonathan Cape, London, 1971. Reprinted by permission of The Peters Fraser and Dunlop Group Limited on behalf of the author's estate; 'Toxins Discharged' from *The Undefeated: An Acid House Romance* in *Ecstasy: Three Tales of Chemical Romance* by Irvine Welsh, Jonathan Cape, 1996. Reprinted by permission of Random House (UK).